Laura Knight

A Life

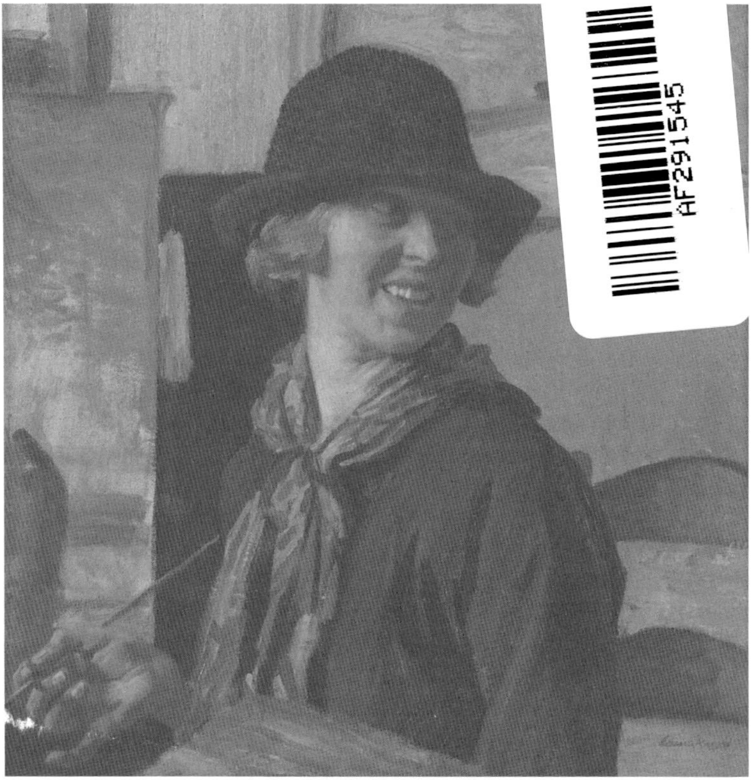

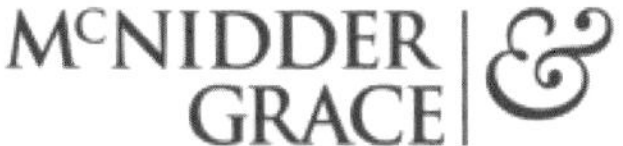

BARBARA C. MORDEN

MᶜNIDDER & GRACE

Published by McNidder & Grace
21 Bridge Street
Carmarthen SA31 3JS
Wales, United Kingdom
www.mcnidderandgrace.com

First published in hardback by McNidder & Grace 2014
Original paperback published 2021, reprinted 2022
© Barbara Morden 2021

A catalogue record for this work is available from the British Library.

ISBN 9780857160492 hardback
ISBN 9780857160508 paperback
ISBN 9780857160669 Ebook

Cover image: Self Portrait, c.1921, Knight, Laura (1877–1970) / Museum of New Zealand Te Papa Tongarewa / © Estate of Dame Laura Knight / Bridgeman Images
Cover design: Tabitha Palmer
Designed by JS Typesetting Ltd
Printed and bound in the United Kingdom by Short Run Press Ltd, Exeter, UK

'I am just a hard-working 'woman, who longs to pierce
the mystery of form and colour, and with full heart
add a mite to the treasure of the world.'

Dame Laura Knight

FOREWORD

I remember my great aunt as someone who was really interesting to listen to. She had gone through many hardships, achieving so much in a period when such feats were restricted or difficult for women to accomplish. In her life she met so many people from all walks of life and she was fascinated by them, especially if they had a skill of their own. Laura had a personality such that all people – be they closely knit communities such as Yorkshire fisher folk and gypsies; or professionals of many varied disciplines such as the ballet, theatre, musicians, authors and writers, circus; captains of industry or the aristocracy – all warmly accepted her and many remained close friends.

Over the past 40 years many people have written a variety of articles and books about my great aunt. Understandably each writer has had to depend heavily on the artist's two autobiographies. These I would personally recommend to enthusiasts, in that they provide a wonderful insight of the wide range of different people she met, major events in her life, together with some fascinating anecdotes, written in her own inimitable style. However, recognising the age of Laura Knight at the time of writing each of her autobiographies (nearly 60 and 88), we must allow for a little clouding of memory. It must also be acknowledged that the artist did not have the research aids that we have today.

Unfortunately, in recent years most of the writers on Laura Knight appear to have relied almost entirely on just the autobiographies and have undertaken little further research. Several writers have made erroneous assumptions and regrettably many of these have over time become so often repeated that lamentably they are now viewed as factual.

On meeting Barbara, I recognised that here was a different writer, one who applied the method of "looking outside the box", seeking evidence not looked at before, and one not prone to making unfounded assumptions. In consequence the reader now has a more accurate record of when events took place, and when certain paintings were executed or exhibited, as well as some material never before made public. This is not a picture book but a biography, so the illustrations included here relate to the phases, events and the people in the artist's long life.

Barbara C. Morden's book is to be recommend to all collectors and lovers of Laura Knight and her works, as well as students of British art of the 20th century.

R. John Croft FCA, great nephew of Laura Knight

PREFACE

In my writing this book and I trust in your reading it, to keep company with Laura Knight has been variously surprising, instructive, entertaining, and above all, engaging.

After publication of the hardback version of *Laura Knight: A Life* in 2014, I was contacted by many people who all in their way enriched the experience by offering further information about the artist not hitherto in the public domain. This paperback version has given me the opportunity to incorporate their contributions as appropriate.

Charlotte Bedford (Gaby) proved to be an invaluable resource, generous with her time and friendship. She shared several family stories, including the belief that Charles Ther was a 'husband of convenience.' Importantly, he was not the father of Big Grandma. She was the illegitimate daughter of King George III: "You only had to look at her to know". Gaby was also at pains to point out that Laura and her sister were not absolutely destitute in their teenaged years. They were always welcome at Corporation Oaks, although in her autobiographies Laura makes a great deal of their 'orphaned' status and deprivation.

One special gift was Gaby's giving me access to Mother's sketch and accounts book from the year 1885. This shows portraits of the three girls as well as a sketch of Uncle Arthur Peter (see Chapter 1). It was a privilege to be able to use this material and to meet and talk with Gaby who sadly died in 2019. Her husband Piers Bedford continues his support and interest in the book.

This revised edition incorporates recent research, images and information which has come to light since the first publication in 2014. With this edition it has been a pleasure to re-visit the text and to present it afresh for readers.

Barbara C. Morden 2021

ACKNOWLEDGEMENTS

The author is indebted to R. John Croft, great nephew of the artist and Chairman of the Trustees of the Estate of Dame Laura Knight who made available valuable information and images for this book. In addition, much is owed to Charlotte (Gaby) Bedford who offered hospitality and friendship as well as a wealth of material relating to the early years of her great aunt.

Laura Knight: A Life has been written with the assistance of the following institutions to whom sincere thanks are due: the Laing Art Gallery, Tyne and Wear Museums; the Djanogly Art Gallery, Nottingham and the National Portrait Gallery, London. I wish to thank helpful staff at the following: the Cadbury Archives, the University of Birmingham; the Imperial War Museum, London; the McManus: Dundee's Art Gallery and Museum; Nottinghamshire Archives; Nottingham Castle Museum and Art Gallery and Tennants Auction House, Leyburn, North Yorkshire. In the process of writing the biography, I have also cause to be grateful to Michael Reid of Chicago; Simon Wood of Brockfield Hall; and Andy and Caroline Peden Smith, publishers, who commissioned the book and saw the project through and beyond with their customary encouragement and enthusiasm.

CONTENTS

INTRODUCTION

"I can twist and turn"

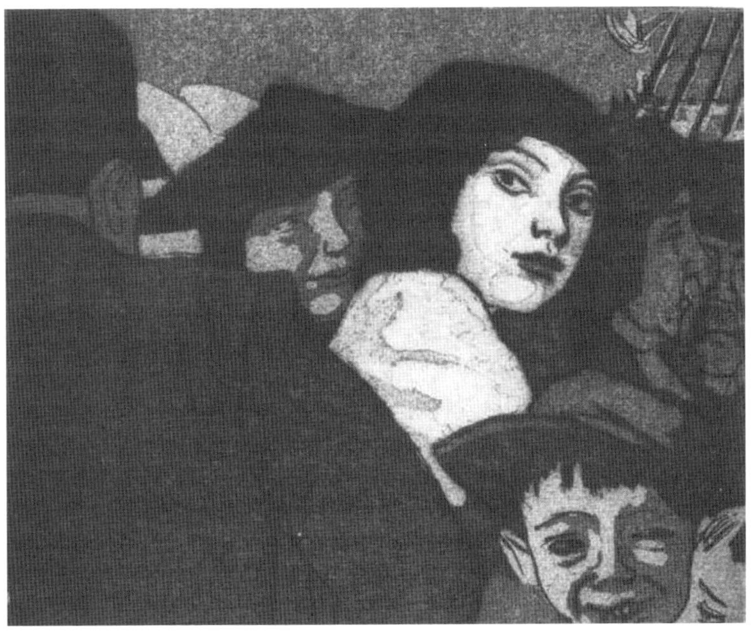

A Crowd, 1923, etching and aquatint. Private collection

This is the story of Dame Laura Knight. A biography rather than a picture-book, it is a pen-portrait of a vibrant and colourful personality who not only lived for and through her art but was blessed with the art of living. Born in 1877 and dying a month short of her ninety-third birthday in 1970, hers was a long life, shaped by the rapid and at times cataclysmic social, cultural and historical changes of the early modern period.

The narrative line of her story tells of a modest and at times impoverished childhood in Nottingham in the 1880s and how finally she was hailed as a national and international celebrity: a woman of achievement. However, the finer detail and nuances of her life are not so easily grasped.

Much documentary evidence is scattered through her two autobiographies: *Oil Paint and Grease Paint*, published when she was fifty-nine in 1936 and *The Magic of a Line* published when she was eighty-eight in 1965. There is one near-contemporary biography *Laura Knight*, written by Janet Dunbar who met and conversed with Laura when she was in her nineties. This was published in 1975 5 years after her death.

Over the decades Laura's correspondence was as prolific as her social circle was wide. In her letters, usually written in haste, she could be effusive or at times abrupt. When she was minded, she wrote well with lyrical and dramatic expression that led to her trying her hand at poetry and writing for the theatre. However diverse and fascinating this material, her versatility, energy and ambition are best expressed through her paintings of children and landscapes; numerous pencil and charcoal sketches, pictures and prints of the theatre, ballet, flamenco dancers, acrobats and circus animals; commercial posters and designs for commemoration mugs and dinnerware. Her repertoire was extensive and her output substantial.

After a period of neglect, her work is now in process of re-assessment, but in the mid-20th century she was a celebrated figure – a "national treasure". Books and articles about Laura Knight were adulatory and often sentimental: "marvellous" was the adjective increasingly applied to her in later years. When she wrote about herself, she could be self-deprecating as well as boldly self-confident, occasionally brash. Her narrative style, especially in the first of her two autobiographies, *Oil Paint and Greasepaint*, is engaging and vivid – the result of her tendency to shift the tense of her sentences from the past to the dramatic present and include snatches of half-remembered conversation. The effect is disarmingly naïve, apparently candid, somewhat scatter-brained, effervescent and sparkling – like the champagne she so enjoyed when elderly and famous.

Hers was a distinctively idiosyncratic character – kaleidoscopic, with facets constantly shifting into new and brilliant patterns so that only very rarely can we grasp a steady, objective view of Laura Knight. She describes her childhood self in these words: 'I can turn and twist through any crowd no matter how they try to catch me – it's as if to say, "They shan't touch me" and they can't, no matter how close I am'. It was a characteristic that persisted throughout her adult life.

In the opening chapter of her first autobiography Laura Knight asserts that she 'was not, as some people think, born in a circus, suckled by an elephant', or 'tossed on the feet of an acrobat'. Nor was she born into extreme poverty or orphaned as a child, which are other myths perpetuated even today. Yet she enjoyed such speculation and mystery and was in no hurry to set the records absolutely straight. Indeed, she herself contributed in great measure to the mythologizing of her life.

Her self-portraits (Plates 1 and 9), whether in words or paint, are shifting and ambiguous. Always it seems she is glancing past us, turning away to engage with the next subject to capture the eye and interest. She is present but with her back turned, face shaded by the brim of her trademark trilby hat, on the margins, in the wings, behind the curtain, directing the sightline away from subjective feeling, delineating herself in primary colours and bold lines, avoiding the shades of deep reflection. Her focus is never analytical or soul searching but dedicated to the communication and affirmation of her single-minded obsession: that she was born to draw and paint. It is as an artist that she wished to be known and as an artist that she is remembered and celebrated. In life, she was reputed to be incredibly good company – I hope that you too will find her so.

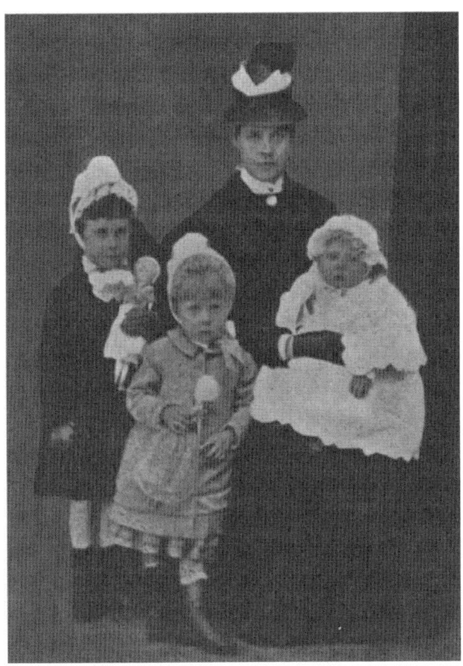

Family photograph (1970s copy) of baby Laura, her mother
and sisters, c.1878. Nottinghamshire Archive

CHAPTER ONE

"Our unconventional household"

The house that Laura Johnson first associated with home was 9, Noel Street, Nottingham. The move there by hansom cab from her place of birth, Long Eaton, Derbyshire, formed her earliest infant memory. She describes the experience early in *Oil Paint and Greasepaint*. Seated in the lap of her great-grandmother, known as "Little Grandma", with her 'old brown nut-cracker face' where the chin and nose well-nigh met, framed by a black cap with lappets and ribbons over her ears, shawl, black silk apron and red-mittened hands, she remembers the clip-clop sound of the horse's hooves beneath her. These sensations, combined with the smell of resin from the drawer that served as her temporary cot on her first night at the house, mark her awakening into consciousness. They are expressed in a manner typically her own in which colour and texture, together with sound and smell coalesce in the narrative line to communicate a sense of immediacy, of "living the moment". This quality was to characterize her personality and her painting throughout her life.

Laura's great-grandmother, "Little Grandma", was Mary Broomhead. Born in 1792, she was the daughter of Joseph and Ann Broomhead of the village of East Leake, a few miles south of Nottingham and close to the Leicestershire border. In the 18th century East and its neighbour West Leake were known for their cottage industries of weaving, hosiery and basket-making. Little Grandma was trained as a stay-maker (corsetry) which, given that the making of hosiery (a word meaning not merely stockings but under-wear generally) was a staple industry in East Leake, is not surprising. At the time of her birth the stay-making industry was in decline nationally, stays becoming much reduced in size and shape because of the growing fashion for the high-waisted Empire style. However, the old fashioned and substantial stomachers which were boned and laced to structure the bust, waist and hips were still worn by older women.

It was family tradition that Little Grandma had visited the Royal Court to measure the Queen for stays. That Queen Charlotte, the consort of King George III, wore the stomacher can be affirmed by portraits. The story is also endorsed by the appropriation of Charlotte as a family name. In 1813 Little Grandma named her first daughter (known to Laura as 'Big Grandma') Charlotte after the Queen. In 1853 she in turn called her second daughter (Laura's Mother) Charlotte, who was to baptise her eldest girl Charlotte Ellen in 1873. All, it seems, can be attributed to Little Grandma's having worked by "Royal Appointment".

It was while she was at Court, most likely at Brighton, that Mary Broomhead met Charles Ther whose surname was variously spelt Ther, Thir, or Thur, reflecting local dialect and the oral transmission of information to registrars. Little is known about Charles Ther apart from his baptism on the 15th August 1792. One family tradition suggested that he was musical and had played the "serpent" (a form of early tuba) in a church band. It was also claimed that he was descended from royalty – be it on the "wrong side of the blanket" – for it was said that he had been brought up in the household of the Duke of Richmond and called the housekeeper "Aunt". Other less romantic stories describe him as an engineer who worked on the first railway tunnel in England and that he was working on another such project when he died aged fifty-two at Ely in 1845. What we do know for certain is that Charles was a militia man and at a time of continuing fear of French invasion would have been stationed at various locations in the south of England.

Born out of wedlock in 1812 Mary's first baby, Owen, died in infancy but the next year another, a girl, was on the way. This was Charlotte (Laura's Big Grandma) whose birth prompted their marriage in December 1813 at the church of St Nicholas, Brighton. Interestingly, however, an alternative version has it that Big Grandma was an illegitimate daughter of King George III, local gossip putting it about that: "You only had to look at her to know …".

In 1818 Charles Ther was with the Royal South Lincolnshire Militia and living in Stamford. The births of three subsequent children, Ann, Charles and Sarah were all registered there between the years 1818 and 1822. There is evidence of an on-going connection with Nottingham, since their second son William was registered in Radford, Nottingham in 1815. This, the year of Waterloo, marked the end of hostilities and the exile of Napoleon to St Helena. The peace brought celebration and the militias were stood-down, so a visit to East Leake and Nottingham to visit family would be in order and appropriate for Mary's latest lying-in. They were certainly back in Nottingham in July 1820 when Charlotte was christened along with her brother William at St Mary's Church in the Lace Market. It is likely that by this time Charles was attached to a Nottingham militia. After the Peterloo Massacre of 1819, continuing social unrest associated with demands for political reform, machine-breaking and food riots meant the mustering and deployment of part-time militiamen throughout the industrial Midlands. The couple's seventh child George was born in Radford, Nottingham in 1824; Hannah in 1826; Elizabeth in 1829; Emma in 1832 and Henry in 1834. Charles' continuing unsettled lifestyle over the years is reflected in the christening and marriage registers of his and Mary's children where he is described variously as labourer, mechanic and lace-maker. To help the reader navigate through this large family, please turn to the end of the chapter for a table which gives the basic details, as far as they are known, of the eleven children of Mary Broomhead and Charles Ther.

Apparently, after Henry's birth, Mary had had enough. She told her husband Charles that she had never liked him and was leaving. Perhaps the decision was finally prompted by Charles' continuing association with the militias. In the years 1831 and 1832 violent protest over the passage of the Great Reform Bill brought the nation close to revolution and Nottingham was a hot spot of agitation. Laura's maternal grandfather Stephen Bates was there in the crowd when a mob burned down the old Nottingham Castle in 1831. The Government lost control of the town for a while until the local militia, whose brutality was notorious, managed to gain the upper hand. As one of them – a militia man in the pay of the government – Charles Ther would be regarded by family and neighbours with resentment, even hate. From this time onwards Mary Ther set herself up as an independent agent.

The 1841 Census describes Mary Ther as living in Radford, Nottingham, with six of her children. In 1848 she is described in *Kelly's Directory* as 'stay-maker of Ilkeston Road, Nottingham'. Now a successful business-woman, by this time Mary's expertise in corset-making would once again be in demand since fashion had returned to a restricted, shaped female silhouette with low shoulders, a narrow waist, with skirts beginning to evolve into the bell shape that was typical of the high Victorian period. Over the years she never lost any of her spirit and spontaneity. This is best illustrated by the tale that in 1845, on hearing that her estranged husband Charles was on the point of death, she set off at once by train to Ely, Cambridgeshire, to slap his face as a last tribute. She arrived too late for these final offices – the coffin lid had already been nailed down. Mary's impetuosity and wilfulness, together with her gruff manner and inclination to utter improper innuendo, mark her as very much a Regency character. This was at odds with the general tenor of respectable Victorian society and the more reserved nature of her daughters. However, it is worth noting that these were character traits inherited by Laura, her favourite great-grandchild.

Sometime in the late 1860s Little Grandma went to live with her daughter Charlotte (Big Grandma) and she remained there until her death aged ninety-seven in May 1889. Short tempered and sharp, Little Grandma had little sentiment in her soul. On receiving the news of the death of her second eldest daughter Ann in Queensland, Australia where she had emigrated with her husband, Little Grandma snapped: 'Well she lived to a good old age' and that was that. All the Ther children who lived into adulthood were in some way associated with the lace or hosiery industry either locally in Nottingham, in northern France or in America. Of particular importance to Laura's story was Elizabeth (baptised in 1829) who with her husband Arthur John (Jack) West (they married at Radford in 1848) ran a lace factory at St Quentin in France. Formally known as Aunt West-Ther (she adopted the French fashion for appending her maiden to her married name), she was a frequent visitor to the house in Noel Street and was to be a good friend to Laura and her sisters. The only Ther relative of her own age to figure in Laura's memories of this time was a cousin Reggie, the grandson of Mother's elder sister, Elizabeth (named after Aunt West). Laura describes him as a 'mardy' boy, a dialect word meaning spoilt and sulky. Clearly young Laura had no time for him.

Out of the extended family of Thers the 'only creature' that Little Grandma 'had ever loved or spoken to kindly' was her great granddaughter Laura. In return Laura writes of Little Grandma with fondness and pride for it was she who was allowed to vigorously comb out the old lady's long hair ('I like the scratching') which had surprisingly little grey. Seated in her chair by the fire, Little Grandma would have a tipple of gin before bed and secrete sugar lumps from the tea-table in her apron pockets for later, while a row of mouldy oranges was ranged on the shelf above her head 'getting ripe to eat'.

In 1837 Big Grandma Charlotte Ther married Stephen Bates, an inventor and engineer of lace–making equipment, at the Parish Church of Radford, Nottingham. Born in Duffield, Derbyshire in 1804, Stephen was from yeoman-farming stock. Derbyshire, like Nottinghamshire, has a tradition of textile production and weaving and it seems that over the generations various branches of the Bates family were associated with this. It is therefore no surprise that as a young man Stephen, recognizing the changing times in which he lived, moved into the expanding textile business. He left the countryside and migrated to where his talent for engineering might have some useful application – the invention and development of lace-making machinery. It appears that his extensive business axis extended from Long Eaton in Derbyshire to Nottingham, the centre of lace production and distribution, some seven miles away.

Over the period when Stephen Bates was establishing himself, Long Eaton in Derbyshire was expanding rapidly from an agricultural village into a thriving lace-manufacturing town, connected to Nottingham by the Erewash Canal and the steam railway. There was plenty of work there for an engineer and inventor in the numerous lace-making factories being set up by entrepreneurs who were attracted to the town by the plentiful supply of workers migrating from rural districts and a lack of unionisation. Stephen is known to have set up a machine-making factory, but whether this was in Long Eaton or in Nottingham is not clear. That there was an on-going connection with Long Eaton is certain because it features in our story as the place where Laura's mother, the younger Charlotte went to school, met her husband and, when newly married, lived. Laura was to be born in Long Eaton in 1877.

Despite this Long Eaton connection, it is the Radford district of Nottingham that is the most important location in the Bates-Ther story. It was there that Mary Ther had her stay-making business, and where Stephen Bates and Charlotte Ther married. In his *Old Nottingham Suburbs: then and now* (1914) the Nottinghamshire historian Robert Mellors describes the men of Radford as 'figuring largely' in the development of the lace machine. In relation to this, in the *London Gazette* of 3rd July 1865 there is an entry that 'Stephen Bates of New Radford, in the county of Nottingham, Lace Manufacturer' has given a patent notice in respect of the invention of 'improvements in the manufacture or production of bobbin net or twist lace made on bobbin net or machines.' The continuing association of the Bates and Ther families with Radford is significant to this story since it is the locality within which Laura and her sisters were brought up and educated.

From the 1790s the expansion of the Nottingham textile industries and the migration of hundreds of workers to support them meant that outlying rural villages to the north and west of the town such as Lenton and Radford expanded significantly. Hence, we have New Lenton, and New Radford as well as the establishment of entirely new settlements at Carrington and Hyson Green further west. In 1845 formal legislation was passed to allow the enclosure of the open fields lying between these village cores and Nottingham town. As a result there was a speculative building boom and the area developed to provide mixed residential property and industrial workshops. Very soon the marshlands of the Vale of Leen and the sandstone rise above the old hunting grounds of Sherwood, were covered with rows of houses. It was in this area, contained by the Alfreton and Ilkeston Roads, bordered by The Forest and Arboretum Parks and quickly to merge with the district of Hyson (originally Ison) Green, that Stephen, Charlotte and their growing family of six children lived.

However inventive, Laura's grandfather had little business acumen and, often neglecting to secure patents for his inventions, his ideas were appropriated by others. He never made a fortune in the way that many did in those heady days of industrialized lacemaking. His business certainly seems to have been conducted in an *ad hoc* manner. For example, in order to fund his projects, he turned his hand to making and selling lace from home, storing the cash in the house until needed. Laura retells Big Grandma's probably highly exaggerated account (it was a trait inherited by Laura) of how 'sacks and sacks of gold sovereigns' were hoarded in their hot-water cistern to avoid the attention of thieves. To celebrate his first achievement at lace-making Stephen bought a grandfather clock that, along with a horsehair sofa and a red plush armchair, survived to be part of the furniture at Noel Street and were to continue as furnishings in Laura's own story.

The Bates had seven children of whom six survived. Laura's Mother was born in 1853, with an elder sister, Elizabeth, three older brothers, Stephen, George and Thomas and one younger, Arthur Peter of whom she was very fond, born in 1854. Not well-to-do but generally comfortable, the Bates family looked askance on neighbours who, having made money during the good times in the lace industry, had aspired to and had purchased smart new houses in The Park estate. Adjacent to Nottingham Castle and originally a private hunting ground, in the middle of the 19th century The Park was developed by the owner the 5th Duke of Newcastle as a residential enclave of exclusive Regency, Victorian Gothic and Italianate style villas: the best address in Nottingham. However, after the Franco-Prussian War of 1870–1 when the French imposed crippling tariffs on imported English lace, there was a major slump in the business and many of the *nouveau riche* residents of The Park found themselves unable to keep up their property or their lifestyle. Living in rented accommodation, the Bates were able to adjust to the fluctuations in the lace trade, reflected in their regular moves to houses each one less distinguished than the last and justified in the remembered litany: 'trade's bad this year'.

Stephen Bates died in 1874, leaving the business in the hands of his two elder sons, Stephen and George, who, by all accounts were ill-suited to the task. His wife Charlotte had to manage the household as finances drained away. It was a struggle, but Big Grandma was capable: 'Mrs Bates you are a marvel' her friends would exclaim. Laura remembered her bright blue twinkling eyes (Laura, too had bright blue eyes) and the white lace cap that covered the silver hair that looped over her ears and was drawn into a knob at the back just like Queen Victoria. It was Big Grandma who found the house in Noel Street and provided stability and assurance for the family when little Laura and her two sisters, Nellie and Eva, arrived there with their Mother Charlotte in 1877. Situated within a mile north of the city centre, number 9 Noel Street is one half of Ethel Villas, a slate roofed, three storied semi-detached house built on the ridge to the west of The Forest. Today this is marked by a faded blue plaque testifying to Laura Johnson's residence there as a child.

Now the site of the annual Nottingham Goose Fair, The Forest was initially designated for public recreational use in the 1840s and from 1865 to 1898 was the place where football was played (Laura and Harold were to be life-long supporters of "Notts County"). During its planning Joseph Paxton, gardener and architect of the Crystal Palace for the Great Exhibition of 1851, was invited to design the network of walkways which traversed the park space. For the elevated houses at the better end of Noel Street it provided a salubrious aspect, overlooking the town racecourse, then in process of construction. Once established, the racecourse offered a glorious phantasmagoria show for the children observing from the balcony of number 9: horses and jockeys in brilliant silks, excited crowds in the red brick grandstand and beyond the tempting sight of fairground rides and sideshows. For little Laura it stimulated a life-long fascination with an alternative world, as she says: 'Doubtless the early association with races, fairs and circuses laid the foundation of much of my later work'.

Born on the 4th August in 1877, Laura was the third child of Charlotte Bates and Charles William (Charlie) Johnson. As a young woman, Laura's Mother had been singled out by her teacher at Long Eaton School as a promising art student who should develop her talent in Paris. For Charlotte in provincial Long Eaton, Paris with its reputation as the place for the student to learn the techniques of art in the teaching studios (*ateliers*) of the finest masters filled her hopes and dreams. The very idea met with scorn, for the Bates' business was seriously unstable at that time and there was no spare money for such grandiose plans. Nor were they considered necessary or appropriate, since it was the strongly held opinion of Little Grandma that a woman's destiny in life was to marry and have children. So, in her innocence

Charlotte sought a man to marry who could support her and maybe help realize her aspirations as an artist. At the age of seventeen she met Charlie Johnson, handsome, worldly and 2 years her senior, at a Long Eaton "social".

Charlie appeared to be gallant and sympathetic, but in truth he was "on the make", fancying that an alliance with the young Charlotte would offer entry into a well-off family who would bank-roll his rakish lifestyle. They were married at St Mary's Parish Church, Nottingham on the 31st December 1872. On the marriage certificate he is described as a "lace draper". To Charlie's disappointment, he discovered that his expectations were without foundation. The family were not rich and the 1870s were hard times for everyone in the lace industry. This fact, however, did not affect his plans. After their marriage he continued to indulge his bachelor habits and his hard drinking to the bitter disappointment of his young wife and despite a growing family. Charlotte Ellen (known as "Nellie") was born on the 7th November 1873, while Evangeline (Eva) Agnes (known as "Sis" or "Sissie") arrived 20th June in 1875 and Laura ("only Laura") on the 4th August 1877. On Eva's birth certificate, Charlie's occupation is described as a "Licensed Victualler", so he had moved on from the wholesale and retailing of lace and become a pub landlord. Charlotte ended the marriage in the December of 1877, not long after Laura was born, and Charlie went out of their lives. In 1883 they heard that he had died (probably from alcoholism) at the age of thirty-seven. Charlotte and the girls made their home in Noel Street, Nottingham with her mother, her grandmother, and Uncle Arthur Peter. In the complicated extended Bates-Ther family genealogy, these persons, along with Great Aunt West-Ther, were to be the central characters in Laura's early life.

Arthur never married and, since his elder brothers were unreliable, shouldered much of the Bates' business, making regular visits to St Quentin in Northern France where Aunt West-Ther and her husband Jack West, ran the French branch of the lace-making business. Big Grandma had been generous in helping them to set up the St Quentin factory and as it prospered, Aunt West was generous in return. Laura writes of Aunt West-Ther arriving like a good fairy with gifts when the girls were small. Once on one of her visits from France, she brought them a toy theatre with many changes of scenery. It was something that Laura, who herself was naturally theatrical, singled out as being a special present indeed.

The house in Noel Street had three floors. On the ground floor was the living room and kitchen, while on the first floor Big Grandma, Little Grandma and Uncle Arthur Peter had their rooms. Young Charlotte and the girls occupied the third storey, which, extending into the upper floor of their next-door neighbours the Gutteridges, provided their sleeping space as well as a studio. Charlotte, now a single mother, was determined to make a living and pay her way. She offered art lessons to the daughters of local middle-class families, teaching them the rudiments of painting and drawing and showing them 'how to copy flowers on to stools, fire-screens and palm-leaf fans'. Always eager to continue her own education, she took up French classes and went to public lectures. In the 1881 census she described herself as "art student" for she was enrolled as a student at Nottingham School of Art, just up the road in Waverley Street, and attended classes in the evenings. When she could, she would take the girls with her on painting expeditions. We can visualize the little troupe, walking (they could not afford a tram fare) 'laden with paints and lunch' out to the river Trent at Wilford two miles away.

Wilford was then a secluded picturesque village famous for its association with the early Romantic poet Henry Kirke White (1785–1806) who in his *Lines Written in Wilford Churchyard* described it as a 'lovely spot' with breezes 'wafting gently o'er the rippling Trent'. Laura remembers her Mother painting a watercolour of Kirke White's cottage while she attempted to sketch the Church, then all three girls settled down on the beach of shingle to imagine themselves at the seaside. It was to The Grange at Wilford that a distant relative, a George Bates was to move. He had made a fortune making mosquito nets in his factory in New Radford and his daughter Marjorie Christine Bates was a gifted artist. However, contrary to a popular Wilford myth, she is most unlikely to have been a playmate for Laura at that time. Not only was she 11 years younger but her family did not live at Wilford until the 1890s. Born in Melbourne, Derbyshire in 1888 Marjorie lived a privileged life, in due course attending the Nottingham School of Art, studying in Paris and exhibiting at the Royal Academy. Despite these similarities, neither the relationship nor other points of connection feature in Laura Knight's reminiscences. Most likely the families were not in regular social contact, if at all.

The Johnson girls did frequent the home of their cousins the Boyells, however. Mother's elder sister Elizabeth (some 12 years her senior) had married a lace-manufacturer, William Richard Boyell (who left her and became a policeman in Paris). The Johnson girls often visited, and their cousin Charlotte Mary often came to Noel Street. Charlotte Mary married James Martin-Langley, who as "Mr Langley" was always addressed by Laura with the greatest courtesy but she disliked their son Reggie – the "mardy" boy. Reggie and his mother were familiar visitors at Noel Street as the family

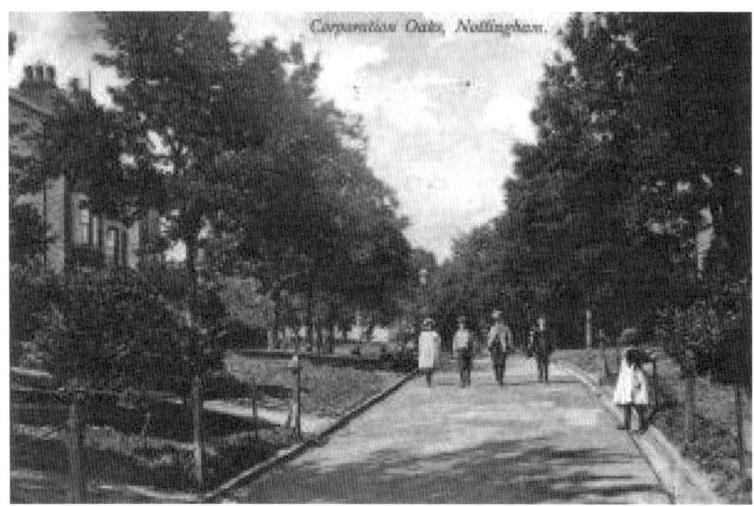

Corporation Oaks, Nottingham, postcard 1910

photograph of 1882 in Chapter Two illustrates. And, the Johnson girls were often at Corporation Oaks, where the Langley's lived, although Laura was, according to family anecdote, at one time "kicked out" for being a nuisance!

The house at Noel Street was crowded and from Laura's childhood perspective as she grew ever more tom-boyish and boisterous, restrictive and frustrating. This was especially the case when she was ordered to be quiet as Little Grandma (through age) and sometimes Big Grandma (through exhaustion) slept in the daytime. Laura's memories of the house focus on a few key motifs: the 'gas jets set in round opal globes' illuminating the dining table where the girls did their homework; Mother at the sewing machine making her own and her daughters' clothes; the attics, where Laura and her sisters played 'with the lumber of past generations', having braved the 'dark creatures' that inhabited the cistern cupboard at the head of the stairs; Little Grandma descending from her room backward down those stairs, nautical fashion, and Uncle Arthur Peter's room, distinguished by a row of bottles of eau-de-cologne purchased on visits to France.

The only man in the house, something of a dandy and man-about-town, Uncle Arthur Peter had a sociable nature and many friends, mostly Freemasons like himself. Laura offers us several images of him: Uncle Arthur asleep on the old horsehair sofa (with which Stephen and Charlotte had set up home), his face covered by a newspaper against the flies; Uncle Arthur

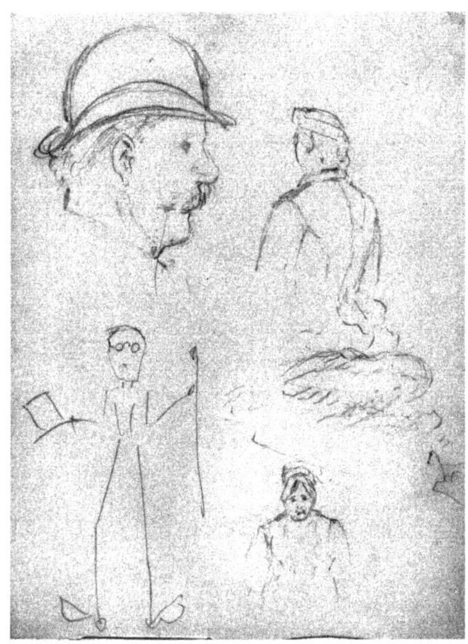

Uncle Arthur Peter, sketch by Charlotte Johnson (Mother), c. 1885

bringing home washing baskets full of roses from his allotment at Hungerhills (a pound a year rental) – enough to fill 'three cut-glass bowls' followed by the harvest of plums, 'as big as peaches'. The youngest of four surviving brothers, Arthur was resentful of his elder male siblings, Stephen and George. Despite having enjoyed a French education at the expense of Aunt West-Ther, in his opinion (probably coloured by a young lady's having rejected his advances in preference to those of one of these brothers) they were ne'er-do-wells. In his opinion they were over-familiar with the factory hands and over-fond of beer. When they visited their Mother, Big Grandma Bates, they did so only to discuss money. At those times Laura learned to keep out of the way because afterwards Big Grandma would be upset. The other brother, Thomas, a good-natured soul who ran the Ram Hotel in Long Row in the centre of Nottingham, died 1883 when Laura was quite small and was remembered only by Nellie and Sissy for his bringing them 'goodies'. Laura recalls being sorry she was too young to have benefitted from knowing him.

Uncle Arthur Peter (the girls' pet name for him was 'Ninkie') was a dominant presence in the household. Severely authoritarian at times and ebullient at others, Laura describes him as a volcanic personality. Fancying himself as something of a thespian, he would often break forth into dramatic renditions, and she would mimic him in voice and gesture. In many ways they were two of a kind. Laura was always keen to perform. Mrs Hemans' dramatic poem 'The boy stood on the burning deck' was her party-piece along with lines from the poet Thomas Hood, in particular 'The Song of a Shirt'. In her renditions she displayed a precociousness that won her both admiration but also reproach from her elders.

Two of Arthur Peter's Masonic friends had a profound influence on the Johnson girls. There was Bill Stevenson who always brought them books and taught Laura the art of calligraphy, inscribing wonderful graphic letters for her to copy in the ledger that she was given for her infant drawing. Bill was funny, intelligent and attracted to Mother. They started to walk out together on a Sunday after church, the girls in their new mantles and Welsh pointed hats with pink and black bows that to their chagrin he called 'jelly bags'. Bill's visits stopped abruptly at the instance of Uncle Arthur whose words to his sister were blunt: '"What, you marry another poor man and come home with another family of children?"'. Laura as a child regretted his loss: 'I could not help wishing that Bill Stevenson had been allowed to marry Mother'. As an adult she was to discover that Bill Stevenson had become a wealthy man.

Then there was the Scotsman, John Cruickshank, like Uncle Arthur, a one-off or in local parlance an "unexpected". A fervid teetotaler, tall, well built, with a red pointed beard and always with a cigarette in his mouth, he was 'gloriously unconventional'. Like a Pied Piper, followed by troops of children, he distributed pennies and sweets from his pockets as he walked. Mr Cruickshank's business was as a paper merchant and he came to Nottingham every 6 weeks, bringing the girls nougat and sacks of drawing paper: 'We worshipped Mr Cruickshank', says Laura, 'and my imagination gave his features to God'.

Laura was christened at the age of five on the 4th November 1882 at St Peter's Church, Radford. In the baptismal register, Laura's deceased Father's occupation was given as "inn-keeper" and the Bates' family address as being number 35 Noel Street. This signals a major downturn in family circumstances. Number 35 was a smaller and cheaper house to rent. It was situated towards the bottom of the hill on what the local doctor declared to be a damp and unhealthy position, having been built on the site of the local cesspit. Life by then was increasingly difficult for the household. Business was bad and the growing children put extra pressure on the finances. Yet despite this, Laura's childhood memories are rich in colour and romance. Taught to read by Big Grandma from *The Arabian Knights*, she devoured books from Uncle Arthur's bookcase such as the terrors of Edgar Allen Poe and the *Ingoldsby Legends*. Her Mother, feeding the spirit of wonderment in her girls, once picked Laura up from her bed to see the blaze of a factory fire in the distance and at another time roused them all to see the sun rise over the Forest racecourse. For Laura Nottingham was a magical place, with its folklore and legends of Sherwood and Robin Hood.

Originally the site of a Saxon settlement, the town of Nottingham was established by the Normans on a sandstone ridge overlooking the River Trent. This was where Nottingham Castle was subsequently built. Its history conjures up a drama of ill-fated campaigns and events starring romantic figures such as Richard the Lionheart who laid siege to the Castle in 1194. In 1330 it saw the capture and arrest of the *de facto* ruler of the kingdom Roger Mortimer, consort to Queen Isabella, the mother of Edward III. It was where Richard III's campaign began in 1485, ending with the fatal Battle of Bosworth. In 1642 it was where Charles I raised the Royal standard, signalling the start of the Civil War.

In Asser's *Life of King Alfred*, 900AD, Nottingham is named Tiggua Cobaucc, which means "place of caves" and for centuries the sandstone rock offered underground passages and caverns used for workshops and storage. An example can still be seen in the centre of the city. Originally a brewery, The Trip to Jerusalem Inn abuts the Castle Rock, with drinking rooms and cellars carved out of the sandstone at the time of the building of the Castle around 1068. Over the centuries more caves were excavated for living spaces, some ornately carved but in 1845 they were condemned as dangerous by Act of Parliament and declared unsuitable for use as dwellings. However, Laura and her sister Sis were able to rent one to use as a studio and bed sitting room in 1895.

Nottingham also has its elegant side. In the centre Georgian buildings are juxtaposed with impressive Victorian red brick warehousing with architectural features taken from the Gothic and vernacular past. In the Victorian period, the female workers in these palaces of industry earned the reputation for being the most beautiful girls in England. This was because its main signature product, lace (the others were to be the manufacture of Raleigh bicycles, Boots' pharmaceutical products and John Player's tobacco), was thought to make the factory girls pretty and feminine. It was a local habit to take visitors to the Lace Market at the end of a shift to view the girls and judge the prettiest. When telling her reader of this, Laura qualifies her remark: 'handling lace was supposed to make them, dainty' she says with a touch of irony – and perhaps with some justice. On leaving school in 1901, the writer D.H. Lawrence (some 10 years the junior of Laura Johnson) took up employment as a junior clerk at Haywood's surgical appliance factory in the textile quarter of the city. He was soon forced to leave, having contracted severe pneumonia after attack by a gang of factory girls! The Haywood factory experience provided material for his semi-autobiographical novel *Sons and Lovers* (1913).

At the heart of Nottingham is the Old Market Square (otherwise known as "Lion" or "Slab Square") of which the saying goes that the stone lions growl when a virgin passes by – which also justifies Laura's scepticism. This was the meeting place and market for the original Saxon settlement and the subsequent Norman town and for 700 years, until 1928, it was the setting for the Goose Fair. This annual event provoked great excitement for the Johnson girls. In the sky 'thick with smoke and October mist', shadows flickered and loomed. In the darkness crowds thronged – women in their 'bustles and the men in 'billycock' hats', while a riot of spangles and feathers distinguished the attire of the show people, all to the accompaniment of the steam organs with their discordant clashing of cymbals and drums. It was a thrilling and a slightly frightening experience, for beneath the make-up and the costumes, Laura's penetrating gaze notes pock-marked and ravaged faces, a life of hardship beneath the glamour.

These people lived a life on the edge, beyond the norms of provincial respectability. Somewhere deep inside it called to Laura. Never staying in one place long enough to be fully known or defined, the fairground, like

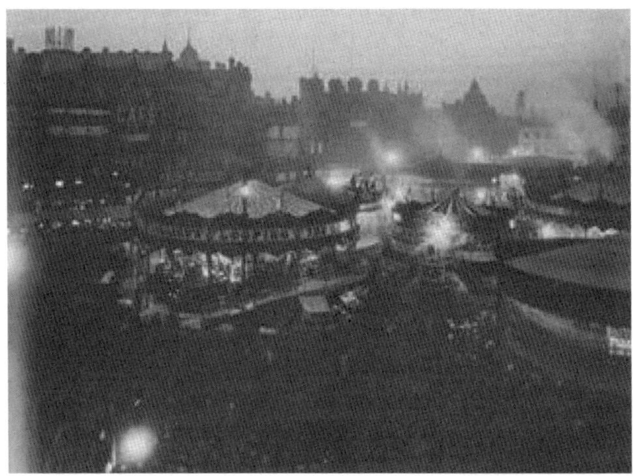

Goose Fair, Market Place Nottingham, c. 1909

the circus and the theatre, had a life-long fascination for her. She delighted in the artificiality, the costumes, the make-up and the lights, the drama of faces glimpsed in the press of the crowd. It is interesting to note that in her representation of *Penzance Fair*, dated 1916 when she was thirty-nine, she pictures herself in that crowd. We see her in three quarter profile, wearing her favourite red jacket, a colour that advances her figure from the riot of shapes and detail. But the image is slightly disturbing: her hair is in pigtails, the stance is nonchalant. It is as if she is affirming her essential self: childlike, spontaneous and insouciant, free of the conventions of the adult world. Her eyes, looking across the gap of years it seems, are fixed on a small fair-haired girl astride a "galloping horse" on the carousel who is also wearing red.

Below: Laura and her Sisters, Nellie and Eva sketched by their Mother in a scribble and accounts book dated around 1885. Note the short hair – the result probably of an infestation of head-lice, not mentioned in the autobiographies! Images courtesy of Charlotte Bedford.

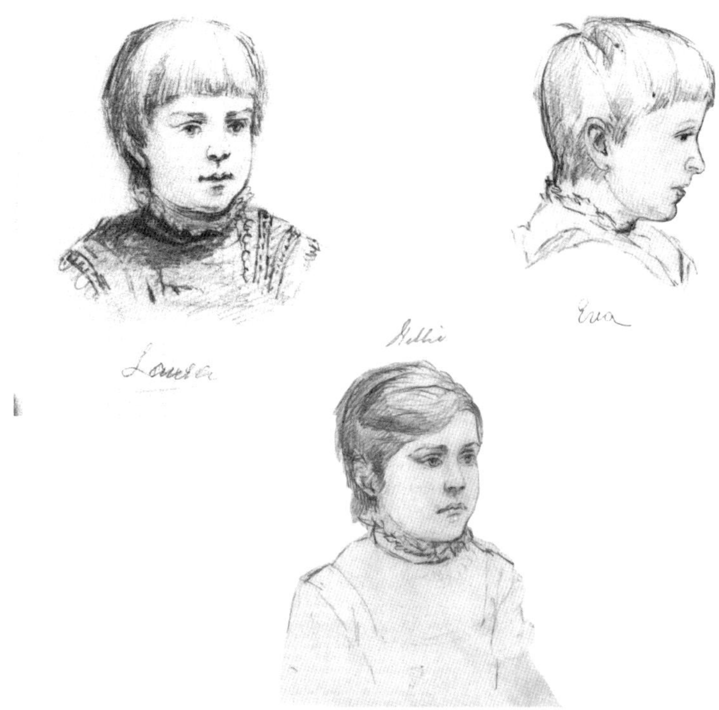

CHILDREN OF MARY BROOMHEAD AND CHARLES THER

Mary Charlotte Broomhead (*Little Grandma*)
Christened 8th November 1792, died 26th May 1889
Married 13th December 1813

Charles George Ther
Baptised 15th August 1792, died 1st July 1845
Had eleven children:

1. **Owen** born out of wedlock 1812, died 17th February 1812 near Dover
2. **Charlotte Ther** (*Big Grandma*) Born 18th December 1813, Nottingham, died 22nd September 1895, Nottingham. Married Stephen Bates 4th October 1837
3. **William Ther** Christened 21st July 1820, Nottingham, died 1882, New Brunswick USA. Married Hanna Coutts 1844
4. **Ann Ther** Christened 20th September 1818, Stamford Lincs. Married William Blazedale 1839, died Queensland, Australia
5. **Charles Ther** Christened 9th December 1820, Stamford Baron Northants, died Nottingham 1884
    1st Marriage: Ann Bennell 8th June 1840
    2nd Marriage: Catherine Needham 27th December 1864
6. **Sarah Ther** Christened 5th March 1823, Stamford Baron Northants
7. **George Ther** Born c.1824 Nottingham. Married Emma Thompson 1842
8. **Hanna Ther** Born c.1826 Nottingham. Married Edward Wakefield 1846
9. **Eliza Ther** (*Aunt West*) Christened 1829 Nottingham, Died 1902, St. Quentin France. Married Arthur John ("Jack") West 1848
10. **Emma Ther** Christened January 1832, Nottingham Died 1907, New Jersey USA. Married Thomas Redfern 1852
11. **Henry Ther** Born c1834 Nottingham. Married cousin Ann Broomhead 1883

This information is provided courtesy of descendants of the Ther/Thir family.

CHAPTER TWO

"Why must girls be pretty?"

Last in line for hand-me-downs, as a child Laura was condemned to wear a black velveteen frock for too many years for her comfort or dignity. She was at first proud of the black velveteen frock since no other children at school wore anything as distinctive, but as the pile wore on the elbows and bodice and it grew every day shorter and tighter, the black velveteen frock became an embarrassment. Once when walking back from school with her friend Norah Truman who lived on the Forest Road, they were caught in a rain shower. Perhaps this was the turning point of her relationship with the black velveteen frock because, expressing concern that the rain would spoil it, Norah's blunt response was 'should think it'd do it good'. That day Laura's pride took a fall.

Laura's oldest sister Nellie, growing into a young woman and blessed with 'ripe-chestnut coloured hair' like her Mother's, was Laura's idol. Her next sister, Sissie's hair was bright gold, so gold it looked 'false'. But Laura's 'bush of yellow hair' refused to be tamed and resisted being curled into ringlets. When it was washed it stood 'bolt upright' in a most amazing way like "Shock-haired Peter" in Heinrich Hoffmann's *Strewwelpeter* (1845). She considered this 'fun' and would 'pull faces and do antics' to frighten her sisters until Mother got angry and ordered her to stop the 'mad excitement'. She had inherited Big Grandma's bright blue eyes but her round pink and white face, was in no way conventionally pretty. Never called out in a game of "postman's knock", she was jealous of one of the other girls at school called Maisie who, having dark curls and melting brown eyes, always was. However, she could soon put such resentment to one side when, with her irrepressible energy and a sturdy frame, she outpaced all runners in school races and was in demand for team games.

Being dissatisfied with her female-dominated family, Laura conjured up for herself an imaginary alternative in which she was flanked by two brothers. She could visualize herself in 'a smocked frock, red on white' but found it difficult to picture the boys: 'they are so much uglier' asking the question: 'Why must girls be pretty?' Laura was famous in her family for being the tomboy. Often swinging on the horizontal bars outside the Boys' High School and joining in their local street games, she would return home dishevelled and with grazed knees. 'She should have been a boy', Little Grandma often said, and Laura just as often wished that she was. When finances were stretched and the household had to dispense with the servant, the girls had to do a share of housework. Laura hated it but spent the penny a week earned on the *Boys' Own Paper* which she read for the adventures and instructions as to how to 'make things'. In winter she delighted in sliding in the gutters and skating over the frozen water meadows of the River Trent. While all three Johnson girls were excitable, Laura was volatile and free-spirited, living life with a passion that earned reprimand and warnings from neighbours that she would come to no good: 'She ought to have a doctor – look at 'er – she must 'ave an abscess growing in 'er 'ead!' Laura's response was typical: 'I was rather proud of having an abscess in my head'.

As a child she was a natural performer – never reluctant to recite or participate in school plays. Wearing her old velveteen frock which Mother lengthened with strips of wadding to simulate ermine, she was made for the part of the "Ugly" Duchess in the "Pig and Pepper" episode of *Alice in Wonderland.* She gloried in the 'raging and tearing about' while 'everyone clapped to see me go mad and I loved it'. In the first version of her autobiography the sequence of reminiscence suddenly changes into the present tense and once again the wild child gesticulates and storms across the stage. Hidden within the same paragraph comes affirmation of her agility and confidence to evade other people's prying eyes and analysis: 'Sometimes when I draw I feel like when I am dodging in a crowd, and in some performances last Christmas, when I was playing the Ugly Duchess in Alice in Wonderland I'd feel the same'. This episode features in *The Magic of a Line* but it is in a lower key and being matter-of-fact reveals no insights into her evasive inner self. There she simply tells of how the first performance being so successful, repeat performances were requested and how in her enthusiasm one night she burst the box of powder which was serving for the stuffing for the baby, covering everything in a 'mist of white dust'. That, she writes in *The Magic of a Line,* 'put the kibosh on the whole thing'.

The girls were all competent artists but, to her Mother's delight, from infancy Laura was naturally gifted, demanding only pencils and paper as her playthings. As a young child she amazed all with her ability to draw household objects and to copy whatever she could get her hands on. As a small girl her exposure to art was confined to book illustrations, her Mother's own water colour paintings and the efforts of Mother's pupils whom Laura joined as soon as she was allowed. Sometimes Mother took them to Church down the hill at Hyson Green, but it was infrequent since the girls would deliberately frustrate and delay preparations and often there was a lack of "Sunday best" clothes. On Sundays, when their neighbourhood 'died … to the clanking of bells', they were not allowed to either to draw or play but could browse some old copies of *Punch* magazine. That this was suitable Sunday reading is questionable since what little Laura enjoyed most were the cartoons: 'I loved John Leech and Charles Keen's drunken men; Dumaurier's drawings I did not like so well, but I could have passed an examination in any of the jokes!' Since Uncle Arthur, being something of a collector, had a well-stocked bookcase, the girls knew Dickens by heart, particularly *David Copperfield* and *Oliver Twist* which were read and re-read. Laura liked Thackeray less, but was much taken by reference in *Vanity Fair* to a 'soiree consisting of cold mutton'. It is noticeable that throughout her life details of food consumed (or the lack of it) is a predominant theme.

In 1879 when Laura was eight, Mother became ill and no one in the house could understand what was wrong or why. A letter dated 22nd July 1885 written by Nellie to Uncle Arthur Peter, who at the time was on holiday with Mr Cruickshank, expresses the hope that that he is enjoying himself and continues: 'We have been to your garden, Grandmamma, Sissy, Laura and I, and took our tea … Mamma is a great deal better, although she was very poorly yesterday'. It was Aunt West-Ther, on one of her visits, who recognized the symptoms of nervous exhaustion. She immediately offered to pay for her niece to have a change of air and scene. The girls were to be looked after by Big Grandma and Mama was to go to St Quentin for a couple of weeks and then stay with family friends in Paris where she was to enrol as a student at one of the painting schools on the Left Bank – all at her expense. Charlotte was to realize her dream.

Paris in the 1880s was an exciting place to visit. Haussmann's recently built boulevards and smart cafés made it the most modern, stylish and progressive city in Europe. As a centre for the arts it had no rival. It was the most fashionable city in Europe and the centre of culture and art with its new Opera House (the Palais Garnier which had opened in 1879); its museums and picture galleries of which the Louvre was pre-eminent; the annual Salon exhibition (the equivalent of the Royal Academy in London) for contemporary fine art and from 1863 the Salon des Refusés which contained artworks that the Salon had rejected that year, allowing public display of the avant-garde. As a result, Paris attracted painters, writers and intellectuals from across Europe and America, all drawn to the *La Vie Bohème*. In the music halls and bars of Montmartre artists, shopgirls and models mixed with the *flâneur*, the philosopher and the revolutionary. The conversation, like the writing, music and painting of this society was charged with anarchic energy. Yet Charlotte saw little of it and recognized even less, for in the *ateliers* art training remained in the past, maintaining the academic conventions. Charlotte, now in her 30s, studied earnestly and took advantage of her opportunity to learn from her masters rather than fellow students.

For the first time she was made aware of oil paint as a medium, mixing and applying colour in ways that she had never before explored. What was remarkable was that in Paris the life-class was open to female students, something unheard of in Nottingham or indeed in London, and Charlotte applied herself diligently. She continued to draw and paint in the way she had always done, preferring to copy old masters in the Louvre, especially landscapes, rather than investigate the ferment that was going on the contemporary art world around her. As a result, even though she must have heard of the names of the new wave artists, Manet, Monet, Renoir, Cezanne, dropped into conversations or furiously debated by fellow students, she remained untouched by their influence.

When the money ran out, Charlotte had to go back to Nottingham. Aunt West hoped that she had developed her skills sufficiently to benefit her teaching and it proved to be so. She managed to get a few hours a week teaching drawing to beginners at the Art College and the cachet of having Mrs. Johnson who "had been trained in Paris" as a tutor for their daughters was not lost on the mothers of the town. Meanwhile, Laura was fascinated by her Mother's stories and particularly by descriptions of the shops and of fashionable ladies in their carriages bowling through the parks. Janet Dunbar, whose text, informed by conversations with the artist later in life, tells of Laura's lasting memory of her Mother's return from Paris 'dressed in a green costume and a bonnet trimmed with flowers, Aunt West's parting gifts'.

While the domestic world of the Johnson girls was confined to the Radford neighbourhood, their experience was not limited. Mother often took them farther afield on holiday painting trips. Once, Laura was taken to Lathkildale in Derbyshire where she practiced skimming stones across the millpond while Mother painted. Occasionally the girls were taken for a holiday to Rowsley, also in the Derbyshire Peak District, where for a few shillings weekly they stayed on a local farm and fed simply on bread, cheese and milk. They walked daily the short distance to Haddon Hall, the long-empty Elizabethan house once the seat of the Manners family. Familiar through Sir Walter Scott's novel *Peveril of the Peak* (1823), the origins of Haddon go back to an illegitimate son of William the Conqueror, Peveril, who ultimately held land – "The Honour of Peveril" – throughout the East Midlands, including Nottingham Castle. It was a fine and mysterious place with romantic associations.

Ballad and legend tell of how in 1563 the 15-year-old Dorothy Vernon, the daughter of Sir George Vernon, "King of the Peak", eloped with John Manners, the second son of Thomas, 1st Earl of Rutland. Sir George disapproved of the union since the Manners were Protestants and the Vernons were Roman Catholic. The allure of their romance resonated throughout and beyond the 19th century in novel and film but for Laura it was a reality. Mother had a passkey to the then empty Hall and made the bedchamber of Dorothy Vernon her studio. There, sitting in the fireplace, the children would feed the mice and rats with crumbs. Interestingly the scenic backdrop painted by Mother (with help from Laura herself) for the production of *Alice* was a scaled–up version of one of her sketches from this Derbyshire holiday, showing the steps down which Dorothy Vernon was said to have eloped.

While better-off Nottingham children like their neighbours the Lees, regularly packed their buckets and spades and made for the coast at Skegness on Bank Holidays (which had been enshrined in law since 1871), Laura saw the sea for the first time at the age of nine. While Nellie was taken to Great Yarmouth by Uncle Arthur, Sis and Laura were invited to join Mr Cruickshank's family on a 6-week trip to Ayr in Scotland. What an adventure that was! Barefoot and carefree, this was their chance to live a life of sheer abandonment. In and out of the water, with the gulls, the smell of seaweed, the hoot of the paddle-steamer and soft white baps for breakfast every day, their horizons expanded and their appetites were sharpened. One day they visited Robbie Burns' cottage at Alloway, coming away with souvenirs, but the promised trip to the Isle of Arran had to be abandoned because of rough seas – the only day of poor weather over the whole stay. On their return train journey, as they travelled over the Border Laura caused great embarrassment to the rest of the party by impetuously standing up in the crowded third-class carriage to recite familiar lines from Scott's *The Lay of the Last Minstrel*:

> Breathes there the man, with soul so dead,
> Who never to himself hath said,
> This is my own, my native land!

> Whose heart ne'er within him burn'd,
> As home his footsteps he hath turn'd
> From wandering on a foreign strand!

Laura could never resist an audience. Ever the self-publicist and always ready to perform, this bravado was an essential part of her character. Time and again she draws attention to herself, presenting to the world a dramatic persona that is all bluster and pomp. She was strong-willed and jealous, often spiteful to her sister Sis. As such she was never an easy child to manage. Without wishing to attempt an analysis of her psychological make-up, it is almost certain that as the youngest child, gifted and made much of, she must, nonetheless, have been curious as to why her Mother had left her Father and wondered (as children do) if she was in any way responsible. Her Mother never mentioned him except to warn the girls against repeating any gossip they heard. Insecurity often shows itself in boldness, exaggeration and a compulsion to show off and what that hides often never comes out of the shadows.

Back in Nottingham after their holidays, Mother greeted their return with consternation, for in those 6 weeks they had outgrown clothes and shoes and there was precious little money available to buy new. Laura too was dismayed to find that while she had been away the two white mice which she had hoped to train to walk the clothesline in the back yard, had been eaten by the cat. Over the next 2 years her domestic world was to contract in other ways. Little Grandma died on the 26th May 1889 in her 97th year. Laura was allowed to see the body laid out in the coffin and never forgot the sight of the gaping mouth beneath the lace cap and the pennies on the eyes, nor the smell of varnish and the glint of brass handles. After the funeral at the General Cemetery the girls were taken for a long walk round the Forest racetrack by Uncle Arthur's friend Mr Cruickshank, returning home to sausages and coconut cakes. It is another early instance of how food is always an important element in Laura's memories, marking events and giving comfort and assurance.

Laura, like her sisters when they left primary school, attended Brincliffe School on the Forest Road at the top of Noel Street. Mother taught art there in return for free education for the girls. Charlotte Johnson still aspired to be a professional artist and attended classes at the Art School when she could fit them in between caring for the girls, earning a living teaching and taking in private pupils. That way she more or less made ends meet. In fragile health, at the limit of her own capacity for teaching and given her own experience of

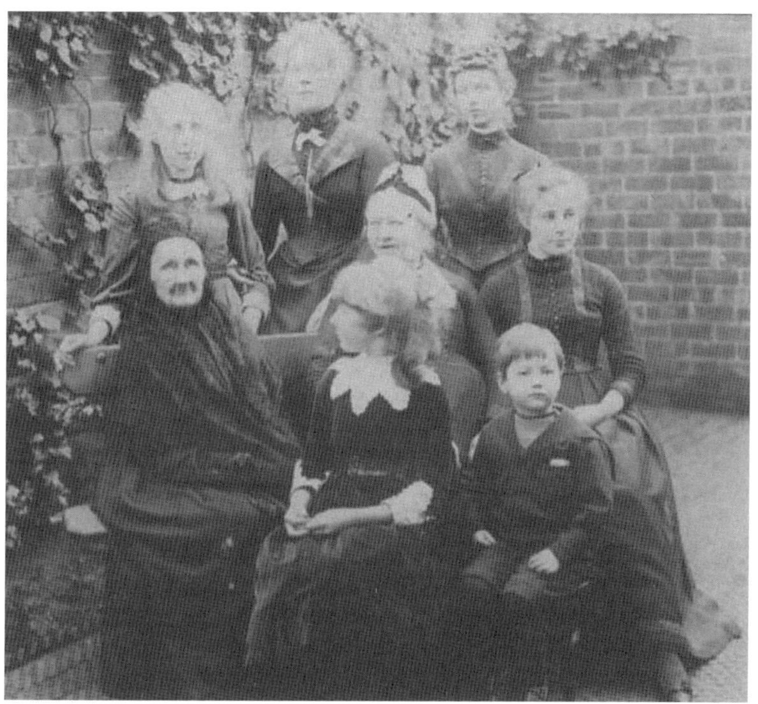

Family photograph, 1882. Back row left to right: Sis, Mother, her niece Charlotte Mary Langley (née Boyell). Middle row seated left to right: Big Grandma, Nellie and front row left to right: Little Grandma, Laura, Reggie Langley (the 'mardy boy'). This photograph is mentioned in *Oil Paint and Grease Paint*, p.20. Courtesy of Charlotte Bedford

marriage, she was determined that her girls be economically self-sufficient. As a result, Nellie left school at fourteen and was found a teaching place at the local Board School where she worked as a pupil-teacher in the day, studying at the University College at night and doing her homework into the small hours. Sis followed the same pattern and became a pupil teacher at eleven rising twelve.

However, when Laura was twelve an invitation came from Aunt West-Ther for her to go to St Quentin. There she would perfect her French in order (wonder of wonders!) go to Paris to study art. Big Grandma, who was very fond of her sister and occasionally visited her in France just as Aunt West-Ther regularly came over to Nottingham, was to accompany Laura on the journey. Laura was ecstatic but, as the eldest sister, Nellie was upset at being overlooked.

When the time came to prepare for departure, Nellie was ill. A major influenza epidemic was sweeping Europe in 1889 and, weakened by relentless work and never robust, Nellie succumbed to what was called at the time the *grippe*. The doctor assured them that despite a high temperature and physical weakness Nellie was not dangerously ill. Therefore, there was no need to postpone the visit. So preparations began. Given that Mother was pre-occupied with nursing the invalid, Laura had, with a local seamstress' help, to cut out and sew her own few clothes, then pack her trunk herself. It seemed to Laura that Nellie was deliberately sabotaging her triumph for there is an element of resentment in Laura's recorded response to her sister's tearful farewell. On the sick girl's pronouncement that they would 'never see' one another again, Laura believed it to be unnecessarily dramatic and, impatient and excited, set out for the lace factory at St Quentin with only a brief backward glance.

After a bad crossing and violent seasickness, they landed at Calais where Laura, much to her disgust, had to kiss a woman who was serving behind the bar at the estaminet. This distant member of the family (possibly a relation of Big Grandma's sister Emma Redfern who with her husband had superintended a lace mill there in the 1850s) 'had a painted face and lots of yellow hair, that looked false'. However, a substantial meal made up for the hair and the kiss, especially the *bouillon* with alphabet letters that you could arrange in the bottom of the plate to spell your name. At Lille they were approached by a plausible woman who told them that they had missed the Basle train and offered them overnight lodgings. Big Grandma, believing that they had indeed missed the connection, accepted her kind offer. But even as the pair left the station in her company, their train arrived and a horrified porter, quickly apprising the situation, violently extracted them and their luggage from her clutches. He had saved them from, what Uncle Jack West dramatically told them the next day, were 'White Slave Traffickers'. For them both, this was a frightening initiation into the dangers of foreign travel. It was a relief to reach their destination.

St Quentin at that time was an historical textile and lace-making town, situated at a strategic position on the River Somme and close to the Belgian border. Over the centuries it had been regularly contested by opposing armies and was to be razed to the ground during the First World War. When Laura visited it was a frontier town reminiscent of the Wild West. Lawless and dangerous with rape and murder commonplace, the streets were forbidden territory to women and children. Great Aunt West kept a loaded revolver at her bedside.

Laura noted that beyond the high wall and trees that protected the factory on one side two gasometers could be seen. On the other side she could see the canal crossing the fields that Aunt West told her had been fiercely fought over during the Franco-Prussian War in 1870. After the battle she had gone out to tend the wounded and dying and, despite there being several Prussians billeted in the house, had secretly protected a young French soldier who had turned up in tears on the doorstep. The story was troubling for Laura. He was only sixteen, the same age as Nellie and, as Great Aunt West said, much too young to fight let alone to die.

The *West-Ther Fabrique de Tulle et de Dentelles* was picturesque in its way with whitewashed vine-clad walls and enclosed by a large garden in which trees and tomato plants fruited and flowers blossomed in abundance. At one end was the house-place, separated off from the works. It was a two-storey building with a long attic running its length where the weekly dressing of the lace took place. This process involved hot glue – a smell which, along with the strong garlic odour of the hands' mid-day meal, throbbed in the reflected summer heat. In those early days Laura was both thirsty and lonely. Because of the threat of typhoid, no water was allowed her – just cherry brandy or tea (brought from England) laced with rum. To her disappointment there were no other children to play with – just those she caught sight of on the brightly coloured canal barges in the distance. There were no books in the house and no animals to play with. Aunt West explained to her that a cat would not survive long on the street for within days it would be served up for dinner as a *fricassée* in one of the local cottages. There was however a guard-dog at the factory, kept as a deterrent to potential intruders and thieves. Chained up in the day and let loose in the extensive gardens at night, he was dangerous and could only be approached by his handler. Nonetheless, Laura in her inimitable way made him her friend over the weeks, but it was a friendship without a future. She was told that he was becoming too tame to be of any use as a guard dog and she must stop the acquaintance.

Awoken with a cup of coffee and slice of bread and butter at 5.00am, those long, hot summer days of 1889 were taken up in observing and sketching on the pad that Mother had given her when she left Nottingham. Big Grandma was no company and slept in the heat, Aunt West was too busy, but at the house there were two people who interested her. There was the odd job man Charles, whom Laura admired greatly for his sloe black eyes and long lashes. She drew him for his beauty and was sad when he was dismissed for stealing. Her other subject was Marie, the many chinned maid whose monstrous build and corset-free rolls of fat were of great fascination, especially on hot days when she would strip to her chemise to do her housework. But, whatever the weather, Marie was never without her big green umbrella. This accessory served as a "poacher's pocket" as she busied herself around the house and every day when she left for home it bulged conspicuously. Marie, who had been born in Nottingham and migrated to St Quentin no one knew when, had little French and the few words she had were spoken with a Nottingham accent. In that adult house there had once been a son who married a local girl. Soon after his marriage he had died in an accident on a "motorised bicycle". Aunt West never got over it. 'Everything young is beautiful' she would often say.

A telegram arrived from England to say that Nellie was worse and was not expected to live. Laura idly speculated on what would happen to Nellie's scarlet hair ribbon which she coveted. Then the next day a black bordered envelope came. Nellie, shining, beautiful Nellie, was dead. Scarlet ribbons forgotten, Laura was stunned because for her dying was what old people did. Girls of fifteen-rising-sixteen did not die. That night she and Big Grandma hugged and cried together. Aunt West and Big Grandma left for Nottingham as soon as arrangements for the running of the factory could be made. It would be too expensive to pay for Laura to return too and so she was to stay there and Marie Légère, the lace-mending overseer, would move in to look after her. When they had gone, in her bewilderment Laura sought refuge in the dyeing shed, her head resting on a bolt of *tulle* while Great Uncle West went to pieces and drank himself into oblivion. This was his one and major weakness.

Despite being unable to read, it was Great Aunt West-Ther who ran the business. She was a formidable presence, dressed all in black, even to the black satin apron, with beetling black eyebrows and hair still blue-black as her Mother's had been. Before she left for England she locked up the cherry brandy. Normally an affable, passive, grey-haired old man, drink, as Laura discovered, transformed Great Uncle West into a 'raving maniac'. In his cups he would become violent and bombastic, Laura often hearing him through the wall in the next bedroom, standing before the mirror, thumping his chest and declaring: 'Jack, you're a man! You're the boss here, understand?' Once, short of money for drink, he had threatened his wife with a carving knife – or it might have been a stick – the two autobiographical sources are not in agreement here. He was subdued by the threat of a judicious blow to the head with the factory keys.

As was to be expected, once his wife and sister-in-law were out of the house and on their way to England, he changed into his Sunday best, ordered an open *fiacre*, took his straw hat and set off on a crawl of the local *estaminets,* until, returning 'rolling drunk' in the evening, he had to be put to bed. Sensibly, Aunt West did not stay in Nottingham long and returned alone (Big Grandma was needed in Noel Street) to find her husband once more out on a spree. The subsequent ructions and shouting distressed Laura terribly. Now without Big Grandma, she desperately wanted to go home, but it was not to be. Even though it was still the vacation, Aunt West decided that Laura was too much to cope with and should be sent to school. So, dressed in a horrendous black mourning outfit that had been copied from her sailor suit by a local seamstress, off to school she went.

There was only one pupil and one governess in residence when Laura arrived at Mademoiselle Mollard's Pension, Rue de Gouvernement, situated behind the Cathedral at St Quentin. Laura's narrative of her time at the Pension in Chapter 2 of *Oil Paint and Greasepaint* is especially interesting. Her distresses and traumas, narrated we must remember by the adult Laura, read as a psychodrama that parallels in so many ways those described by Charlotte Brontë in her fictionalised accounts of her own experiences at school in *Jane Eyre* 1847 and, as a young woman in a Belgian Pension in *Villette* 1853. Laura's forthright and angry persona and her isolation in a foreign environment, mark her out as a rebellious and disturbed child, very much in the mould of Jane Eyre. The parallels are remarkable. Like Jane at Lowood, Laura bonded with a fellow pupil at the Pension. In Laura's case it was an Irish girl, Ethel, who was her sole companion in the otherwise empty school. There 'was a bond between us: her mother was dead and I had lost Nellie' she writes. In addition, very much in the pattern of Lucy Snow's inner turmoil in *Villette*, Laura describes the inner confusion created by her Protestant upbringing and the attractions of the ceremony and ritual of Roman Catholicism. There is however a subtext in Laura's case, a suggestion of deliberate spitefulness in her refusal to go to the Protestant Church.

Like a Brontë heroine, Laura describes her lonely victimization, being made the butt of the school for her odd appearance: fair-skin, blonde bushy hair and strange clothes. The returning pupils laughed at her and kicked her hat around the dormitory. Since Laura's close friendship with Ethel meant that they conversed in English, she was slow to acquire the necessary colloquial French to express herself or give a riposte and hold her ground. When it came to washing, she was met with shocked dismay and was chastised for her flagrant immodesty. Being used to an abundance of soap and hot water at home, she had stripped to the waist and anticipated a "good sluice down". However, her fellow pupils remained shrouded in their nightdresses and merely flapped at themselves with the corner of a damp towel. Feet could be washed fortnightly and for a franc (Laura never had one to spare) you could go to the public baths once a month. She could never understand how the French girls looked so clean and neat. She was made to feel different and inadequate, even by Mme Mollard, whose worst insult was to deliberately mistake her for a retarded pupil, the *cretin* of the school, once again echoing an episode in *Villette*.

Two things alleviated the pain, the first was sharing with Ethel the basket of pastries which regularly arrived from Aunt West at the *Fabrique*. These had to be eaten straight away before the ants attacked them. The second was the chocolate which Ethel bought with the five-shilling postal order sent to her by her Aunt who, they said, was a Countess. The chocolate was a welcome addition to their otherwise meagre diet, disguising, for one day at least, the texture of the dry bread. Despite gnawing hunger, they could not stomach the horsemeat and surreptitiously parcelled up and threw it over the garden wall into the cemetery on the other side. There was English tea on Sundays but the same tea leaves were boiled up and served daily over the rest of the week. Laura preferred to drink the brackish water which of course came with a health warning that she resolutely ignored.

Lonely and home-sick, malnourished and bitterly cold once the freezing winter set in and long icicles hung from the dormitory ceiling, Laura became angry and violent. Once pent-up emotion drove her to attack a thin and rheumy-eyed teacher, hitting her on the behind with a hairbrush one night as the poor woman said her prayers. Somewhere inside Laura's confused mind was the certainty that she had done wrong. Every day she expected to be struck down by the hand of divine retribution, but it did not come. Instead, she externalized her detestation of those around her, especially the head mistress with her slavering pendulous lip and 'passionate tempers', by sketching them surreptitiously with a Hogarthian virulence, tearing up the pages of her sketch book as she went. And, so, quickly she learned to 'hate'.

Laura, the grown woman, personifies her predicament at that time in a strangely allegorical sentence: 'I shook hands with hate; he and morbidity were my bedfellows…' Here we have a dark night of the soul dramatized in the same way as the mental anguish of the heroines of Charlotte Brontë's novels. Feeling, 'dirty, untidy, and an outcast', at this stage of her young life Laura is close to breakdown. She is drawn to self-harm and imagines killing herself: 'I must go to Nellie, whatever happens'. She plans to climb out of the window and throw herself into the canal. Or, a more practical plan, one night she secretes into her bed the penknife that Uncle West had given her for sharpening her pencils. She runs the blade over her wrists but fails to press it deep and imagines instead a macabre piece of theatre: herself. discovered in the morning by the other girls, lying in a pool of blood. It did not happen and she endured.

A dunce at most things, so she was told, Laura's low self-esteem was ameliorated by the fact that she could draw better than any of them. She was, after all, destined for Paris to study art! In the meantime, Aunt West had arranged twice weekly classes for Laura at the studio of a local artist, Monsieur Lucien Schmidt. This meant copying his work or, for homework, portraits of famous men from the magazine *Le Petit Journal*. Mother had always said that Laura must draw from the life and not be merely a copyist. It was frustrating and what is more she missed out on some of the formal school lessons and so was unable to progress, as well being unable to join in the outdoor walks with the other girls. Still, she liked Monsieur Schmidt and found solace in visits to his home and family on a Sunday. There the food was good and plentiful, and the floors polished to a high gloss. Meanwhile she practised drawing from the life by sketching her fellow pupils and selling them their portraits for a few *sous*. A highlight of her artistic life was the day when, quite unexpectedly, Uncle West (bless him) sent her an extraordinary large paintbox that was even better than Mother's. Her pride and joy, that paintbox was to be her companion and emotional prop for decades to come.

Occasionally, Laura went back to the factory for the weekend to have a proper wash, a change of clothes and to be fed. Once, Ethel too was invited. Aunt West cooked a feast that day but the girls could not do it justice – they were wearing tightly laced new stays which impeded their full enjoyment. Afterwards they went to the Circus. It was an English Circus and the two girls were enchanted when the clowns singled them out of the audience. Ethel said that it was the happiest day of her school life and for Laura too it marked a stage in her accommodation to circumstance. Perhaps it reminded her not just of home but that there were other ways of living and working, people who could, when the time came, pitch tents and move on.

The months passed. Spring tipped the poplar trees with a soft mist of buds; Easter eggs were dyed; Laura's French improved and, further easing herself into her situation, she even began to forget what Mother's face looked like. However, shortly after Easter 1890, news came of the impeding bank-ruptcy of the Nottingham business. It was a bad shock for the whole St Quentin household. Aunt West set to in order to salvage what she could of her sister's financial situation as well as to protect the French interests. She announced that she could no longer pay for her niece's education or keep her in France. Laura would have to go back home. With a typically heroic gesture, Laura offered to work in the factory and send Mother her earnings if that would help save the business. But Mother would have none of it. The Nottingham business was beyond saving. To compound the anxiety, in early June a message came to the Pension, ordering Laura to return to the *fabrique* at once. Aunt West was in distress, her sister Charlotte, Big Grandma, had contracted influenza (the *grippe*) and was not expected to recover. They had to set off at once.

Laura duly packed with the aid of Ethel whom she assured would see her back again soon. Wearing a pair of Aunt West's flannel drawers that were far too large (to keep her warm when crossing *La Manche*) and a man's peaked tweed cap, her pigtail hanging beneath, she must have cut a droll figure when they boarded the ferry. Crossing the Channel, she now viewed the idea of home with dread and embarrassment, for there would be no Nellie and most likely no Big Grandma either. What is more, Aunt West said that they would all – Mother, Uncle, Sis and herself – be moving again – this time to an artisan's cottage at the bottom of Noel Street because even number 35 had become too expensive. When she returned everything looked small and narrow. Even Sis, who was Laura's elder by 2 years looked diminished for, while away, Laura had grown a full two inches taller than her sister. Unused to hearing let alone speaking her native tongue, Laura felt disabled and very much a stranger there. She recoiled from Mother's gesture of embrace and Mother cried. It was a bad business. Yet one good thing was that Big Grandma was holding on. There she lay in her familiar cap and ribbons, propped up in the walnut bed with its canopy and curtains of blue silk. It was all reassuring except that the same bed, along with all the family furniture that was not essential was due to be auctioned off within days. Laura's hopes and expectations of Paris were carried away with the tide of misery that swept through them all.

The evening after her return a family conference decided her fate. She was to be enrolled at Nottingham School of Art as an "artisan student" which meant that there were no fees to pay. A special dispensation had to be obtained from the authorities for her to go there rather than to go back to conventional school. Attendance was from 9.30 in the morning, with a short break at noon and a 2-hour break in the afternoon before the evening session began at 6.30, finishing at 9.30pm. Laura was in fact delighted, if taken aback, at the speed of events. Barely thirteen, she was to be the youngest pupil to attend the prestigious Art School and was admitted that very night.

CHAPTER THREE

"The only serious girl student"

Established in 1843, Nottingham Government School of Design, as it was originally called, had been the first art college to be set up outside London as a government initiative in response to the decline in the textile industry. The original aim, as stated in the *History of the College*, published in 1951, was to 'provide elementary instruction in design for manufacturers, and in the history, principles and practice of ornamental art'. The School had originally been sited at various locations in the town centre until 1863 when a new purpose-built college (now a part of Nottingham Trent University) was built in Waverley Street. Adjacent to the Arboretum and within the neighbourhood where the Johnsons lived during Laura's childhood and adolescence, the College was an important feature in her life.

Traditionally, art education was the province of men, although women were allowed to attend from 1873. As we have seen, Laura's Mother described herself as a 'student' at the School of Art (as it was now designated) in 1881. Given that its pedagogic approach was taken from the London Royal Academy Schools, the foundation of art education at the Art School was based on the study of classical models and drawing from the life. In England, on the grounds of propriety, this basic training was restricted to men. Women's art was regarded as trivial, their repertoire as students restricted to what was ornamental and decorative. Drawing the body from life was forbidden and so they were to study drapes, heads and faces only. When an undraped life model was being studied in class, the women were exiled to the statuary room. In time Laura Johnson was to challenge that male prerogative. Reflecting on the effect of copying merely inert plaster casts, the older Laura was to note that it was detrimental to her artistic development, bringing 'woodenness, a dead look to all my studies'.

On her arrival at the School in 1890 one young man of seventeen stood out as the most gifted student. He had won bronze, silver and gold medals in the national competitions run by the South Kensington College of Art

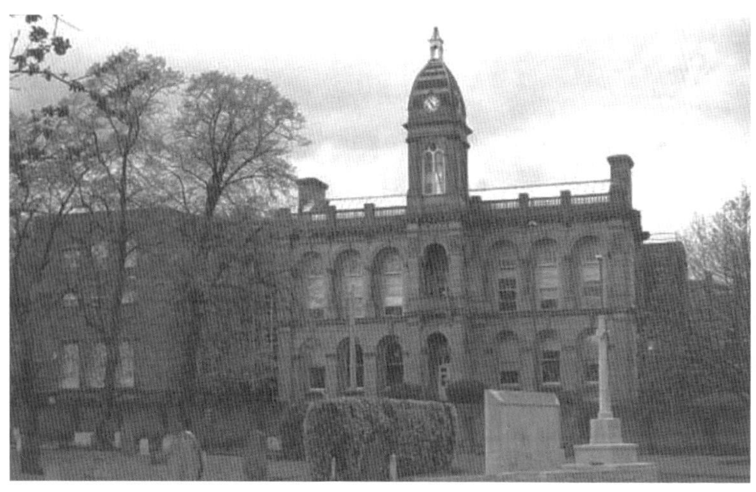

Nottingham Art School today. Public domain

for provincial art schools and was, they said, headed for greatness. This was Harold Knight, the son of a local architect. The Knights were known to the Bates as both families had lived in Radford for many years. Indeed, Harold's and Laura's grandfathers had stood together during the Nottingham Chartist riots when the old Nottingham Castle had been burned down. Slender and dark, with a pair of *pince nez* on what Laura describes as his 'aristocratic' nose, he could be sardonic, even cruel when in her now halting English she attempted to strike up a conversation. Nonetheless she insinuated herself into his space, setting up her easel behind his so that she could follow his example. Harold's technique of building up the structure of a portrait head was copied meticulously stroke by stroke. Laura even imitated his stance and hollow good looks by sucking in her cheeks in an attempt to look slim, hopefully pale and most certainly interesting. When questioned as to why she was pulling such a face, the attempt was abandoned but the hero-worship continued unabated.

Harold was the star pupil of his year and when he drew a pencil study of a girl student, Lily Poyser, the life studies master Wilson Forster (newly returned from studying in Paris and Antwerp) judged it to be 'beyond criticism'. Laura, becoming obsessed with this paragon and desirous of being noticed by him as well as Forster whom she admired and liked, worked hard and long hours. She too drew Lily Poyser. At the end of the day she was the

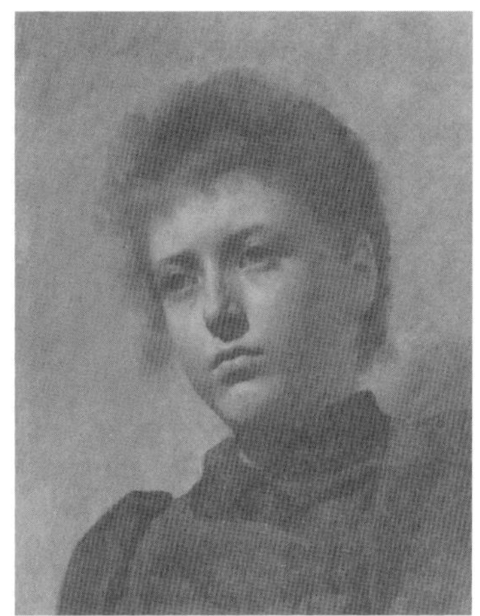

Laura Johnson, *Head Study of Lily Poyser* c.1891.
Public domain

only girl left amongst the students in the "head" class. The young men appear to have treated the 13-year-old with ironic indulgence. She tells of how one night they light-heartedly did her due obeisance by kissing her shoe. Harold affirmed his own act of homage by spraying the place with the fixative that they used in pastel and charcoal drawing. For Laura this signified a moment of recognition that affirmed her place at the School and within the precincts of Harold. That first year was one of the happiest of her life.

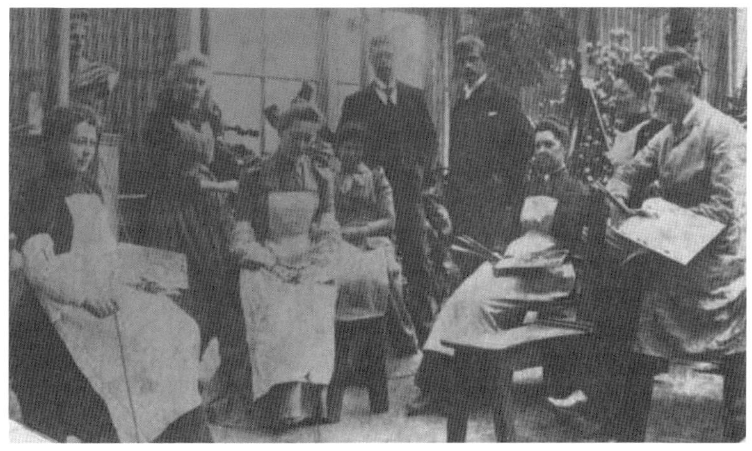

Nottingham Art School: a group of young painters in the studio, c.1892.
Laura, left standing, and Harold seated with palette, right. Nottinghamshire Archive

However, joy and satisfaction were no sooner grasped than they were taken away when the authorities at the School decided to provide the women and the men students with separate classrooms. Laura felt the disappointment of relegation deeply since the master did not spend anything like the time with female students that he did with the men. In the women's class she was criticized for drawing with too heavy a hand. She had no 'feminine refinement' they said and drew like a man: 'Why don't you develop your feminine side? You must draw from your wrist, not your shoulder.' Reprimanded and reduced to tears by Head of the School, she decided at once to ditch art and audition at the Theatre Royal to become an actress. Whatever her dramatic talent may have been, the idea was outrageous – a whim born out of resentment and disappointment. The next morning her temper subsided and she grudgingly accepted her lot, but only for a few weeks. The idea of a career on the stage persisted and in *The Magic of Line* she describes her younger self practising an audition piece: Byron's poem *Waterloo* in front of a mirror. But her anticipation of an acting career was not to be fulfilled.

Given the family's financial difficulties, Laura was offered up as a companion to the live-in cook of the Bates' rich relation, Mr John Ashworth of Belgrave Square who was on vacation in Bournemouth for a month. The only compensation for the trial of sharing the cook's room was the breakfast – a breakfast such as Laura had never experienced: 'Twining's best tea, smoked Wiltshire bacon, and above all, steamed whiting with its tail stuck through its eyeholes, which I had never tasted before'. In Chapter Seven of *The Magic of a Line*, Laura recounts how this munificence was to end. One night Laura declaimed *Waterloo* to herself a time too many: 'On and on I went, until the cook forgotten, I let go and in a full blast of drama, bellowed: "Arm, arm, it is, it is the cannon's opening roar"'. The cook, terrified out of her wits, went at once to Noel Street: '"That Laura of yours 'as never to come back to Belgrave Square ever anymore – she's raving mad – 'as got to be put in an asylum – she's dangerous – is going to kill somebody – that's not going to be me"'.

Apart from Laura's personal frustration and unhappiness, there was a new mood of optimism in the Bates household. Uncle Arthur had started up a new business manufacturing bobbins and parts for lace-making machines and Mother was attracting several new pupils. On the strength of Uncle Arthur's success, they had again moved, this time to a slightly larger house about half a mile from 35 Noel Street on the other side of Forest Road in Oliver Street which led to Cromwell Street. These names, given that it was at the Royalist stronghold of Nottingham Castle that the standard of Charles

I was first raised, illustrates how divided loyalties in the town during the English Civil War were perpetuated even into the early 19th century when the houses were built. At number 6 Oliver Street there was a reasonably sized ground floor room that Mother could use as her studio and teaching room. It was also a slightly more respectable address but cheap because it was overlooked by the General Cemetery where Stephen Bates, Little Grandma and Nellie were buried.

The pressure off and Mother in good spirits, she and Laura managed a sketching trip to the coast at Flamborough in Yorkshire. Done on the cheap, they got there by a roundabout route that took advantage of a series of cut-price tickets. Laura loved the sea, the wide horizons and open air and was reluctant to return to the confinement of Nottingham and the airless rooms of the Art School. However, both she and her Mother were attending classes in that new term in 1891 and Laura was pleased and proud to have Mother as her companion and colleague. This pleasure turned into distress as over the weeks it became obvious that her own ability was way ahead of Mother's and she grieved on that account. Yet, however conscious Mother might have been of this disparity, she was always loving and accepting. One moment glows in the memories of this time with an image of her Mother drawing, radiant with cheeks 'flushed with the heat of the stuffy life-room'.

Mother's classes were doing well and in the summer holidays of 1892 she took a group of students to Winchester to draw and paint. Big Grandma, now seventy-nine (she had survived the influenza and continued to keep house for the family) received a message that Charlotte had fallen and broken a leg in two places. Laura was told to go to Winchester at once. Laura did not want to go, having made plans for the holidays, sketching landscape and climbing trees at Wilford and she said so. But to Winchester she was sent only to find Mother confined to bed in her lodgings. In both of her accounts of this time Laura brings to mind an ancient rowan tree in the Cathedral Close that was at that time attracting attention for its spectacular display of scarlet berries. Weighed down by this abundance, its dry, brittle trunk had snapped just like the patient's leg. That tree became a symbol of Mother, glorious and generous in its yield and dying in its final flush. For, on their return she was diagnosed with cancer.

The family's response to the news was one of devastation. The Winchester doctor had hinted and, when Uncle Arthur Peter took his sister to a specialist in Birmingham, he confirmed that it was too late for remedial treatment. One local clergyman advised that they put their faith in God. The sentiment was punctured by Sis' (growing up she dropped the "Sissie") unusually forthright response: 'We don't believe in God'. Laura records her 15-year-old self as being shocked by her sister's blunt rejoinder, reflecting self-righteously that, unlike herself, Sis could not be expected to be *au fait* with the niceties of good manners: after all she had not been to France.

Big Grandma was Mother's nurse but often the girls had to take over at night when Grandma was exhausted. As the disease advanced some nuns offered to help, but Mother lingered and they left when her pain was too great for them to bear. One incident from this terrible time appears in both autobiographies but they differ in substance. In *Oil Paint and Greasepaint* Chapter 3 we are told that Uncle Arthur Peter was very badly affected by his sister's suffering and one night suddenly got up and went outside to a piece of nearby wasteland where he was violently sick – a fact that Laura was 'told later'. However, in Chapter Seven of *The Magic of a Line* she tells of how she herself was at his side, the pair walking 'hand in hand over the rubble for hours in complete silence'. Perhaps there were two such nights, but the later version is invested with a dramatic poignancy that is typical of Laura. Her tendency to self-dramatize shapes and colours the second narrative account, elevating it into a moment of mythic significance. Milton's *Paradise Lost* was a text which Laura knew, enjoying the music of the words even if she did not understand all of the content and returning to it at times when she needed reassurance. At the end of Book XII, exiled from Paradise, Adam and Eve walk hand in hand and with 'wandering steps and slow/ Through Eden took their solitary way'. The familiar trope marks a discontinuity in things, a loss of innocence and, above all, an uncertain future. Laura too had reached a critical juncture in her story.

Mother was moved downstairs to the studio; the piano having been shifted to make space for her bed. Lying beneath a length of St Quentin's tulle which kept the summer flies away, to Laura's eye she had 'a lovely look'. In *The Magic of a Line* those days of Mother's illness are further memorialized in an emblem of her sister by the bed and staring out of the side window over the cemetery, a 'Rubens-cupid little figure, with its close-fitting cap of golden hair!' she says. We notice here the exclamation mark that signifies a self-conscious, dramatic gesture on the part of the narrator, the older Laura. This is a significant stage in the build up to a major transition in her young life from child/student to teacher/ breadwinner. It was then that a 'dread of life and an awful fear of the future was born in me'.

At the age of fifteen Laura had to take over Mother's art classes. Her childhood over, it was necessary to put up her hair and 'pretend to be twenty'. The significance of this phrase as marking a rite of passage is indicated in its use as a heading for Chapter Seven of *The Magic of a Line.* Most of the families whose daughters Mother taught were prepared to accept her as the substitute, but she suffered agonies of self-consciousness and feelings of inadequacy as she attempted, without any real knowledge of the medium, to teach the art of water colour and other desired artistic accomplishments to provincial middle-class young ladies. However, there were compensations – such as going once a week to Melton Mowbray on the train to teach one of Mother's rich pupils. This was an opportunity for self-indulgence and she regularly bought a trashy comic to read on the journey and enjoyed the slap-up lunch provided at her destination.

Her self-confidence left her, however, at the thought of having to go in her Mother's place as Drawing and Painting Mistress to Brincliffe, her old school. Some of the girls had previously been her fellow pupils and they treated her with sniggers and contempt. She dealt with the humiliation by telling herself that they were resentful because she had superior talent and was now training as a student of art. In fact she had few teaching strategies and was reduced to showmanship, 'swanking' that she could draw two sides of an object simultaneously on the blackboard. At the end of the year while she was paid her thirty guineas for her work, there were complaints from parents that she was unsuitable for the post and she was dismissed. Without that money, the family resources were again dangerously depleted.

Even though her time and energies were much reduced, Laura still kept up her studies at the Art School and took her share of sitting with Mother through the long nights. Sis, not as robust, was showing signs of strain and her health was deteriorating. The doctor diagnosed tuberculosis and she was sent away to the better-off relatives, the Ashworths (whose cook Laura had alarmed), where she was to remain for some months. These same relatives sent a meat joint to Oliver Street every weekend. As a consequence, the preliminary to Sunday dinner was Uncle Arthur's sonorous grace that gave thanks to their benefactor, cousin John Ashworth. Laura felt degraded. She felt degraded and embarrassed to admit where she lived, let alone their dependence on what she calls the 'crumbs from the rich man's table'. This was all the more galling when her acquaintance with Harold Knight took a new turn.

Harold without doubt found Laura trying at times. For a serious and inhibited young man, her over-ebullience and intrusive presence was often an irritant. However, he had painted a study of her in the art class, an image that shows her characteristically turned away from the viewer, her mane of hair tied back with a ribbon (Plate 2). In her second autobiography Laura makes much of this as marking the start of their relationship: 'While he was painting it, I first got a hint that I meant as much to him as he to me'. She elaborates this with the detail of how Harold, now eighteen, was apparently 'frightened' by her deep blushes – a confession she tells us he made to her many years afterwards. The nuances and implications of this event are made retrospectively. They are shaped by her desire to discover or impose a significant turn in the plot line of her life and give it a colouring that at the time was more of a neutral tint than of a deeper hue.

They took to walking together, not in any formal way, but as comrades. Of course the neighbours misinterpreted their companionship, bringing the news that Laura had been seen 'walking the streets with a young man!' Uncle Arthur Peter, apparently taking his role of man of the family seriously, attempted to have a quiet word with this youth and find out his intentions. In the event Uncle Arthur was amicable and Mother did not mind in the least, pleased that Laura had someone to talk to and give her support at this difficult time. When well enough, she encouraged Harold's visits to her sickroom and enjoyed talking to him about art and especially about Laura, her talent and prospects. A tacit assumption developed, whether welcome or no, that he would take responsibility for her when her Mother died.

They did not, says Laura 'exchange rings; neither of us could afford such expense', adding 'had we thought of it.' That added rider is significant because it, and the previous 'I was tormented by the feeling that too much was being taken for granted' indicates the adult Laura's need to objectify how things stood between their youthful selves. This was in no way a stereotypical boy-girl relationship, but in reflecting upon it she is tempted to impose the narrative trope of the birth of a love-affair on her story. It is very unlikely that she was 'tormented' in the way she describes, her feelings not developed enough to be subject to the social and moral imperatives of formal courtship. Rather it is her way of adjusting and presenting for the public a version of what was for her a confusing and complex emotional situation. At the time, we must remember, she was, for all her apparent confidence, an immature girl of fifteen.

Often after evening classes, Harold would, in his gentlemanly way, walk her home and join the Johnsons for a hot drink. It seems that he found that unconventional household congenial after his own conventional, stiff and proper home. Laura describes Harold's family in her later autobiography *The Magic of a Line* and Janet Dunbar (who met Dame Laura latterly and apparently conversed with her at length) also describes that first visit to the Knight's Villa. The versions differ markedly. In Chapter Three of Dunbar's book, she describes the experience as 'disquieting' for Laura since she could not comprehend the atmosphere in the house, so different from her own open and affectionate family. Formally seated, Harold and his brother were grave and silent while his sisters merely articulated offers of bread and butter and cake. Harold's Mother smiled equally politely while Mr Knight alone spoke. From this version it seems that William Knight, a highly successful architect, was the archetypical Victorian *pater familias* with a severity of manner that Dunbar suggests masked vulnerability. She suggests that he was a repressed and frustrated man because of his wife's pathological fear of sexual relations and that Harold's obvious artistic talent gave rise to jealousy. Unable to read the situation, Laura was mystified how such well-off people could be so unhappy.

However, in *The Magic of a Line*, Laura describes a very different scenario. Harold's Mother is described as a welcoming, beautiful lady, generous too since she made her son's friend a present of a silver bracelet. In this version Laura stays beyond tea to enjoy supper. This allowed her to discover that William Knight enjoyed a game of tiddly-winks and was subject to 'uncontrollable fits of laughter'. His tendency to explode with humour is enlarged upon as Laura reminisces about a later time when, sitting next to him in church, he ceremoniously put a handful of small change in the plate. This caused such an audible cacophony of sound that the congregation turned only to witness his own outburst of amusement. He is even described as laughing out loud at his wife's funeral on the sight of Harold's baggy trousers. Can this be the same man?

It is difficult to reconcile the two, but the lack of congruence can be understood when we consider that Dunbar's mediated version was published in 1975, 5 years after Dame Laura's death, while *The Magic of a Line* was published in 1965, 4 years after Harold Knight's death in 1961 when Laura was eighty-eight. Dame Laura's recollection is low key, sentimental and with indulgent comic touches. These are the observations of a Grand Old Lady whose memories, occasionally occluded, are tidied up for posterity. By contrast, Dunbar's analysis of Mr Knight seems to take a Freudian standpoint, explaining his demeanour in terms of repression and sexual frustration. In addition, she places Laura herself in the role of a romantic protagonist, the description of Laura's bewilderment being more novelistic than biographical.

Dunbar frequently allows the reader to be privy to her character's inner thoughts and inserts scripted dialogue which we are to assume are authentic, being reconstructions taken from conversations with Dame Laura herself. For today's writer of biography this is what is called 'faction', or (a delightful term) 'truthiness', meaning a shaping of facts or making up for the absence of facts to satisfy what the writer, the editor and perhaps the reader would like to be the case. However, whatever the inconsistencies, dislocations and ambiguities in these versions, they do not detract from but add to the enigma of our subject – contributing to the multi-layered shifting tectonic plates of her personality rather than describing a stable and coherent character. Even though the facts of the first meeting between Laura and Harold's family are unclear, what is certain is that their partnership was tacitly and, it seems, symbolically affirmed around this time. Harold's acceptance into the family circle appears to be endorsed by a portrait (never before made public) that he painted of Big Grandma between 1893–4 (Plate 3).

Aware that time was running out for her, Mother requested that both Harold and Laura come to her room and gave them her final blessing. She died on the 22nd September 1893, having made full provision for her own funeral arrangements and organised for her daughters' mourning outfits to be measured and made up. The cheap deal coffin that Charlotte herself had ordered to save money was countermanded by the undertaker who said that it would cost more than an off-the-peg oak one. And so she was buried, in the same plot as Nellie, Little Grandma and Stephen Bates in Nottingham General Cemetery just next door. She had died a month before her forty-second birthday.

For Laura, Mother's death brought no real sense of closure. In the final hours Big Grandma made sure that she was kept out of the way and afterwards she was sent to a friend of Mother's while the household underwent another major change. On the death of Uncle West, at Aunt West-Ther's request Uncle Arthur Peter left the business he had set up in Nottingham and with some reluctance agreed to manage the factory in St Quentin. Since Sis was still recuperating with relatives, now the household comprised Laura, Big Grandma and Thomas, the Persian cat. In early 1895 they were to move again to 39 Tennyson Street.

There Laura took control, using her artistic flair in arranging the furniture – Mother's piano was to be positioned at a fashionable angle in the corner of the room and draped over it was the old Indian shawl that had served as a blanket for all the girls in babyhood and as a wrap for Nellie when she went to her first dances. Grandma, who liked Harold, invited him to Tennyson Street for tea and supper at the weekends and after tea would leave the two of them together in the sitting-room. A short vignette is offered us in *The Magic of a Line* – a reflection in the mirror over the fireplace where, lit by the glow of the fire below, Laura's own commonplace face is juxtaposed with Harold's 'fine looks'. Things were going well for him, he was winning prizes and medals and in 1893 had been awarded the Queen's Prize at the National Art Training School in South Kensington. Laura too submitted work and won a prize that year. It was, she admits in each of her autobiographies, a hopeful and peaceful time, 'one of the most beautiful' periods of her life. Like all beautiful things, it was not to last long.

Big Grandma, now eighty-two, was having severe attacks of chest pain. She had suffered from angina for years but now the attacks came more often and she was noticeably thinner, failing, yet in no way less interested in everything that Laura did at the Art School. She was particularly taken up with one of Laura's paintings which she named 'Yellow Boys'. In *The Magic of a Line*, Laura describes it: 'I chose an unusual lighting effect for the popular girl model Lily Poyser. I draped her in a veil of yellow muslin costing tuppence three farthings a yard. Grandma's sole employment became the furtherance of my progress; she helped me shape and stitch the yellow veiling and on my return home from Art School her first question was "How's 'Yellow Boys' getting on?" John Croft, the artist's great nephew, has supplemented this with the information that some of Laura's Art School studies 'were recently discovered in a bricked-up cupboard of a house in Nottingham that was being pulled down. Among them was the yellow veiled work that Big Grandma had christened "Yellow Boys" – a portrait of the head model Lily Poyser. It is a wonderful picture'.

Sis returned to Tennyson Street and together the girls waited for what was inevitable. When Big Grandma died, it was Laura who was keeping watch as the church bells rang out from All Saints Church that Sunday, the 17th February, 1895. In *Oil Paint and Grease Paint* she describes the moment when 'Death' took Big Grandma, but in the later version she enlarges on this with a ghostly vision of Grandma in her nightcap and gown standing in the middle of the room even as she lay on her deathbed. It is an occasion for exclamation marks and dashes, as the poignancy of the episode is communicated in the present tense: the laying out, Grandma with pennies on her eyes and the window open to let her soul free into the cold air. It is 'fearful' to imagine her without covering and death is 'ugly' so Sis and Laura put her feet into beautiful oriental slippers. Since Laura has coveted those slippers for years, it is a great but necessary sacrifice. Laura cannot sleep until the coffin lid is nailed down and frequently returns to the room to listen outside the door for sounds of life. It was unthinkable that Big Grandma had left them orphans. But orphans they were. At the funeral no other relatives apart from Sis, Laura and Uncle Arthur were present, and afterwards Uncle Arthur had to return to the factory in St Quentin. Having arranged a sale of the household goods and chattels that would not be needed by his nieces, he promised to send them £5 a month to help them out. He never failed to do this, but other relatives in the town seem, according to Laura, to have been without concern for the girls' welfare. Apparently, they had to fend for themselves, find accommodation and somehow survive. This has been disputed. It was not in the interest of Laura's narrative to be over frank, and she keeps up the story of her own and Sis' deprived youth but from evidence of one of Laura's own paintings (Plate 4), it appears possibly otherwise. That the two girls were welcome at Corporation Oaks and visited there in their teens is evident by the painting which shows the spire of St Andrew's on Mapperley Road. This is the church nearest to Corporation Oaks (identified in discussion with Neil Walker at the Djanogly Art Gallery). However, Laura's tale is of unrelenting hardship.

The first place they found sounded promising, the landlady telling them that she would 'be as a mother' to them, but there could be no pets. Laura was distraught that her cat Thomas had to be re-homed (within weeks he pined away and died) although she was excited by the prospect of independence. But independence has its risks. At night in the new lodging there were unexplained knocks on the door and voices in the corridor. It dawned on them that this new mother was running a brothel and so they barricaded themselves in their room by shoving the chest of drawers against the door. To cook in the shared kitchen was impossible supposing that, after rent, there was any spare money for food. Their diet consisted of eggs boiled in front of their gas fire. They had one outdoor coat between them and so had to take turns to go abroad to shop or to classes. It was all humiliating not to say dangerous for two young women, but they did not wish to trouble Uncle Arthur or Aunt West in France. Nor was Harold to know of their predicament, for apart from the shame of letting him know how low they had sunk, his Mother was fatally ill.

Then 'like a Great Big God' Mr Cruickshank descended. Realizing their plight, he insisted that they write at once to Uncle Arthur, gave them £5 and suggested they take a holiday by the sea. Together with Harold, Sis and Laura went for a few days to a farm near Skegness. There they reverted to their childlike selves, running through the sea and sand-dunes, feeding well and gaining health and strength so that on their return to Nottingham they had fresh resolution. Uncle Arthur had also sent money over for the girls to help them move and they found reasonably priced, yet respectable, bright rooms with a kitchen over a dairy in Park Street, Lenton about a quarter of a mile down the Derby Road and bordering The Park. At Park Road Dairy they set about making a home for themselves. They still had some pieces of Bates' furniture. One was a 17th century oak chest which was to remain with Laura until her death in 1970. In her Will she gave this information about the chest: 'Charlotte Johnson her sisters and brothers and also Laura Knight and her sisters learned to walk in it'. There was Mother's cottage piano, a crimson plush chair and other special relics of past prosperity: the Worcester vases and a Crown Derby Chinoiserie *pot-pouri* jar which had been so often the repository of petals from Uncle Arthur's roses at the allotment. With these and a bamboo fern flourishing in the window, a menu of tea, porridge, bread and butter sufficed and worn-out shoes could be remedied by some black paint on the toes to mask the gaping holes.

Meanwhile, Laura's private teaching was not going well, there were fewer and fewer pupils, and her own art was at an impasse. She felt deeply her position as a female student, denied the advantages and opportunities available to the men. Once more she considered giving up art and going on the stage. Given that Laura sang (a German friend Fraulein Gutjahr had given her lessons and taught her to sing *lieder*) and both she and Sis played the piano, she formed a plan that they might form a duo and give concerts. More practical was Sis' intention of learning to type. Laura too turned to commercial outlets, sending examples of her illustrative work to the editors of magazines and periodicals in the hope of commissions, but all were re-turned with a refusal. Even so, there were moments when together Sis and Laura could be the children they in fact still were: 'Glorious moments when we romped and played and chased each other over and under our beds, jumped over chairs and did high kicks. We were irrepressibles.'

In the South Kensington College of Art competition of 1894, when she was seventeen, Laura had a breakthrough. She won silver and bronze medals. One of these was for a painting of a young model Julia Sowerby 'dressed as a Swiss girl counting her beads' (as Julia's sister remembered in a letter to the *Nottingham Evening Post* on 19th June 1936). Most splendid of all was the gold medal awarded the following year for her painting of the cast of sculptor Hamo Thorneycroft's figure of the Trojan archer *Teucer* or *Teukros*. More than this, since out of all the girl students she had won the most prizes, she was awarded the Princess of Wales Scholarship. This amounted to a prize sum of twenty pounds a year for 2 years. Laura was ecstatic but Harold rather cruelly brought her down to earth, warning that she should not get too big-headed since he had been to the competition exhibition and the standards were pretty low. Perhaps it was this dose of realism that made her sell the gold medal for the sum of five pounds and seven shillings.

The money, which the girls speculated could have got them to Paris, sadly had to be spent on a doctor. Dunbar states that the illness was a recurrence of Sis' tuberculosis and in *The Magic of a Line* Laura writes that she herself had caught a bad chill on one of her teaching visits. She recalls that the doctor was without sympathy for her, advising that what a robust girl like her needed was more outdoor exercise. Possibly so, but more likely was the lack of a varied diet for both sisters, since porridge continued to be their staple food, alleviated only by Harold's Saturday visits. He would arrive carrying pork pies, sausages, maybe cake and certainly copies of the latest magazines. *Harper's Bazaar* was much prized as the source not merely of American fashion and events but because of the illustrations and photographs.

All three, Sis, Laura and Harold would, after their grand tea, sit around the table reading in companionable silence. Sometimes he would bring with him his sisters Ethel and Agnes (known as 'Tet' and 'Tag') who liked being with these open-faced girls. They remained friends for life. It was an interesting group of young people, bonded together not just by the arts, but more importantly by family association. Not for nothing does Laura tell her readers that the Grandfathers Bates and the Knight had both found themselves caught up in the Nottingham Chartist riots in the year 1842. In the rioting Knight came close to being killed by the militia. It was only the fur collar on his coat that had protected him from what might have been a fatal blow to the neck. He survived to marry, have children and grandchildren, one of whom was Harold. So providentially, Laura Johnson's future destiny as Mrs Laura Knight was assured.

In the summer of 1895 while Sis was with Aunt West at St Quentin, Laura, Harold, his sister Ethel and younger brother Edgar decided to go to Skegness once again. However, this time it was not so successful and even though the young artists took their painting equipment, they could find neither inspiration nor challenge in the dun-coloured landscape. Flat and dull themselves they returned to Nottingham. They were growing up and new horizons beckoned. Already Edgar was planning to emigrate to America and, before leaving the Art School, Harold had been awarded a British Institute Travelling Scholarship of £50 per annum for 2 years. The first year, despite finding the family domestic arrangements uncongenial and his Father more than difficult, he stayed in Nottingham to save money. He rented studio space for himself and began an ambitious large work. This must have galvanized Laura into considering her own position. She too decided to leave Art School and set herself up as an independent artist with her own studio.

Since Sis' health was again fragile, Laura took the initiative and identified just the place for them to live. At the south entrance to The Park some of the caves at the bottom of Castle Rock had been boarded out and made available as living spaces. Entered up a flight of steps, the red-brick façade opened up into two good size living rooms with a large room above, previously used for dancing classes. With a skylight opened in the ceiling, this room would make a perfect studio space. Laura organized it all. It was a good address and she had high hopes of persuading some of the wealthier citizens from The Park to come to sit for portraits. She also hoped for private pupils, who would come in their droves (it would hold twenty!) to stand at their easels and learn from her tuition. Until then she and Sis had to survive, and so she started painting in earnest and considering where she stood in terms of marketing and selling her work. It was at this time that she painted a beautiful portrait of Sis (Plate 4), which family tradition suggests was Laura's gift to her sister on her twenty-first birthday. Never before seen in the public

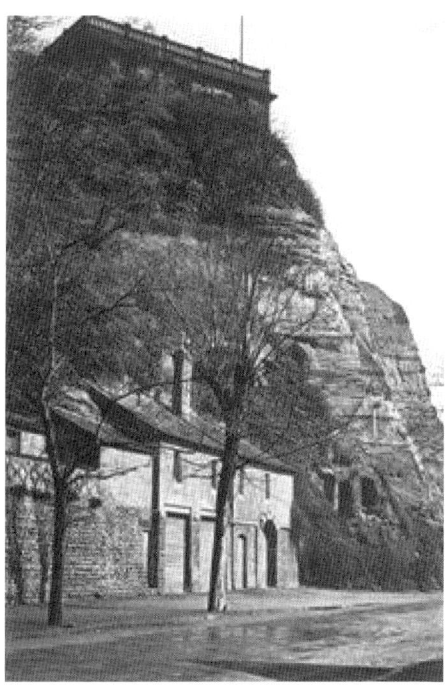

Cave dwellings: Castle Rooms, c.1910, Possible location of Laura's studio.
Image courtesy of Nottingham City Council

domain, this illustrates Laura's talent for portraiture as well as her refinement of technique.

With their mothers' permission, she paid local children to skip school and model for her at the Castle Rooms for six pence a day, a cup of cocoa and bread and butter. Daring she certainly was in asking one of the male models from the Art School to pose for her: the partially sighted Jack Price. It was her very first nude study and she was embarrassed and apprehensive, but there was no need. Jack was respectful and happy to accept his pick of her artwork in payment. He selected the first oil produced in the Castle Rooms: *Dressing Dolls*, painted in 1895–6. Laura had thought this picture of children playing good enough to send to the Royal Academy Exhibition, but it had been rejected. It was therefore a relief that her 'patron' Jack opted to take it in return for a 'considerable number of sittings'. On the other hand, in that year Harold was successful with his first Royal Academy acceptance: the painting *When the Cat's Away*.

In her cave studio she found herself perplexed about how to set out to be a practitioner and businesswoman. She had no one to talk to about how

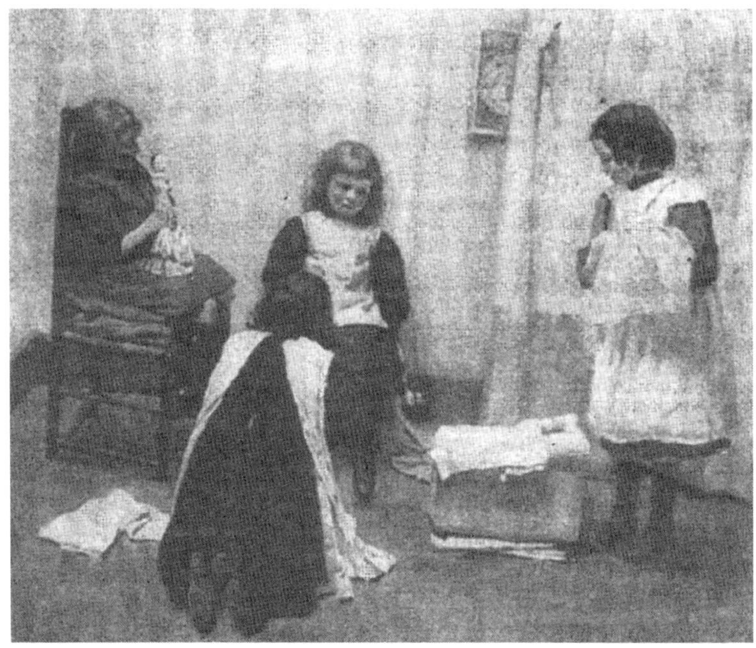

Laura Johnson *Dressing Dolls*, c.1895-6. Private collection

to choose subjects and develop techniques that would appeal both to the current art market and meet the standards of the academic elite in London. With knowledge of fine art restricted to the formal tuition of the Art School, a fleeting visit with Mother to the London galleries and the local exhibitions at Nottingham Castle, her exposure to painting was limited to Victorian sentiment, conventional landscapes and groups of naked figures claiming to be in the genre of 'history' painting. As she herself writes 'the proper subjects to paint are water nymphs and mythological people'.

Neither she nor Harold knew about the several break-away artistic movements then current. Nor did they know about the Slade Art School in London which, established in 1868, had introduced some radical new ideas for tuition. As a result, there was a new generation of *avant garde* British painters who were open to the influence of French Impressionism and who painted out of the studio in the open air. When in 1894 Laura and Harold had gone to an exhibition at Nottingham Castle Gallery of pictures by the Newlyn Group – a community of artists in Cornwall who had embraced the techniques of painting in the open air (*en plein air*) – they were unaware of its ground-breaking nature. These were artists of a different kind, taking as their subject ordinary working people and painting in radical new ways. However, at that time Laura neither had the perception nor the confidence to grasp its significance. What she took away from the exhibition was overwhelming old-fashioned sentiment. One picture in particular, Frank Bramley's *A Hopeless Dawn,* moved her to tears.

Reluctant to ask his father for more funds, but eager to take up his place at the famous *Academie Julian* under the tutorship of Jean Paul Laurens and Benjamin Constant, Harold travelled to Paris with the meagre sum of £75 to support himself for a year. The parting was painful for them all, not least for Laura who took him for granted as an essential element of her life. She found a new friend however in Rosie Good who had enrolled as one of her pupils at the Castle Rooms. From a well-off middle-class background, Rosie often stayed over, romping and laughing with the Johnson girls. Often, because she wanted to escape the restrictions of home, she brought along her future husband, Harold's friend Oliver Sheppard who was a master at the Art School. Rosie was no artist herself but contributed to the household purse and to its air of youthful vitality. But life at the Castle Rooms was still a struggle. Despite one or two portrait commissions from local businessmen who paid £5 a painting, the scrabbling for loose change to pay for food continued to be a way of life and the endless diet of porridge took its toll especially on Sis whose health continued to be poor.

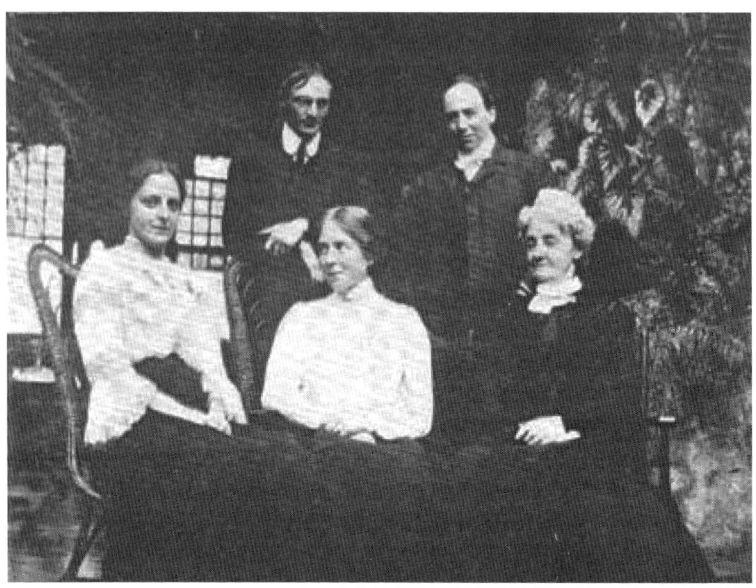

At Rosie Good's House, 1897. Left to right: Rosie, Harold, Laura, Oliver and Mrs Good.
Private collection

In July 1897 Harold returned, haggard, ill, threadbare and down at heel. He had set off with high expectations. Once in Paris, he realized the impossibility of affording tuition as well as food and lodgings with his very restricted budget. He came home after 10 months. On his return he was reticent about his months in Paris, for they had been destructive to his self-esteem as well as his health. He had nothing to say about the modern ideas and artistic movements that were making Paris the vital and glamorous centre of Europe in this *La Belle Époque*. He had experienced only the pain and none of the glamour of Bohemian life. On the other hand, he did bring Laura one memorable souvenir – news of a hairstyle that was all the rage in Paris, made fashionable by the glamorous celebrity, ballet dancer and post-card beauty, Cléo de Mérôde (1875–1966). Laura at once set about taming her unruly bush of hair to conform to the fashion so obviously admired by Harold and the *beau monde* of Paris. With the hair drawn back severely from the face, parted in the middle and brought into a knot at the nape of the neck, "the Mérôde" was for several years Laura's preferred style.

One morning Aunt West arrived unexpectedly straight from the ferry, alarmed at having news of Sis' illness and that the girls were not merely struggling but starving. She had no idea where the Castle Rooms, their cave dwelling, was to be found but with her usual good sense enquired for directions. She was duly directed to the place where 'the two round faced fair young ladies lived' and soon remedied their desperate situation. With food in the pantry and Aunt West's comforting presence, things seemed to be made right once again: "to think of you poor children not having proper food. It shall never happen again; it breaks my heart to think about it. You shall be all right in the future." What is more she insisted that they all, Harold and Rosie too, should take a seaside holiday. Having argued and fallen out badly with her "co-manager" Uncle Arthur and desiring that he *cuire à l'étouffée* ("stew in his own juice"), she had time at her disposal. But where to go? That was the question. Laura and Harold needed a place that would offer the inspiration they had failed to find in Skegness. The answer came from a master at the Art College, Thomas Barratt, who said: 'Go to Staithes … there is no place so splendid for an artist in the whole of England. I have a cottage there I go to every summer. Harold and you will want to spend all your time painting'. And so in the late summer of 1897, the year of Queen Victoria's Diamond Jubilee, to Staithes they all went.

CHAPTER FOUR

"A place and a people apart"

Arriving on the station platform at Staithes, the travellers were at once buffeted by the coastal blast. Skirts billowed, hats were blown away, and 'every breath we drew seemed to wash the whole of our insides'. This was sea-air that not one of them had ever before experienced, raw and relentless, carrying with it the heady smell of the brine and the cry of gulls which hovered and swooped on the wind. Walking over the cliff and down the steep incline of Staithes Bank, they could almost touch the chimney pots of the nested houses that clustered below. Deep within a cleft where the Roxby Beck ran down to the sea between Cowbar and Boulby Cliff on the left and the sweep of Penny Nab Cliff on the right was the settlement of Staithes or Steers as it was pronounced locally.

Tracing its origins to the Viking invasions sometime around the ninth century AD, every aspect of Staithes' geography and its indigenous population testified to centuries of hardship and endurance. It is not a natural harbour and takes the full brunt of the Nor'easters as they rage across the sea, so that even today despite newly built breakwaters, the waves can sweep through the narrow alleys and gunnels of the village. Then the fishing cobles would be moored up the Beck, tied to the rickety trestle bridge that straddled it but in bad weather (which was frequent) the boats were hauled manually up the beach by the villagers – men, women and children – all hands were needed. As Laura and Harold soon learned the North Sea can be unforgiving and in a savage storm boats, bodies, rocks, and houses would be engulfed and tossed in the violent waves, the debris strewn over rocks and in coves miles away.

Always a place of hardship and graft, in the early 19th century Staithes was one of the largest fishing ports on the North East Coast, its economy boosted by the mining of minerals – chiefly of alum and potash – from the lias cliffs that run from Scarborough north to Saltburn. By the mid-century this economy was in decline since what were effectively small

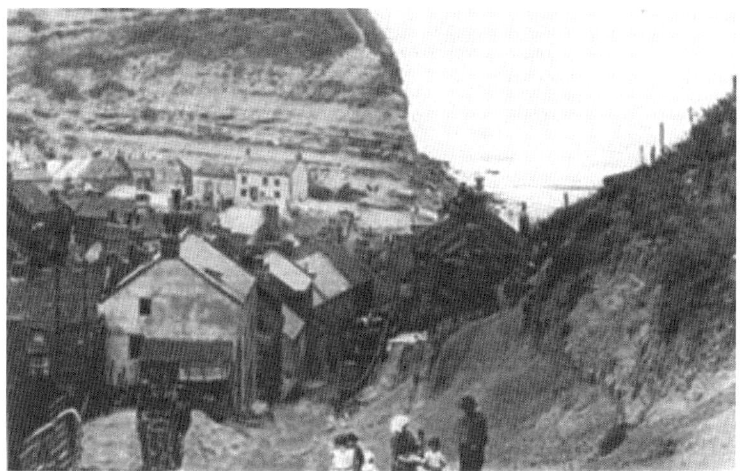

Church Street, Staithes c.1925. Private collection

cottage industries gave way to large-scale mining operations, shipbuilding and textile manufacture in urban industrial centres connected by the expanding rail network. When the railway came to Staithes in 1883 some three hundred fishermen were working out of the port, with the Whitby, Redcar and Middlesbrough Union Railway running three trains a week from the

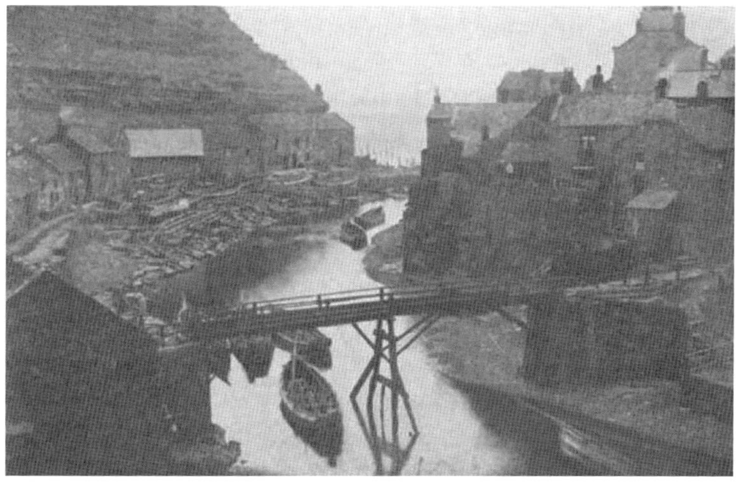

Staithes c.1900. Private collection

station at the bank top to transport the catch to markets nationwide. Yet the community below maintained its self-contained isolation. They considered even those who lived and worked "up top" as foreigners. Even so, for all its apartness, Staithes could not ignore the trickle of outsiders who came to the village: painters attracted by its picturesque character, its dramatic weather, strong light and long days. Seeking out remote, rural and coastal places, they were part of the new movement that was transforming the art-world at home and abroad. They brought with them modernity and a whiff of revolution to this remote place.

As we have seen, Harold Knight and Laura Johnson with their provincial upbringing and training at Nottingham School of Art were largely unaware of the new art movements sweeping across Europe in the last quarter of the 19th century. While formal art education in centres such as Antwerp, Paris and London continued to be based on academic principles and practice, over this period many gifted young artists, dissatisfied with the repetitious and sterile programme of study on offer, deliberately chose to work outside the academic context. Leaving the confines of the *atelier* and rejecting the tradition of copying the masters, they looked beyond the studio and took as their subject the every-day activity of ordinary folk in their natural setting. Equally innovative were the new techniques they devised to capture that experience. The emergence of these *avant garde* movements was due to a significant cross-fertilisation of artistic ideas and practice between London and Paris over the course of the nineteenth century.

In the lace trade too, there was an on-going exchange between the lace-making communities in Nottingham and France. At times of slump in the industry Laura comments that some 'manufacturers left the failing trade of the town (Nottingham) and set up business in northern France – Lille, Caudry, St Quentin'. This was a feature of her own recent family history. As we have seen, in the 1850s Aunt Elizabeth and Uncle John West settled in St Quentin to establish the lace factory and around the same time her sister Emma and husband Thomas Redfern moved to Calais to run another. Aunt West and Laura's Big Grandma regularly ran the gauntlet of the excise man on their trips to and from France, Laura commenting on the big trunk in the attic within which, interleaved with clothing, substantial quantities of "Valenciennes" lace were smuggled: 'We were closely connected with France; someone was always coming or going' she says.

In the early 19th century the relationship between the lace trade and the art world can be illustrated by the life of the painter Richard Parkes Bonington (1802–28). Born the son of a lace-maker in the town of Arnold, four miles from Nottingham, he was something of a child prodigy and at the age of eleven exhibited paintings at the Liverpool Academy. In 1817 Bonington's family moved to France where his father set up a lace factory in Calais and in 1818 the family moved to Paris to open a lace retail outlet. Continuing his art education in Paris, Bonington began studying at the École des Beaux-Arts in 1820 and exhibited his first oils at the Paris Salon (the French equivalent to the Royal Academy in London where he also was to exhibit) that year. At the Salon of 1824 he won a gold medal as did John Constable (1776–1837) whose *The Haywain* created a public sensation in Paris. Both painters were popular in France to the extent that Bonington is often claimed to be a French painter and Constable sold more paintings in France than at home.

Encapsulating the contemporary Romantic mood, both English artists took the natural landscape as their subject rather than merely employing it as a backdrop to human events and actions. They portrayed the ordinary, the simple and the humble subject rather than the intellectual, sophisticated and heroic and sought to capture in paint the transitory and shifting nature of subjective experience in new ways. Bonington, Constable and, we must add, J.M.W. Turner whose work was also starting to be known in Paris by the 1830s, can be credited with introducing a new sense of light and colour into French art. All these artists developed innovative techniques that were predicated on the artist moving out of the studio in order to paint what they saw out in the open air.

In France over the 1830s and '40s many disaffected painters, at odds with the establishment and escaping from political ferment, especially during and after the revolutions of 1848, sought the open road and the rural subject as well as exploring new methods to transfer their experience onto canvas. In this they were aided by the invention of the portable easel and the availability of paint in tubes. These gave freedom to live and work in the countryside where they found a rich source of material in the peasant way of life. Free from tradition and the dictates of the Salon, Jean Baptiste-Camille Corot (1796–1875) and Jean-Francois Millet (1814–1875) set the pattern by moving out of Paris to settle in the Forest of Fontainebleau near the village of Barbizon. From the 1830s to the 1870s other disaffected artists gathered there, forming a community that earned the name of the "Barbizon School". It was the prototype for the many artists' colonies that were soon to proliferate throughout northern Europe, dedicated to painting *en plein air* and taking as their subject what was "true" rather than contrived and idealized: the art of "Rustic Naturalism".

Perhaps the most influential painter associated with this "Rustic Naturalism" in the succeeding generation was Jules Bastien-Lepage (1848–84) whose methods and reputation brought itinerant artists from across Europe to the art colony of Concarneau in Brittany where he settled in the 1880s. Painting without an attitude or any subjective feeling, his work was judged to be true to the Barbizon desire for "the authentic" – an authority founded in simplicity. Central to this was his technique of "square brush painting" in which a wide brush (some 2" in width) was used to cut across shapes rather than moulding their contours. In this way both the background and figures are treated in the same way, creating the matt effect of a photograph. This technique did not originate with Bastien Lepage, being previously known in Paris and in England, but his exploitation of the method together with his *plein air* philosophy won him the admiration of the next generation of *avant garde* painters in far-flung artists' colonies across Europe, such as Staithes, Laren in Holland and Newlyn in Cornwall into which Laura Johnson and Harold Knight were subsequently to be absorbed.

Laura is commonly described as an "English Impressionist" painter and her early work illustrates the way that *en plein air* painting is associated with that other revolutionary art movement in late 19th century France: "Impressionism". Impressionist painters, Claude Monet, Edgar Degas, Pierre-Auguste Renoir, Camille Pissarro, like the Barbizon painters consciously rejected academic tradition and took to the open air. In their case the aim was not to render a subject with photographic realism, but to express the feeling, mood and a subjective perception of the object; to capture its transitory and ephemeral qualities and, delighting in the shifting effects of light, explore the science of colour harmonies. Their "broken colour" technique applies fine brush strokes of complementary or opposing colours in the spectrum and in doing so forces the viewer to adjust perception and create a play of hues and tones across the canvas.

Famously brought to the Parisian public's notice with the first *Impressionist Exhibition* in 1874, several of the early Impressionists painters had made London their home during the Franco-Prussian war in 1870–1. When in London those French artists became fully aware of the importance of Turner's experiments with colour and light and in their own way absorbed his influence. It was in London that Monet and Pissarro met up with the Barbizon painter Daubigny who was also residing in the capital and he in turn introduced them to the art dealer Paul Durand-Ruel who was to be an important agent in the familiarisation of both Britain and America with Impressionist art.

Whereas once it was dependent on patronage, art in the modern world was becoming commercialised. There was a new clientele: manufacturers, industrialists, urban upper middle-class buyers who had developing tastes and money to spend. It was in this context that new exhibiting spaces were set up such as Sir Coutts Lindsay's Grosvenor Gallery which opened in 1877 and Ernest Brown & Phillips' Leicester Galleries founded in 1903. These provided opportunities for artists not in the mainstream to display and sell their work. The Leicester Galleries was to be a crucial outlet for Harold and Laura's work from 1904 onwards.

One early example of how artists themselves were taking control of the market by self-exhibiting was the formation in 1885 of the New English Art Club. The Club's founder members included Frank Bramley (painter of *A Hopeless Dawn* which so moved Laura at the Nottingham Exhibition in 1894), John Singer Sargeant, Philip Wilson Steer, George Clausen and Stanhope Forbes. Combining Barbizon *plein air* technique and aspects of Impressionism, their aim was "authenticity", painting rapidly to capture the subject (meaning the total environment – figures, setting, atmosphere) in one continuous painterly process across the surface of the canvas. Like the Barbizon School their subject matter was taken from the environment – rural, maritime, Naturalistic studies of ordinary life. In attempting to capture the "instantaneous" image they emulated the new art of photography, just as "art photography" modelled itself on *plein air* painting. From the 1870s to the first decade of the 20th century there was a happy association between "photographic art" and "art photography", illustrated by the synergy that can be appreciated in the years 1875 to 1910 between paintings of local life by Staithes artists and the photographs taken of the same local life by Frank Sutcliffe.

The cluster at Staithes, its neighbour Runswick Bay and Whitby was just one of the many artist's colonies that proliferated in Britain in the later 19th century. Others include Newlyn and St Ives in Cornwall, Walberswick in Suffolk, Cullercoats in Northumberland and Cockburnspath in Kirkcudbright. In those remote places *plein air* painters discovered subject matter from a pre-industrial age: tight-knit communities operating at a slow pace and according to atavistic instincts. By 1880 three influential artists were working in the Staithes-Whitby area: Gilbert Foster, Frederick Jackson and Mark Senior. They established what was to be a loosely associated colony of painters, resident there for over 30 years and known as the "Staithes Group". Harold and Laura were associated with Staithes for over 10 years (from their first visit in 1897 to their removal to Newlyn in 1907) and it was at Staithes that both of them threw off the restraints of academic art and provincial attitudes. As Laura affirmed, Staithes was for her a 'tremendous influence on work, life and power of endurance'.

When the Nottingham party first arrived at Staithes in 1897, it was a revelation to them all and they were a revelation to Staithes. The figure of Aunt West with her Frenchified clothes and manners and the unusual outfits that she had organized for Sis and Laura (knee-length frocks that would allow freedom of movement) were odd even in this remote place. When Aunt West tried to buy a soda siphon at the general store, the shopkeeper Frankie Seymour was 'fair flabbergasted!' Nonetheless, the local folk were getting used to painters coming and going, taking lodgings and hiring rooms for studios. By 1895 they were doing quite well out of the visitors, who paid not only for food and accommodation but offered money to anyone prepared to model for them. The local economy was the better for the arty folks' presence.

They found rooms in a cottage just up from the chandler's shop in Church Street where James Cook had worked as a young man. Their land-lady was a Mrs Crooks who charged ten shillings a week all-in for the ladies and twelve for Harold although he had to sleep in a flea-ridden bed in rooms further up the hill. Food was good and plentiful: fresh caught fish and cured kippers, home baked bread and fruit loaf – just the thing to satisfy appetites made sharp by the sea air. For Laura the whole experience was overwhelm-ing. The senses bombarded on all sides by elemental turmoil and emotional confusion, it was like plunging into a whirlpool.

Here was a wealth of subject matter – outlandish figures, nets, boats and the shifting sea with its varying textures and colours, strong, clear light and the dangerous, thick dark – so much that it was beyond Laura's capacity to absorb let alone paint. In both autobiographies she spends time describing in word pictures the qualities of the place for the very good reason that it was at Staithes where she found herself as an artist: 'It was there I found myself and what I might do'. This untamed, strange and what she calls a 'wildified' place, spoke to her inner nature. It suited her well. 'I loved it passionately, overwhelmingly', she writes, 'I loved the cold and the northerly storms when no covering would protect you. I loved the strange race of people who lived there, whose stern almost forbidding exterior formed such contrast to the warmth and richness of their nature'.

Aunt West soon became restive and, anxious that Arthur would not be managing without her, returned to St Quentin early and, once the month was up, the girls had to go back to Nottingham leaving Harold behind. His spirits were high, raised by the new environment and the opportunities it offered to mix with fellow artists, and, as a result, he requested Laura to approach his Father for more money to finance his stay until Christmas. Surprisingly his Father obliged. Without distraction and having, he said, finally thrown off the trammels of Art School training, Harold worked intensely. By contrast, back in Nottingham all seemed stale and torpid. Even so, Laura refused an offer from Rosie to finance a trip to Paris. If the opportunity had come 2 months earlier, the chance of experiencing the metropolitan sophistication of Paris and work in a professional studio would have been grasped with delight. But now that Laura had tasted life of a very different kind, Staithes beckoned her back.

With Sis and Rosie in tow, she determined to go back to Mrs Crooks, maybe even rent a small cottage. Above all she anticipated attaching herself once more to Harold who would be her tutor. So, the girls sold up their furniture, left their Nottingham Cave and were off. In Staithes they took Ebor Cottage for a small rent, delighting in placing what bits of furniture they had and bargaining for other necessaries. Even though the bed she purchased collapsed almost immediately so that for some time Laura slept on the floor, it was her idea of heaven. When she remembers the atmosphere, the light, colours and character of Staithes, the girl who was Laura Johnson is literally in her element. Observed from the studio room looking onto the wooden *staith* (old Norse for landing stage), the life of the village becomes immediate. It is keenly observed and relished.

At this point in her first autobiography the tense again changes to the dramatic present and we can capture with her the sounds, sights and emotions generated by an imminent storm; hear snatches of dialect and glimpse patches of colour, washed out blue, red and russet; visualise the bare arms and strained muscles as once again they are braced to pull on the ropes. She is fascinated by the tall and impressive stature of the men in their fishermen's jerseys, boots and oilskins, nets slung over their shoulders; the sturdy upright women, with their red skirts hitched up beneath their aprons, plaid shawls and lilac bonnets with broad flaps shading their faces. She marvelled at their poise as with a padded ring on their heads they balanced tubs filled with mussels from the beach, or with sticks to make a fire for cooking the fresh-landed herring. She focuses on wives knitting; babies being nursed and children plodging and splashing in the water; groups gathering on the steep and crooked steps of what was called "The Barrass" on a summer's afternoon; and all of this is dusted with fish scales, glittering in the sunshine. So limpid and plangent is the prose-poetry of the original, no paraphrase is adequate.

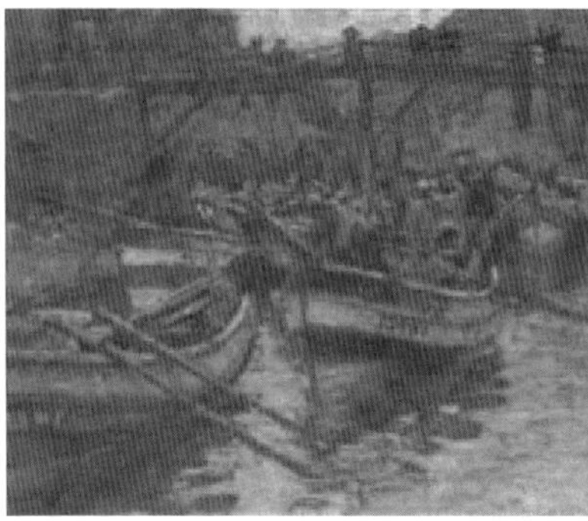

Harold Knight, Boats in Roxby
Beck and the trestle bridge, Staithes.
Photographic copy

There are also, of course, darker shades of hardship and the black cloud of imminent death in the Staithes sequences. Each day as the cobles go out there is fear that some may not return. Every man's clothing is marked with his name so that his body could be identified when the sea delivered the drowned sailor. The Death Wail of a woman's keening is common in the alleys. Many are the widows, their status signalled by black bonnets (which

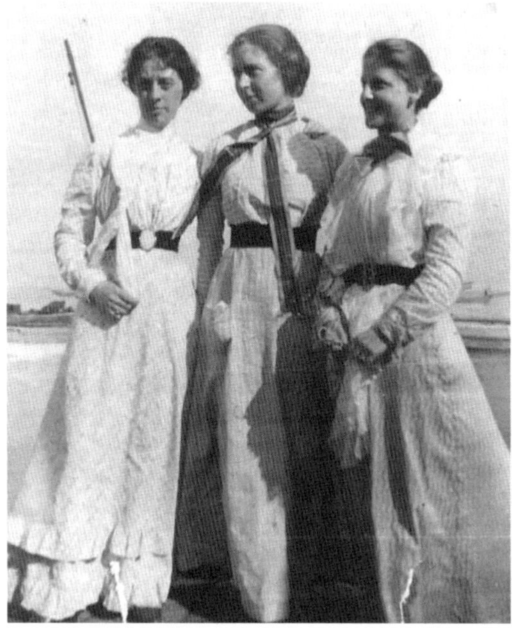

Laura, centre, Rosie Good, right, and another student, 1898. Private collection

Laura considered to be very becoming) and tragedy stamped on their faces. One woman stands out and apart, 'tall and straight, an unseeing look in her dark eyes, her neck a white column. We all wanted to paint her'. Harold did. Known by the simple title of *Grief* his painting of her is indeed a masterpiece, a testament to the dignity and nobility of the women of the Staithes community facing the capricious power of the sea on a daily basis. Now in a private collection, the painting featured as the publicity image for an exhibition on *The Staithes Group* in 1993.

Bad weather brought a continuous sequence of disasters, when the water boiled and the currents carried the cobles way out beyond the safety of the harbour. Laura describes the drama in the village when three men of the Unthank family, the father and two sons, failed to return. The description of the retrieval firstly of the coble stripped of its contents and then, over time, the bodies being salvaged from the sea is harrowing. Especially moving is the scene in the Unthank's cottage when the bier bearing the body of the drowned Father is returned. Laura shared these personal sorrows with her neighbours just as she shared their times of celebration and hopeful expectation: the excitement of the annual fairs and Chapel *love feast* (a faith supper and revivalist gathering); the bustle and eager anticipation as the herring shoal passed down the coast and quieter, reflective and companionable times

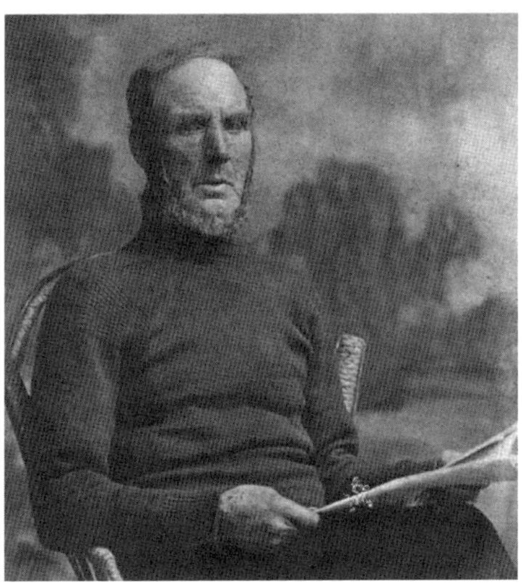

Argy Verrill, the Staithes fisherman, Studio portrait.
Courtesy of N. Suckling (All rights reserved)

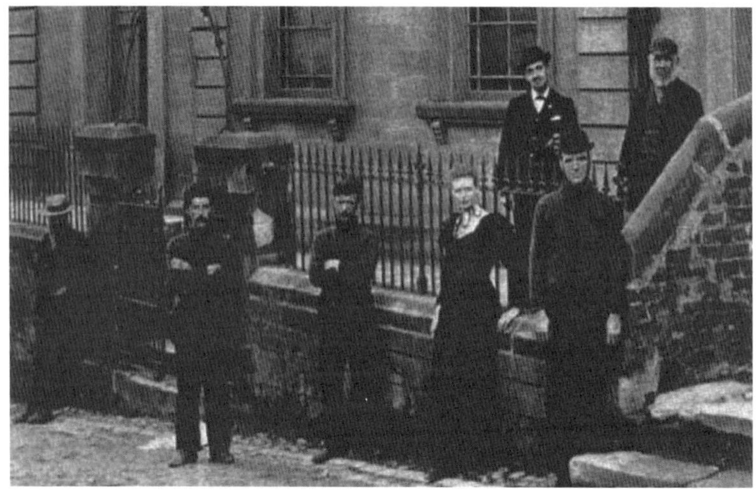

Outside Staithes Primitive Methodist Church, Courtesy of N. Suckling (All rights reserved)

when two or three gathered together to knit or mend nets and share tales of curious and great deeds of past times. She imprinted herself on their life, identifying with their marginal existence and both in words and paint illuminating their life and communality.

Invited to join the Primitive Methodist Church congregation by "Ranter" Argy Verrill who led the singing, Harold, Laura and Sis further embedded themselves in the community. It was at this time that Laura claims to have been almost religious, unsurprisingly since the whole of the village lived at an intense level of fatalism and providential faith. Singing in the chapel, her absorption into Staithes life was total. Many of the Staithes characters in the congregation are given dramatic presence in the autobiographies, especially in Chapters 5, 6 and 7 of *Oil Paint and Grease Paint*. There is Frankie Seymour with his cross eyes and loose dentures, whose general dealers was one of the centres of village social life; Isaac Unthank – six foot three in his socks; Sally Hicks the fish-buyer – 'a grand spender when she's oot' as her friend Mrs Porritt averred on their return from a day out in Middlesbrough; 'Pore Tom' with his withered arm and a paralysed leg whose slow wit at times revealed practical common sense; the old man with a ruff of facial hair around his otherwise unwashed but clean-shaven face who tended the lamps set on the cliff to guide in the boats. Then there was Argy himself whose fireside offered warmth and good company on a winter's night; and, of course, the Cornishman Jimmy James the fish auctioneer. He had settled locally after spending his sea-life following the herring shoals. It was Jimmy who told Laura about southern shores, and about the Cornish colony of artists at Newlyn. She vowed to go there someday.

In the early months, Laura learned to row and Harold invested in a 'leaky pilot boat', a vessel that several times brought them close to being flung into the waves that constantly heaved and broke around Cowbar Nab. Displaying thoughtless bravado, the pair of them would often climb Penny Nab on the south side of the harbour, until one day Harold dislodged a sheet of shale and hung precariously over the cliff edge. After that such extreme pursuits were curtailed. Harold was at ease in Staithes, painting enthusiastically in his studio, having a pint with the fishermen in the Cod and Lobster pub of an evening, conversing with his fellow painters – Fred Jackson and Harry Hopwood, Fred Mayor, Arthur Freidenson and Charles Mackie. Laura wanted to join them but it seems that Harold did not encourage this. He found their company congenial and at times found her assertive presence very irritating. What is more, he soon put paid to the idea that he would act as her critic and mentor.

Staithes artists were typically provincial painters trained in the academic tradition but these had struck out independently as *plein air* painters. Manchester-born Fred Jackson had, like so many others, studied at the *Académie Julian* in Paris. He regularly exhibited at the Royal Academy and had spent time in an artists' colony in the Conway Valley in North Wales before discovering the Yorkshire Coast. A founder member of the New English Art Club, he was a friend of Philip Wilson Steer and Walter Sickert. Harry Hopwood had lived in Manchester and had also studied at the *Académie Julian.* He was an inveterate traveller, over his lifetime visiting Japan and Australia, North Africa, and France. Fred Mayor too studied for a time at the *Académie Julian* in Paris. He went to North Africa in 1890 and discovered Staithes in 1897. Resident there in 1899, he shared lodgings with Arthur Friedenson and Harold Knight.

Friedenson had come to Britain with his family from Russia in 1881. He studied art in Antwerp and at the *Académie Julian* in 1890–2 and again in 1896. Taking up residence in Staithes, he at first shared lodgings with Harold Knight and Fred Mayor at the house of Mr and Mrs George Porritt in Gun Gutter. Later he moved his base to the next bay down the coast: Runswick Bay. It was at Runswick that the Staithes painter Rowland Hill and Tyneside artist Ralph Hedley met. Hedley was not the only Cullercoats painter to frequently visit Staithes. The respected female artist Isa Thomson discovered Staithes around 1892 and introduced her husband-to-be Robert Jobling to the place. Once married, they spent every working summer there. Charles Mackie was well travelled. While a traditionalist, he was curious about, sought out and was responsive to recent developments in the art world. For instance, when in France he was one of the first British artists to meet Gaugin at the international colony at Pont-Aven in Britttany. But his home was Edinburgh where he maintained a studio. When Harold and Laura were first in Staithes, he, his wife and son rented a cottage at Roxby on the moors above Staithes for the summer season. He was a kindly man and acted as a father-figure and mentor to younger artists who were regularly invited to his home.

It was hard for Laura to be outside what amounted to a charmed male circle, yet several of them took an interest in her and were generous with their time and advice. Jackson and Mayor were happy to discuss techniques with her and Friedenson obtained for her a first commission, but it was Charles Mackie who offered her the most valuable and consistent tuition. She was struggling with the confusing range of possible techniques of which she was becoming aware. For instance, having got hold of a book about Seurat, she at once set about painting in the *pointilliste* manner by experimenting with the technique of applied dots of colour. Unhappy with the results, she lost heart until Mackie advised her to forget other painters' 'isms and 'paint simply and directly' what she saw. He then offered to set her a programme of study. Firstly. she was to methodically explore the effects of colour in relationship and juxtaposition; then to experiment with one colour on another and the effect of a pale spread against a darker spot. He showed her how to place her colours on the palette, and how to avoid garish effects by selecting a subtle juxtaposition of pigments to create an illusion of a colour. He displayed how a spot of red will give green tonalities to the hues in its vicinity and showed her how harmonies of grey could be effectively used to capture the subdued tones of the Staithes atmosphere. Under his care, Laura started to find her way and in *Oil Paint and Grease Paint* she pays him tribute: 'I never paint a picture now without thinking what he taught me … (he) lifted me out of a Morass'.

When writing of her life in Staithes, in both autobiographies Laura is highly selective in whom she mentions of the community of artists there. We are offered information only about painters who directly impacted on her life and work over those years. However, all those mentioned (apart from the wives of male painters) are men. There is no mention of the important and influential female artists who lived in Staithes during her time there.

Hannah Hoyland (who married Fred Mayor in 1902), for instance and Isa Jobling were painters of distinction in their own right and were, like Laura and Harold to be founder members of the Staithes Art Club in 1901. Isa Jobling, says Laura Newton in her book on the artists' colonies of the late 19th century *Painting at the Edge*, was a role model for young female artists at Staithes. She points out how Jobling's stark and uncompromising treatment of Staithes life, particularly that of the women, can be detected in the work of Laura Johnson but Laura does not mention her in either of her autobiographies.

What was the reason for the 'obvious biases and careful omissions' which Newton detects in Laura Knight's narrative? Probably, as always, it was the result of her solipsistic nature. By omitting information, it is unlikely that she was being consciously biased or that was she being devious. It is more probable that it never occurred to her that her reader would want to go beyond the parameters of her own orbit. We must also remember that the first autobiography, *Oil Paint and Grease Paint*, is not the product of objectivity and careful planning and the second, *The Magic of a Line* is the reflective narrative of a very old lady. We do not go to either of them for documentary facts, but to get a sense of who and what she was. The personality who emerges from the texts is evidence of the essential Laura Knight and not an objective history of her life and times.

Over the following seasons Laura tells us of how she remained in Staithes, tirelessly working from morning until night, destroying as many

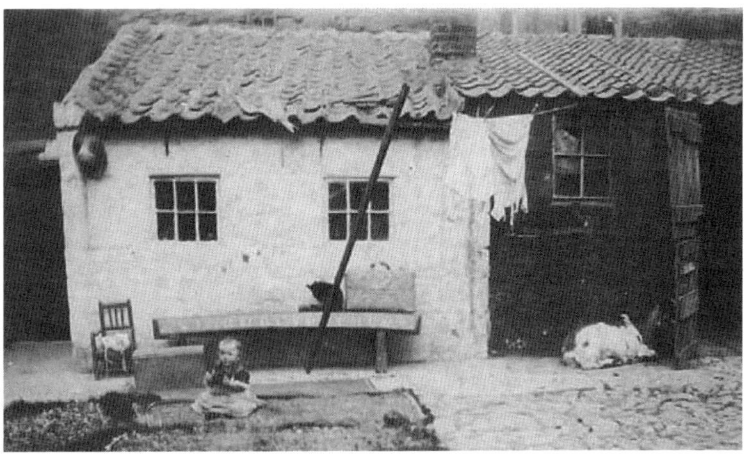

Laura's studio at Staithes, 1898. Private collection

sketches and paintings as she completed. Harold occasionally went to London and Sis to St Quentin, sometimes Ethel, Harold's sister who was always a good companion, came to visit Laura who clung on there like a limpet. For a while she took a room in the cottage on the moor that had been the Mackies' summer base. Each morning she would walk the three miles down to her studio in Staithes and return each evening exhausted and hungry but happy. She filled sketch books with closely observed studies of the dynamics of movement, whether of a hand, a thumb, or a rope, or made rapid water-colour "blottings" (as Fred Mayor, who set the trend, called them). Observing and perceiving for herself, she discovered the transformations required when rendering perceived colour through pigment. She rid herself of some assumptions, realizing, for example that 'all shadows in sunlight are not blue, but sometimes warmer than the light itself'.

She was taken by the picturesque, painterly qualities of domestic life: women employed in everyday tasks, peeling potatoes, plucking fowl; a girl playing with a cat; a tender moment between a mother and her child. They were happy to oblige her for the payment of a few pence. At this time, a muted palette and soft, feathered brushwork employed alongside often strong linear moulding, create a series of intimate studies of interiors in which grey, brown, ochre and golden hues predominate, illuminated by windows through which a pale, yellow light falls. Laura grew in confidence and her output was prolific, so much so that from time to time both she and Harold, running out of storage space, had periodic bonfires. Over the years working in Staithes, what they considered as good they sent for exhibition to Nottingham and the very best were submitted to the Royal Academy Summer Exhibition with modest success. There was also the annual selling exhibition organized by the Staithes Art Club, of which Harold and Laura were founding members.

Artists from the Staithes and Runswick Bay colonies were initially associated with the Yorkshire Union of Artists based in Whitby, where they held annual exhibitions. But in 1901 the Staithes Group broke away and set up their own association, with Laura and Harold as Founder Members. The Staithes Art Club held its first exhibition in the Fisherman's Institute and this was the location for subsequent exhibitions in 1902 and 1903. They were highly successful, attracting favourable reviews in the *Whitby Gazette*, with proceeds from the entrance fees going to the Institute. So popular was the initiative that by 1904 membership of the Staithes Art Club had grown to a point when the Institute could no longer cope with the demand for hanging space and so in that year it moved to the Anderson Gallery in Whitby. The

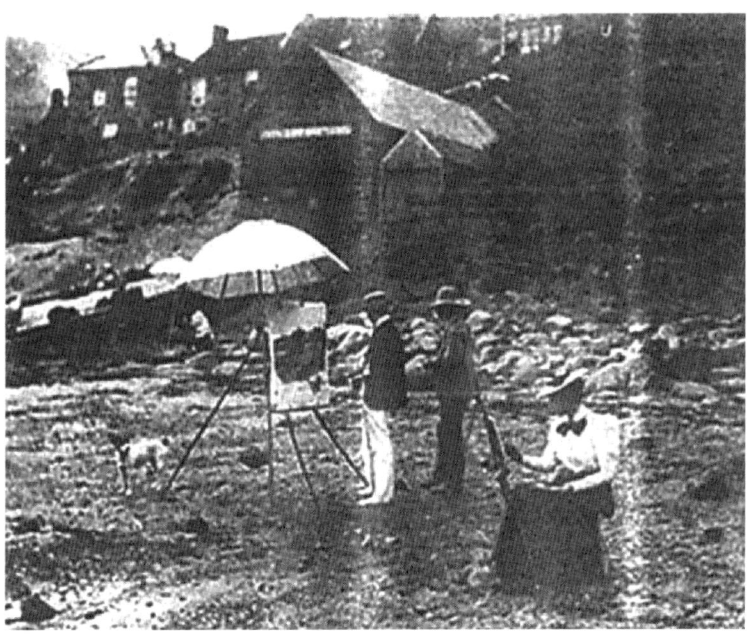

Laura Painting at Runswick Bay, photograph taken by Fred Jackson. c.1900.
Private collection

last independent Staithes exhibition was held in Whitby in 1905 and then it was absorbed back into the Yorkshire Union of Artists. After 1907 the Art Club was disbanded and its members mostly drifted away to other venues.

While most Staithes artists came and went by season, Laura and Harold lived in Staithes more or less continuously. They were accepted by the community and shared the day-to-day activity as well as the highs and lows of village life, the celebrations and deep sorrow. In Staithes, says Laura, she participated in the drama of life – the 'spiritual ecstasy' and 'sordid tragedy'. This was the 'black and white of life' and 'neither was to be despised – without the one the other could not be'. Black, white, the beauty of line: Laura's observations continued to be sharpened and enhanced. She records the abstract beauty of line displayed by a girl poised over a rock-pool, oblivious of watching eyes; the proportional relationship between limbs, head and body of an infant crawling on the sand; the brown hard-edged profile of a fisherman and the texture of his blue knitted "gansey"; the gemlike glow of a pebble washed by the tide. Unsentimental and yet deeply engaged, she gathered up her visual experiences and assembled them as a platform on which to build her confidence as an artist.

Harold found Staithes life congenial. He was able to paint as he wished, and he enjoyed the conversation and company of fellow artists and the locals over a pint at the pub. But he also found it emotionally draining. He felt, although did not overtly display, an empathy with the anxieties and suffering of those around him. While Laura engaged, he more often than not walked away from the relentless emotional battering that the community suffered on a daily basis. It was too much to bear. That Harold felt the tragedy of their existence is found in his paintings at this time, so that when representing a group activity, a fish sale, or a crowd of fisher-folk he directs the viewer's attention towards an individual with a face etched with pain and anxiety, body braced and battered by the storms. Harold not only testifies to their life of endurance in these sensitive portraits but reveals his own sensibilities. When the time came, he would be glad to leave.

One winter season Laura, Sis and Harold's sister Ethel who was staying with them moved to the Redmund's farm up on Roxby Moor. Here Laura found another kind of freedom in the bright, cold air, the heather and gorse moor, stretching to the open horizon. She tells of drinking fresh milk straight from the cow and snuggling down in the cowshed for warmth. She painted a lot but nothing of great note was kept, for pleasant as this might be, Staithes

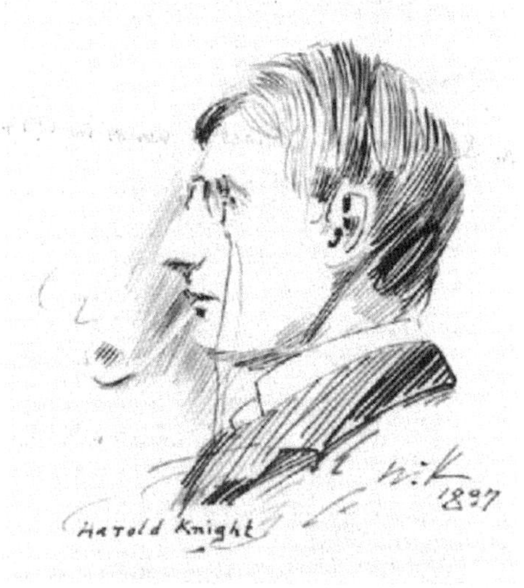

Laura Johnson, Pencil Sketch of Harold Knight, 1897. Private collection

down the hill was her preferred environment. Her early works at Staithes – pictures dating from before 1903 – such as *Under the Bridge, Unloading Nets, Whitby Market* – illustrate how the artist was exploring technique while maintaining a fairly restricted brown, and ochre palette, relieved occasionally by the occasional lilac of a Staithes bonnet or the splash of primary red in an infant's pinafore. There is at this time a definite correlation between Laura and Harold's work.

They both continued to exhibit locally, sent work to the Royal Academy and to the Nottingham Society of Artists. In 1901 Harold's paintings *Boys Fishing, Staithes* and *Hauling a Coble up the Beach* were given very positive reviews by the Nottingham press and in 1902 *The Last Coble* was purchased by the Holbrook Bequest and presented to Nottingham Castle Art Gallery. However, despite Harold's association with Staithes and *en plein air* genre painting, his main forte was portrait painting and he was keen to pursue this, travelling wherever a commission took him. In 1903 he was paint-ing portraits of dignitaries in Nottingham and in Newark. In the same year Laura showed an oil study, *Mother and Child*, at the Nottingham Society Exhibition. Believing that it was her best to date, she then submitted it to the Royal Academy Summer Show. To her delight and astonishment *Mother and Child* was accepted. What is more it was purchased by the well-known artist Edward Stott for the undreamt-of sum of 20 pounds. For Laura it seemed that the path forward was clear and when Laura Johnson was moved, like the storm breakers at Staithes, nothing could stand in her way.

Harold was now twenty-nine and Laura twenty-six. Neither of them in the first flush of youth, she had often hinted at marriage (goaded most likely by the fact that in 1902 they had attended the wedding in Nottingham of Rosie Good and Oliver Sheppard) but Harold always prevaricated, saying that marriage required financial stability. Now with her twenty pounds and Harold's portrait commissions she had an answer to the objection and de-cided that the time had come to be married. Sending a telegram to Harold who was working on the portraits in Nottingham, she got the first train out of the station in order to join him. Whatever Harold might think (and his first reaction was to point out that twenty pounds was not such a fortune), over lunch she proposed the idea and Harold accepted. They were yoked together as a couple, already joined together in a companionship based on years of shared experience and shared obsession: the desire to make a life in art. Marriage was inevitable.

Laura's impulsive will determined the next course of action which un-folded with startling rapidity. She took lodgings in the village of East Leake (where Little Grandma had been born and raised), and the wedding date was set for June 3rd leaving only a short time to make arrangements. With the help of Harold's sister Ethel, she made her wedding dress on the old Jones sewing machine from a linen sheet that had been part of her Mother's trousseau. Sis was in France at this time, staying with Uncle Arthur who, on the death of Aunt West-Ther in 1901, had taken over full management of the lace factory in St Quentin. He came over to England several times a year and Sis had returned with him as his housekeeper and administrative assistant. When the news came of the impending marriage, she hastened back to Staithes to help Laura clear the cottage. There was a doorstep sale of goods and chattels, which seems to have been a symbolic statement on Laura's part: she was cutting free and moving on. Unburdened by household goods she and Harold were to forge an identity together as free agents. Travelling gear was requested instead of pots and pans as wedding presents – luggage, writing cases, collar boxes were preferred.

Uncle Arthur Peter was to give Laura away and other guests included Harold's Father and his sisters, Ethel and Agnes, an old Nottingham friend Fred Milmine and Laura's former singing teacher Fraulein Gutjann and her niece. The wedding party was ferried in relays to the medieval church of St Helena in West Leake in the ancient horse-drawn village cab, the driver sporting a white buttonhole and a white ribbon on his whip. The setting for the wedding has some charm for West Leake, like its neighbour East Leake,

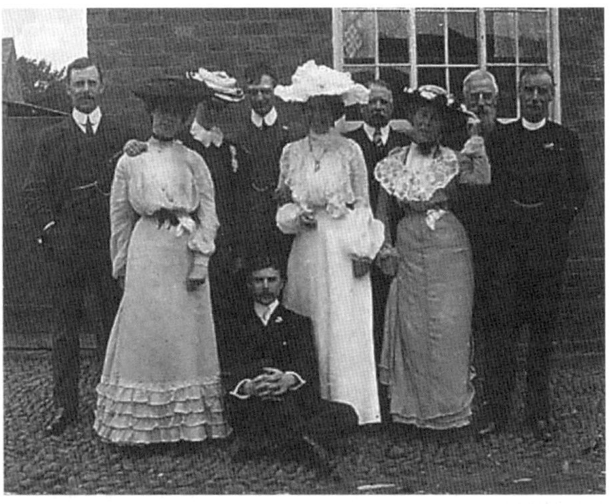

The wedding of Harold and Laura Knight, 1903. Private collection

lies on a tributary of the River Soar and "Leche" – the ancient form of its name – comes from the Anglo-Saxon word for a water-meadow. Laura's narrative of the event, however, has no romantic sentiment and her tone when writing of the wedding is more comically flippant than serious.

She tells us of how Uncle Arthur and she arrived fifteen minutes too soon at the church and had to stand awkwardly at the back while the vicar struggled into his surplice. Harold at last appeared 'splendid' in his grey Fifty Shilling Tailor's suit and, confusion continuing to reign, it was he who walked down the aisle to the customary bridal march. In the wedding photograph, the bride looks suitably radiant, the dress complemented by frills of St Quentin lace and the large-brimmed white hat embellished with a piece of St Quentin tulle. The self-effacing bridegroom stands at the back, shyly dignified in his suit. The Church has a small bellcote rather than the usual tower or spire and it contains two bells, so maybe the wedding was celebrated by the ringing of the old bells over the village and the water-meadows but Laura does not indulge in such lyricism. What she does tell us is that after the ceremony a modest reception was held at the farm where she had been lodging. Whether the marriage breakfast comprised raspberries or strawberries and cream is uncertain since the sources differ, but the drink apparently was coffee. A quantity of rice was thrown over the couple as they left on honeymoon to a fanfare of squawking and fluttering from the delighted chickens in the farmyard. For Laura it all seemed to be most satisfactory.

Setting off on their honeymoon to London by train, she in her navy pinstripe and Harold in his wedding suit, they travelled first-class courtesy of Uncle Arthur. Soon they were walking arm in arm down the Strand, facing the future together in that summer of 1903 as Mr and Mrs Harold Knight. On the way to the Arundel Hotel there was a diversion to a shop in Charing Cross Road so that Harold might buy some pyjamas which he had omitted to pack. Two pairs in real silk at a guinea a pair, these pyjamas were a startling 'rose red' and 'celestial blue' – clearly Laura's choice and endowing the occasion with a painterly glow. What Laura felt at that time was essentially the joy of having Harold to herself and to be able to visit art galleries and stand in front of individual paintings together without being concerned about anyone else or having to watch the clock to 'catch a trip train home'. Being with Harold was 'a privilege' and an 'enchantment' – a juxtaposition that suggests the tension between consciousness of her new official status and her excitement at its novelty.

Laura's 'enchantment' was made complete by an exhibition at the Guildhall which appealed to them both. It was of contemporary Dutch paintings, of interest because several of their acquaintance at Staithes had connections with artists working in and around Amsterdam and The Hague. One artist appealed above all others: Matthys Maris (1839–1917), a visionary painter who was recognized at the time as combining the *plein air* qualities of the Barbizon School with Pre-Raphaelite romanticism. Selecting simple subjects taken from nature, his paintings are invested with a dreamy and mysterious quality. The effect was achieved through his method of selecting a rough textured canvas, over which a charcoal outline was rubbed down so that the white ground emerged only to be brushed over with touches of vermilion or cobalt. The technique was interesting to Laura of course but the link with Harold's pyjamas seems to be significant too. Since she often re-members events in terms of colour, Maris' work fits into the spectrum of her joyful memories of that time – colour and food both. Laura, as we know and understand given her history of starvation rations, always describes meals enjoyed as the markers of high points in her story. So she tells us how after a short trip to Rye, the honeymoon was rounded off with a meal at *The Monico Restaurant* where veal and ham pie, followed by meringue a la crème was on the menu – setting a precedent for many subsequent celebratory feasts.

CHAPTER FIVE

"Watering the seeds of our ideas"

After their honeymoon Mr and Mrs Harold Knight went back to a wet and dreary Nottingham where Harold completed his portrait commissions. They then made their way back Staithes, lodged with Mrs Bowman at Roxby and took a studio behind the Post Office. The rain continued throughout the summer months and into autumn, followed by winter gales and early snow. The time spent there was flat and unproductive.

They enjoyed some cheer however when, now a couple, they were regularly invited by Henry Hopwood, Fred Jackson and their respective wives to their homes at Hinderwell, the next village from Staithes along the Whitby road. These friends offered them food, warmth and good conversation. Indeed, pretty soon Laura was taken in hand by Hopwood's wife who rifled through her own wardrobes and found her one or two up-to-date dresses – more than Laura had ever possessed. These were received with varying degrees of approval, but the fashionable toque hat that was pressed upon her head was too much for Harold to bear. He advised Laura to take it off even before they had passed through the garden gate. Of the two painters, Jackson's dedication to *plein air* painting earned Laura's admiration. She describes how Jackson, a 'more robust influence' than Hopwood who was more temperamental, would go out in all extremes of weather: 'Under the mittens he wore, his hands were swollen, stiff and chapped, as were the edges of his ears and the wings of his nostrils'. There were to be future times when Laura Knight would do exactly the same in pursuit of a subject or a particular effect.

Up on Roxby Moor Laura and Harold commonly awoke to snow on the pillow, ice in the bath and a depressing lack of sales for their work. Very early in her Staithes experience Laura had realized that the coming of spring lambs and primroses was no guarantee of warmth in the sun or relief from the cutting edge of North East winds. In that spring the cold and penetrating damp of the North East Coast invaded every corner and every bone of their bodies. For relief they went back to Nottingham for a few weeks and tried to sell some pictures, renting a room on South Parade as an exhibition space. But, apart from meeting up with old friends and colleagues, there was little to keep them there and so they made their way to London to try to interest dealers in their work. The dealers did not like or even understand what was offered. Only one, Ernest Brown at the Leicester Galleries was positive. He was courteous and spent time assessing their paintings, accepting several to sell. It was a good omen. Meeting Henry Hopwood in the capital, he told them of his intention to travel to Holland the following year and suggested that they might join him. Given their circumstances such a trip seemed to be out of the question. However, true to his word, Brown sold some of their paintings and offered to mount an exhibition of their work the following year. Buoyed up by this success and with just enough money to cover expenses, in June 1904 they sailed with Hopwood to Amsterdam.

Regaining their land-legs after a rough crossing, the flat picture-book polders were slowly revealed as the sun burned off the mist. In Amsterdam Laura once again brings us into the dramatic present as she describes the costumes of the people in the street which, together with the old canal ways and squares, create for her a medieval townscape. The smells and the sensations mingle: coffee and canal water, cigar smoke and strawberries. True to his name, Hopwood excitedly jumps about the thoroughfares, directing their attention to a line here or a colour there, 'cupping his hands in a square to frame a view', oblivious of anybody or anything moving around him. They go to the Rijksmuseum, where the scale and dignity of Rembrandt's group portrait of *The Nightwatch* impresses; the jewel-like interiors of Vermeer entrance, and animated portraits of Franz Hals amaze. The joy and excitement of the experience is orchestrated through a series of exclamations which herald the arrival of new perspectives and dimensions for Laura, and presumably for Harold too, but this is Laura's story and his responses are unrecorded.

The capital was expensive for them and so they decided to take the train some 30 kilometers east of Amsterdam to one of the artists' villages, Laren. Along with other well-known locations in Holland such as Katwijk and Volendam, Laren had become a popular place for artists to work in the 1880s and was well-used to itinerant painters coming to visit or stay. Accommodation for the foreigners was available at the Pension Kam and the locals were happy for a painter to set up an easel in a barn or kitchen, both at modest cost. This was a farming and weaving community and the population continued to wear their traditional clogs, caps and head-dresses. It was a picturesque subject.

There had been colonies of artists in Holland from the 1840s. When the painter W.J. Bilders established himself at Oosterbeek, a town south east of Laren, others, inspired by the 17th century Dutch painters and influenced by the Barbizon school, joined him there. These included Paul Gabriël, Willem Roelofs, Jozef Israels, the brothers Willem and Matthijs Maris (whose work Laura had so admired at the Dutch Exhibition in London) and Anton Mauve, a cousin-in-law to Vincent Van Gogh. Around 1870 some of them migrated to The Hague and together with a younger generation of artists established themselves as the "Hague School". Characteristically, their work has a low-key tonality suited to the pearl grey skies and atmosphere of landscapes and skyscapes of the northern coastal climate. This palette can be recognized in earlier work produced earlier by Bilders at Oosterbeek and is the same harmony in grey that Charles Mackie recommended to Laura as being appropriate for work on the North East Coast at Staithes. She was therefore in a familiar painting environment.

At Laren in 1904 'serious work was being done' by the artists in residence at the Pension Kam. Run by the English born widow of a Dutchman, this was where all the incomers stayed and ate. Laura's image of the artists seated around the communal table creates a characteristic Dutch interior. At the head of the table sits the patriarchal figure of the American painter Wilder M. Darling (1856–1933): the "Great Oracle". Originally from Ohio, Darling was a great expert on 17th century Dutch painting as well as being keenly interested in the Barbizon and Hague Schools and a practitioner of *plein air* painting. He had been staying at the Pension Kram for 10 years and was therefore something of an institution in Laren. A man of few words, what he did say was always insightful and pertinent and listeners hung on his words.

At the other end of the table sat the proprietor, Vrow Kam. The newcomers were seated next to her, but Laura notes that the most stimulating conversation was to be enjoyed at the other end of the table and she clearly wished to progress towards Mr Darling's end. The patriarch offered to show them around the village the next day and with his help they were advised of likely houses where they would be able to set up easels and work at a cost of 5 guilden a week. As Laura says, such households were used to painters working in their homes and barns, accepting them as a necessity to boost family earnings: 'the peasants were as used to painters as the air they breathed'.

In Chapter 10 of *Oil Paint and Grease Paint*, Laura describes their first morning in Laren – the sun glancing across red-brick walls and coloured shutters, giving a lightness and sparkle to the lime trees that raised the spirits. Then there is a contrast as she moves into what she recognised as 'Rembrandtesque interiors': a barn which not only contained animals and fowl but the family too in the summer months. She notes the large fireplace at the far end, its Delft tiles blackened by soot; plates ranged along the chimneybreast; a small table where a cat sits by the coffee pot, dipping its paws into the milk jug; a woman scrubbing milk cans at a pump. In the company of Mr Darling whose knowledge of the 17th century Dutch Masters was considerable, clearly Laura's perceptions are now primed to absorb the configurations of her surroundings and transform them. She was confident that 'something more important might be achieved'.

Unused to the pungent smell of the animals at the farm where she first set up her easel, Laura retreated feeling very sick. Finding a more spacious and airier establishment, she set out at once to paint the housewife preparing vegetables for the pot. What follows is a scene taken straight from one of Jan Steen's "kitchens": family and workers seated around a table, grace said, all delving into the pot with bare hands, everything 'ending in a hubbub, as the children screamed and fought for scrapings, and the housedog nosing round for the fallen scraps'. For both Harold and Laura the work done in those 6 weeks at Laren was 'promising' and at the end of their stay they determined to return the next year.

After their trip, they had little money left and no option but to go back to Roxby where Mrs Bowman allowed them to stay with her 'on tick'. What money they had was to be hoarded to pay for the carriage of their best work to London for the next Academy Exhibition. To their joy, the paintings were accepted but it seemed that to go to London for "varnishing day" when the picture was hung and finishing touches could be made was a luxury they could not afford. In the event Harold borrowed five pounds from his Nottingham friend Fred Milmine with the promise to repay. It was Easter weekend and no trains ran through Staithes, so they had to walk and finally run across the moor and through a downpour to catch the train from Whitby to York and on to London. Once on the train they sat with soaked and steaming clothes which they had to wear for the next two days. They bickered all the way, Laura blaming Harold for their discomfort and Harold replying with his usual sarcasm. Spirits lightened, however, when they discovered that Harold's painting *A Cup of Tea* had sold. The Royal Academician Sir Frank Dicksee had bought it for the Brisbane Art Gallery which, having been inaugurated in 1895, was acquiring a collection. Dicksee had paid the grand sum of £100 and that was a fortune which would allow them to return to Laren the next year.

Laura's accounts of the whole Laren period are dislocated and telescoped. In *The Magic of a Line* she dedicates a whole of chapter to 'Holland' and in the process condenses events and experiences to such an extent that subsequent writers offer conflicting chronologies of the years 1904–6. What is certain is that there were three visits to Laren and each one of these had a profound influence on her development and confidence. In 1905 they stayed at Laren for 6 months, once again lodging at Vrow Kam's pension. This time they were able to take their seats at the much-coveted Darling end of the table. The company was made up of some familiar faces and some new ones. What is notable from Laura's record of some of the artists who were in the Laren group at that time is its international flavour.

There was the English woman Julia Beatrice How (1867–1932) who normally divided her painting life between Beverley in Yorkshire and Paris and whose specialism was in painting children. Although Laura calls him 'Henri' Villain, another member of the community was the Barbizon inspired painter George-Reneé Villain (1854–1930), whose good looks and vanity (Laura tells the story with some satisfaction) were damaged when an Amercan girl's bulldog attacked his nose. A number of Americans featured in the company, most of whom were scholarship students. One was Albert Henry Krehbiel (1873–1945), a graduate of the Art Institute of Chicago who was travelling on an American Travelling Scholarship. In 1903 he began studying at the *Academie Julian* in Paris. Much decorated with praise and honours, it appears that he had taken time out of the stuffy atmosphere there to explore *plein air* painting and was in Laren at the same time as Laura and Harold Knight. Krehbiel returned to the United States to paint at a variety of coastal colonies and was eventually to become head of the Chicago School of Art.

Laura was impressed by one 'radiantly boyish' character called Mackay who had arrived from America filled with enthusiasm. This young man embodied all the excitement and hope that she herself felt in this new season at Laren. Energetic and enthusiastic, Mackay is a generic type that was always attractive to Laura. Another young American painter at Laren and for whom we have some details was Clarence Hincle (1880–1960). Having won a travelling scholarship to Europe from the Pennsylvania Academy of the Fine Arts, he arrived at the colony in 1905 and stayed for 3 years. His work of that time, a palette of browns and greys, like Laura's own, reflects the influence of Dutch landscape and weather. But, again, like Laura, Hincle was to emerge from this subdued tonality when he moved back to the States and settled in the painting colony of Laguna in California where he discovered light and colour. Soon Laura too was to break out of the fog of Holland to find a new vitality and a brightened palette at Newlyn in Cornwall.

Then there was fellow Englishman John Everett (1876–1949). A nephew of the Pre-Raphaelite artist John Everett Millais, he was a marine painter and an adventurer. Everett's 'pale blue eyes, fair skin, rough tweeds and thick boots singled him out astonishingly as he went his own way'. Laura identified him as a fellow spirit, for not only did he know where to get the best bargains, he had a buccaneer swagger and charm. She admired him greatly. A versatile artist (he was commissioned to illustrate a biography of his friend Thomas Hardy in 1924–5), long after Laren, Everett continued to be a friend of the Knights, more particularly of Laura, and in the early 1920s they 'started etching together'.

In 1905, having arrived early in the season Laura and Harold were able to take their pick of farms and cottages and negotiate where they were to set up their painting pitch (Plate 5). Their competence in speaking Dutch appears to have been halting, Laura describing what little they knew as "Boer Dutch". In fact, in *The Magic of a Line* she occasionally refers to native Dutch people as "Boers" which of course is mistaken. However, what must be remembered is that the South African or Boer War was for her a contemporary event, starting in 1899 and resolved of a fashion in favour of the British in 1902. It is likely that the smattering of colloquial "Boer Dutch'" that Harold possessed had been picked up in the company of acquaintances in Nottingham who had fought in the Boer War. This is evidenced by what he is reported to have said in response to the pestering of a local guide who wanted to show him the sights of Laren. His riposte in Boer of 'not bloody likely' was not quite what he had meant to say as a gentleman. That Laura continues, mistakenly, to use the word "Boer" as a synonym for "Dutch" so many years later in *The Magic of a Line* is the result of ingrained British imperiousness and her artist's assumption that a place like Laren was a resource to be exploited, like gold in the Transvaal.

The golden days of that summer were spent painting with great intensity, but on Sundays they took a day off, travelling on the train to Amsterdam. In the company of fellow painters and sometimes Mr Darling, they trawled the galleries Tand closely studied the painters of the Golden Age: Rembrandt at the Rijksmuseum; Vermeer in the Mauritshuis at The Hague; and Franz Hals in Haarlem. Selecting specific works, they paid particular attention to technique and composition, attempting to apply what they had learned on their return. Laura found this 'irksome', preferring to work intuitively rather than by rule. She could find little to say about the Van Gogh canvases she

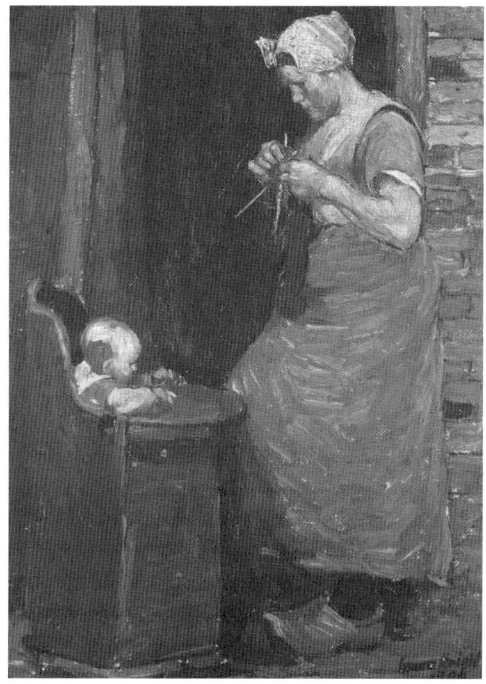

Black and white photographic copy of *Mother and Child* by Laura Knight.
Private collection

saw except to note their brilliant colour and simplicity. Compared with the old masters, they seemed to her to be purely decorative.

What she did enjoy were the regular evening gatherings in the dining room at the pension: playing parlour games and joining in the painting talk generated around Mr Darling while he drank his customary three bottles of beer. In both texts she enthusiastically tells of joining in with the games of baseball (more like rounders, she admits) that were played on the dunes after work by some of the residents at the Pension Kam. Laura was quite a star and 'the only girl who stuck to the team' for she was good at catching if not so good with the bat. This expertise she puts down to Harold's and her own 'favourite form of exercise', regular games of 'dodgy catchers' on the beach at Staithes. This delightful image of the two of them – approaching thirty – committed to regular and enthusiastic ball games on the beach testifies to their jolly companionship, free from strait-laced conventions, artless in their pursuit of art.

Soon enough the period of their stay was over and they returned by the packet boat to England. Their trunk was filled with a substantial number of paintings, interlaid with rolls of tobacco which, to help their finances, they planned to sell once back in England. Just as they were about to leave, Harold (always susceptible to teeth and mouth problems) developed a tooth abscess which swelled and caused him extreme pain for the whole of the journey. It seems to have been an eventful passage in many ways. Two difficult Dutchmen on the boat caused great unpleasantness, trying to make 'everything as uncomfortable as they could' for fellow passengers. They earned the disapproval of the captain by bringing their own rations on board and at all stages were prepared to bluff their way out of paying for anything. The atmosphere aboard was tense but for Laura interesting.

Then, on reaching the Thames, there was a series of potential disasters: a near collision in the fog; a 5-hour delay in berthing at the docks and the worry (given their contraband) of cross-examination by customs – unnecessary in the event because it was late and the dock was largely deserted. What is more, two drunk watermen whose craft was to carry them to the wharf, nearly dropped the trunk in the river. It was saved by the quick thinking of their Laren friend and fellow passenger, Albert Krehbiel, who manfully hauled it on board, watched from the deck by a mournful Harold, his jaw swathed in a poultice to relieve his abscess. This is the story we are told in *Oil Paint and Grease Paint.* However, in *The Magic of a Line* Dame Laura calls this saviour 'Raphael'. This must refer to the American painter Joseph Raphael (1872–1950) who, originating in North Carolina, had studied in Paris and worked in Laren from around 1902, dividing his time between Europe and the west coast of America. The confusion about which artist was their fellow passenger can of course be put down to Dame Laura's age at the time of writing. It is also interesting that in this same later version of the incident she also indulges in a dramatic, even sentimental, aside which is not quite in character either for her or her husband. Harold, she says, was fully expecting 'boat, boatmen, Raphael and his beloved wife all tossed in the ink-black water of the Thames'. They and their luggage survived, which was just as well since their future was packed into that trunk.

Their 'Dutch pictures' as they called them were some of the best they had done and as soon as they landed, Harold arranged for the Canadian flower painter A.F.W. Hayward (1836–1939) to view their cache of work with the intention of buying. He bought several and paid over a cheque for close on £100. When he had gone, Harold is reported to have waltzed Laura around their sitting room in a mood and that affirmed their relief and youthful high spirits. Solvent again, Laura bought herself a green suit that she had identified in a shop on Shaftesbury Avenue and Harold was to have a new overcoat. While in London they negotiated their first exhibition at the Ernest Brown and Phillip's Leicester Galleries, *Dutch Life and Landscape*, which was held in June 1906. The future was brightening.

Back on the moors, they were pleased to be once again exposed to the bracing air after the lung and throat-clogging fogs of low-lying Holland. Harold found a studio down in Staithes for his painting, but Laura, now with the habits of Laren, decided to set up her easel and paint within the cottage of a local family. She found one up Cowbar Hill, renting it and the inhabitants as models by the week. The father earned a pittance as a miner at the local ironstone mine and with four small children and a baby on the way to provide for, the little money that Laura offered them in payment was a lifeline. These were good people, loving and loyal in spite of their marginal existence. She describes the plight of the exhausted mother and to read her account of the hardship, graft and physical suffering is heart rending. But, typically, she maintains an artist's objectivity, explaining that the family ben-efitted from her being there, adding as a self-justification and as a sop to the reader's sensibilities that had the family 'not been of such unusual interest to paint, I could not have borne to see the suffering of those wretched people'. It is an ambiguous sentiment.

One painting in particular from time spent with the miner's family at Staithes testifies to Laura Knight's growing accomplishment: *Dressing the Children*. The picture illustrates much of what she had learned from her working in Holland. The mother and three children pose before the fire in a room that is bare of any other furniture apart from a settle and a rag rug on which an infant sits. The light source at the window shines on the hair of the small girl having her dress fastened and casts its brightness across the otherwise monochrome interior. A cat crouches on the floor. It was a feature that Laura apparently required for the composition, although the family did not own one. So, a feral cat had to be coaxed into the room, where it spat, scratched and hurled itself at the window.

That cat proved to be Laura's most difficult sitter and she could make little of it, Harold commenting that 'It looks as though someone had trod-den on it and squashed it flat'. However, the grey and beige tonal harmonies of cat and interior are beautifully modulated, the only colour being the red of the embers in the grate echoed by the red ribbon tied in the hair of girl seated with her back to us. Closer inspection reveals that red features within the brushstrokes of the girls' pinafores; it is present in their mother's bonnet and is an important ingredient of the shadows in the room. As a result, the interior has a soft grey-pink ambiance – a tenderness that belies the harsh reality of their lives. The painting was a success at the Royal Academy Summer show in 1906 and the *Dutch Life and Landscape* exhibition at the Leicester Galleries sold well. The Knights determined to return to Laren. But, before they went they loaned the sum of £5 to the family so that the father, now ailing and unlikely ever to go down the mine again, could buy a horse and cart and set up a business selling fish. He did well and was soon able to repay part of the loan. The rest was a gift.

On their third trip to Laren in 1906 they ate but did not stay at the Pension Kam, taking two rooms on a farm instead. In Laura's general comments on Holland, some of the more practical difficulties associated with this are aired: the fleas which tormented Harold and the smell of the peasants who never washed – ever – many being sewn into their clothes until they dropped off in tatters. Smells linger over the pages in *The Magic of a Line* at this stage of her story: coffee and tobacco mixed with the pungent odours of the farmyard and the bitter smell of humanity. In their concern for personal freshness, Harold and Laura travelled with an india-rubber bath that they managed to persuade the reluctant Vrow, 'certain that we were going to kill ourselves', to fill for their own ablutions. The accommodation was a partitioned space at one end of the great barn, with a latched door that when opened each morning allowed all the rich odours of family and farm to reach their nostrils along with the pervading smell of coffee. Equally sensuous, is the description of the compacted threshing floor lit from without by golden streamers of morning sunshine radiating through the great barn.

For all this, the stay in Laren was disappointing for Laura's work. She had begun to be annoyed by Mr Darling's proscriptive judgements on her painting and his negative attitude towards her desire to discuss her thoughts and discoveries about composition and colour. This reveals a clear growth in confidence to form her own independent style. At this point in *Oil Paint and Grease Paint* Laura pays Harold a great compliment, perhaps the greatest she could make. He was, she affirms, 'the best critic', not forcing opinion upon her but working to understand the thinking and effort behind a painting. He is gifted with an 'extraordinarily sensitive and sympathetic nature'. Then follows a delightful sequence describing their enjoyment in exploring Holland, visiting markets and shops in Delft and Amsterdam, haggling for bargains, and going to the sea at Enkhuysen at the edge of what was then the Zuyder Zee (soon to be drained as polder) and imagining how it was when Rembrandt and Franz Hals were there. Nonetheless, it is clear that

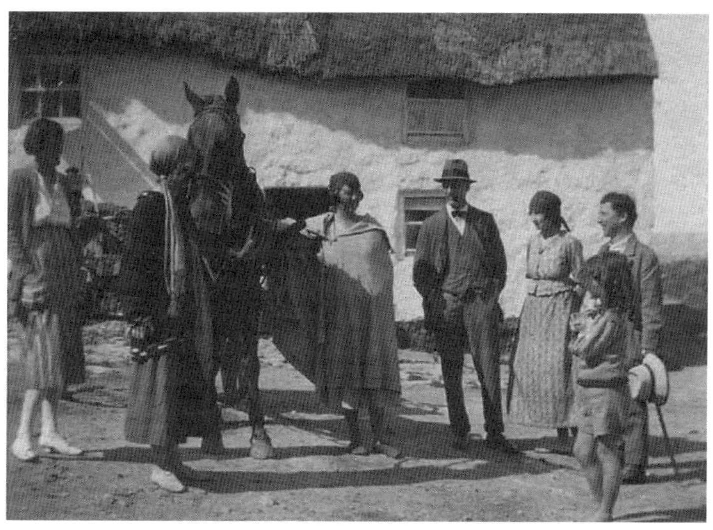

Group photograph at Staithes with horse and cart 1905. Laura centre with
Harold in bowtie and hat to her left. Private collection

she is starting to see the Dutch landscapes and costumes as picturesque in a
hackneyed way. Harold, by contrast, was happy there. For him Holland was
an affirming experience as he began to refine his own style through a study
of 17th century Dutch interiors and specifically those of Vermeer.

The winter of 1906–7 was extremely cold, the Zuyder Zee froze over,
as did the water in the india-rubber bath. Laura and one of the girls she
used as a model went skating on the 'Rink' at Laren and a few from the
pension played baseball in the snow. While sledges decked with bells coasted
over the frozen landscape, Harold and Laura huddled close to their stove.
Christmas 1906 was spent with festivities at the farm where Laura, Harold
and Raphael gave a party for their host family. They had never experienced
such a thing – sitting up late well beyond their normal bedtime and with
the artists who had changed into their best clothes – they having been sewn
into theirs for the duration of the winter! Then there was a Christmas meal
at Vrow Kam's, after which Harold, always inclined to what was called at the
time "biliousness", was sick.

Leaving Holland in January 1907, they left an Amsterdam covered in
snow, the house gables outlined white against a leaden sky as in the old pictures. They sailed just as a thaw set in, leaving behind another community of
artists and another stage of their painting life.

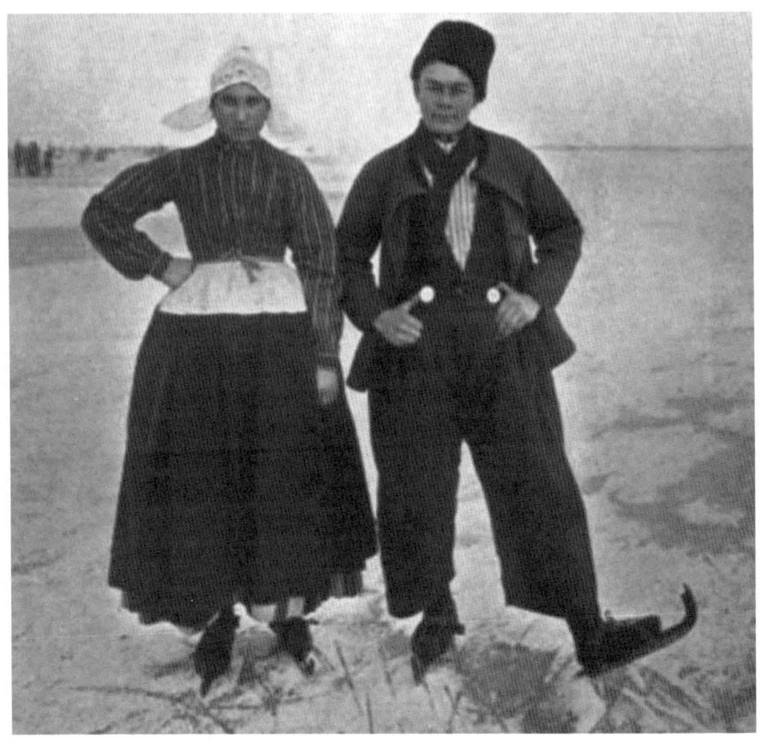

Dutch Skaters c.1903. Public domain

Back in England, they finalised the arrangements for their second exhibition at the Leicester Galleries to be held in October 1907, titled *Life and Landscapes by Harold and Laura Knight*. They made their way back to Mrs Bowman up at Roxby and in June were painting at Runswick Bay. But there they found the coast permanently shrouded in mist and cold enough to nip Laura's nose as she attempted to paint glimpses of light coming through the clouds. It was little different from Laren. The autumn came in with severe gales and storms, and, unable to face the strenuous walk back and forth from Roxby to Staithes, Harold and Laura took a room above Featherstone's Post Office and worked in their old studios. Then after one gale too many when the winds and foam lashed the staithe and foamed up the narrow, cobbled ways, once again there was the sound of keening in the streets as yet one more fishing boat was thought to be lost.

That it proved to be a false alarm when the crew arrived next day hale and hearty, having landed down the coast at Port Mulgrave, was no consolation. The Knights had had enough of the raw pain of the place and, now that the winter set in, missed the companionship of other artists that they had enjoyed at Laren. Harold in particular was emotionally drained, tired of watching the never-ending tragedy of life on the Yorkshire coast. Yet Laura was reluctant to leave, for she owed so much to the place. Staithes had offered her emotional and professional nourishment and throughout her life she would think back to her time in that 'wildified place' as marking a rite of passage. It was there, she says that 'I … found my own way of seeing and trying to speak of it in pencil and colour, instead of copying other people, particularly Harold.' The time had come to move on. So, they burned their unwanted canvases and looked south and west with the promise of warmer climes, longer days and brighter skies of Cornwall.

CHAPTER SIX

"Life was going with a swing ..."

Newlyn is situated on the Cornish peninsula, 10 miles south of St Ives and less than a mile away from Penzance and the railway. Despite being within easy reach of suburban and metropolitan London, Cornwall has a quality of "otherness". A place of legend and magic, the quality of light and the geography of its landscape have more in common with Brittany than mainland England. Writing to his mother in 1894, the painter Stanhope Forbes described Newlyn as 'a sort of English Concarneau, and is the haunt of many artists'. Aware of the work of Bastien-Lepage and keen to explore *plein air* painting and rustic naturalism, Forbes had travelled to Brittany in 1891–2 in the company of his friend Henry La Tangue. They visited the artists' colonies of Quimperlé and Concarneau where Jules Bastien Lepage had settled in 1883. On his return to Britain, Forbes made his way to Newlyn and found there another colony dedicated to *plein air* realism and the square brush techniques of Bastein-Lepage. He decided to stay.

The first resident artist in Newlyn had been Walter Langley who had moved there in 1882, but it had certainly been 'discovered' by artists earlier. For instance, the Slade student Caroline Burland Yates wrote to her future husband Thomas Cooper Gotch (both were to be good friends of the Knights) about the 'delights of Newlyn' in 1879. By September 1884, when Forbes arrived, there were some twenty-seven artists residing in the colony. These included Frank Bramley, Norman Garstin, Thomas Cooper Gotch, Fred Hall, Edwin Harris, Harold Harvey, and Henry Scott Tuke. Many more artists came to visit or reside in Newlyn over the following years often with their wives (usually artists in their own right) and their families. Many others, while recognised as part of the "Newlyn School", were based in St Ives or Falmouth.

Above all his fellow artists, it was Forbes who took the discipline of *plein air* painting to extremes. It was his confirmed belief that the more successful the picture, the more uncomfortable the artist had been in painting it.

For instance, his celebrated painting *Fish Sale on a Cornish Beach* of 1885, cost him many hours of physical discomfort as he battled with the elements to achieve authenticity. When hung at the Royal Academy the following year 1886, *Fish Sale on the Beach* was highly praised, Alice Meynell writing that it 'manifests the finest quality of natural art' (an article re-printed in the *Art Journal,* 1889). However, such Naturalism was fiercely attacked by a few pro-Impressionist members of the New English Art Club, notably Walter Sickert. The full force of his venom was reserved for Frank Bramley's *A Hopeless Dawn.* When Harold and Laura saw *A Hopeless Dawn* in Nottingham Castle Gallery in the Newlyn Exhibition in 1894, they did not realise how contentious the painting had been as a focus for serious division within the New English Art Club. Five years previously, the success of Bramley's picture at the 1889 Academy show provoked Sickert into vitriolic comment not merely on the painting but on the whole technique and philosophy of Naturalism. As a result, to a man, the Newlyn contingent left the New English Art Club in 1890 in protest. This was to have a positive impact on the colony, affirming both the identity of Newlyn painters as a group and renewing their loyalty to the Royal Academy. The colony at Newlyn had been in a period of decline but the controversy injected new life and it grew in strength and influence nationally and locally.

The fishing community of Newlyn benefitted from the presence of the artists who boosted the economy by renting studio space in disused net lofts, paying for food and accommodation as well as hiring local folk as models. This impact of the last is delightfully illustrated in the 1891 Census where 84-year-old Elizabeth (Betsy) Lanyon described herself not as "fishwife" but as "artist's model". One problem for some was that the incomers did not keep the Sabbath and this attracted violent protest at times, with easels smashed and canvases ruined. They were, as one villager commented, 'a godless though profitable nuisance' and on the strength of this, old Newlyn opened itself to the economic pressures of modernity.

By the 1880s the infrastructure of the fishing village was itself in the process of modernisation. The old harbour walls, so appealing to visiting artists, were replaced by two new piers – one with a lighthouse, which, while offering greater safety and efficiency for the fisherman, were neither picturesque nor painterly. Because of this, many visiting artists continued to paint the harbour as it had been and in doing so brought into question the whole philosophy of Natural Realism – the direct and truthful representation of the subject. This erosion of ideals continued when one entrepreneurial artist, Benjamin Arthur Bateman, purchased a meadow in the town and built several studios on it. These were constructed with a large surface area of glass so that artists could continue to paint apparently *en plein air* while keeping warm and dry. While this was regarded as a benefit by some, others regarded it as a betrayal of the *plein air* ideology, a speculative build that attracted the wrong sort: 'Swells came down for a holiday and called themselves 'Artists' and almost crowded the workers out' reflected one anonymous contributor to the *Magazine of Art* in 1898.

The Meadow soon became the location for artists to exhibit their work in advance of the Royal Academy shows, and this was to become a major social occasion for the villagers as well as outsiders. In 1895 this arrangement was superseded when a dedicated exhibition gallery was built at the request of some of the Newlyn Group at the eastern end of the town, funded by the philanthropist and businessman John Passmore Edwards. Once more, however, the constitution of the colony was professionalized and its original spirit compromised. Gradually the Group began to disperse.

The Newlyn colony was revived in October 1899 with the opening of the Newlyn School of Painting by Stanhope Forbes and his wife Elizabeth. They hoped to attract new blood to the place by offering residential art tuition to students. Forbes, called the "Professor", was the titular master but Elizabeth was an essential part of the business. She not only tutored pupils and posed the models but had an important practical role in mentoring the young women who enrolled, many of them away from home for the

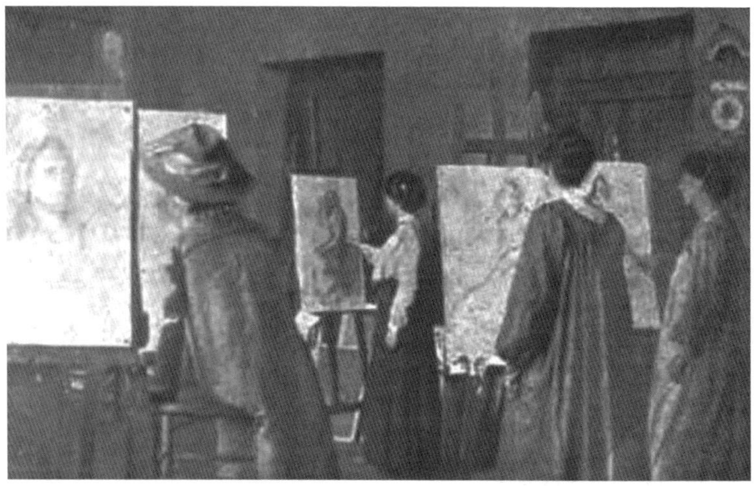

Newlyn Art School, Female Class led by Mrs Stanhope Forbes c.1899. Public domain

first time. The School was highly successful and over some 40 years saw hundreds of aspiring artists pass through its tutelage. Some were to achieve professional accolades, many others remained accomplished amateurs. What is significant is that the art education offered there, while being driven by the ideals of *plein air* painting, also imposed a strict academic regime on the student.

Training at the School comprised three teaching stages in mastering representation of the human form. Three separate "huts" were designated for the pupils: the first was for the novices who were set the task of copying plaster casts; the second was life study of the clothed model who posed outside when the weather was clement; the final "hut" was for the most talented who were allowed to paint the nude. Since local girls were reluctant to pose unclothed, for this exercise models were brought down from London. This meant another structural change in the community. Joining the local village people, the established professional artists and the young middle-class students (male and female) at Forbes' School, came dancers and actresses, supplementing their income with a summer job as artists' models. It was an interesting mix that created an energy and vitality attractive to a new generation of artists who came to Newlyn, drawn there by its climate, clarity of light and bohemian lifestyle. By the time Harold and Laura moved there in 1907, Newlyn was flourishing.

The effect of Cornwall on the work of the Knights was described in 1913 by a fellow Newlyn artist Norman Garstin. In an article published in *The Studio,* Garstin comments that their vision was in no way clouded by the notorious Cornish damp and windy weather – a climate epitomised by his own famous picture of 1889 *The Rain it Raineth Every Day.* Rather 'there came over their work an utter change in both their outlook and method: they at once plunged into a riot of brilliant sunshine, opulent colour and of sensuous gaiety'. This transformation was to be spectacularly evident in Laura's work and was due to her immersion in a very different lifestyle as much as to the discovery of the joys of painting outdoors on the Cornish coast. Harold, free of the emotional pressures of Staithes, was certainly more at ease in Cornwall and Laura, with mood lightened and formalities put to one side, soon became absorbed into community life – indeed one of its prime movers.

When Harold and Laura arrived in Newlyn in the late autumn of 1907 the November weather was not promising. They came by train to Penzance station and would have travelled by pony and trap along the wet and windy promenade to Newlyn. Looking out of the window of the Mount's Bay

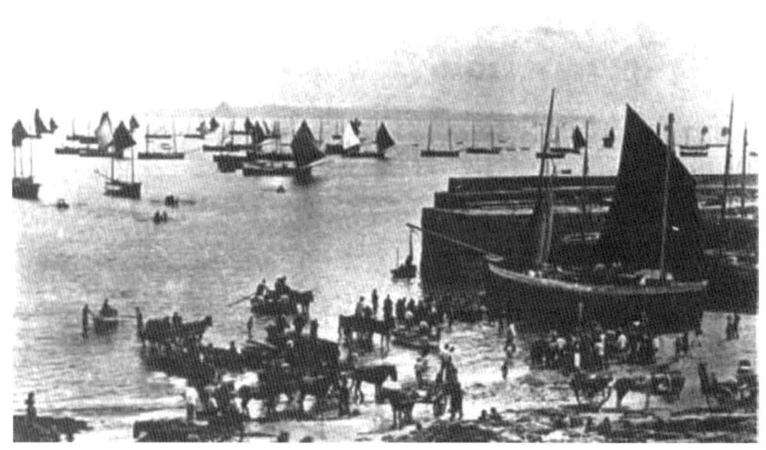

Newlyn harbour c.1900. Private collection

Hotel on their first morning, the outlook was 'forbidding and grey', but their welcome from Stanhope Forbes was cordial. He suggested lodgings for them and then conducted them around the site of the School to see the work of his students. It was a good start and it was also encouraging that they were able to make contact with some of the local fishermen by mentioning the name of their old friend Jimmy James, the fish buyer at Staithes. Nonetheless, at first Newlyn was a disappointment for Laura. While many of the houses clustered on a steep side of Paul Hill to the West and narrow lanes (called "opes" as opposed to the "gunnels" of Staithes) led in an arbitrary way to the beach, the perspectives here were broader; the slate and thatch roofed houses did not snuggle down in rocky clefts with the seagulls and the fisher-folk displayed none of the statuesque dignity of their counterparts at Staithes. Worse, as she looked over Mount's Bay, the light seemed to be washed out and colourless rather than aglow and vibrant as she had expected. In the opening of the 12th chapter of *Oil Paint and Grease Paint* she gives expression to her sense then of being cut adrift from the place which 'had been one of the most vital influences on my life'. But even though she looked back with regret, the break with Staithes had been made.

With the coming of Spring, however, the mood changed. They were visited by Uncle Arthur and Sis, who, with the sale of the St Quentin factory had returned to England to look for a suitable retirement home with a garden for Uncle Arthur. Sis would accompany him as his housekeeper and

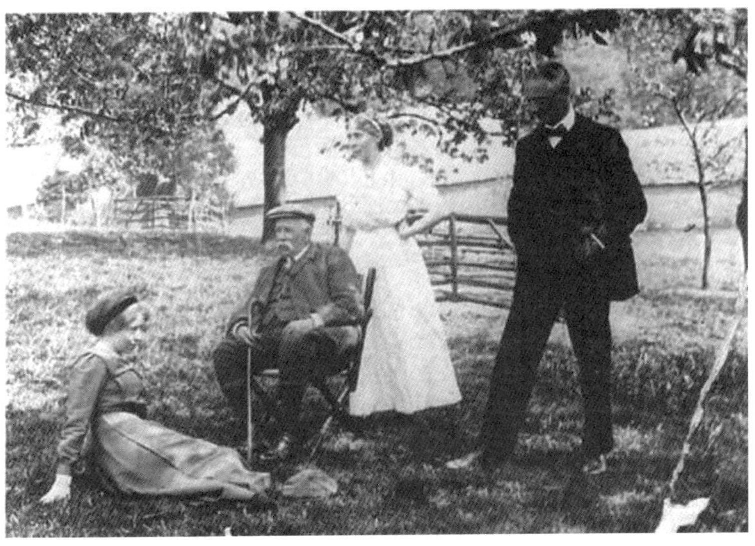

The orchard at The Limes, Nonington (Left: Laura, Uncle Arthur Peter, Eva (Sis), Harold.
Private collection

companion. The house he purchased was in Nonington, Kent and Laura and
Harold visited often.

When they were together they made a good party. Uncle Arthur
had the same sense of humour as Laura and all four would converse in
a hybrid language that was incomprehensible to any outsider – a mix of
Nottingham-English, patois French, Boer Dutch and Laura's own personal
idiolect in which she appended *'ified* to any available adjective or adverb:
'wildified', 'cloudified', 'hungrified'. A sense of enjoyment and purpose
prevailed. Daffodils and narcissi blew in the wind, blossom appeared on
the orchard trees and for Laura the streets were 'crammed with interest'.
Responding to the spring sunshine, her palette brightened and light suffused her canvas. Almost at once she started on a big picture. She did not
in fact begin it from scratch but worked up a subject originally conceived
in Staithes.

The Beach (Plate 7) brings together studies made at Staithes and at
Newlyn. The children have, as Elizabeth Knowles comments in *Laura Knight
in the Open Air*, been taken 'out from a dim cottage interior into the brilliant light' and the North Yorkshire coast re-located, like Laura, to southern climes. The painting communicates not only the clarity of light and

pastel freshness of a Cornish afternoon in early summer but also (contrary to Stanhope Forbes' belief in the necessity for struggle and discomfort in the production of a painting) the artist's pure elation and physical pleasure in undertaking the task. Sensed in the surface shimmer across the canvas, the painting displays a naturally acquired Impressionist technique, capturing the brisk breezes, the glancing sunshine and eyes of the children, as well as the physical and emotional energy of the painter. Relishing her new-found strength of body and purpose, she was liberated, free to ride 'in harmony with the mood of the wild' and 'sling' paint onto the canvas without restraint as she says in the opening of Chapter Fourteen in *The Magic of a Line.*

Such profligacy with painting materials was a previously unknown joy. It was justified by her discovering that at 'Primrose Court', the studio room she took on arriving at Newlyn, there was a residue of excess oil paint which a former inhabitant ('she must have been very rich') had smeared liberally on the rafters. It was still useable and Laura made full use of the free gift, particularly valuing the copious amounts of cadmium yellow which was expensive. In 1909 *The Beach* was accepted by the Royal Academy and earned great approbation. That year too Laura was made a member of the British Colonial Society of Artists. This was a committee set up to facilitate the purchase of contemporary art for newly commissioned art galleries in the Empire. As a consequence, examples of Laura's work can be found in galleries in South Africa, Canada and Australia. Today this seeding of European culture in far flung colonies is often regarded with distaste with the result that the future of at least two important paintings in South Africa – *Flying the Kite* (Cape Town) and *The Boys* (Johannesburg) is at present uncertain.

Soon after their arrival, the Knights found satisfactory lodgings at Penzer, or 'Beer' House, so-called because their landlady was a delightfully eccentric and warm-hearted Mrs Beer who took to them immediately. Even though the accommodation had been previously booked by other visitors, she chose to ignore that and welcomed them as paying guests. Her food was delicious ('French cooking my dears'), the beds and linen comfortable and clean. Once Mrs Beer was on your side 'there was no end to the trouble she would take' or, it seems, what she would endure, for on some nights their room next to hers was filled with music and talk. Over those first months at Newlyn Laura discovered 'student life in surroundings such as we had never dreamed of; a carefree life of sunlit pleasure, and leisurely study'. She was thirty, and, making up for lost youth, relentlessly pursuing her desire to fully participate in the social activities of the artistic set, most of whom were younger than herself. She determined to make the most of her opportunity,

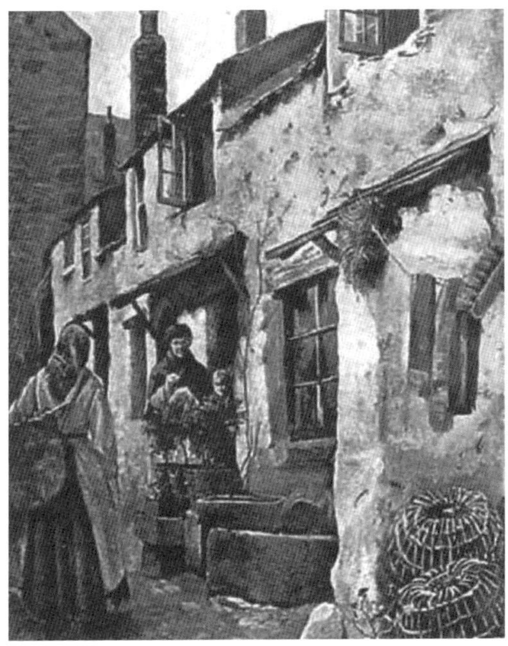

'Primrose Court', Newlyn, c.1890. Private collection

for whilst she was old in terms of life experience, they were so much more advanced in their capacity for fun and enjoyment.

Her husband, by comparison, was more restrained in his responses. Harold was then thirty-four and, as Laura notes, his hair increasingly 'greying'. Harold remained true to his vocation, painting portraits and working on delicate studies of indoor domestic subjects. Influenced by the Vermeers that had so affected him in Holland, he often chose to paint a domestic interior with a figure sitting or standing in front of a window, the sun shining through the glass. That image has been used (without any justification) as a metaphor for a withdrawn personality – cutting himself off from the round of parties, music, dance and rowdy gatherings so much relished by Laura. In fiction, *Summer in February* by Jonathan Smith, and in Tom Cross' overview of Newlyn painters, *The Shining Sands*, Harold is portrayed as locking himself away from the social crowd, living in a private world from which he views Laura's sometimes indiscreet and childish antics with disdain, even resenting her success. All of this is hearsay, opinions formed without any evidence. Cross takes this further by judging Harold's work in a highly

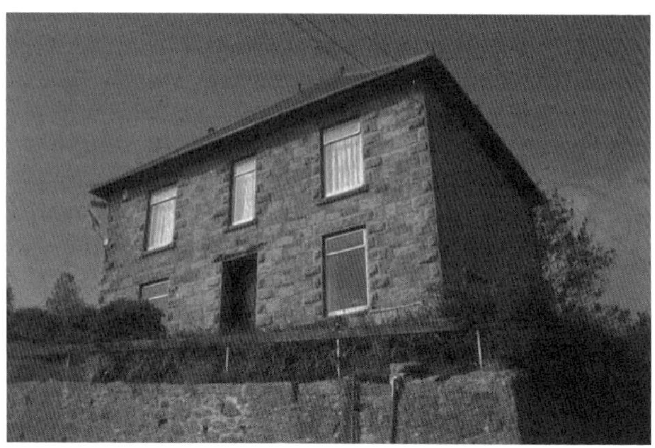

Penzer House, 'Beer' House today. Private collection

prejudiced way, saying that he 'too frequently produced dull conformity', lacking the 'spontaneity' of Laura's newly found uninhibited style, giving as an example one of Harold's Newlyn paintings: *In the Spring*.

Painted in 1908–9, *In the Spring* (Plate 6) shows a couple drinking coffee at a table under an apple tree. Structurally pleasing, the shadows create an architectural contrast for the blossom which, like Cornish clotted cream, forms a canopy overhead. Admittedly, despite its being an outdoor subject, the composition is formal and contained, but this seems appropriate for a study of affectionate intimacy in a public space. Harold's artistic achievements have never been fully explored or evaluated in depth, despite his being a highly accomplished painter, better it might be argued than Laura, and a great portrait artist. Nor has Harold Knight been treated fairly in his own right, too often being represented as withdrawn and repressed, existing in the shadow of his flamboyant wife, a muted background against which Laura performed her vibrant excesses.

Yet those who met and knew Harold considered him to be, in the words of John Croft (Laura's great nephew): 'by nature quiet, sober, mild-mannered but not afraid to speak his mind'. He was a good conversationalist, well informed, not just about art but about national and international affairs, 'displaying a lot of common sense, pragmatic and highly respected both as a man and as a painter'. Laura herself was to say in later life that Harold gave her the stability and discipline she needed, for as she admits towards the end of *The Magic of a Line*: 'Mine was a stormy attitude of mind; he possessed calm … I know at times I do need putting in my place'.

In 1908, their first full year in Newlyn, the Knights, determined to establish themselves and their funds, exhibited pictures not only at the Newlyn Art Gallery and the Royal Academy but at the New English Art Club, the Royal Hibernian Academy in Dublin, the Walker Art Gallery in Liverpool, and the Royal Birmingham Society of Artists. At the end of 1908 to Laura's delight she was elected Associate of the Old Water-Colour Society and in the new year travelled to London to receive her diploma, staying overnight with old Nottingham friends, Ernest Gillick, who had been a fellow student at the Art School, and his wife. Dedicated to the *plein air* philosophy, she could not resist prolonging her visit so that she might paint the recent snowfall in the street outside their house in Cheyne Walk. At once she went out to buy canvas, brushes, paints and galoshes and set up an easel on the pavement. The temperature was sub-zero, but she worked all that day and the next, numbed by the cold. *Cheyne Walk*, a picture of a red pillar box on the slushy pavement, was subsequently exhibited at the Academy in the summer of 1909 and purchased for Leeds Art Gallery. It is a testament to her physical endurance and will power. She returned to Newlyn, buoyed up by success and ready for more ambitious projects.

Over the season 1909–10 Laura worked on two large canvases – *Flying a Kite* and *(The) Boys*. With these she was beginning her signature technique of enthusiastically 'splashing' out in the open air. Carrying the canvases balanced on her head seemed the most natural thing to do as she scrambled over rocks and climbed up and down dunes to reach her locations. *Flying a Kite* is set on the cliff top overlooking the harbour at Newlyn with Penzance in the background. The topographical detail of the landscape is so accurately detailed, commented Laura, that Joey Carter-Wood, (another Beer House resident, inclined towards botany and biology rather than painting), would have recognised each and every 'patch of plough and grass and heather'. Significantly, the children in the foreground are slightly blurred, out of focus, at one with the brisk wind. One, a small girl in a red pinafore, is in process of turning away from the spectacle of the kite high above the beach, as though a speck of sand has blown into her eye or because the light is too strong. The painting has become familiar in Britain through its being featured in the publicity and as the cover of Elizabeth Knowles' Catalogue for the exhibition *Laura Knight in the Open Air*. This was first shown at Penlee House Art Gallery, Penzance in 2012, moving from there to the Djanogly Art Gallery at the University of Nottingham and then to Worcester City Art Gallery. *The Boys* – sometimes known just as just *Boys* – (Laura's paintings can be variously titled, causing confusion at times), the viewer is taken down to the harbour where a group of young boys are grouped around upturned boats, drying off and dressing after a swim. Here a pale golden light bleaches the sea, boats and limbs of the children. It dazzles – a sensation echoed in the motif of a tiny girl shading her eyes from the glare. She displays the same pose as the infant in the red pinafore in *Flying a Kite* but is in pastel tones and distanced from us.

With these paintings we see other aspects of the artist's method. It appears to the viewer that in each the sunshine and sea breezes, the quivering excitement of the children have been captured in one vigorous sweep of the brush in the open air. While every part of the paintings was indeed executed *en plein air,* in fact the sketches of the children were undertaken separately from the landscape study. They were then blended in the studio, where, with a dramatic, bravura gesture all the elements – the children, landscape, the air and the sea merge with the artist's own energy and passion across the canvas. Another, smaller painting *In the Sun, Newlyn* uses the same motifs as in the *Kite* painting. It shows some of the girls in their white pinafores and straw hats posed before a wide perspective of the bay. These figures are less dynamic and the sea of a deeper aquamarine than in the *Kite* painting, suggesting a more intense and shimmering heat. All these are happy paintings for once more Laura had found her natural element and she had a rapport with children, being childlike herself.

One evening soon after Laura and Harold's arrival, they were invited by Stanhope Forbes and his wife to the fine house they had built overlooking Mount's Bay, Higher Faughan. Forbes played the cello and he and other artists would give musical evenings; as well as founding a Beethoven Society, the artist Charles Simpson organised concerts with invited soloists; and there were amateur dramatics too: the Newlyn Players. This activity was very popular and time consuming, Forbes complaining at one stage that he was so busy learning his lines that his art was neglected. Laura was soon drawn into the theatricals since she was adept in the costume department, re-modelling her old Staithes lilac print frock for a production of *Cranford* as an instance. Invitations also came from another established artist Thomas Cooper Gotch at Trewarveneth Farmhouse on Paul Hill. There they met his wife Caroline, herself an artist and musician (who 'gave a regal air to any studio') and his daughter Phyllis who entered into the unconventional spirit of any social occasion with gusto. The food was plentiful for each guest brought a contribution – a 'mess of parcels of food on tables and chairs in the dining room', Laura comments in amazement. There were many such parties, when, with the furniture pushed back to the walls and a gramophone set up, dancing, singing, acrobatics, laughter and general high spirits were the order of the evening and late into the night.

At first Harold and Laura excused themselves from staying late at these jollifications on the principle that they had to work the next day. Soon, however, Laura, feeling easy in her new environment, became very much the life and soul of any party. Once she is recorded as playing the comb and tissue paper accompanied by an unusually extrovert Harold on a pan lid. Summer parties were held in the garden at Wheal Betsy, the Gotches' new home. It was there at one 'gypsy Beano' beneath the Chinese lanterns, that 'little Mrs Knight' is reported to have been 'the wildest of the wild' with 'hair streaming and ragged skirts a-whirl'. At another time, on the instigation of Phyllis Gotch who was always full of enthusiasm and ideas, she agreed to participate in an outdoor dancing display. It was to feature some children from the local dancing class, with Phyllis and Laura as "principals" (although at that time Laura had never had a dancing lesson in her life), dressed in floating 'Grecian' drapes – their costume and style emulating the free interpretive dance manner of Isadora Duncan, the scandalous American dancer then making a name for herself in Europe. The evening proved to be something of a damp squib: while the audience became cold, damp and bored, the children were 'sneezing, grumbling and crying behind the bushes'. Still, for Laura 'Life was going with a swing, and we had health and strength for hard work and for play' as she enthuses in Chapter 4 of *Oil Paint and Grease Paint*.

She made friends with a group of four younger women living at Myrtle Cottage, a Georgian house on the hillside overlooking the harbour in the centre of Newlyn: Doris Shaw ("Dod") who was to become a close ally; Fryn Tennyson Jesse who was a great-niece of Alfred Lord Tennyson, later a writer and journalist and the source of the revealing insight into the behaviour of the wild behaviour of 'little Mrs Knight'; her cousin Cicely Jesse and another girl called Clare Waters, colloquially known as "Still". Dod's mother, Mrs Eunice Shaw, kept a relaxed eye on them all. When the "Myrtage" girls, as they described themselves, had arrived in 1907 they were in a phase of wearing amber necklaces, Liberty fabrics and silks of dun and brown – the "art" colours to which were added those "unheard of greens" that Max Beerbohm described as being *de rigueur* for the aesthetic set. An elite group, they 'talked literature, some wrote tales and poems, some did woodcuts, some painted' and they communicated in their own distinctive patois, playfully inverting and shortening names and words. It was a habit of speech that Laura understood well.

Pretty soon there was a change of mood at the Myrtage: the young women suddenly threw off Romantic aestheticism and embraced a less demure image. In 1910, they took to wearing bright frocks and suits of a 'dashing cut'. They sent out to Norwich for cosmetics: lipstick, face powder and 'even eyelash cream!' Laura exclaims. Still Waters arrived at one party in a white ballet dress, attracting all the attention and 'taking away all our partners – she was so fascinating', Laura complained. They were smart, fast and occasionally outrageous. This was most disconcerting for one gifted young painter, Ernest Proctor who had been attracted to the Romantic beauty of the young ladies at the Myrtage, especially to Doris Shaw. After a short absence he returned to Newlyn to discover a total transformation in the object of his admiration who had adopted a completely new personality and appearance. For reassurance he fled at once to the Knights at Beer House, which tells us that Laura, despite her wild moments, had some status as the wise elder in the community of the young. Ernest must have had good advice and adjusted to the situation. He married Dod in 1912.

And what of Laura Knight as this time? Not only was she being recognised as a painter in the national art world (*The Beach* was accepted for exhibition by the Royal Academy in 1909 and in 1912 it was featured in *The Studio),* but she was also exhibiting on an international stage. Alongside painting by Vanessa Bell, Laura's work was selected for the Venice Biennale in 1910 and in 1914. As a female painter she opted to exhibit with the Women's International Club, which had been established in Paris in 1899 to arrange exhibitions of a professional standard for women artists at a time when such opportunities were few. Both Harold and she were selling pictures and as a result 'there was no shortage of cash' and she could 'go a-bust on canvases and paints'.

She was exhilarated in finding a new or rather long repressed identity, expressing itself not only in her application of paint on canvas but in her dress and behaviour. Writing that all 'the gaiety I had missed in youth came suddenly', the wild child of Nottingham days was resurrected as an equally irrepressible woman. She took up singing again, since 'I loved making a noise' and at the slightest provocation, as we have seen, would pick up her skirts and dance. She sought out other 'irrepressibles' and the Myrtage girls were excellent company. She was especially taken with Dod Shaw who she describes as having a 'brilliant complexion, enormous dark eyes and long, slender legs'. Dod was as 'swift and active as a gazelle'. Laura's admiration is expressed here in language and imagery that are characteristic, her senses and feelings ever responsive to instinctive animal vitality in whoever she met.

This was a quality that she herself possessed in abundance.

With the arrival in Newlyn of the painter Alfred Munnings, the Myrtage circle found its hub. His reputation went before him. At the end of Chapter 13 of *Oil Paint and Grease Paint*, Laura writes: 'there were dreadful tales about A.J. Munnings' – that he threw parties at which young men 'got tight'; that he wore an outfit more suited to a horse-dealer than an artist – a yellow neckerchief and a loud check suit with black velvet collar; that he had an equally loud mouth from which emerged a constant stream of anecdotes and songs, and that his energy knew no bounds. Munnings kept several horses and rode to hounds, frequented the racecourse, and lived with the gypsies. The arrival of "AJ" (as he was familiarly known) on the Newlyn scene changed the tone and the configuration of the place. Not only the Myrtage girls (who soon adopted the yellow neckerchief themselves) but Laura too found him 'irresistible'. She could not, she admits, take her eyes off him: 'He was the stable, the artist, the poet, the very land itself!' What is more Munnings was most admiring of Laura's work. Having seen *The Beach* at the Academy, he greeted her with 'praises piled one upon the other' and she, always susceptible to flattery, lapped it up.

Much speculation has been aroused by Laura's obvious fascination with AJ as well as the attitude of Harold towards him. Clearly, AJ's vivacity and magnetism were something with which Laura identified. Both were from modest, working class backgrounds (AJ was the second son of John Munnings a miller of Mendham in Suffolk) and both had displayed precocious artistic talent from a very young age. Physically and in temperament they were two of a kind, never still, with a boundless capacity for work, always seeking outlets for their excess energy (Laura, said Munnings, 'possessed the energy of six'), both inclined towards childish excess and self-display. His great love was horses, riding and painting them with an understanding of every muscle and fetlock. He kept company with gypsies and itinerants and was ever ready to abandon the comforts of domesticity and take to the open road.

A free spirit, Munnings was charming and dangerous. He had a piratical panache enhanced by his having only one eye – the result of an accident with a thorn hedge. Few could resist his charismatic appeal. Harold, it seems, could. He appears to have maintained his self-restraint even when Munnings managed to persuade Mrs Beer to give him a room at Beer House and convinced her that the Knights would be delighted to share their sitting room with him. When Harold had first found him resident in their armchair, he was appalled, but warmed to him and often he and Laura joined AJ and his Welsh terrier, Taffy, on long walks over the cliffs. In fact, contrary to idle conjecture, Harold was not antagonistic to AJ and over the next years was his friend and counsellor. As for Laura, Munnings fitted her childhood image of the brother she never had.

While on the one hand conceited and boorish with a considerable drinking problem, Munnings was on the other hand well-read, able to recite and perform (his recitation of Edgar Allen Poe's *The Raven* was a tour de force), dance and sing. In his first year at Newlyn, as his contribution to the festivities Munnings directed a full-scale "Dickensian Christmas" at the Gotches which Laura describes as "a glorious holiday, full of fun. Dickens reigned overall, and AJ carried him and the entertainment on his back". Wherever a group gathered around him a party would spontaneously ignite. In the summer AJ initiated picnics to Lamorna Cove – a walk along the coastal path from Mousehole; introduced the girls to point-to-point races at St Buryan and, humane and yet game for the chase, enraged the Master of the Western Hunt by refusing to allow the final kill once the fox had been given a good run. For Laura he combined the "irrepressible" and the "unexpected" (the qualities identified in Uncle Arthur and his friends) and she loved him for it. When difficulty came, Laura could be a devoted and loyal comrade to those she "loved" and Munnings was to be one of these.

There was a stir in Forbes' school and the whole artistic community when in 1909 a very beautiful young woman, herself an artist, arrived to visit her brother Joey Carter-Wood at Beer House. With the face of "Botticelli's Venus" and a manner of refined elegance, Florence was much sought after as a model. Harold Knight painted her several times over the next 2 years. When AJ saw her he was enchanted, for Florence epitomised his romantic attachment to Cornwall: the sound of the surf, the warmth of the rocks, the wild thyme and sea-pinks trembling in the wind. By this time, having outgrown Beer House in all ways and requiring a less proscriptive studio and living space, Munnings was working in Lamorna. Lamorna Cove at that time was remote and picturesque, with its small-scale granite harbour and fishermen's cottages, a trout stream running down the Valley to the sea. Important to AJ was that there was also an agreeable public house – the Lamorna Inn, a smugglers' haunt known colloquially as 'The Wink'. Mr Jorey the publican was jovial and indulgent. However, there was constant antagonism between him and his estranged wife, Jessie Jorey, who ran the Cliff House Temperance Hotel a hundred yards or so up the valley. It was at the Temperance Hotel that visiting professional artists and respectable visitors stayed.

Painters had discovered the Cove around the turn of the century, the

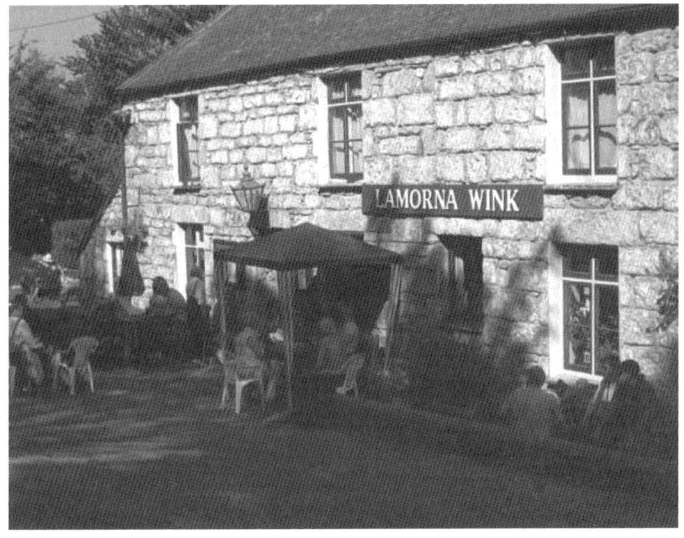

Lamorna Wink at Lamorna. Private collection

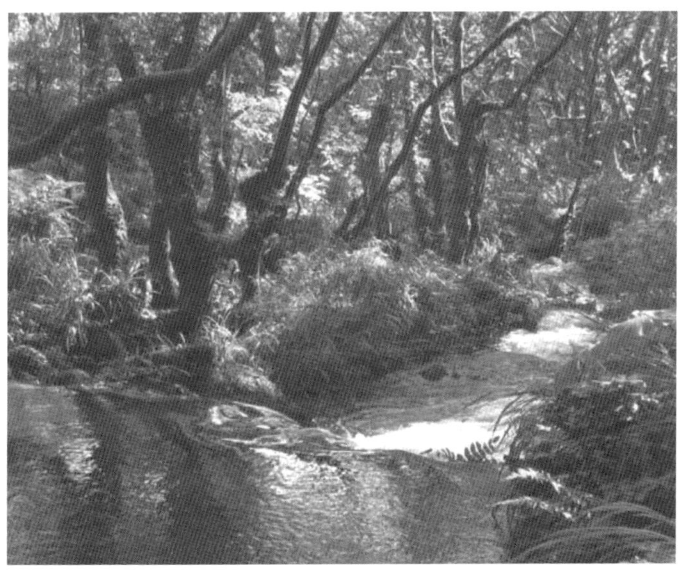

Lamorna stream today. Private collection

most distinguished being Samuel 'Lamorna' Birch (so-called in order to distinguish him from another painter Lionel Birch). Marrying in 1902, he and his wife rented the former harbour-master's house, Flagstaff Cottage, where the painter built a studio by the stream. The couple soon began the practice of inviting local artists to their home on Sundays, offering good food, talk and light-hearted entertainment. "Mouse" as Mrs Birch was known was an accomplished cook and Laura, ever attentive to food, recalled the fish pies topped with cream, the delicious pasties 'the like of which I never tasted', the fresh trout (caught by Birch) lightly fried in oatmeal and the game pies and casseroles (the product of Birch's hunting). Almost as soon as they arrived in Newlyn, the Knights had been introduced to Birch and, ever hospitable, he invited them to lunch the next day. Laura was to describe this first visit to Lamorna in an article she wrote for the Old Water-Colour Society's Club's annual volume in 1957. It was November and yet, on turning into a narrow lane, they found themselves at the head of a densely wooded valley 'already speckled with the yellow of early primroses and white anemone … it would seem that we had suddenly entered Paradise'.

When Munnings arrived in this paradise he at once identified the old mill as a place to set up his base. Given his background as a miller's son, it seemed to be an appropriate place to stable his horses, set up his easel and, it transpired, to chase a dream: Florence Carter-Wood. Naïve, conventional and religious, Florence was from a wealthy brewing family, with properties in London and a country estate in Cumbria. Her background and experience were the complete antithesis of his own. Yet, against all sense, he at once pursued her as his ideal. He was to paint her, wearing the same outfit and hat, on horseback, four times. To picture Florence in the green glade, easy in the saddle and with statuesque composure was for AJ a perfect subject, combining his two loves: his favourite horse and a beautiful woman. With the allure of a dryad and the mystique of the centaur, the vision of Florence on his hunter was, however, a chimera, an illusion. It was to be a disastrous relationship.

Brought up in a sheltered home and knowing little of the world, Florence's father had intended her for marriage into the aristocracy. When she expressed her desire to be an artist, thinking that under the protection of her brother Joey she would be safe and would grow out of the idea, he agreed for her to go to Newlyn. Once there, knowing little of the dynamics of relationships with men and less of the "facts of life", she was out of her depth amongst the bohemian crowd and did not have the emotional intelligence to cope. Her surface composure masked an increasing disassociation from the implications of her situation and her own and others' behaviour. This was made the more complex by being assailed on the one hand by Munnings and by another, less ebullient, contender for her favours, Captain Gilbert Evans.

A permanent resident at Mrs Jorey's establishment Cliff House, Evans was the land agent for Colonel Camborne Haweis Paynter (1864–1949), who had been a fellow officer in the Boer War. Paynter owned the great house and estates of Boskenna, comprising around 2,000 acres, including thirty-two farms and numerous houses (including Clapper Mill which Munnings rented) and much of the coastal land between Land's End and Penzance. In passing, it is worth mentioning that this landscape and Boskenna House itself provide the setting for Mary Wesley's well-known novel *The Camomile Lawn*, published in 1984. As a child, Wesley stayed with the Paynter family at Boskenna which provides the raw material for her books. While not a painter, Gilbert Evans was a valued member of the artistic community because of his organising abilities. Handsome and gentlemanly, at twenty-six he was clearly suited in background and demeanour to Florence – also known as "The Bloat" or "Blote" (an unfortunate name bestowed on her by an uncle). Meeting him at the Cliff Hotel where she too was staying and at the artists' evening parties, Florence responded with gentle interest. Yet inexplicably in 1911, she agreed to marry the importunate Munnings.

Laura and Harold were witness to this bizarre pairing: the courtship and the lengthy trials imposed by Florence's father on Munnings, of whom he disapproved. Unable to consent to his daughter marrying an itinerant artist, he demanded that AJ prove himself by earning £1000 in a year, then, perhaps he might talk to him again. Goaded, Munnings worked tirelessly to

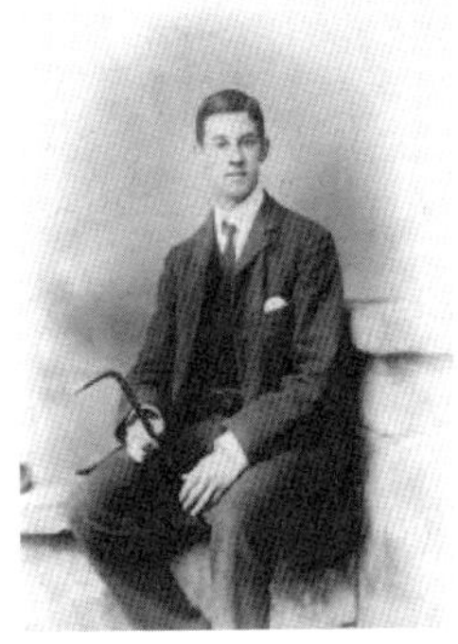

Captain Gilbert Evans

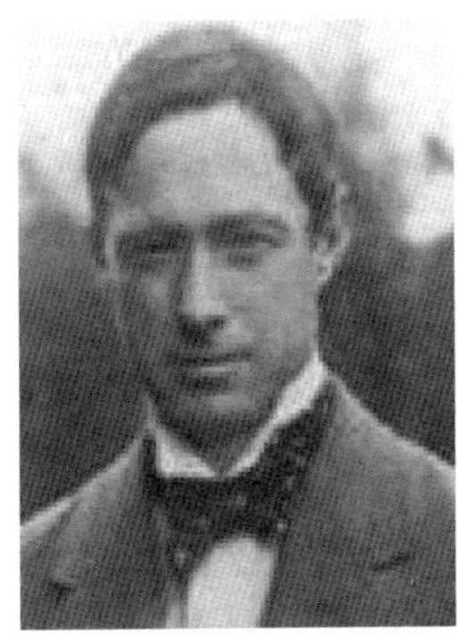

A.J. Munnings

prove himself, producing a series of watercolours and oil paintings that sold well and raised the required sum. However, as Jean Goodman writes in her *Life of Alfred Munnings 1878–1959*, in that year he was so taken up with the task and maintaining his hectic social life that 'he had little time alone with 'The Bloat' – too little, perhaps, to allow for suspicion that the charming aloofness and sophisticated manner might mask an impenetrable coldness to the opposite sex'. As a result, the relationship, while continuing in name, could not develop.

They were married in January 1912 at the Church of St John the Evangelist in Westminster and spent their honeymoon in London at the Artillery Mansions Hotel, Westminster, which was owned by Florence's parents. For some reason, Harold and Laura Knight were staying in the hotel at the same time. Odd though it may appear, this may well be another instance of AJ's free manner and generosity of spirit – allowing the Knights to enjoy a free London stay courtesy of his parents-in-law. Or it may be because the relationship was so fragile that both bride and groom were in need of support. As it transpired it was fortunate that Harold and Laura were there since that night Florence attempted suicide by taking cyanide. Between them they managed to save her, and although Laura draws a veil over the incident, the event and what was to follow cast a dark stain on Laura's bright vision of Newlyn.

Returning from London, AJ and Florence were to live at Mrs Jorey's Cliff Hotel and nothing was said, Laura and Harold having elicited a promise from Florence that she would never attempt such a thing again. Maybe it was talked through – maybe not. Florence was not the sort of person to be intimate with women friends – although she did become close to a woman called Joan Coulson, whom Munnings' biographer Jean Goodman describes as 'lesbian-inclined'. Florence was equally remote with men – including her husband. Munnings accepted his situation and continued his itinerant painting life, leaving Florence at the Cliff Hotel. However, in 1912 Laura and Harold had to leave Trewarveneth Farm, which they were renting. One of Harold's on-going infections became very serious and he was sent to hospital in Plymouth where Laura too fell ill. They were away from Newlyn for 6 months – an episode that we will revisit in the next chapter. While they were away and in Munnings' absence, Gilbert Evans' care and concern for Florence Munnings became more intense. They went for long walks together, talked for long hours and, perhaps, declared their love.

The details of the affair have been much speculated upon. It is the subject of Jonathan Smith's novel *Summer In February* which was published in

1995 and the film of the same name of 2013. In these the story which Laura Knight herself described as having the potential for 'terrible scandal' are developed. The facts are detailed by Jean Goodman as follows. On the 23rd July 1914 a fancy-dress dance was held at Trewarveneth Studio at which all the leading players were present. Around midnight, as the organiser of the party Geoffrey Garnier wrote to his friend Reginald Pound, Munnings was heard to shout in response to Florence's request to go back to the Cliff Hotel because she was tired: 'All right, you bloody whore, buzz off!'. At this she left in tears. The next morning AJ and Florence breakfasted as usual downstairs and then Florence went up to their room. Munnings found her there on the bed half an hour later: unconscious. She had once again taken cyanide. The doctor was called from Penzance and the Knights arrived, Laura attempting artificial respiration for hours in an atmosphere 'stinking of cyanide'. It was to no purpose.

After Florence's death, Munnings admitted to a friend that he never ceased loving her even though their marriage was never consummated. Some suggest that her sexual dysfunction was the result of disgust and fear on hearing the details of childbirth from the wife of Charles Simpson, another Newlyn painter. She was, it was agreed, depressed, possibly as a result of thyroid deficiency, or the result of an underlying mental disorder. Others maintain that she had passively gone ahead with the marriage, despite realizing her mistake, because she felt locked into the arrangements. A more dramatic explanation (which the novel and the film appear to endorse) is that in the summer of 1914 Florence found herself pregnant by Gilbert Evans, and, given that her marriage was unconsummated, was unable to see a way through. Once again one can merely speculate on the truth.

Now, more than a century after the events, such possibilities present the material for "tragic romance". Then it was a tragic reality and it affected the Knights deeply, its shadow never quite leaving them. Whatever the truth, a letter written by Laura in response to Munnings' second wife Violet's request for facts, indicates Laura's sense of waste, her personal hurt but also her realism and straight-talking: 'Bloat, beautiful and fascinating as she was' she wrote, 'had no stability of character or sense of responsibility either – call it madness of a kind, if you will. Even suicide was not denied to her in her crazy desire for experience'. Munnings believed that Florence's neurosis was the result of morbid obsession, but Laura puts a slightly different perspective on things, observing that Florence had a capacity to inflict 'refined cruelties' on AJ. This is an aspect of Florence that is not brought out in either the fictional or screen versions, nor is the fact that Laura and Harold knew of and had to watch how those 'refined cruelties' played out and the suffering of all the parties concerned.

In January 1914, Gilbert Evans was appointed to a Colonial position in West Africa. He left Newlyn for London and sailed to take up his posting in the March. Whether this exile was self-imposed because he was troubled about his developing relationship with Munnings' wife and its implications, or whether, as is likely, Colonel Paynter had got wind of what was going on and sent him there for his own good or maybe as a punishment since West Africa was the worst of postings. We are not to know. Whatever the case, AJ himself managed to bury his hurt in his work and he kept faith with Evans, gifting his friend the earliest of his iconic images of Florence, *The Morning Ride*, which had been exhibited at the Royal Academy in 1912. In his three-volume autobiography: *An Artist's Life* of 1950, *The Second Burst* of 1951 and *The Finish* published in 1952, Munnings makes no mention of the episode. Laura too avoids reference. All she says in *Oil Paint and Grease Paint* is: 'Suddenly the death of a much-loved member of our colony put an end to all joy…'

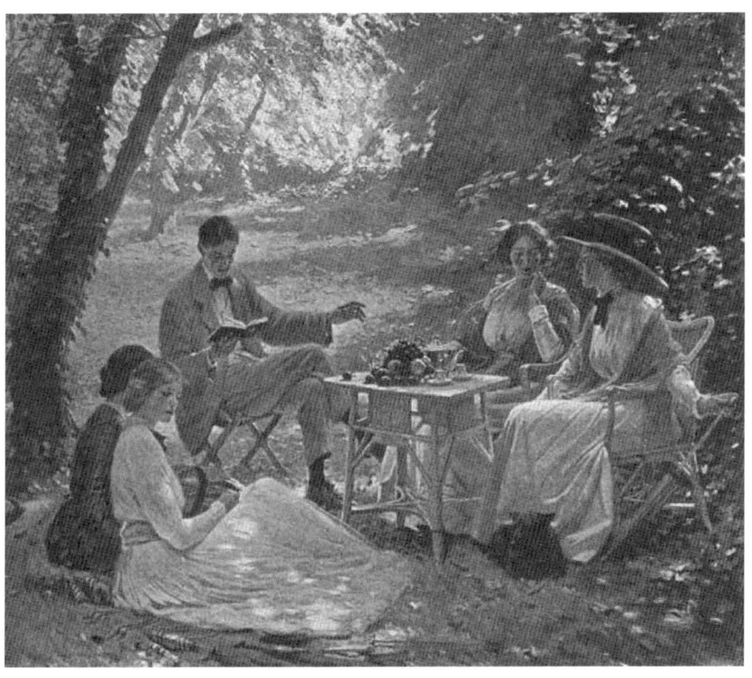

The Sonnet by Harold Knight. Alfred Munnings reading poetry, to his left are Laura Knight and Florence Carter Wood. Painting exhibited London Royal Academy 1911 and reproduced in *The Studio* December 1912. This work was later used as an advertisement for Players cigarettes.

CHAPTER SEVEN

"Daring grew, I would work only in my own way"

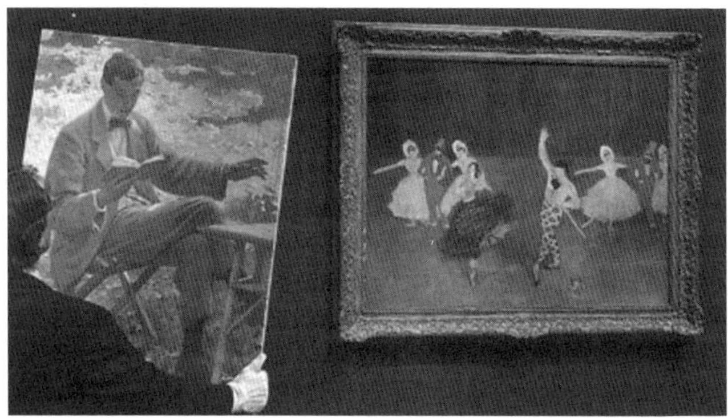

Evening Standard, 14th December 2009

Some have speculated about the nature of Laura's close friendship with Alfred Munnings, speculation that was re-ignited in 2009 by the discovery of a fine portrait of AJ reading in a garden, painted by Harold Knight around 1911. It had been deliberately concealed behind a canvas by Laura of a performance of the ballet *Carnaval*, painted in 1915. Why this act of subterfuge? The question elicits two possible answers. Firstly, perhaps it reminded the Knights too keenly of the happy and apparently carefree time enjoyed before Florence Munnings' death. Secondly, maybe Harold had indeed taken against Munnings and had wanted to get rid of the picture. Whatever the reason, Laura was prompted to cover up the portrait, to protect it, AJ, her husband and herself from unnecessary hurt. What her motives were will never be proved. This is, as she confesses at the end of *The Magic of a Line*, maybe one of the 'corners' of her life 'into which I dare not peep' as well as 'friendships and great (the) love still known today'. With this thought, it seems to be the time to engage more directly with her personality, her sense of identity and relationships – with her own and the opposite sex. It also allows us to consider the positive shaping experiences and friendships that Newlyn offered to Laura during the halcyon days before and the difficult years during the Great War.

Laura loved Munnings just as she was to "love" a variety of men and women with whom she had a bond – both professional and personal – throughout her life. What was the nature of that "love"? Her relationship with AJ was not of an erotic kind. Dunbar puts this down to her upbringing which 'instilled' a kind of Puritanism, so that it 'is unlikely that she had any kind of affair with Munnings, or with anyone else'. In conversation with Dame Laura, then an old lady, Dunbar raised this very issue and records Laura Knight's response to "propositions" from men: 'I always told them, 'not in my line. I'm married, and even if I weren't, it's still not in my line''. She always protected herself from unwanted attention by affirming her married status and her loyalty and love for Harold. That is never in question. The question is rather what she meant by the rider 'even if I weren't'. That has invited speculation from those in the later 20th century and since for whom it is *de rigueur* to probe into the 'dark corners' of artists' lives to satisfy salacious curiosity.

Dunbar, writing in the early 1970s when society and culture were becoming open to discussion of sexuality of all kinds, feels compelled to pursue the issue. She homes in on what she describes as Laura's 'partly masculine nature'. It is true that Laura was physically robust, wilful and, one of her favourite words, 'irrepressible'. All that boisterous energy needed to find its outlet. So, in the early chapters of *Oil Paint and Grease Paint* for instance, she describes how she so much wanted to be a boy and play boys' games. Then at Art School she was criticised by the Master at College for having too heavy a painting hand: 'Why don't you develop your feminine side?' she had been asked, reducing her to tears. The implication of the Master's comment is that she was to rectify her tendency to express herself with vigour and reduce her expectations in line with what was considered appropriate to her sex. Here we have the implementation of the blunt instrument of gender convention to assure compliance with the principle of male privilege which in education, like all public institutions of the period, was the established norm. Its reinforcement at this time was the more urgent because in the 1890s confidence in social stability and national prosperity that for generations had been predicated on the trope of the dominant "manly" male and the weak "feminine" female was under scrutiny.

Throughout Europe it was commonly supposed that Imperial decline, racial degeneration, "male effeminacy" (summed up in the word "Decadence") and the "manly woman" (demanding women's suffrage as well as female equality in wider society) threatened the very fabric of society and ultimately the species. This *fin de siècle* mind-set generated much anxiety, debate and theorising in relation to the model of Darwinian evolution. It was suggested that evolutionary changes through time did not necessarily lead to the betterment of the species. They could also work in reverse: the theory of "degeneration". This widely held theory was set out in the internationally influential book *Degeneration* by Max Nordau published in Hungary in 1892. Nordau highlights the belief that it was the negative influence of art which was encouraging the weakening of gender boundaries and therefore sapping the moral and physical health of civilised society. It had to be reversed. Art was to be brought back into line, to reassert the hegemony of the masculine over the feminine and re-establish boundaries. As a consequence, even in provincial British Art Colleges the proprieties of what was fitting for female students to study, their style and subject matter had to be maintained and male hegemony protected.

It was this stultifying doctrine of gender conformity that shaped Laura Johnson's experience during her time at Art School. Yet there was a cosmopolitan artistic movement afoot which deliberately set out to break out of the straitjacket of definition by gender: 'Modernism'. Virginia Woolf, for example, perhaps the quintessential Modernist writer, famously sought to neutralise her narratives and achieve an androgyny of mind and method. In her book *A Room of One's Own* (1929) she draws on Coleridge's belief that 'a great mind is androgynous' (*Table Talk* 1832). A mind that is purely masculine cannot create, any more than can a mind that is purely feminine, she argues. To achieve true creativity all artists must free themselves from the trammels of gendered discourse. Unaware of such intellectual stirrings and independent of any "movement", Laura was to cut through the conventions on her own initiative and find a way of living and working in her own way. She had an instinctive desire to think, live and work "out of the box" of gendered stereotyping. Hers was an androgynous spirit and yet, not surprisingly, from the start it was as a "female" painter that she has been and continues to be viewed and judged.

Over the decade's critics have consistently discussed her and her work in gendered language and according to the binary conventions of feminine or masculine style and subject. For many, echoing the Art Master at College, she is aggressively masculine: 'Dame Laura Knight is virile and there are many vigorous passages' says a reviewer in the *Pittsburgh Gazette* on the 11th March 1931 in respect of her contribution to the International Exhibition at the Carnegie Institute. In December of that year in an article about modern women painters by Helen McCoy in the *New York Times*, Laura Knight is described as lacking 'refinement and subtlety'. She belongs, McCoy writes, to that school of women's painting 'in which feminine qualities have been carefully ex-purged'. This obsession with pictorial analysis and evaluation by gender, was countered by Laura herself who, in an interview in 1930 for *The Queen* magazine stated unequivocally that 'art should be regarded as international and sexless'. Then a mature and experienced practitioner, Laura was much exercised by this issue. In an article in the *Nottingham Evening Post* in December 1930, there is a report of Laura Knight's response to a speech made by the then Headmaster of Eton School, Cyril Alington. He had made the outrageous statement that there had 'never been any great feminine poets or artists' and Laura's reply was direct. For centuries, she asserted, women had not achieved greatness because of lack of encouragement and opportunity rather than lack of ability. She could have added that it was the gender paradigm that above all put obstacles in the way of women achieving the realisation of their creative gifts and achieving "greatness".

In our highly sexualised society similar gender stereotyping persists, now of course no longer binary, but stereotyping nonetheless and of a kind that seriously misrepresents Laura's life and work. This was very apparent in some of the recent skewed and flippant reviews and responses to the National Portrait Gallery exhibition *Laura Knight Portraits*. On the 7th September 2013 *The Spectator* commented: 'Any suspicion that she might have been lesbian is offset by her evident adoration of Squire Munnings. But was that admiration for his great skills as a painter, or for his unusual personality?' Meanwhile, an online posting on curatedlondon.co.uk: stated 'Although married, Knight's clear affection for her female subjects and her depiction of women 'on top' lends the show a definite queer sensibility'. Such innuendo and over simplistic assessments of both the artist and her work require to be objectively addressed.

Laura Knight was a passionate woman – her feelings were strong, her senses acute, her capacity to appreciate the physical body – whether male or female, of babies or the elderly, black or white and all shades in between – generous, and, in her pursuit of successfully rendering these in her art, an all-consuming obsession. This was not sexual desire, rather an urgent physical and emotional need to prove her talent and fulfil her destiny as a professional artist. This drive was as fundamental for her as the need to have food and sleep, perhaps more so since it was only through art that she could afford to have either. When at the Art School in Nottingham, her mettle had been sharpened with resentment that as a girl she was considered to have second rate talent and denied the basic academic training of life studies thought to be essential for an artist aspiring towards distinction. It was at Newlyn that she began to exercise her freedom to gain mastery of the human form and to do so 'in her own way'. She sketched and painted her friends, models, a couple of tramps who came by – whoever was willing and patient enough to pose draped or in the nude, giving her the chance to make up for denied opportunities. There was no other agenda but this.

In 1913 when Laura and Harold were living in Lamorna, without any self-conscious sense of daring, she stated as a matter of fact that she wanted to 'paint the nude out of doors'. Lamorna Cove was particularly secluded and therefore suited to this professional challenge. Laura brought some female models down from London, housing them in the next-door cottage. The girls' naïve understanding of country ways and domestic arrangements caused some amusement in the neighbourhood but they also attracted unwanted attention from local youths and the disapproval of more staid members of the community. One memorable instance occurred when two "respectable" ladies, walking the coastal path, came across Laura painting one of her models posing naked on the rocks. Their consternation and dis-composure were such that they made a formal complaint to Colonel Paynter who, as the landowner and magistrate, was urged to stop such disgraceful behaviour. Colonel Paynter, himself only thirty-seven, had a more open mind and announced that, since it was his land and he had every confidence in Mrs Knight, he would not interfere. He was generally supportive of the artists in the colony, welcoming the brightness and vitality they brought to the place.

It was on the granite rocks at Carn Barges in Lamorna Cove, that Laura, her friends and models 'swam and dived in the deep pools at low tide or lay in repose'. She sketched them in pencil and thin oil pigment, desiring to master the flow of their sensuous bodies, and experimenting with effects of light and sun on the texture of their skin. In addition to being a necessary professional exercise, it was a spiritual exercise too: 'How holy is the human body when bare (of no other than *sic*) {to} the sun', she writes in *The Magic of a Line*. It was 1911 and she was working on a study of a group of semi-naked girls transfigured by unmediated sunlight – a painting she would call *Daughters of the Sun*. Her first attempt was not to her satisfaction, and she destroyed it. With the second it seems she found her painting rhythm and a successful

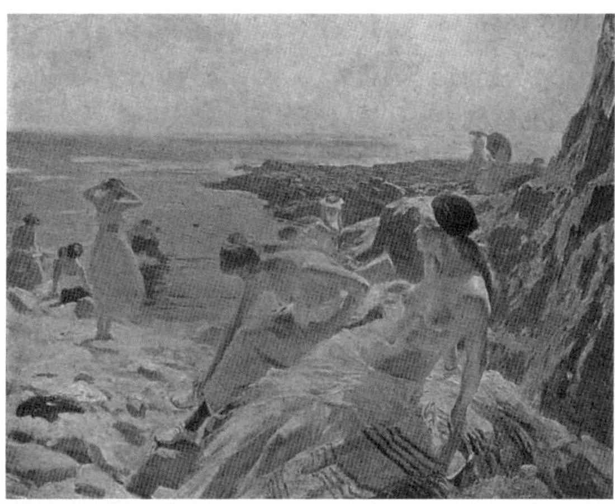

Daughters of the Sun, 1911, oil on canvas. Destroyed by Laura. Reproduced from *The Studio*, December 1912. A colour print of this has recently been discovered

method, telling us that: 'Reversing the usual methods of painting sunlight, I made the direct light cool and almost colourless; in the reflections from the rocks into the flesh shadow, fullest warmth and colour was given'.

The effect of the figures bathed in a gloriously white-golden glow won guarded admiration when the painting was exhibited at the Royal Academy Exhibition. No one appeared to be too disturbed by the nudity, since it was an essential element of professional academic painting, and no one commented on the gender of the artist. An offer was made to buy the picture at a premium of £300 which Laura, putting an over-high monetary value on her work in the hope of enhancing her reputation in the marketplace, refused as being 'an indignity'. It did not sell and over the following years the picture did the rounds of provincial art galleries and became so damaged in the process that she eventually cut it up and put it in the dustbin: 'I felt a murderer', she says. All we had was a black and white photographic reproduction, printed in *The Studio* in 1912. However, more recently a colour reproduction has been discovered in *Allies in Art* of 1917. This gives us some sense of the way Laura was developing her ability to communicate the radiant dazzle of a Cornish summer and challenge conventional cultural assumptions about the female nude.

Daughters of the Sun has a clear relationship with the painting tradition of representing naked female bathers observed as objects of desire and possession through the 'male gaze'. Examples span the centuries, from Titian's

Diana and Acteon painted between 1556–9 and Renoir's *Women Bathing* of 1887. In these the female is posed for the private enjoyment of the presumed male viewer. However, with *Daughters of the Sun* there is no such voyeurism, for the observer (male or female) is invited into the dynamics of the group. That the viewer is welcome to enter into the pictorial space is signalled by the attitude of the foreground figure, her body sloping towards the artist/viewer, her head turned as a gesture towards the other bathers. The significance of *Daughters of the Sun* lies in this inclusivity. It is neither erotic nor tacitly gendered, standing as a testament to Laura Knight's independence as an artist: 'I had found something all my own' she says with satisfaction.

The definitive statement of Laura Knight's independent status and a direct challenge to academic tradition was a ground-breaking picture of 1913, *Self Portrait,* also known as *The Model* (Plate 9). Representing herself in the process of painting a female model "from the life", the artist is seen from the back standing at her easel. The model was her friend Ella Naper, also viewed from the back and there is a third presence, the replicated image on the canvas. The tri-partite arrangement of Laura the artist, Ella the model and the painted image on the canvas draws on a trope of classical art: "Three Graces". In addition, its figurative concept makes reference to Velazquez' *Toilet of Venus* (also known as the *Rokeby Venus*), painted circa 1647–51 and in the National Gallery Collection. As an iconic female nude, the Velazquez *Venus* had something of a cult status at the time. In terms of gender politics, it was a contested site and generated strong   emotions. In 1914 it was badly damaged by the suffragette, Mary Richardson, whose violent attack earned her the title of "Slasher Mary". The Knights appear to have accepted the *Venus* figure as a point of aesthetic reference since they were wont to make a direct comparison between it and Ella, who modelled for them both.

In *Self Portrait* long-established conventions of painting the female nude are set up and then deliberately subverted. For here the gendered conventions are neutralised and abstracted. On the right the nude is set against colour blocks of red and brown, echoed in the striped rug on which she stands. Against the abstract shapes, the model's pose is echoed on the canvas on the left. This provides a neutral background for the painter who wears her favourite red jacket and black fedora. Her face in profile, she looks across and out of the picture. It is a sight line that provides another horizontal axis. Pamela Gerrish Nunn in *From Victorian to Modern* (2006) observes that with this painting Knight displays 'modernity' not 'explicable simply in terms of realism versus abstraction' but 'in the vigour and energy of her treatment of traditional motifs, in particular her radicalising the woman artist's agenda'.

The painting testifies to two things: Laura Knight's grasp of what a "life study" should mean in the new century and her self-confidence as a professional artist.

This time, however, Laura's bravado caused discomfort, even repulsion, in the male art establishment for what was seen as a blatant denial of all the proprieties. It was unthinkable for a woman painter to expose herself in this way. Representing all that was contrary to the social and artistic standards enshrined in the Royal Academy, it was refused by the selection committee. Not too disheartened, however, she changed the title to *The Model,* directing attention away from the personal and making a gesture towards anonymity. Under that name it was accepted for exhibition by the International Society of Sculptors, Painters and Gravers. Over its history the *Self Portrait* has been hung and catalogued under a variety of titles: *Artist and Model, Myself and Model, Self and Model and Self and Nude.* It has also been the object of much criticism and denigration. But today, under its original name, *Self Portrait,* it is valued as a ground-breaking image in the history of female portraiture. Laura never parted with it and it was exhibited from time to time, most notably in her major retrospective at the Royal Academy in 1965. On her death it was purchased by the National Portrait Gallery in London.

Timothy Wilcox has noted in his Catalogue to the exhibition *Laura Knight at the Theatre* that in conception this painting may well have been a response to Matisse's painting *Red Studio* that Laura must have seen at the *Second Post-Impressionist Exhibition* held in the Grafton Galleries in London in 1912. When living in Staithes, the Knights would go up to London to deliver paintings for exhibition or for Harold to negotiate and execute portrait commissions. Usually, they travelled third class there and back, often in a day. When in Newlyn, and a little better off, however, they would visit the capital regularly, staying for a few weeks to go to the theatre and take in the latest summer art exhibitions. In 1910 Roger Fry, the art critic and soon a leading figure in the "Bloomsbury Group", had shaken the cultural elite and the general public with his first Post- Impressionist Exhibition *Manet and the Post-Impressionists.* Fry showcased paintings by Cézanne, Van Gogh, and Gauguin, illustrating their connection back to Manet and forward to the *avant garde* painters Matisse and Picasso, who were also represented. Hardly reconciled to Impressionism, the British art establishment was shocked and the public baffled by Fry's development of modern taste, which was further endorsed by the second *Post-Impressionist Exhibition* of 1912.

Neither Harold nor Laura was unaware of either of these exhibitions which had such impact on the cultural scene. Harold, it appears, remained untouched and though Laura's mind was open, she was wary and, a little scornful of Bloomsbury with its patrician self-confidence, she distanced herself from it. In her memoirs she acknowledges Roger Fry as a figure on her horizon, even if she dismisses him as an 'interesting personality'. When he vacated his studio in Gower Street around 1919, she took it over. She never actually worked there and yet continued to rent it for 'several quarters'. Why she did that is a mystery, for she was not one to ally herself to 'Movements' and had no sentiment in her soul for "Bloomsbury". Nonetheless, Modernist ideas did shape Laura's development, not least in her belief in the "artist's vision" and the inter-connectedness of life and art which was a key tenet of "Bloomsbury" within which Fry was to play a significant role.

Never a conscious theorist, it is however significant that towards the close of her later autobiography *The Magic of Line* Laura explores the idea of the "artistic vision". Firstly, she establishes the principle that 'mere imitation is no work of art' but rather the result of intense emotional and physical investment. She goes on to describe how, after weeks of unsatisfactory effort, with one stroke of the brush the whole can come together in 'a miracle of revelation' (the image that Laura uses to express this is the ignition of a 'glorious flame'). And so, with one stroke the constituent elements of the picture are brought into relationship. What those constituent elements are was identified by Roger Fry in his *Essay on Aesthetic*, first published in the *New Quarterly* in 1910. Privileging none, he identifies the elements of *rhythm, mass, space, light, shade* and *colour* which, when brought into meaningful relationship by a single *accent,* create a *unity* and *harmony* that communicate with the viewer's emotions and feelings. This he called the realisation of "significant form".

Fry's was a Modernist challenge to the Classical "rules" for art that had been accepted by the Academies of France from the late 17th century as the way to assure a standard of excellence in painting. They were enshrined in 1695 with the *De Arte Graphica* by Charles Du Fresnoy, a textbook that was subsequently translated, affirmed and re-stated many times. Its tenets were to become the cornerstone of instruction within European Academies of Art for generations of students. Its objective was the acquisition of the intellectual discipline and practical skills essential to the creation of morally sound, narrative and representational painting – the rules of *design, drawing* and *composition.* Formal and hierarchical, these were designated "male" and privileged over secondary "feminine" painterly effects of *colour* and *expression.* Here is the source of the ingrained sexualisation of the arts which we met earlier in this chapter. It is significant that Fry's aesthetic neutralises the elements of the visual arts just as Woolf was to do with language and narrative. The arts should be androgynous.

Around the same time Laura Knight was independently becoming more conscious of the key constituent elements of her art – *colour* and *line*, and how these are used to communicate the sense of spatial dimension and substance: *mass*. But, more than that, she was moving towards the representation of *duration*, that is the existence of mass through time as well as in space. Formal academic training was based on the assumption that to convey *mass* the painter had to master the rules of *perspective* and *chiaroscuro* in order to represent a two-dimensional body as though in three-dimensional space. Such a representation was 'inert', as Laura, who herself never suffered from inertia, had learned from the way her efforts in figure drawing and painting were 'wooden'. Now she sought a way to convey the dynamic of bodies in movement. This was her *significant form*. While never a self-conscious intellectual or in debt to the Modernist aesthetic, she was a woman of the early 20th century at a time when developments in science, philosophy and technology were transforming perceptions of time and space, specifically in relation to representations of the image. It is this context that informed Laura's artistic development at this stage of her life.

When we view Laura's Newlyn paintings of the period 1910–12, we share in the evanescence of her visual and sensual experience: the shimmering brilliance of sunshine on wet sand for instance, the elemental force of wind and, above all, in the impish shapeshifting of small children at play. In such examples mass appears to be energised, time telescoped and the past becomes the present. How is this achieved? As has been noted in relation to *Flying a Kite,* 1910, and is evident in a painting such as *Untrodden Sand,* 1912, there is a conscious blurring of the image, as though the children have been focused through a lens but are reacting to the sting of wind-whipped sand or simply quivering with agitation and excitement. They are shapeshifters and cannot be fixed as in a photograph. Laura herself when photographed occasionally displays an inability to be still and impassive. This is clear in the very early Bates family picture that we have in which she alone turns her head away from the camera. It is also evident in a formal photograph of herself, Harold, Rosie Good, her fiancé Oliver Sheppard and Rosie's mother taken at Rosie's home in Nottingham in c.1898 (see chapter 3). The twitch of her mouth, knowing eyes and a sideways glance breaks the petrifying spell of the lens. This same anarchic spirit is replicated in Harold's painting *Afternoon Tea* which was painted around 1910. In these images Laura is consciously subverting the assumption that a personality or an event can or should be immobilized like this.

In her own way she was responding to ideas that were headline news not only in scientific papers but in the press: Einstein's theory of "relativity", Freud and Jung's theories of the multi-layered consciousness and Ostwald's research on the "allotropic" nature of matter which won him the Nobel Prize in Chemistry in 1909. On this evidence, nothing is motionless and static, not least the laws of time and space. For the general public such ideas were made real through rapidly developing technologies of cinema. This phenomenon not only invested the image with movement but changed the way that the public perceived and responded to actual visual experience. What is more, just as the camera "still" had done in the mid-19th century, so "moving pictures" were to have a profound effect on practitioners of the visual arts in the early 20th.

Over the first decade of the 20th century the rapid growth of the phenomenon of cinema transformed popular entertainment as well as public perceptions and expectations. In London between 1906 and 1914 over a thousand picture halls opened up in London, in adapted shops and chapels as well as established theatres. It was the fashion for music halls to feature the latest Biograph, Cinematograph, or Bioscope reels alongside the staple fare of song, dance and comedy turns. Soon purpose-built "picture palaces" began to proliferate across the nation and in 1906 – the year of the Knights' arrival – Newlyn saw the opening of its own cinema: *The Gaiety*. For the artists in residence at the colony this challenge to conventional image-making must have provoked much excitement and discussion. It transformed some of the established ways of thinking about visual representation and gave a new metaphor for the processes of painting.

It is significant that Laura herself uses the word *projection* when talking about her relationship with her various subjects: 'Painting, music, theatre, circus … what joy to project oneself in each', she writes in Chapter 42 of *Oil Paint and Grease Paint*, 'to feel the daring of an acrobat, the control of the artist, in understanding and sympathy to live many lives in one!' It was a way of viewing and understanding the world – a blending of frames from a reel of film, an ongoing process. In her paintings and her writing she displays this quality – kinetic like the elements that sweep across and through them.

In *Oil Paint and Grease Paint* she writes in Chapter 15 of warm summer days when groups of children – including Lamorna Birch's two girls, Mornie and Joan – came down to the rocks. As they splashed in and out of the water, she observes how their 'bare flesh showed, amber or purple – rich against pale rock and water and pearl pink against dark shadow or the blackness of some deep gully.' Then in affirmation of her energy and sense of purpose, she continues: 'I revelled in studying all, determined to make up for my lack of knowledge of the nude, filling dozens of sketchbooks with notes of every pose, movement and effect'. She was equally engrossed in the line and modelling of one lithe model, 'her torso as if carved in black shining marble' and 'poised ready to dive', or curving through the air from some great flat rock to plunge into depths below. The effect of this paragraph is kinaesthetic, melding the energized line with shifts in colour tonality: 'a weed fringe, like coarse hair of greenish-brown colour, which curled and uncurled as the water surged up or receded'.

Even the most apparently static representation from this period betrays a sense of imminent movement. The painting *Rose and Gold*, for instance, is not just a portrait image of the model Dolly Henry but what could be described as a happening "event". Laura commented that Dolly was a fascinating model with hair as golden as the sunflowers in a Lamorna garden and she painted her several times. In this picture, her figure emerges out of the textured surface of the canvas, with its opulent colours and effects of glinting sunshine on red-gold hair hardly distinguishable from the background hedge of roses that in their turn merge with the green velvet jacket. From their first meeting, Laura recognised in Dolly a familiar vital spirit that quivers beneath the apparent composure of the portrait with its twitch of barely suppressed amusement, shrewdness of eye and a spark of fiery temper. It is, in all senses, a moving picture.

Rose and Gold was painted in 1914 just before Dolly had gone back to London in a panic which at the time the Knights could not understand. What happened next was a shocking event. On her return, Dolly had been tracked down by her lover, the artist John Curry, who, maddened by her waywardness and cruel taunts, gunned her down before shooting himself. It was headlined by the newspapers as "The Chelsea Crime". Not everyone in Newlyn was surprised: 'We all got sick of her,' commented Augustus John. 'She was an attractive girl, or used to be when I knew her first, but she seems to have deteriorated into a deceitful little bitch'. But the Knights were appalled, believing that they were party to the crime for, misjudging the seriousness of Dolly's claims, Harold had given Curry her address.

Laura's models could be a source of anxiety but they were also an inspiration. She had a particular rapport with a dancer from London, Dolly Snell. With a fine-toned physique together with a glorious head of red-gold curls, a sunny disposition and endless patience, she shared Laura's boundless energy and humour. This 'Dolly' had been one of the famous "Tiller Girls" – the most popular dancing troupes of the 1900s who, with matched heights and precision routines, earned national and international fame. Laura, always eager to try out new things, wanted Dolly to teach her to dance, especially the trick of kicking the back of one's head – a feat that she particularly envied. To this end she set up a *barre* in the living room at Trewarveneth on Paul Hill which the Knights were then renting. There in the space previously used by Stanhope Forbes and Thomas Gotch as a studio, they practised ballet steps and acrobatics much to the curious amusement of their friends and neighbours. Harold's younger brother, Edgar, came to stay with the Knights at this time, newly returned from America where he had travelled and worked since his late teens. Edgar was now thirty and a very different person from the shy and reticent youth they had known. He was mature and extrovert, determined to enjoy a holiday of several weeks by the sea. Laura found in him a fellow spirit, ready to join in the fun and always prepared to lend a hand.

Edgar was especially attracted to Dolly (they were to marry and settle in America) and was eager to be of assistance when Laura set her heart on painting her model dressed in an emerald-green dress of her own fashion and making. It was to be another over-sized canvas, painted *en plein air* in a single day and it would put her talents to the ultimate test. She sent to London for a canvas measuring seven foot by five, immediately prepared it with linseed oil and the next day had Edgar transport and set it up in the field near her painting-hut. It was an overcast October morning but Laura was happy. She set out to create a work in tonalities of grey that set off Dolly's outfit: the bright green gown, neat black jacket and hat with a fine emerald feather.

Dolly stood imperturbable, sustained by Edgar's coffee, bread and cheese that were snatched in very short breaks in the otherwise continuous process. Then the sun came out and totally altered the effect: 'the heavy clouds broke apart, showing an intense bright blue'. Laura was undaunted. She repainted the whole canvas with sunlit clouds in the sky, the resulting shadows, the shot-silk effect of the sun on Dolly's skirts and the soft glow of her complexion against the green feather of her hat. She painted for a further five hours until the light faded. 'I used nearly three pounds of flake white that day', Laura records; 'Edgar squeezed it out for me as he saw it disappear from my palette, now and again handing me a clean one'.

The following morning there were only a few areas to touch up. The weather had again changed and there was a brisk wind and the threat of rain. Dolly had difficulty keeping her hat on her head, the emerald gown blew over her head and Edgar had difficulty in restraining the canvas itself, but it was soon satisfactorily finished. *The Green Feather* was indeed the work of a day, an "action painting" that Laura was proud of and she returned home elated. Harold was not impressed. He had no time for extravagant bravura. It was a work of vanity that would make her ill. Laura was devastated since Harold's approbation mattered and she writes that in the subsequent weeks she 'could not abide the thought of ever taking up the brush again'. She did of course, and was soon arranging for *The Green Feather* to be exhibited – not in Britain but in America at the annual Carnegie International Exhibition in Pittsburg. It was awarded an "honourable mention" and later bought for the Canadian National Gallery, Ottawa, where it still resides.

1911–12 saw mixed fortunes for Laura and Harold. Always susceptible to problems with his teeth and inclined to poor health, in the late summer of 1911 Harold appears to have suffered a severe illness. A recently discovered series of letters from Laura to an American acquaintance staying in Newlyn, suggests that Harold's health problems were more serious than mere dentistry could mend. Laura wrote: 'My dear Mrs Howland, may we come to you another night later on instead of Friday? Harold has had a nervous breakdown and was fearfully ill last night. We had to send for the doctor who ordered complete quiet'. It is thought that Laura's diagnosis of a 'nervous breakdown' was exaggerated, although certainly Harold was suffering from nervous debility. On the 11th September she writes again to Mrs Howland: 'Unfortunately Harold still seems dreadfully weak, he has hardly left his room yet, so it seems impossible to fix a date … the slightest worry or excitement seems to upset him, however the doctor says that he will be quite well soon again – after a good rest'. In a letter dated October 6th Harold is still 'in bed', having been set back 'weeks' by getting up too soon: 'Today we carried him out into the sun on a bed, which is a great improvement, probably now he can get out of doors for a little time he will pick up very quickly'.

In the early summer of 1912, Harold had to be admitted to hospital in Plymouth and to be near him, Laura took lodgings there. But she could not work – and work was her resource, her life. Just as Harold was making some progress, Laura, in a state of high tension and exhaustion, was herself diagnosed with nervous collapse and spent some time in a nursing home. Both were ordered to rest and refrain from painting for what Laura describes as a 'hateful six months'. Financially however they were in a better position and Harold decided that they could afford a car. So, when Laura came out of the nursing home in the early spring of 1913, she was picked up in a brand new "Belsize" and together they drove up to Wyresdale in Lancashire where

Harold had a commission to paint Gertrude Ormrod. Gertie was the daughter of J.G. Lyon, a manufacturer and philanthropist from the Pontefract area. He had been an early patron of the Knights in Staithes days and Harold had painted his portrait in 1909. They spent a month, painting and recuperating at Wyresdale. It was a beautiful location and Laura enjoyed her time there, but even so she found it 'strange ground' and had been pleased to return to Newlyn. After the months away from Cornwall (these were the months when the "affair" of Florence Munnings and Gilbert Evans apparently became serious), they returned to find Trewarvaneth farmhouse rented out in their absence. However, Colonel Paynter had knocked three cottages into one for them at Lamorna Gate: Oakhill. Until the cottage was ready for them, the Knights stayed with the Sidgwicks. Alfred Sidgwick, a retired Oxford professor, and his novelist wife Cecily lived at Trewoofe (pronounced 'Trove') Orchard.

A young couple, who were to become close friends of the Knights, had just bought a plot of land next to the Orchard and were building their own house, called simply Trewoofe. They were Ella and Charlie Naper: she an accomplished enameller and jewellery-maker in the Arts and Crafts tradition and Charlie an architect and artist. Over time the Sidgwicks became very fond of Ella and treated her like a daughter. She called them 'Aunt Cis' and 'Uncle Alfred' – Laura called them 'the Sidgys'.

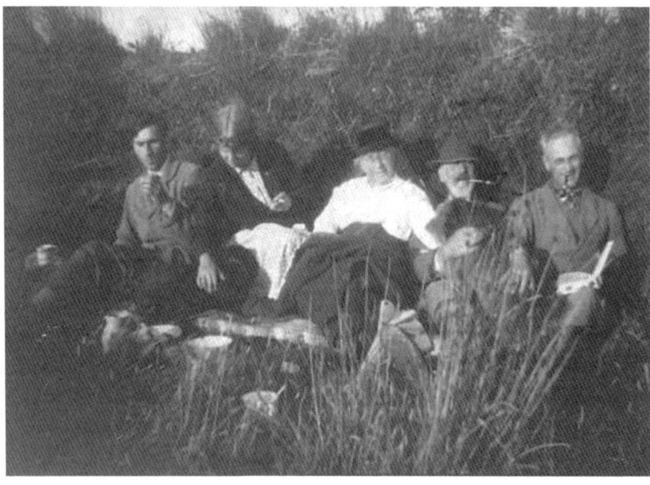

Charles Naper, Laura Knight with Tip, Cecily and Alfred Sidgwick and Harold Knight at Dozmary Pool in August 1914. Courtesy Maryella Pigott

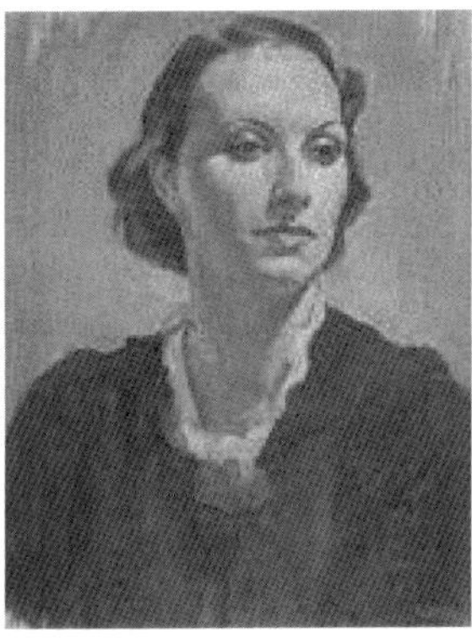

Harold Knight, *Portrait of Ella Naper.*
Photographic image courtesy of Tennants Auction House

The newly extended cottage, Oakhill, was in many ways the Knights' first 'home' which they (meaning Laura) could furnish to their own needs and taste. She did so in style, with a blue and white signature colour scheme for curtains and pottery, ordering her 'furniture, linen and silver' from Harrods' catalogue! "Mrs Alfred Sidgwick gave us a handsome bow-fronted mahogany chest of drawers as a house-warming present (she writes) which we still have, and the big blanket she gave us is on my bed at the present time … At Oakhill, we kept open house as we had always done; almost every evening people gathered round our fire. The gramophone was constantly playing for dancing on the rush matting that covered the stone floor."

The garden was cleared and planted out with sunflowers, geraniums and lobelia by 'Mr Ernest', a tramp who, with his wife, had come recommended to the Knights by their Plymouth doctor who had treated his epilepsy. Handsome, tall and strong, Mr Ernest was a great asset. Having no inhibitions, he and his wife were happy to pose naked for Laura and Harold to draw. They adopted the Knights in return, initiating Laura into the tramps' secret sign code and regaling her with stories of their Saturday night tramps' gatherings. They stayed for a while until the urge to move on overcame them. But, over the years, Laura was to receive letters telling of their news and exploits on the road, for Mr Ernest was able to write and spoke several languages.

Work went well, for in addition to providing upgraded accommodation for the Knights, Colonel Paynter had a studio-hut built for each of them – one for Harold at Oakhill and a larger one for Laura at Trethinnick down the

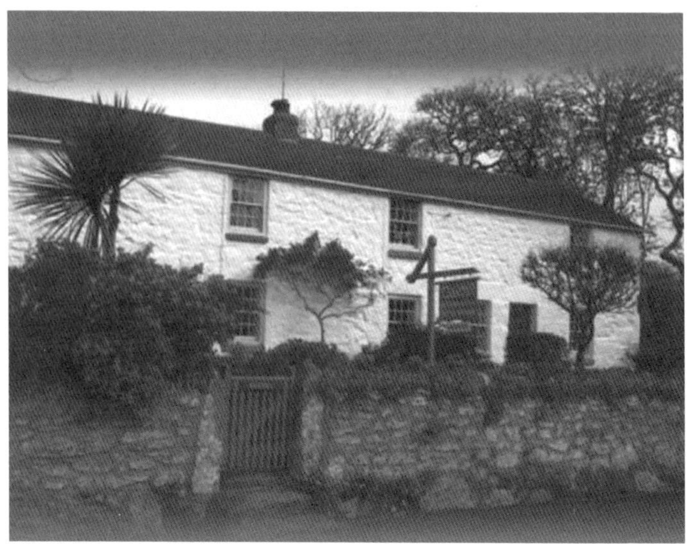

Oakhill today. Private collection

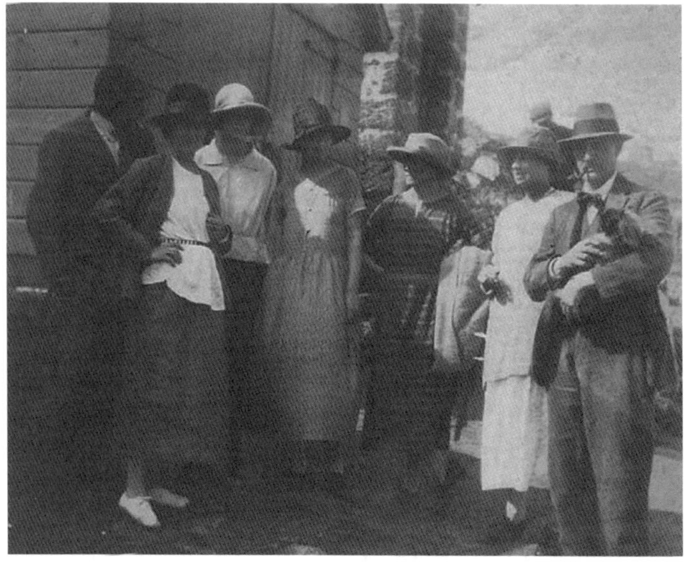

The Knights with the Napers and friends, including Tip the dog c.1912. Private collection

valley. In December 1912 Norman Garstin's article in *The Studio* 'The Art of Harold and Laura Knight' promoted their work and reputation significantly, identifying them as a couple to be watched. This increased the confidence of both and perhaps it was this affirmation that suggested to Laura that it was the time to make a public statement of her having come to an important stage of her painting career. *Self Portrait* was painted at Trethinnick. It was, says Laura a time of 'tremendous output' and increasing prestige for them. In 1913 she sent two paintings to the Carnegie International Exhibition in Pittsburgh and they had a third joint exhibition of watercolours at the Leicester Galleries with very satisfactory sales. They were upwardly mobile, had money to spare for once, and Laura started to fashion a public and professional identity for herself as "artist". What, at the age of thirty-six, was that image?

We last considered Laura's appearance at the period just before she and Harold left for Staithes. Much had happened in the intervening years. Graduating (or perhaps regressing) from the Parisian 'Merode', her preference in Newlyn seems to have been to wear her hair free or in plaits, which were soon to be curled about her ears as 'earphones' – a style with which she was to be identified for many decades. She still made her own clothes on Mother's old sewing-machine but, unlike the cotton prints of Staithes, she now sought out unusual and colourful fabrics on the market stalls of Penzance and made them up into curtains or frocks to wear and share. The emerald silk dress was one of her creations. It illustrates the fashion for the slimmer line that, rejecting the "S-curve" of the corseted Edwardian 'Gibson Girl' silhouette, began to be popular in the years just before the First World War. Laura's day dresses were simply styled to the floor or just above the ankle, loosely waisted and with minimal ornamentation.

Harold often dressed his models in gowns created by his wife and these found their way to a common costume and prop-box. One of Harold's paintings, *Reading a Letter* for example shows Phyllis Gotch wearing the dark blue silk taffeta dress that is worn by Laura herself in *Afternoon Tea* where she is seated facing us at the tea-table in the company of Florence Carter-Wood wearing green. Laura's outfit is topped by a wide-brimmed hat decorated with tulle that is highly likely to have been an incarnation of her own wedding hat. That image is a piece of play-acting – one of Harold's "interiors". In the early years at Newlyn in reality Laura was more likely to be seen in a painter's smock worn over an old frock. On her feet she inevitably wore stout hobnail boots, a necessity when climbing over cliffs and rocks, although something of a trial when riding her bicycle!

Over the next couple of years, however, as Laura grew in confidence, her image was adjusted. She began sporting the black, wide-brimmed hat worn in the *Self Portrait*. A cross between a *fedora* and a *trilby*, this was to become her trademark. The *fedora*, a key element in the costume associated with Parisian artists (Toulouse-Lautrec being the obvious example), had been appropriated by women after Sarah Bernhardt wore one in the 1889 American production of the play *Fedora*. It was quickly adopted by women's rights activists in the 1890s. The *trilby*, a smaller crowned version, with a slightly narrower brim angled down at the front and turned up at the back was called so in homage to George Du Maurier's novel *Trilby*, 1894. The eponymous heroine of the stage version wore such a hat and, as a result the style was soon synonymous with its theme of "artistic obsession". Both forms of headgear are heavy with symbolism. Can we therefore read any significance into Laura's wearing a hybrid version of them? Some may well wish to do so but I suggest that rather than being a badge of political affiliation to women's rights or a reference to her own artistic obsession, her hat was nothing more than a statement of her individuality. It was bohemian, practical and suited her well, like the bright red jacket, known as her 'Cornish scarlet', which, purchased for 2/6 at a sale in Penzance, did excellent service in and out of the studio for many years.

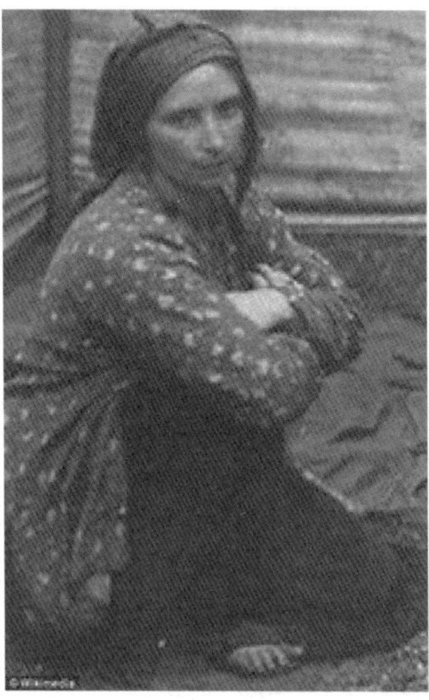

Dorelia John, c. 1913. Public domain

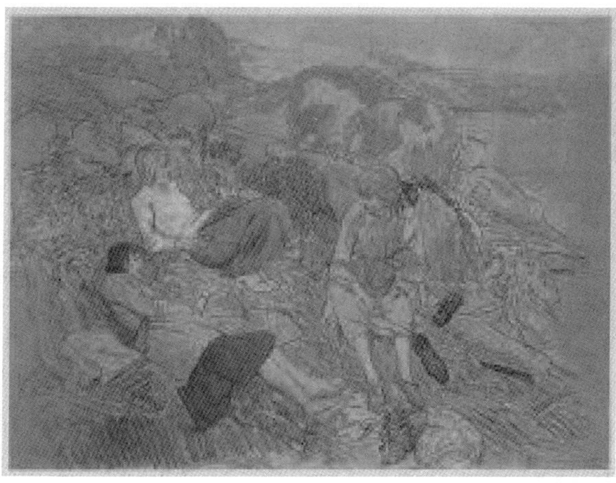

Laura Knight, figures on a cliff, including Tip, In Cornwall 1916 (print). Private collection

When Augustus John and his wife and muse, Dorelia, arrived in Newlyn in the autumn of 1913, they caused a stir not only in response to the larger-than-life presence of the notorious John but to beautiful Dorelia. Laura and Harold first met them at the invitation of Munnings at Mrs Jorey's Temperance Hotel where the Johns lodged for a short while. Laura was much impressed by Dorelia's 'startling' looks, notably her ivory skin and jet-black hair. Dorelia's appearance set a new trend in the colony, which enthusiastically embraced her gypsy looks and fashion: a tight bodice and gathered full skirt, often enhanced by bandana around the head, long silver earrings and a black cloak. Laura also notes that during her time in Newlyn, Dorelia was responsible for an even more revolutionary trend when she cropped her hair and took to wearing woollen jumpers over a knee-length skirt. This gamine look marked a significant shift in female fashion which was to gain ground in wartime.

It was a costume that appealed to Laura and her circle, as several pictures from this time of girls perched aloft at the cliff's edge, illustrate (Plates 10 and 11). In her walks over the cliffs, she was often accompanied by their dog, Tip, who, like Laura herself, had a mind of his own and could disappear for days on forays far-afield. She 'adored' Tip and tells us that for all her life she carried with her 'the feel of his black india-rubber nose, and the rough hair of his back'. Tip is immortalised in several of her so-called "cliff-top" paintings. By working there Laura was taking a risk since wartime restrictions put coastal sketching off-bounds and trespassers could be arrested and interrogated as alien spies. However, from 1916 onwards Laura was able to secure official permission to paint on the coast, presumably through the good offices of Colonel Paynter.

One image, 'Looking Out to Sea' (also known as 'On the Edge of the Cliff' painted in 1917, epitomises her work at that time. The lone figure, turns away from the painter/viewer, scanning the dark sea below. The wind blowing her skirts, she stands confidently (even heroically) dominant in full sun, her shadow cut by the hard rock edge. Wearing a short skirt and jumper in the 'modern' style with hair in a casual plait, at the base of the cliff waves eddy and ripple outwards only to be truncated by the picture frame. A contracted palette of intense blue sea and the sepia rocks, together with the white and muted blue dress and rich auburn hair of the girl complements the narrow spatial focus. This, after all, is a war picture.

It was in the context of war conditions that Laura sought to fulfil a long-held ambition to capture the 'effulgence' of spring. She had first had a longing to do so on seeing the primroses emerge down at Pearly Bottoms at Staithes. This time she wanted to cram all the drama of spring in Cornwall onto the canvas: the frothing blossom of the blackthorn; the shifting cloud shadows over the quickening fields but, as she herself says, no primroses 'because I could find no place to put them'. The painting was an amalgam of motifs. In an interview for the *Cornishman* newspaper given in 1935 (when the picture was purchased for the sum of £400 by the Chantrey Bequest for the Tate Gallery), Laura tells, somewhat dramatically, of how, 'hiding in the bushes', she made forays from her painting-hut in Lamorna to sketch details 'while coast-watchers were searching the whole coast with their telescopes'. It was back in the studio that she arranged the lambs (she always 'adored' lambs), trees, a single magpie (the connotations of which caused Gert Harvey, who was highly superstitious, much concern: 'you will never sell that picture with just one raven in it') and a rainbow arching over the sweep of moorland. In the hollow of the foreground she placed her good friends Charles and Ella Naper: Charles in tweeds with his fishing rod and Ella wearing a "Dorelia style" costume in a striking attitude that was typical of her – hand on hip, her legs gracefully positioned.

Perhaps because the painting was put together piecemeal without Laura's characteristic 'splash', it carries with it a sense of contrivance and picture-book naivety. Laura knew that and was to re-paint it several times over the following years. Nearly 20 years later, she was to paint out Charles Naper and replace him with the figure of a local boy. This amended version was exhibited at the Carnegie International Exhibition in Pittsburgh and was reproduced as a Medici print. However, in 1935 when the painting was purchased by the Chantry Trust for the Tate Gallery, Charles was put back into the picture.

Contrary to her fabled technique of creating her canvases in one burst of energy, she did in fact return to some of her canvases. As a result, some larger scale paintings such as with *Spring* and *Lamorna Birch and his Daughters*, became palimpsests – canvases revised and painted over many times and over several years. The Birch picture (Plate 8), for example, was begun in the period 1913–16 but not completed until 1934 when it was voted "Picture of the Year" at the Royal Academy Summer Exhibition. The overpainting of the picture has created a complex layering of textures across the canvas. This is not a delicate painting which explains why when it was exhibited at the Carnegie International in Pittsburgh in 1935, the reviewer from the *New York Times* wrote: 'This is vigorous "outside" painting: naturalism honestly and bluntly, and ruggedly hammered home'. The colour 'frank and harsh', it is in no way 'esthetic'.' Once again there is a subtext: for the critic the effect is 'unfeminine'. For a more balanced recent assessment we go to Rosie Broadley's *Catalogue* entry for the work, which describes *Lamorna Birch and his Family* as 'a strikingly modern family portrait'. Relaxed and informal, we see here Laura's compositional skill as well as her unsentimental gift for painting children. What is more, this is the 'primrose' picture that she had so long wanted to paint. It is owned by the University of Nottingham.

These were happy days in the company of their Newlyn friends. In Ella's company Laura found a sympathetic and dependable companion as well as a model. Harold painted her too, for Ella, so the Knights declared, had a figure to rival the *Rokeby Venus* and they took photographs to prove it. These were taken in July 1914 up on Bodmin Moor, where the Knights, the Napers and Harold and Gert Harvey were camping. Laura had just returned from the inquest on the death of Florence Munnings which affected her deeply. Harold had packed the Belsize with a tent and they drove inland to Dozmare (Dozmary) Pool where the Napers had a favourite camping spot: a ramshackle hut which Charles had built on their first arriving in the area and where they had lived a "gypsy life" before building the house at Trewoofe. On their way to the Moor, the Knights and Harveys stopped in Truro, where Gert (always practical and sensible) bought provisions and Laura a rainbow-coloured blazer. It was meant to be a cheering thing but she 'could not stop weeping'.

Once up on the Moor, however, there was respite from the pain and upset. They bathed naked, cooked on a makeshift stove and, despite wartime restrictions, made excursions to the coast: to Sennen (always a favourite place for Laura and painted several times) and to Mousehole. However, it was Dozmare itself that enchanted Laura: the 'density of an ink-black pool, gold spotted where the sun pierced some little hole in the fir branches overhead, turning the peat-stained clear brown water into little patches of pure colour'. It was a magical place steeped in Arthurian legend. This was the pool, they say, from which Arthur received the sword Excalibur from the Lady of the Lake and to where it was at length returned by Sir Bedivere after the final battle of Camlann. Tales were told of its reappearance from time to time and Laura was susceptible: 'I saw it myself, or imagined I did' she claims in *The Magic of a Line* in the chapter 'Cornish Light and Shade'. It was a period of seeming contentment for Laura and Harold – a life lived in the fresh air and sunshine. One of the snapshots of that time shows Laura, hair in plaits and in a short frock seated outside the makeshift hut and in another the pair of them, Laura giggling, holding onto Harold's arm and Harold, looking middle-aged in a hat and sucking his pipe. It is a loving image, but the pool was troubled.

After his illness Harold's nervous debility appears to have become more serious. He was inclined to bouts of depression and occasionally Laura's non-stop energy and ebullience were too much. They had both been through

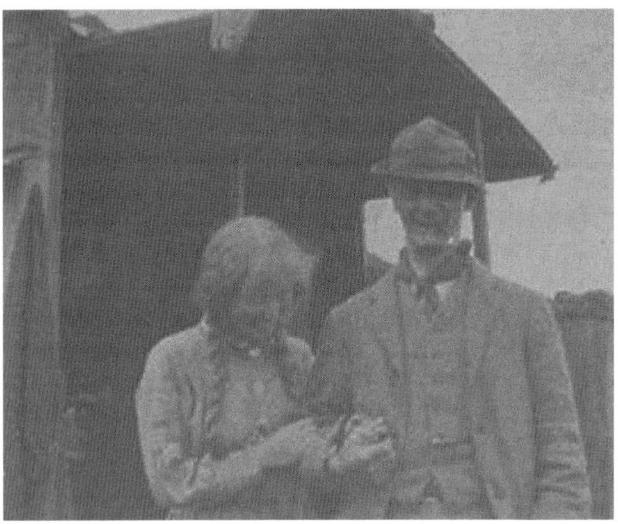

Laura and Harold at Dozmary Pool, 1914. Public domain

the traumas of Florence's suicide and Dolly Henry's murder. All this took its toll. Now we come to another contested issue. Friends, notably the Birch family, put his depression down to an unrequited passion for Ella Naper – or so Dunbar claims. She reveals Harold's secret passion in a dramatic narrative gesture that can be explained in part by her publishers requesting that she add extra "spice" to her manuscript to give it popular appeal. However, there is no evidential basis for the claim and if anyone in the Knights' social circle did observe any sign of his feelings for Ella, they chose not to make it public and Laura chose to keep silent. We have to address once again that matter of "love".

We could say that both Laura and Harold "loved" Ella. Harold could hardly help "loving" her. She was beautiful physically – the perfect model and he painted her often. We know that Laura too thought her to be physically beautiful as the *Self Portrait* (or *The Model*) of 1913 illustrates. John Branfield's book on the Napers and their life at Lamorna addresses this. He points out that Laura describes Ella as 'an adorably lovely slim creature', alerting us to the use of the word 'creature', suggesting 'she saw her as instinctive and physical, with an animal vitality'. We have met this before in relation to Laura's admiration for Dod and should come to a similar conclusion. However, as Branfield also says, Laura's sensuous appreciation of women's physical beauty can be 'easily be misinterpreted … but her interest never went beyond the aesthetic'.

There were overtly lesbian artists in Newlyn, Hannah Gluckstein (known as 'Gluck') for one and Joan Coulsen who had befriended Florence Munnings before her death, another. But Laura Knight was not one of them even though to the cynical eye it might seem so. As we have already noted, she and Harold painted Ella, often nude, out of doors and in the studio, many times. Whether from this we can imply a sexual interest or obsession in either of them would be unreasonable and presumptuous since, as we know, both were unselfconscious about painting "from the life" – it was something accepted as part of the professional artist's repertoire. On the other hand, it is also important to note that many men and women (including 'Gluck') found Ella sexually attractive, but she was not interested and did not seek such attention or physical gratification. What seem to have been her most important qualities were her patience, sympathy and gentleness of character. Harold found her presence soothing and Laura liked and admired her greatly.

Laura's reflections on that summer at Dozmare, when they seemed to be 'a complete community in ourselves', so remote that 'the news of the day did not reach us', carries a tragic irony. On the evening of the 3rd August 1914, War was declared. The Newlyn community itself continued normally, convinced, as so many were, that the war would soon be over. Gradually however able-bodied young men disappeared from the community to go to the Front, taking with them the ideals of heroism, chivalry and the honour of the British Empire. Few returned. 'Memory of that horror', Laura writes in retrospect, 'blots my pen'.

However, lightening the mood, in that year the Knights made the acquaintance of a personable young man who, having come to Newlyn to have his portrait painted by Munnings, was to become a life-long friend. This was Barry Jackson, then in the process of building up an important project. In 1913 he had established the Repertory Theatre in his home city of Birmingham ('the Old Rep'). It was to be the start of one of the most important provincial theatres in Britain and of a distinguished theatrical career. Knighted in 1925, he founded the Malvern Festival in 1929 and was made Director of the Shakespeare Memorial Theatre in Stratford in 1945. Over succeeding years Barry Jackson was to open up many opportunities for Laura socially and professionally and the connection with Malvern was to be significant for both Harold and herself, especially in their later years. At that stage however he with his companion Scott Sunderland were simply two pleasant and charming new friends, who they met very occasionally when they went up to London to negotiate picture sales and exhibitions.

As the war developed it was clear that this was not the time to try to sell pictures. Money and rations dwindled and economies had to be made. The car was sold and, unable to keep up the rent for Oakhill, the Knights were forced to find cheaper lodgings. One day in late November 1915, rations being short, Laura went out on an egg-hunt. Returning in the dark with one precious egg in her pocket, she had a bad fall and broke her ankle in two places. Harold, preparing the vegetables for supper heard her cries and alerted their neighbours, Walter and Ruth Simpson, who immediately left their dinner table and came to help. Others soon arrived and a doctor was sought while Laura lay in great pain on the wet grass. It was a traumatic event that had echoes of her Mother's accident in Winchester. However, she avoids any such assumption when in *Oil Paint and Grease Paint* she records her main concern: the Simpson's leg of lamb, a 'luxury almost unknown', which remained untasted and congealing on the dining table. The egg survived without a crack and Harold had it for his breakfast the next day.

For Laura, who constantly walked, climbed and stood long hours before her easel, a broken ankle was a disaster. Now, forced to lie for weeks on a couch in the sitting-room, she nonetheless enjoyed the attention of friends – Ella Naper, Eleanor Hughes, Ruth Simpson and Gert Harvey. Munnings too gave due attendance and read to her every day, sometimes bringing with him a fish that he had managed to get hold of from John Jeffreys, the sole fisherman then working out of Lamorna. One 'beautiful grilled herring' is remembered well as, once again, Laura marks moments of significance with memory of food relished or desired.

That winter they went to stay at St Hilary's Rectory, five miles east of Penzance, at the invitation of the recently appointed Rector, Bernard Walke and his wife Annie who was also an artist. The Knights had been introduced to the Walkes by AJ and at once they had a rapport. The friendship was long lasting and, in later years when they had moved permanently to London, Laura and Harold often entertained Ber Walke. After the War, in the 1920s and 30s, he and his wife had the idea of rallying local artists to decorate the interior of the Church of St Hilary with images of Celtic saints. Artists who worked there include Harold Knight, Ernest and Dod Procter, Alethea and Norman Garstin, and Roger Fry who designed the reredos screen.

Back at the Rectory in early 1916, Laura with her leg in plaster was trundled around by Ber in an old bathchair to see the frozen pond where she sketched the children skating and sliding. She was to work these drawings up into her first major oil painting after the accident, helped in the process of rehabilitation by her newly acquired habit of cigarette smoking. Laura and her cigarette were henceforth to be another of her trademarks. The leg mended and work once again took precedence and it seemed that all would be well. However, in 1916 Harold received his call-up papers. He had prepared his response: convinced of the immorality of fighting, he would refuse to fight. Because his health was poor, his doctor advised that since he would never be passed as fit for combat, he need not take that step. But Harold was a man of stubborn principle, and, refusing to make what he considered to be excuses, went public as a 'professed Conscientious Objector'. At that time in the popular mind the word "conchie" carried with it the stigma of "coward" and "traitor". To be officially identified as such meant imprisonment or, at best, manual labour of some kind. Harold had to present himself before a Tribunal and it was only after prolonged and demeaning questioning that his motives were considered to be genuine.

As a Conscientious Objector, Harold suffered terribly. Former friends and acquaintance turned away from him in the street and refused his hand in greeting. He found some support from other local artists who, also refusing to fight, were required to work on the land. Later, however, he was obliged to hoe fields on his own and some distance from Newlyn. It was heavy, back-breaking work, and, above all, terribly lonely. Dunbar fills out the detail here, based presumably on Laura's own words. They had already relinquished Oakhill, so she found a place to stay close to the farm in north Cornwall where he was sent to work and busied herself sketching and painting. His hands rough and calloused, Harold himself did not touch a paint brush. He hardly spoke and retreated far into himself to a place that no one could reach. At this point Dunbar once again invokes the spectre of Harold's unrequited "love" for Ella Naper. This, she believes, was the source of his depression. But for a man as sensitive and intelligent as Harold, the implications and realities of the War, let alone his own physical circumstances and ill health, were quite sufficient to trigger a major breakdown.

Laura was very concerned for Harold, even if, when he had first taken his stance as a pacifist, she had felt anger and frustration at what she felt was an unnecessary gesture. Anxiety was compounded by the fact that no one was buying their paintings and they were again literally "on their uppers". A possible solution to their plight was offered in 1916 when Laura received news of a commission to go to Witley, the Scottish-Canadian Physical Training Camp in Surrey. There she was to make some studies for the Canadian War Records with a payment of £300. It was impossible to refuse. Laura tells us that she gratefully accepted and left Harold in the capable hands of their 'landlady'. This is slightly disingenuous for the actual arrangements were sensible and in no way heartless as might be at first thought. Charlie Naper was away with his regiment in Italy and Ella, unhappy living at Trewoofe on her own, had joined the Sidgys in a rented cottage at Sennen Cove. The Knights took the cottage next door. Therefore, when Laura went off to Witley Camp she in fact left Harold in the capable hands of Ella and the Sidgys. So, with a clear conscience she set off on her journey to Witley to begin her work as an Official War Artist.

CHAPTER EIGHT

"Armed with my sketchbook and full of confidence"

The commission to paint at Witley Camp had come about through a series of fortuitous meetings. Laura had first met Paul Konody, the art critic for *The Observer* and *The Daily Mail*, in 1913 when he was negotiating the purchase of her painting *May Blossom* for the newspaper magnate Lord Rothermere. She met Konody again when he arrived to do a picture evaluation for the Ormrods while she and Harold were staying with them in Lancashire. In 1916 he was working on behalf of Lord Beaverbrook, the Anglo-Canadian press baron, who in turn was acting as agent for the Canadian Government, identifying potential artists to contribute to the Canadian War Archive. Laura had come to mind. Her subject was to be 'Physical Training Camp' – men bathing in the river in sunlight. When she got there however, she saw precious little sunlight and no athletic males bathing: 'the ugliness everywhere was devastating – row after row of brown huts, and khaki figures drearily standing about in the mud' she comments towards the end of Chapter 17 in *Oil Paint and Grease Paint*. Several painters had been invited to contribute canvases but at first Laura could find no other artists and despaired of finding a subject. It was miserable.

Then in the camp barber's hut, she came across a boxer – Joe Shears. Showing all the characteristics of his profession – nose, ears and lips all 'mashed', Joe, bantam-weight champion of all the forces at that time, had an interesting lived-in face and a tightly-sprung, well-formed physique. Like all his compatriots he was delighted to be offered a diversion from the relentless boredom of the camp and dreary news from the Front. He agreed at once to pose. Laura set up her studio in the gymnasium and soon, in her trademark red jacket she was a feature of camp life. That jacket had been dubbed the "Cornish scarlet" by Konody, recognising it as a distinctive primary statement in several of her paintings of the blue skies and sea of Newlyn. Worn by

Laura and her models for years and washed numerous times, it was still shone bright and at Witley Camp was 'the only spot of colour for miles'. Then, one bitterly cold day, Joe thoughtfully provided her with a hand-warmer, so hot that a large hole was burned in the pocket of the scarlet jacket.

Laura was something of a novelty in the Camp and readily made friends with the soldiers who gathered around to watch her at work. She writes in one letter: 'I like the Canadians, they are ripping men, today I have been drawing the Kilties, as they call them, the Scotch Canadians, their dress is such a fine one.' But her strongest bond was with Joe who treated her with the greatest courtesy and offered her the privilege of 'months of studying of the male figure – in action too!' He would regularly escort her the 3 miles back from the Camp to the Angel Hotel in Godalming where she was lodged and just as regularly, she would invite him and the other soldier-models for 'little dinners' there. Laura's output was rapid and prolific, her many sketches soon covering the walls of the Gymnasium. Joe was very proud,

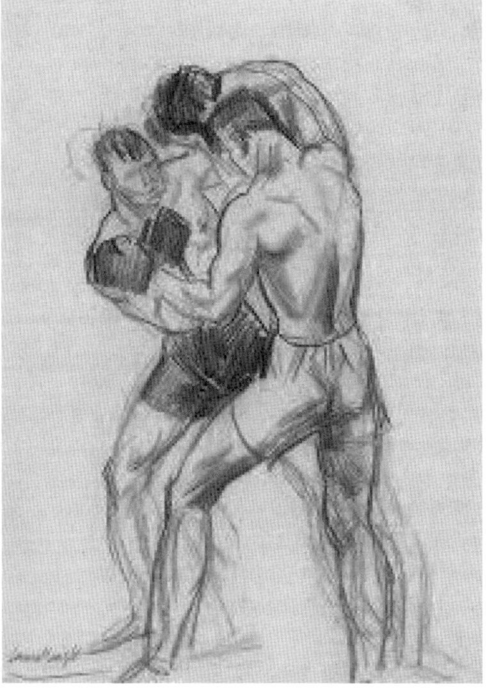

Boxers. Private collection

even suggesting that they open a shop in Leicester Square to display and sell her drawings of him. With Joe as chief 'barker' soliciting business, together they would make a fortune! In reality, for her exhibition at the Leicester Galleries in 1917 Laura had a fine collection of boxing studies as well as Cornish pictures to display. At the Grosvenor Gallery in the same year a portrait of hers earned the interest and admiration of Jacob Epstein who requested the name of the sitter since he too wished to use her as a model. 'That', comments Laura, 'is how I came to make the Epsteins' acquaintance'. With acknowledgement by such a high- profile fellow artist it seemed that nothing could stop her now. But something did.

In the winter of early 1917 the pandemic, known as the "Spanish Flu" began its sweep of Europe and America. Harold caught it and then in early 1918 Laura, in London to see the hanging of the exhibition at the Leicester Galleries, went down with it and developed serious complications: pneumonia. Moved to a nursing home, Laura once more conjures an inner psychological drama with the chapter headed 'Delirium' in *Oil Paint and Grease Paint*. The sequence, which has strong echoes of Laura's mental anguish when at school in St Quentin, is highly charged. It shifts into the dramatic present tense, moving from air-raids over London streets, to mud-filled trenches and bursts of machine-gun fire, while dead babies and shrouded bodies invade her space. Death looms. At that point her voice surfaces into confession: 'It's my own wickedness …. I thought of myself too much –I have realised how much more others are suffering'. And so, she proceeds 'from semi-madness to sane thought of extraordinary clarity' and, thinking 'of Mother', finds Harold at her bedside. He came with food, champagne and news of excellent sales at the Leicester Galleries, sales good enough to buy Laura her first fur coat – a musquash that became a much-loved staple of her wardrobe. So dressed, she re-surfaced in Cornwall.

Laura's severe illness had meant that her life-size oil painting of boxers at Witley was not completed. Yet, though debilitated, she was determined to see it through. Because the preliminary charcoal sketches of the work had been accidentally destroyed, she had to persuade Joe to come down to Lamorna to pose again. Ever resourceful, he managed to do this by claiming "sick leave". During his stay he terrified the locals and respectable acquaintances such as Colonel Paynter and guests who, on paying an unexpected call to enquire after Laura's health, were disconcerted by the sight of her in her sick-bed painting Joe stripped for combat. Laura's several oil studies based on her boxing sketches were to be well received – her painting of Joe, *The Boxer*, winning the Silver Medal at the Olympiad in Amsterdam in 1928 (from 1912 the Arts were an Olympic category as in the original Games). Above all, it is *Physical Training Witley Camp* 1917 in the Canadian War Museum Ottawa, that confirms Laura's accomplishment as a sporting artist. Indeed, in 1923 she was to become the Vice President of the United Amateur Wrestling and Weight Training Club in London (her membership card is in the Nottinghamshire Archives). But all this was but one facet of her developing fascination with the 'magic of a line' delineated by the body in movement.

In 1922 the American magazine *The International Studio* published an article based on an interview with Laura Knight which she gave during her first visit to the United States in that year. The reporter was interested in her boxing pictures: 'Laura Knight admitted her admiration for the sport' it reports, 'and her art revels in the athletic limbs, the highly developed muscles and intricate postures of those who contend in the roped arena ... It demonstrates her interest in all phases of life and her feeling for attitudes, for rhythmic movement, and form and colour'. This provides us with a convenient transition, for it is but a step from Laura's portrayal of fine footwork and athleticism in the boxing ring to her greater love of fine footwork and physical grace of the dance.

Dancing for Laura was an intuitive form of expression. In the early days at Newlyn, she was notorious for suddenly breaking out into wild gyrations

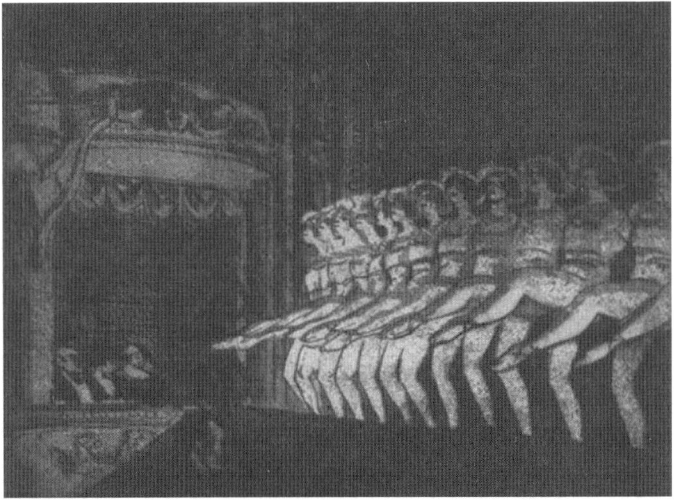

Tiller girls, print. Private collection

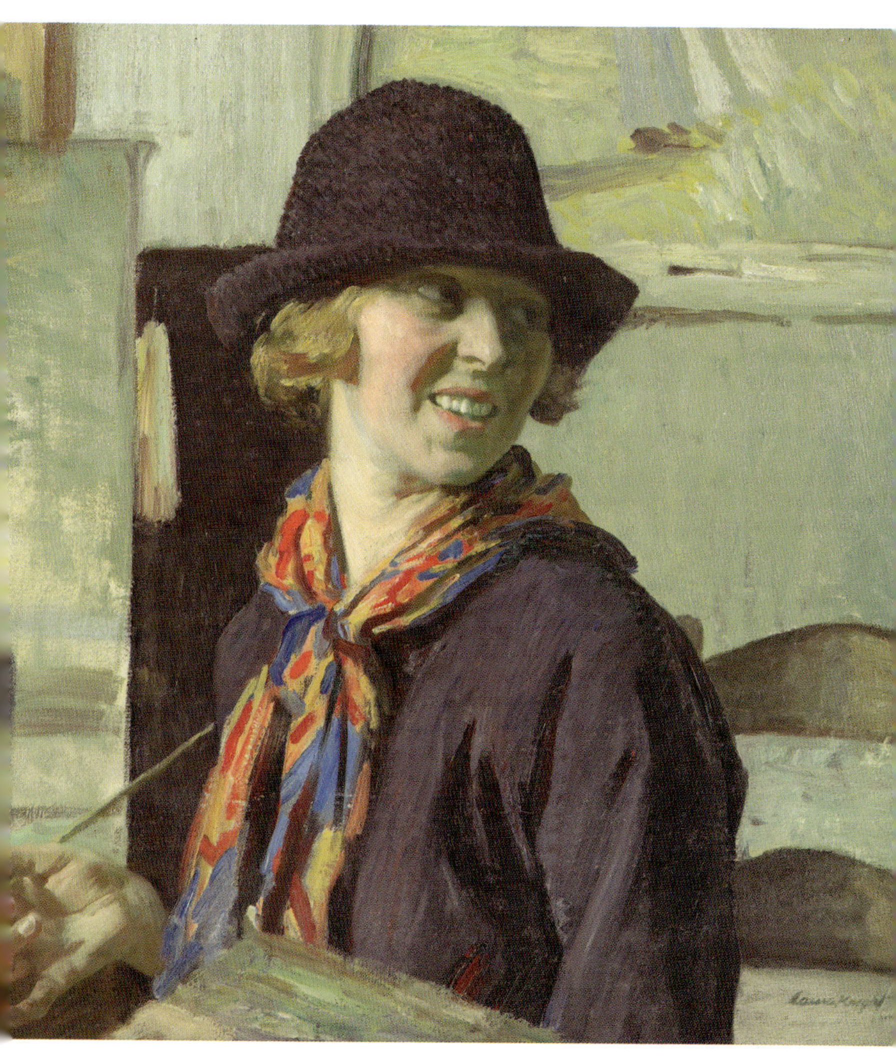

Plate 1. Laura Knight Self Portrait, *c.1921, oil on canvas. Museum of New Zealand,*
Te Papa Tongarewa.

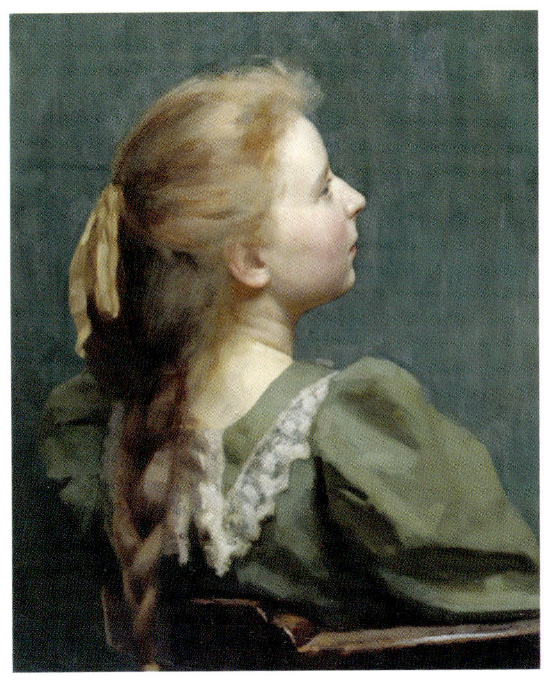

Plate 2. Harold Knight Laura, aged 14, *1891, oil on canvas. The Royal Academy, London.*

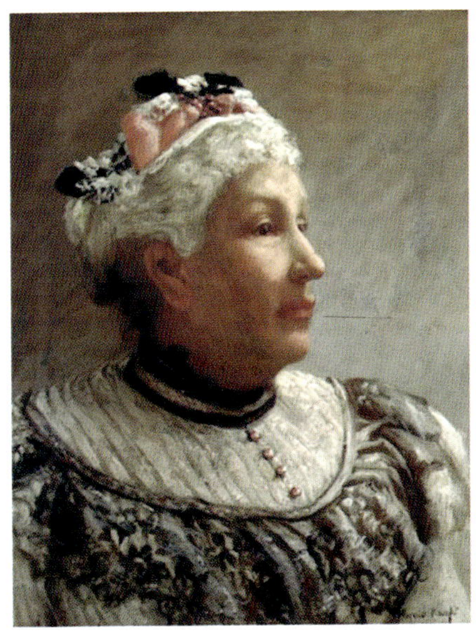

Plate 3. Harold Knight Charlotte Bates ('Big Grandma'), *1893–4, oil on canvas. Image reproduced with the kind permission of Mr & Mrs J Wheeldon.*

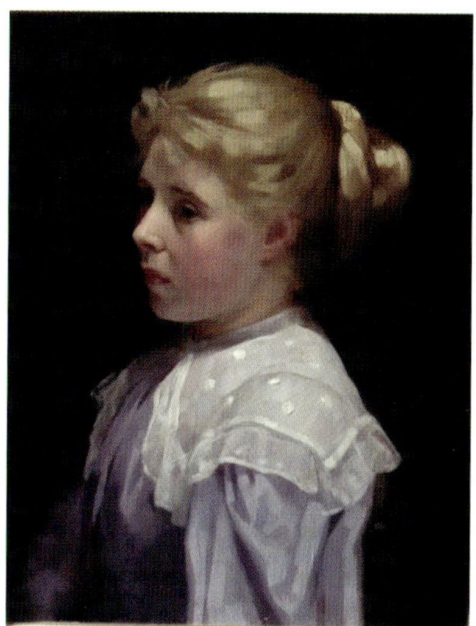

Plate 4. Laura Johnson (Knight) Eva Johnson *('Sis'), 1896, oil on canvas. Private collection.*

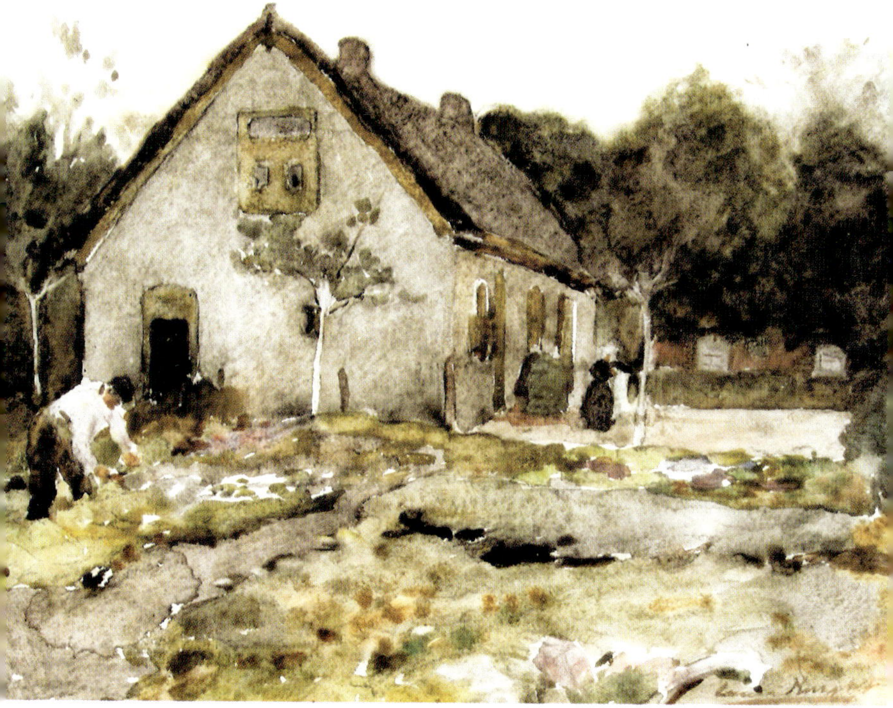

Plate 5. Laura Knight A Cottage on Laren, *1905, watercolour. Image courtesy of Mr and Mrs J Edwards.*

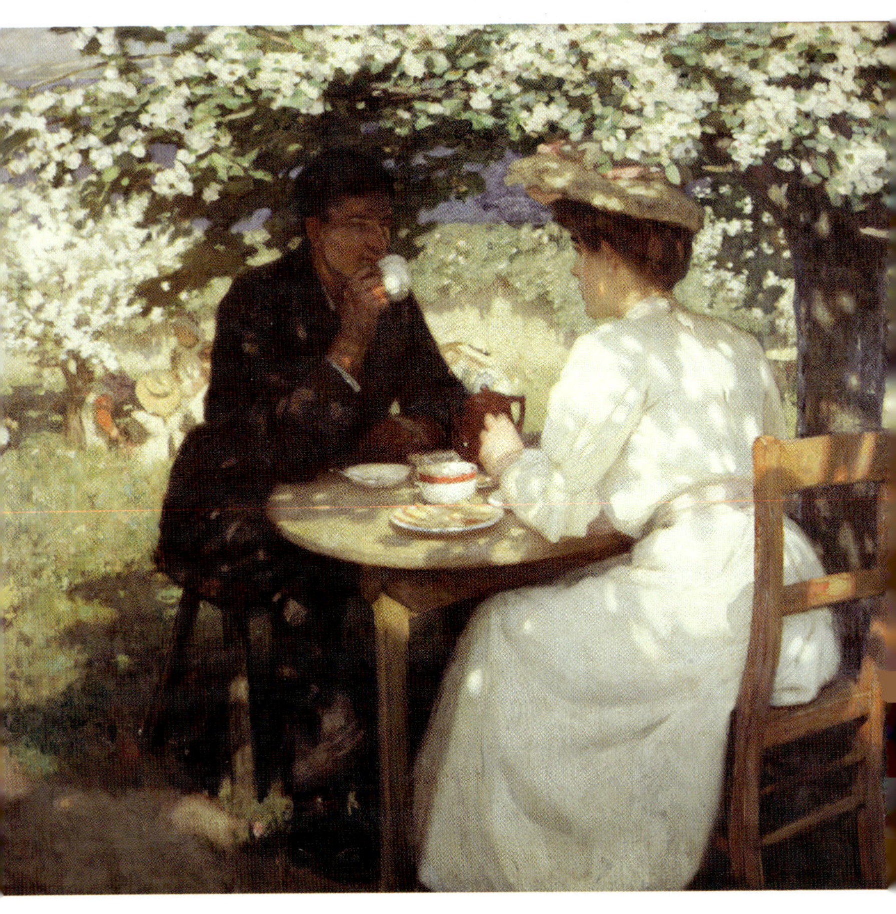

Plate 6. Harold Knight In the Springtime *aka* In the Spring, *1908, oil on canvas. Laing Art Gallery, Tyne & Wear Museums.*

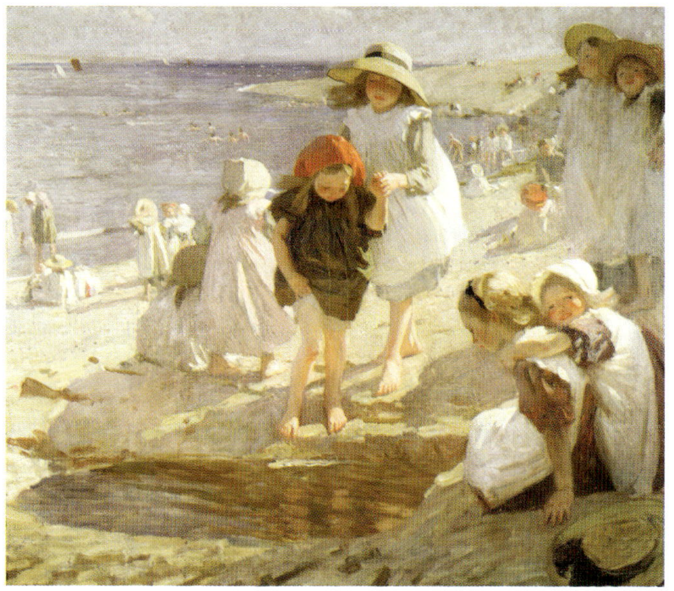

Plate 7. Laura Knight The Beach, *1908, oil on canvas. Laing Art Gallery, Tyne & Wear Museums.*

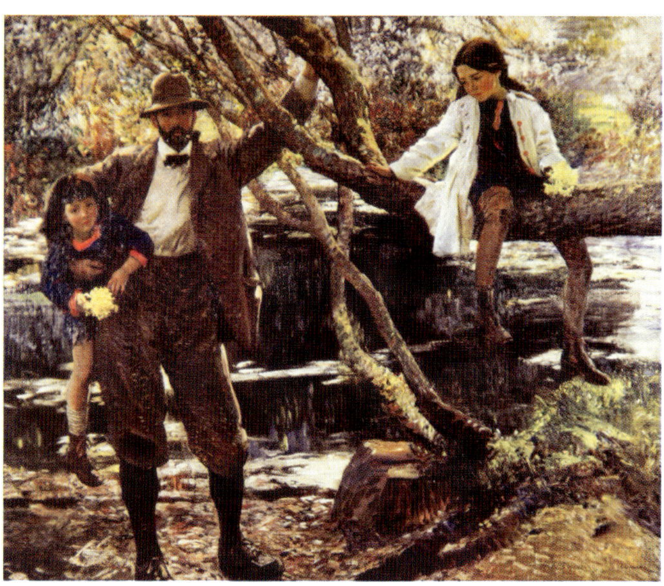

Plate 8. Laura Knight Lamorna Birch and His Daughters, *1916 and 1933, oil on canvas. Nottingham University.*

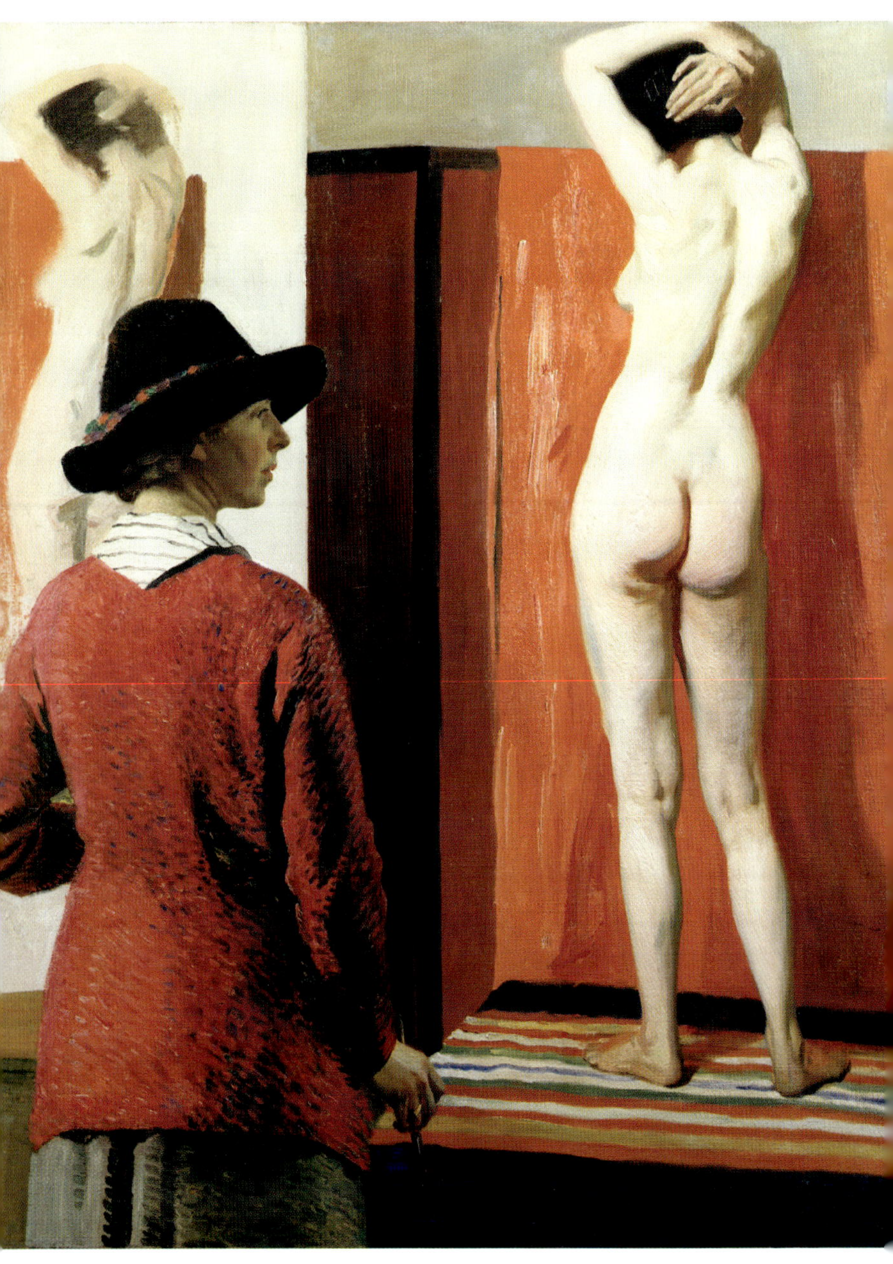

Plate 9. Laura Knight Self Portrait, *1913, oil on canvas. National Portrait Gallery, London.*

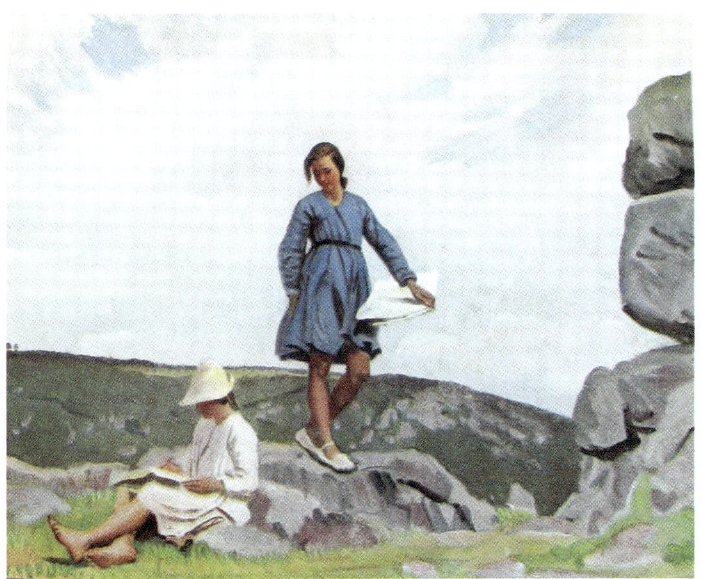

Plate 10. Laura Knight Young Artists, *1921, oil on canvas*. From Modern Painting 1: The Work of Laura & Harold Knight, *1921. Private Collection.*

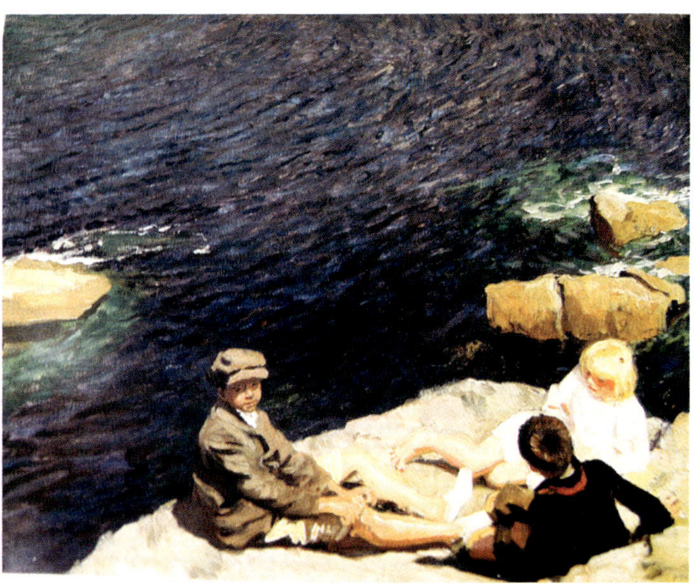

Plate 11. Laura Knight By the Sea, *1921, oil on canvas*. From Modern Painting 1: The Work of Laura & Harold Knight, *1921. Private Collection.*

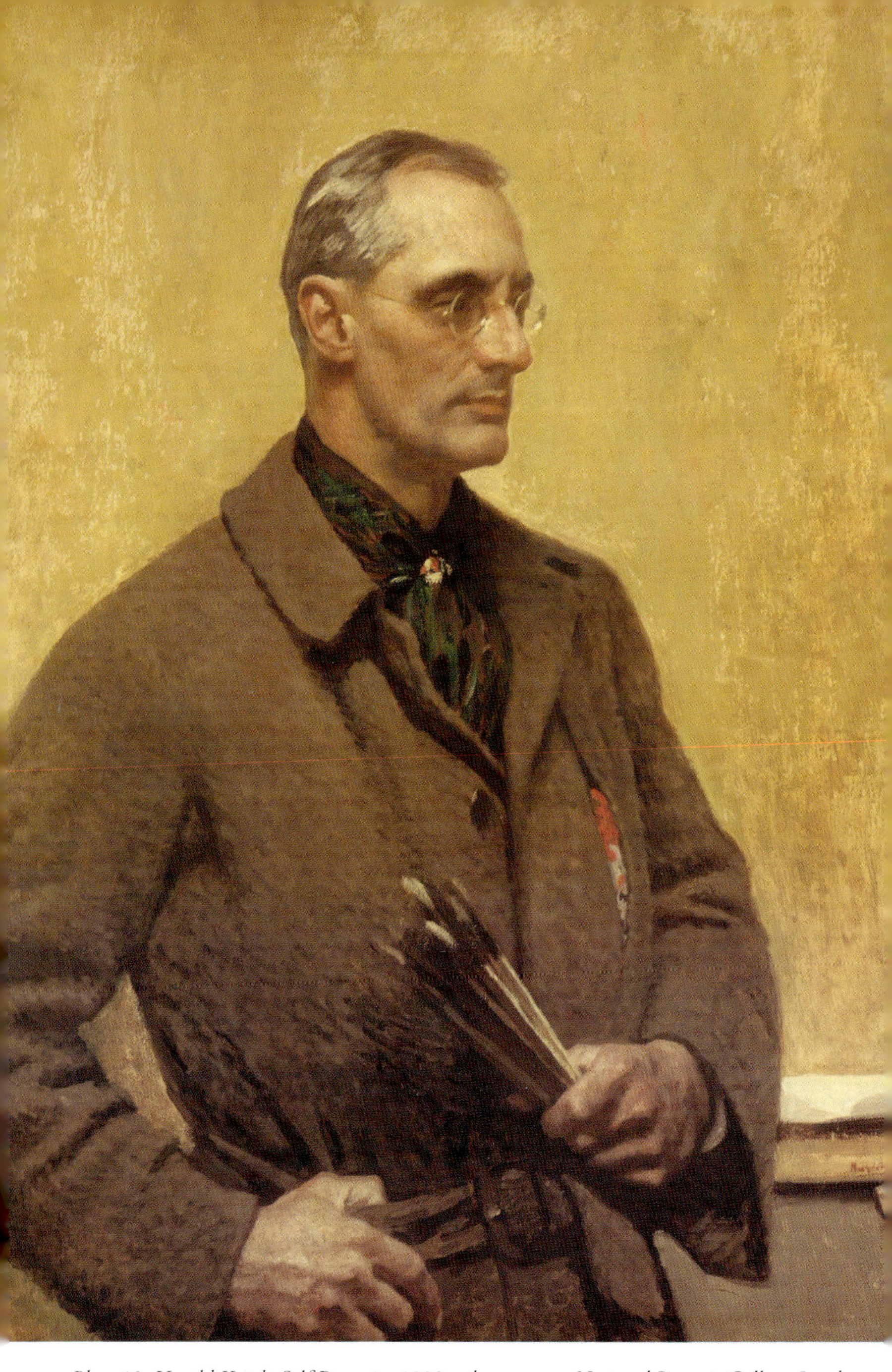

Plate 12. Harold Knight Self Portrait, *1923, oil on canvas. National Portrait Gallery, London.*

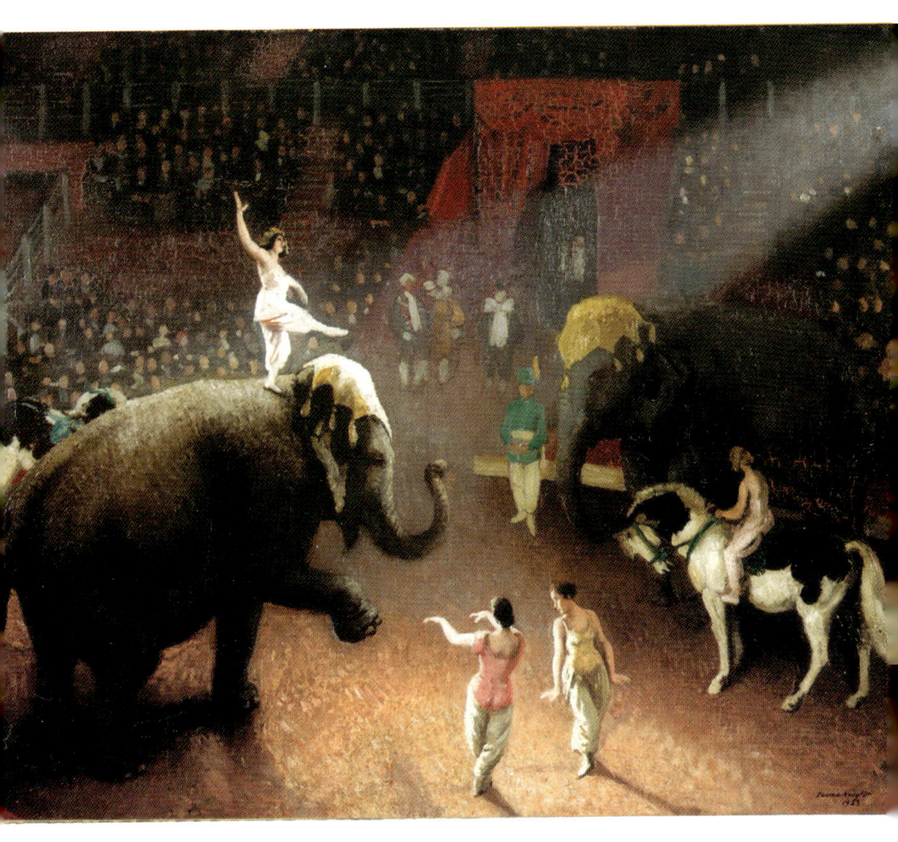

Plate 13. Laura Knight Salt and Saucy, *1923, oil on canvas. Private collection.*

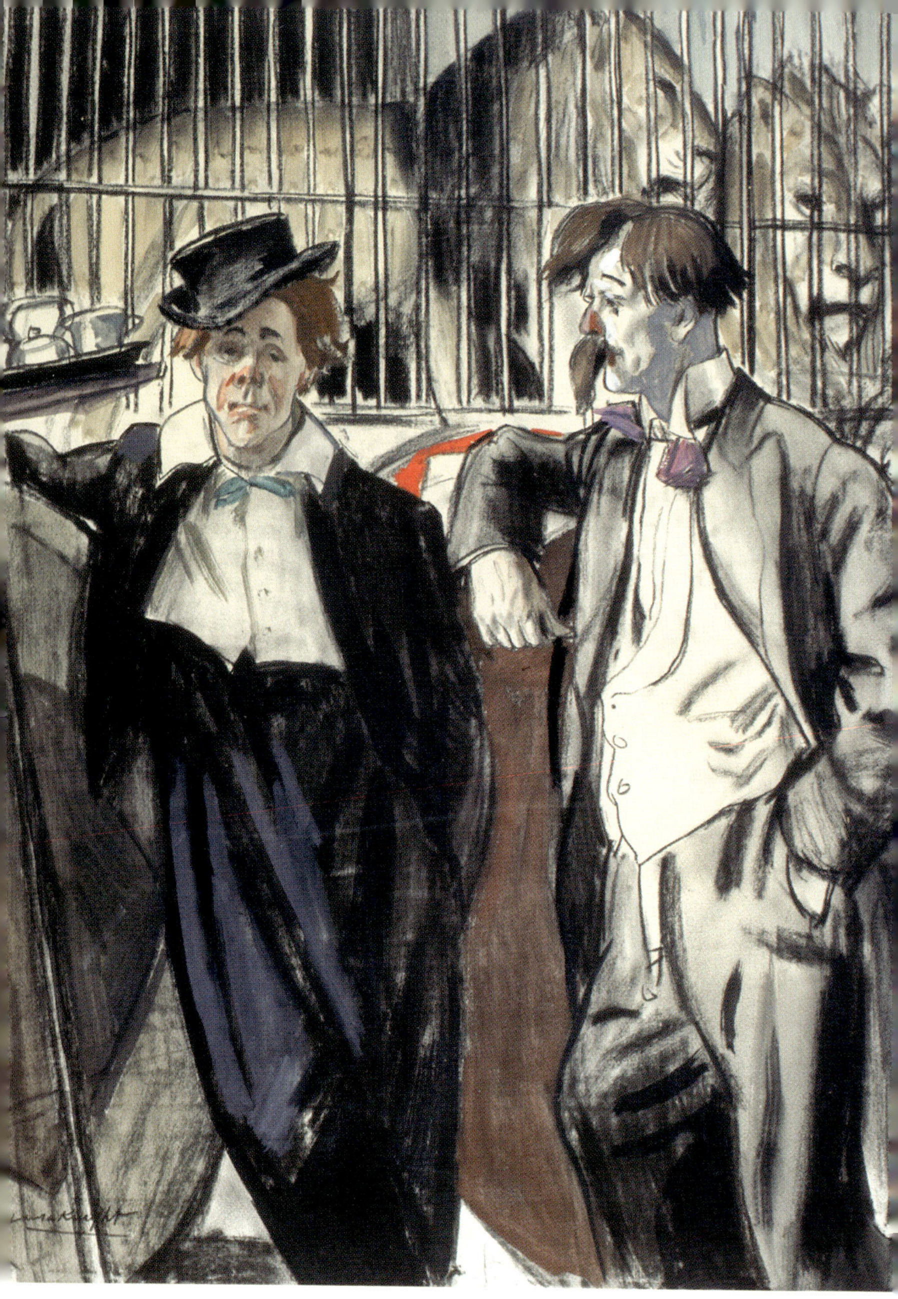

Plate 14. Laura Knight Two O'gust and Two Lions, *1930, watercolour. Laing Art Gallery, Tyne and Wear Museums.*

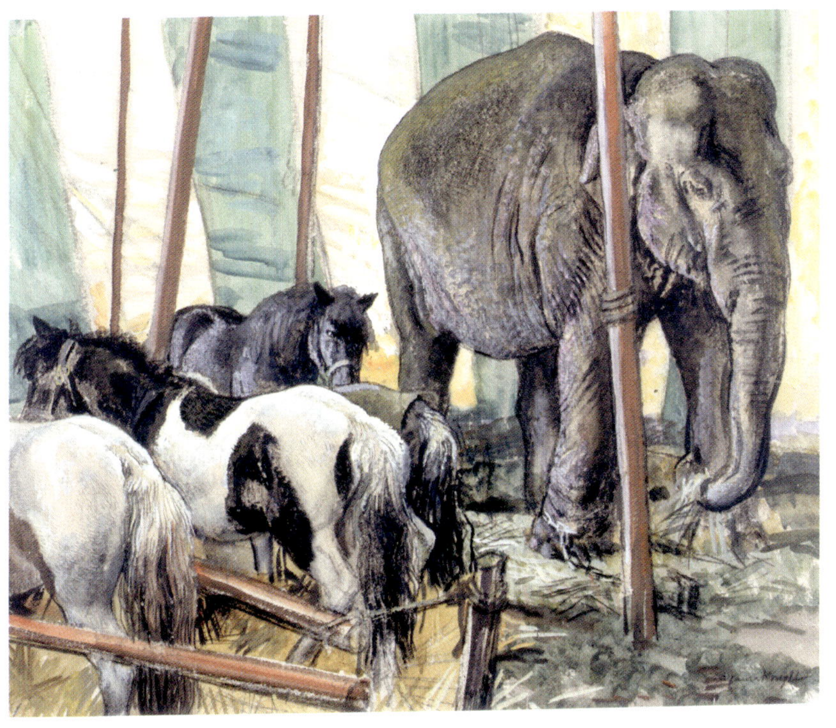

Plate 15. Laura Knight Mary and the Shetland Ponies, *1930, watercolour. Laing Art Gallery, Tyne & Wear Museums.*

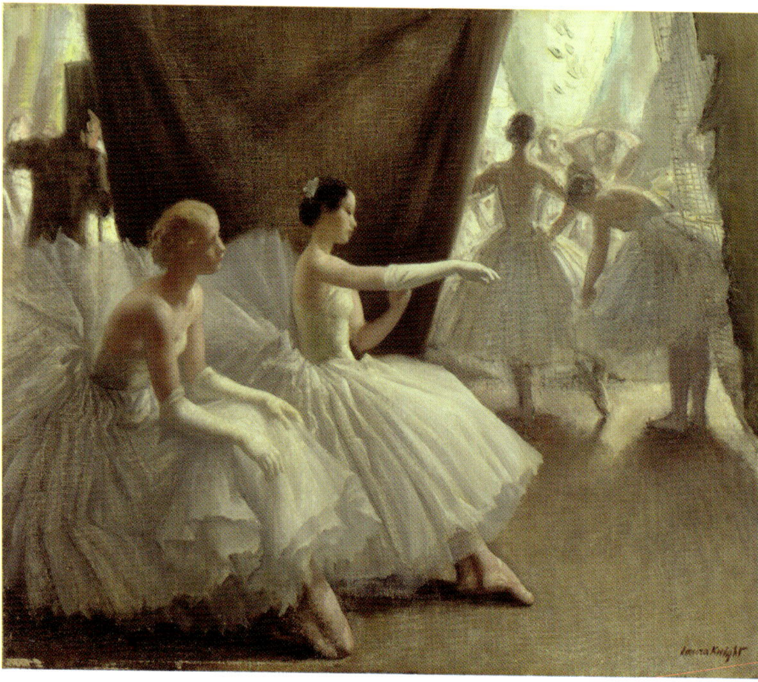

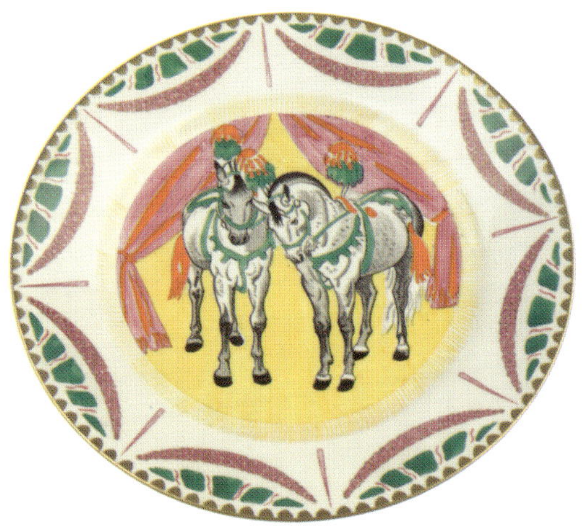

Plate 16. Laura Knight Ballet, *1936, oil on canvas. Lady Lever Art Gallery, National Museums Liverpool.*

Plate 17. Laura Knight 'Circus' plate, 1935. Laing Art Gallery, Tyne and Wear Museums.

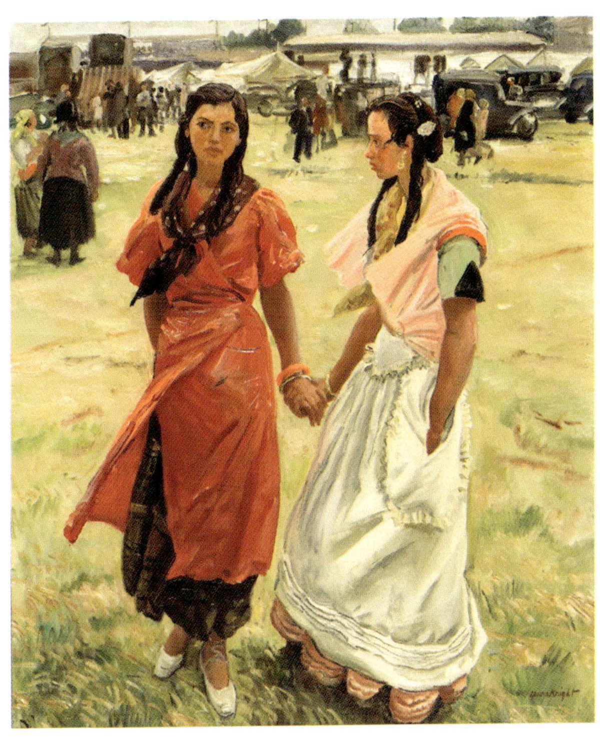

Plate 18. Laura Knight Ascot Finery, *1936/8, oil on canvas.
Dundee Art Galleries & Museums (Dundee City Council).*

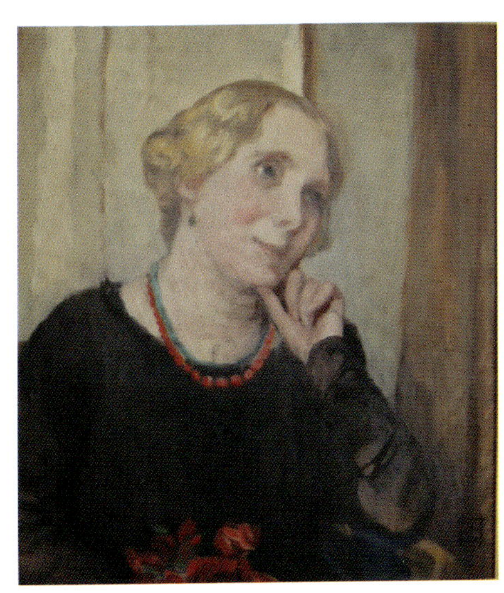

Plate 19. Laura Knight Eva Crofts
*(née Johnson) ('Sis'), 1946, oil on canvas.
Private collection.*

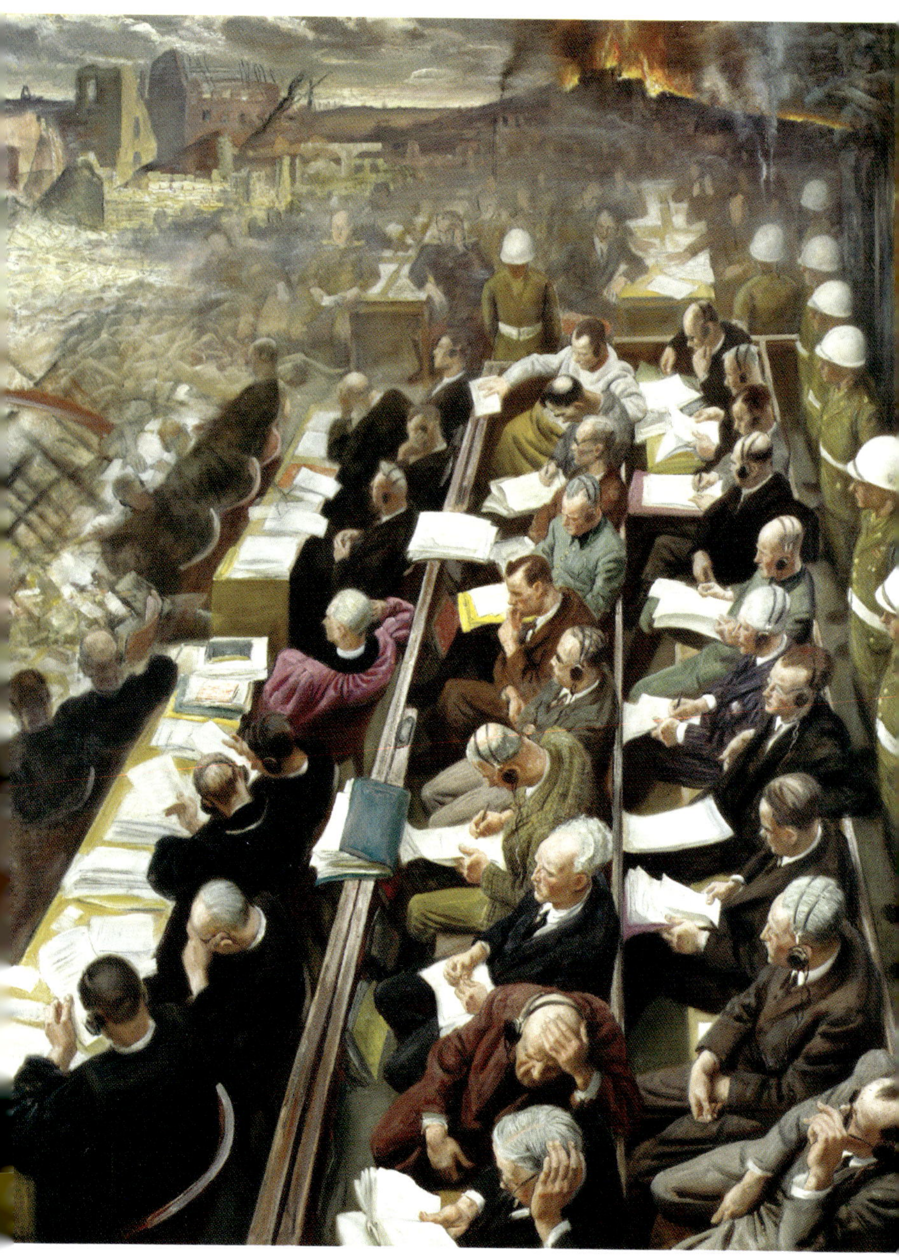

Plate 20. Laura Knight The Nuremberg Trial, *1946, oil on canvas.*
© *Imperial War Museum, London.*

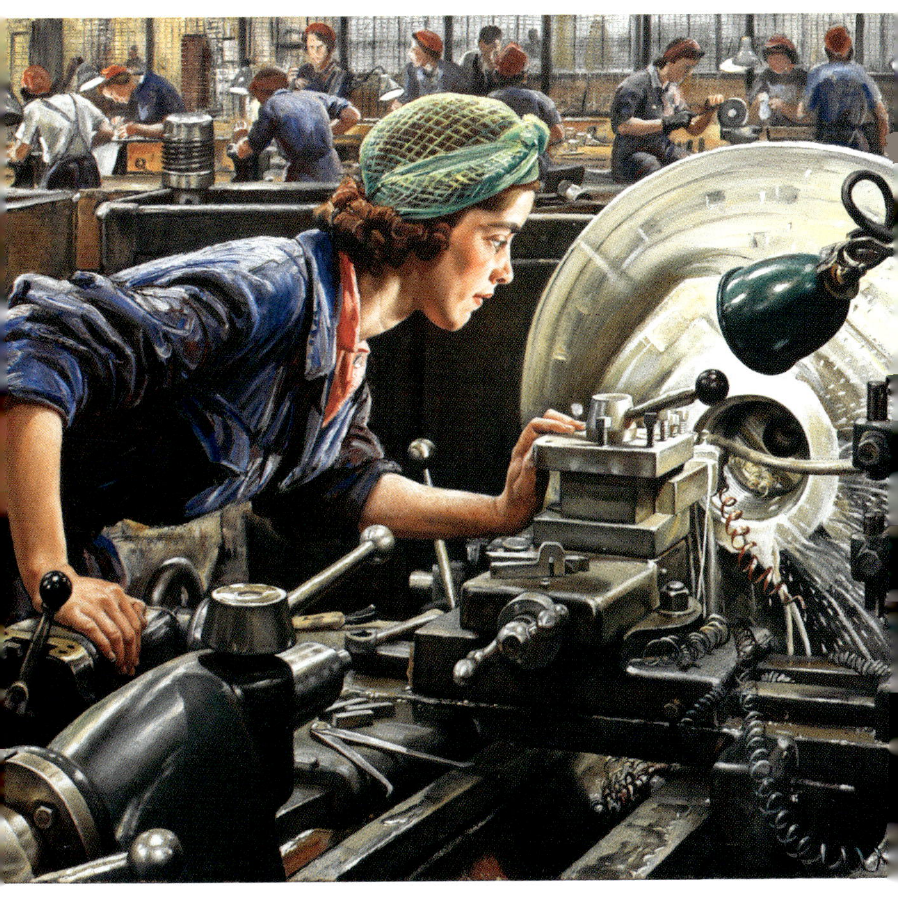

Plate 21. Laura Knight Ruby Loftus Screwing Breech Ring, *1943, oil on canvas.*
© *Imperial War Museum, London.*

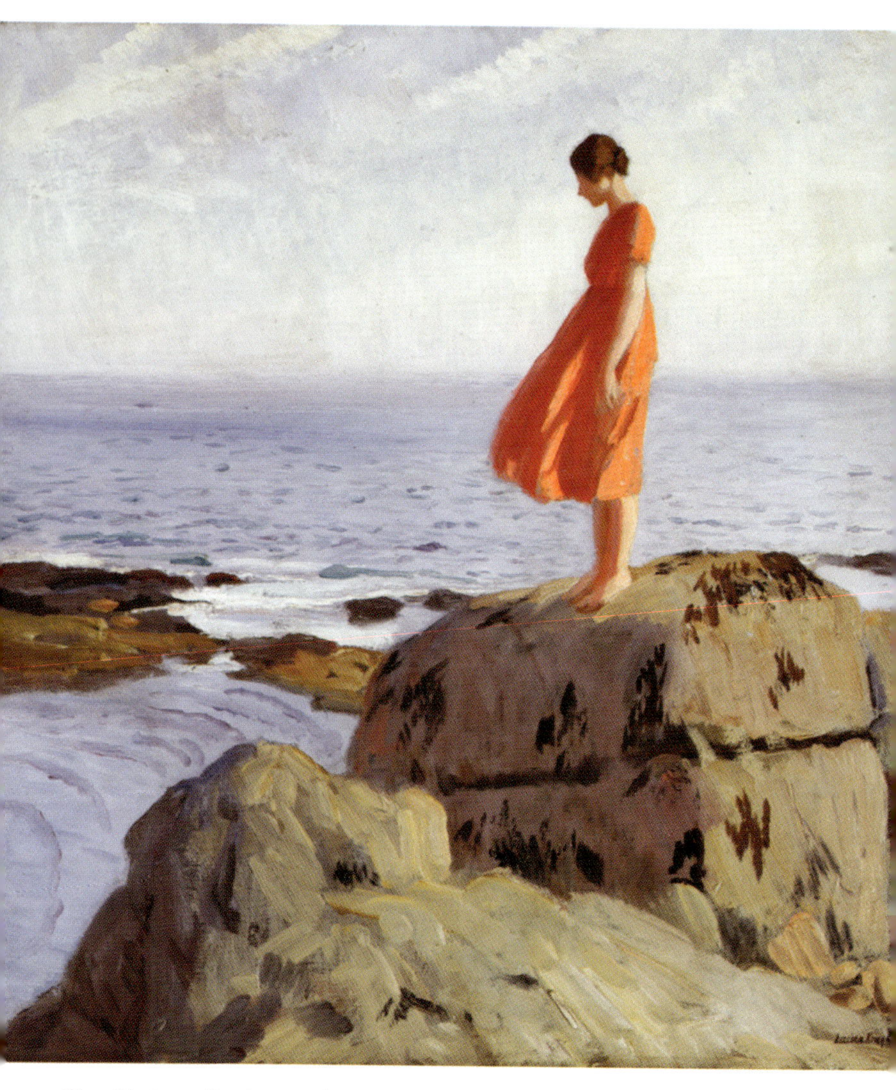

Plate 22. Laura Knight A Dark Pool, *1908–18, oil on canvas. Laing Art Gallery, Tyne & Wear Museums.*

for the sheer joy of being alive. That physical exuberance was encouraged by her friendship with her model Dolly Snell, the Tiller Girl with whom she practiced ballet steps, high kicks and somersaults in the living room at Trevarveneth. It was further focused when, in 1909 on a visit to London, Dolly arranged for her to attend Tiller's practice room in St Martin's Lane. Laura was entranced by the sights, sounds, smells and distilled energy of the whole experience. She paid for two terms' dancing lessons, but, to the distaste of the dancing mistress, had sat herself down in a corner to sketch rather than join in the dance. It was, she says, a scene for Dégas: the resined floor, the line of dancers dressed in a motley array of old costumes, and herself with sketchpad and pencil. That image was imprinted on her memory and fixed there, accompanied by the odours seeping out of the adjacent Crosse and Blackwell jam and pickle factory!

Performance of all kinds (especially her own) had been a passion with Laura from childhood. At Newlyn had joined in the amateur theatricals with gusto, play-acting, costume-making and willingly co-operating with Phyllis Gotch in a display of modern expressive dance. When she and Harold went up to London, Laura would take in as many shows as were on offer – and those offerings were extensive and varied. Before the War she tried to see as many performances as she could of the *prima ballerina* Adelina Genée at the old Empire Theatre, Leicester Square. She inveigled her way back-stage to sketch the dancers – one in particular, Phyllis Beddells, who joined the Empire company in 1907 and became prima ballerina there in 1914. Beddells was to write a lively autobiography record of this period in her life, *My Dancing Days* which was published in 1954. She does not mention the artist who shadowed her every move with her pencil, but Laura remembered her well for her kindness and patience.

Repertoires of London theatres from the late 19th into the next century reflected the changing tastes in popular entertainment of the period. In 1896 the Empire showed the first moving pictures by the Lumière brothers and, by the time Laura knew it, the theatre was fast becoming a popular picture-palace as well as a venue for live performance: music-hall acts, light opera, ballet, clowning and pantomime. Laura's tastes were in no way "high-brow" and she could enter into the spirit of whatever was on offer. She loved pantomime – its anarchic fun, laughter, spectacle and of course audience participation. She was susceptible to the glamour of it all – "glamour" used in the old sense of fairy enchantment – spell-bound by the lights, colour and spectacle, just as she had been as a child at the Fairground in Nottingham. She could enter into this alternative world and reconfigure the boundaries of her life in the way that her favourite stage character Harlequin could, with a wave of his "slapstick" bat, set the stage machinery moving for a grand "transformation scene". In later years Laura was to design party invitations featuring the Harlequin figure in his suit of "motley" –for Harlequin epitomizes her own bravura and sense of style. She was drawn to the fanciful and capricious characters of the Italian *Commedia dell'Arte,* the knockabout farce, acrobatics and spectacle.

Then, in 1911, in their first season in London, Diaghilev's *Ballet Russes* danced Schumann's *Carnival* with its combination of music, dance, pantomimic fun and sentiment. Harlequin was danced by Nijinksy, Columbine by Tamara Karsavina, Bronislava Nijinska (Nijinsky's sister) as Papillon; Adolf Bolm played the sad clown Pierrot; and the great Russian choreographer and teacher, Cecchetti, played the old Pantalon. Laura was in raptures. The *Ballet Russes* had debuted in Paris in 1910, featuring Nijinsky, Karsavina, Nijinska and Anna Pavlova. In that season, productions of Rimsky-Korsakov's *Schéhérazade* (with choreography by Fokine and costumes by Bakst), Vaslav Nijinsky's *Danse Siamoise* and Stravinsky's *The Firebird* created a sensation. The stage exploded with a riot of colour and exoticism.

Then in 1911 Diaghilev and Stravinsky collaborated to create the ballet *Petrushka,* in which the fairground puppet was danced by Nijinsky. His was a vital role in the processes of change and modernity in European ballet. However, this form of dance which show-cased the male dancer rather than the ballerina was not well received by an audience brought up on the classical ballet. For instance, Nijinsky's languid choreography and sensual interpretation of Debussy's *L'après midi d'un Faune* in 1912 caused consternation and was described as obscene. Even more notorious was *The Rite of Spring*, also choreographed by Nijinsky, which premiered in Paris in 1913. Stravinsky's experimental a-tonal score, the provocative costumes and insistent, elemental rhythms of the dance, were considered to be an affront to all decency and civilized society. It was howled off the stage.

The dancers of the *Ballet Russes* had first appeared in London for two seasons at the Royal Opera House, Covent Garden, during the Coronation celebrations for King George V in 1911. Over the following decade they returned regularly with breaks only during wartime. Then, after a financially disastrous production of *The Sleeping Princess* in 1921–2, there was a 4-year gap. In the subsequent seasons of 1926, 1927 and 1928 the company only performed short pieces as part of a variety bill. It was but a shadow of itself and when Diaghilev died in 1929, it dispersed. Over the years the *Ballet Russes* performed at a range of venues – in the first flush of fame at

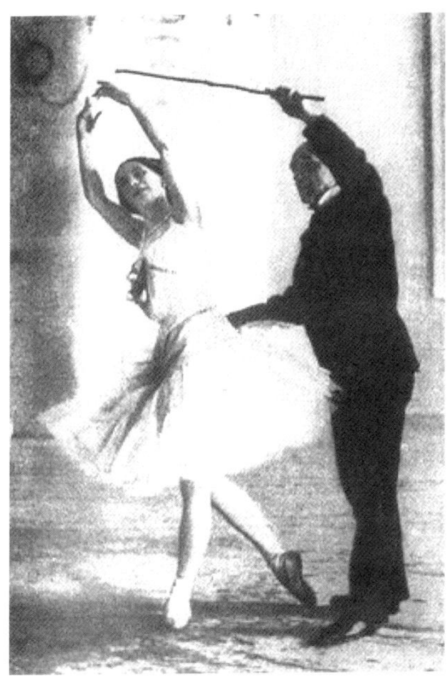

Enrico Cecchetti teaching Anna Pavlova, 1907. Public domain

Covent Garden and Drury Lane and then after the War in 1918 at the London Coliseum. In later years, from around 1926, a reduced repertoire was presented at the Lyceum, the Haymarket, the Princes, the Empire and Alhambra Theatres, but now as part of a programme of variety acts. Laura was there from the start in 1911, managing to get a free ticket for the first autumn season, courtesy of Mr Steer, her picture-framer. It was then that she saw Anna Pavlova and Nijinsky dance together – but for the last time. Always an uneasy relationship, the partnership could not sustain two such super-egos. In 1909 Pavlova had become Diaghilev's principal dancer, but she had refused the lead part in *Firebird* as she could not come to terms with Stravinsky's score, so the lead was given to Tamara Karsavina.

In 1910 Pavlova set up her own *Anna Pavlova Company*, making its debut on 18th April at The Palace Theatre. It was there that Laura first saw Pavlova partnered by Mikhail Mordkin, performing a classical *pas de deux* that received ten curtain calls (remarkable for what was after all a music hall) and then a shockingly modern piece of abandonment, the *Autumn Bacchanal.* In 1911 she was at the premiere of *Les Sylphides,* danced by the Diagilev company with Pavolva as soloist. This production is the likely source of studies worked up into her painting *Les Sylphides* of 1915. Pavlova's final break with the *Ballet Russes* came in 1912 when Nijinsky mocked her acceptance of the invitation to appear at the first Royal Command Performance at the Palace Theatre, which, like so many others, was best known for music hall. For Laura, unaware of any such tensions, to experience the *Ballet Russes* was nothing short of a miracle and she felt 'sorry for anyone who did not see Diaghilev's first seasons' in London. It was an experience that gave her the 'feeling of being born again to a new and glamorous world, with complete satisfaction in every sense'.

In many respects the Knights' artistic paths diverged from this time. Harold was much in demand with ongoing commissions to paint the portraits of public figures politicians, churchmen and the aristocracy. These took him away for days, sometimes weeks. Laura, meanwhile, explored her latest subject, setting up her studio in the precincts of the footlights. From a reserved seat in the stalls, in the second season of the *Ballet Russes* she managed to sketch and complete a painting of Nijinsky partnering Karsavina in the *Pavilion de Armande*. But, for Laura the picture was unsatisfactory- it was too static and, in one her 'destructive rages' to which she was occasionally susceptible, she destroyed it. The petulance was regretted later for she had recorded 'something wonderful'. In 1912 she exhibited her first ballet pictures at the Leicester Galleries and in 1914 nine of her ballet drawings were exhibited at the Carnegie Hall Pittsburgh. At this time, she was driven by her compulsion to sketch from the wings and backstage so that she might try to transform physical *mass* into the rhythm and energy that is dance.

Her experiments with 'pure line' developed into what she describes as a technique based on 'rhythm, repetition of a line, accented beat and cross rhythm, as in music'. Laura credits herself with the coinage of the word *rhythm* in relation to the visual arts. Having tried it on Paul Konody, apparently this word 'was seized with avidity by the Art Press and used in every art criticism – we had never heard it in the same connection before'. However, Roger Fry had identified *rhythm* as the first component of *significant form* in his 'Essay in Aesthetics' published in *The New Quarterly* in 1909. It was a concept much debated at the time within the context of Modernism – an attempt to integrate the arts – literary, visual and musical – and in doing so break through the barriers of academic 'discipline' and achieve a unified aesthetic. Laura's ballet sketches extended the concept and brought the human body into play. She refined the lines of the dancers' movements, drawing with great rapidity to capture each frame of the action. One further experiment, emulating and encouraged by her friend Ella Naper, was her work with enamels: exquisite small pieces some 12 centimetres wide featuring the dancers Nijinsky, Karsavina and Pavlova in brilliant colours of red, green and gold, all bearing the mark LK&EN. These were displayed at the Fine Art Society in 1915 and still shine jewel bright. One example, showing Harlequin and Columbine from *Carnaval*, can be seen at Penlee House, Art Gallery, Penzance.

After the War, while maintaining a base in Cornwall, the Knights re-located to London and within easy reach of live theatre and the galleries. Their first rooms were at 10 Abbey Road (a location best known through the Abbey Road Studios of Beatles fame) and then in 1920 they took two studios with living space at numbers 1 and 2 Queen's Road off the Finchley Road in St John's Wood. This building bore a plaque testifying that Thomas Hood the humourist and poet had died there. This seemed to Laura to be particularly appropriate since one of Hood's poems had been a staple of her childhood recitation repertoire when she would regularly declaim from *Faithless Nelly Gray*, 1826: 'Ben Battle was a soldier bold, used to war's alarms. A cannon ball took off his legs, so he laid down his arms'. Then when, having left College, she and Sis were living in the Cave Studio, Laura had contemplated a painting to illustrate Hood's famous poem *The Song of a Shirt* as she he recalls in Chapter 4 of *Oil Paint and Grease Paint*: 'It was to contain all the pathos of "Stitch, Stitch, Stitch!" I had not forgotten my old friend Thomas Hood'. The Knights retained the 'Thomas Hood Studio' for many years.

When the *Ballet Russes* returned to London in 1919–20, Diaghilev himself gave permission for Laura to work back-stage at The Coliseum. It was at this point that she consciously developed her natural facility with pencil and charcoal to work 'the magic of a line'. This was important work, for in her later autobiography, which takes the phrase as its title, she writes: 'I firmly believe the most valuable study I ever have had was in my attempt to draw the ballet. Never before had I tried to make the pencil speak in a language all its own.' In 1920, on the initiative of Paul Konody, some of her ballet drawings were published as *Twenty one drawings of the Russian Ballet by Laura Knight with an introductory note by PG Konody* (Davis & Orioli). This is now a very rare publication, largely because many copies have been broken up and plates sold individually.

It was the start of a new and exciting phase of her developing career as a painter of ballet. Lydia Lopokova (later the wife of the economist Maynard Keynes) was particularly helpful in response to Laura's request to be able to work backstage and invited her to sketch in her dressing-room. In the

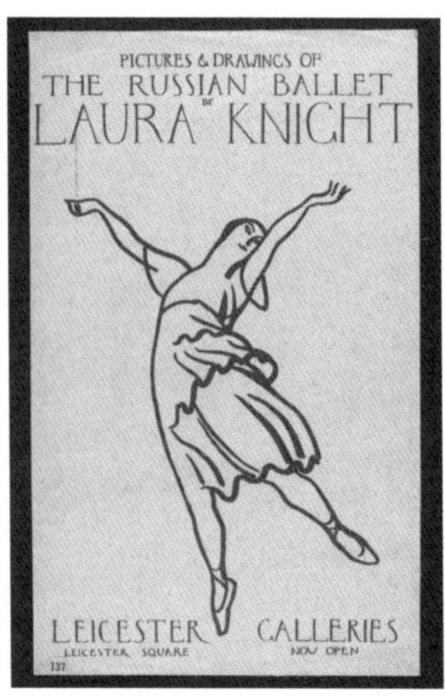

Poster. Public domain

'Coliseum' chapter of *Oil Paint and Grease Paint* Laura writes: 'For many months the pink walls of Lopokova's dressing-room held my interest. I sat in a corner, silent like a shadow, studying and making notes of everything that happened from taking off the day dress to the final fantasy'. The outcome, she writes, was to make great strides in draughtsmanship. It also offered strong contrasts of light, shade and vibrant colour which she was to use to great effect in her work. Paintings from this time include *Before the Mirror*, *Before the Curtain* and *Peeping Through the Curtain*. In each of these images the artist communicates to us the strange littoral spaces of theatre, where artifice and reality confront one another across the orchestra pit.

Backstage everything 'was glorious to paint; the contrast between the stagehands, the black-clothed dresser and the artificial brilliance of net and tulle; the character of the make-up table, its little candle to heat the eyelash black, the white enamelled furniture and the white drugget on the floor – even the old red-plush arm-chair was a thing of joy. While Laura was much taken with the ephemeral vision of the *corps de ballet* on stage, delicate floating creatures in ballets such as *Les Sylphides* and *Giselle,* more interesting for her was life back-stage, in the wings, behind the flats and in the dressing-rooms. She was fascinated by the metamorphosis achieved through costume and make-up, the processes of transformation on which the illusion of theatre depends. She describes the atmosphere in Chapter 21

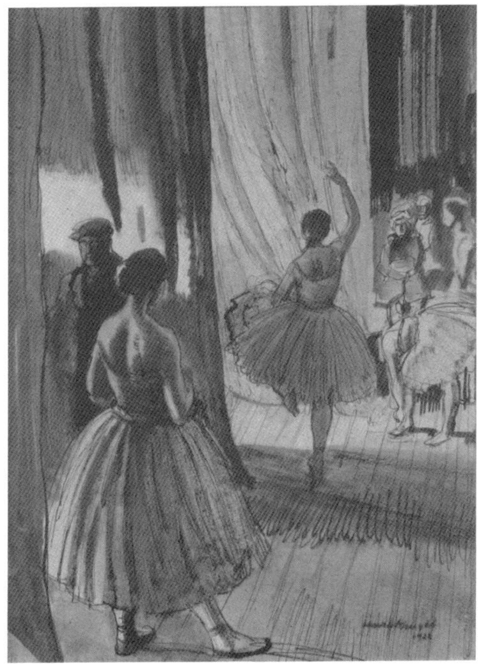

Laura Knight, *Ballerinas*, 1922. Public domain

of *Oil Paint and Grease Paint*: the crowded rooms where 'girls in every stage of dress and undress from bare body and tights to "ready"'; the dressers, working within their own sub-culture, dependable, cheery for whoever is in this week: 'Panto- opera – ballet – just another crowd to hook up and peel'; and the *sylph* applying her black mascara and rouge before the harsh lights of the dressing table. These are no spirits but physical human beings working to exhaustion to conjure glamour for the audience.

Brilliant colour, strong contrasts of light and dark appealed to Laura as over the succeeding seasons the *Ballet Russes* repertoires at the Coliseum, the Alhambra and the Empire offered a programme of exciting 'modern' ballets – short and stylish. *La Parade* premiered in Paris in 1917 with music by Satie, 'cubist' design and costumes by Picasso with some 'surreal' input from Jean Cocteau. It came to London in the 1918–19 season at the Alhambra Theatre, together with *The Three-Cornered Hat*. The drama and the passion of this last, with its choreography that incorporated Spanish *fandango*, the *sevillanas* and the *farruca* was all to Laura's delight. Diaghilev followed this

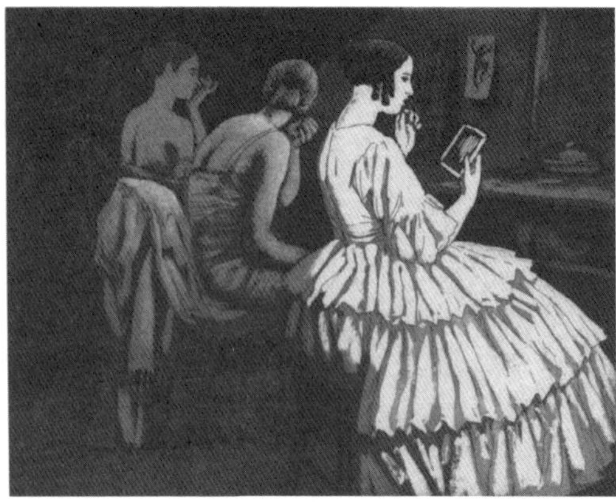

Dressing Room No 2,
etching and aquatint. Laing
Art Gallery, Tyne & Wear
Museums

up by bringing a troupe of Spanish gypsies to London. This show was hugely popular with the public who were known to mob the stars. Laura loved the excitement and controlled wildness of the dance and captured it in her sketches of the time and in the splendid aquatints she made of *Flamenco Dancers* in the early 1920s.

Her study of the rhythm of a line was much aided by Lopokova's introducing her in 1920 to the maestro Enrico Cecchetti and his master classes at Chandos Hall in Maida Vale. Cecchetti had enjoyed an esteemed career as a dancer within the Imperial Ballet in St Petersburg, before developing his

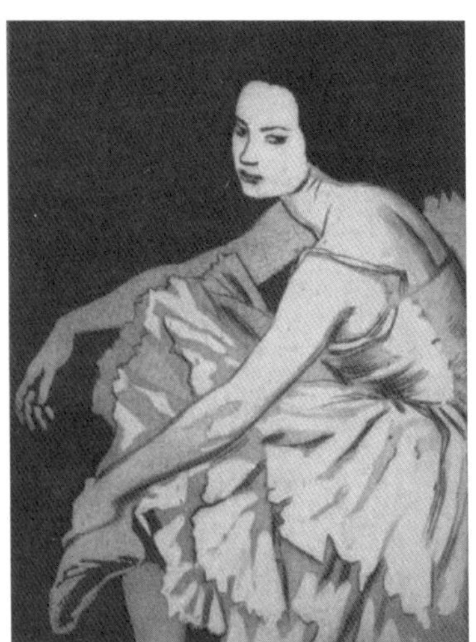

Dancer Resting, 1923, etching and aquatint.
Laing Art Gallery, Tyne & Wear Museums

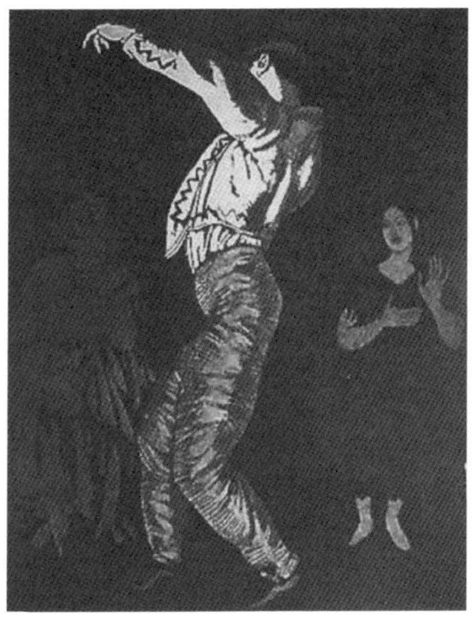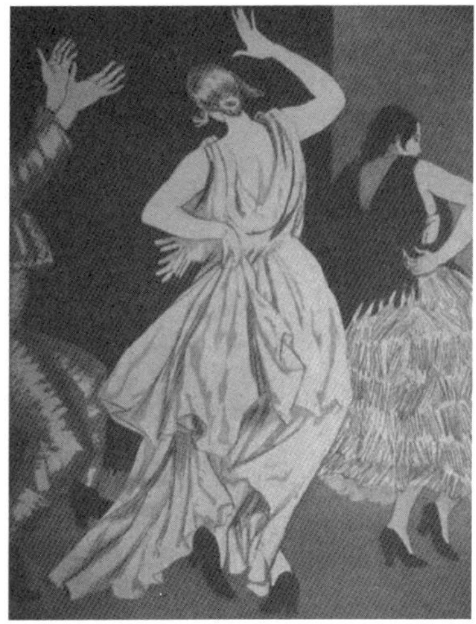

Russian Ballet Nos.10 and 14, 1920, drawing. From *21 Drawings of the Russian Ballet*, 1921.
Private collection

particular method of teaching which was based on an awareness of anatomy and expressive line in the dance. For this very reason he and Laura shared common goals and he acknowledged that, demanding the greatest accuracy of position and balance in his dancers as well as in her drawings of them. Cecchetti and his wife soon became friend of the Knights, entertaining and being entertained by this distinguished and charming couple. Laura worked in the Dance School for 2 years until Cechetti's retirement in 1924. As well as a wealth of drawings, *A Dancer Resting* and *A Dancing class at Maestro Cecchetti's School* belonging to this period. She credited his tuition and per-fectionism in refining her own technique and standards: 'I speak so much of Cecchetti's classes because they had an immense effect on me. Perfection of balance and line became my ideal also, and I revelled in the joy of line for its own sake; the infinite possibilities of composition as exemplified by the human body in movement filled my mind'. *Comme la photographie!* was the great man's comment one day as he watched her work. She was uncertain how to react – did he mean as in a "studio" photograph or, as perhaps she hoped, did he mean as in a "moving" picture? If it was the latter, then he understood her absolutely.

Meanwhile, the great *prima ballerinas* – Lopokova, Karsavina, Tchernicheva and Pavlova – provided Laura with further affirmation of her own commitment and expectation of distinction in her own art. They were

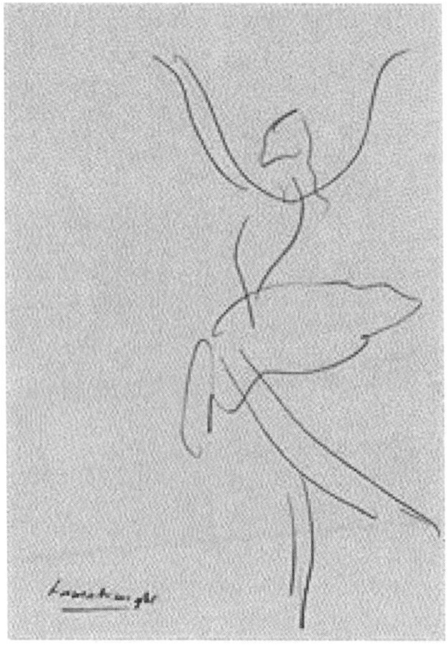

Laura Knight *The Magic of a Line*: from series of Balletic Sketches. Public domain

her role models, as Timothy Wilcox writes in *Laura Knight at the Theatre*: 'For Knight they were more than performers; they embodied the female artist at the very summit of her profession, a position Knight had not yet reached, but knew to be within her grasp'. It was Laura's association with Anna Pavlova that was particularly significant in determining for her the role and status of a professional artist. Pavlova had danced with the Imperial Russian Ballet until 1909 and was *prima ballerina* in the *Ballet Russes* on its first European tour in 1910. After forming her own company, she toured widely in Europe and the United States and as a result was and continues to be revered internationally as the greatest ballerina of all time.

After the Great War the independent Pavlova Ballet Company performed at Drury Lane, and in 1920 Cechetti had introduced Laura to Anna Pavlova herself, who gave permission for her to work back-stage. Imperious though she might be, the great lady acknowledged Laura's presence, inviting her into the dressing-room at Drury Lane to sketch. From 1921 Laura also regularly visited her at her home, Ivy House in Hampstead with its famous ornamental lake and tame swan. While Pavlova was the quintessential *Giselle*, her reputation and association with swans is due to her role as *The Dying Swan* – a role that had been choreographed for her in 1905 by

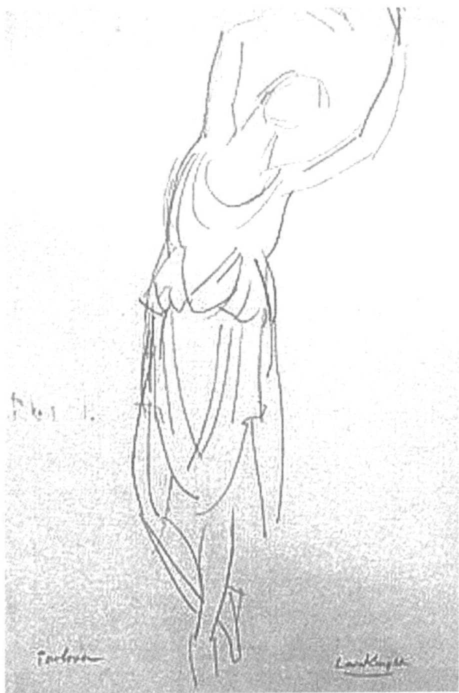

Laura Knight sketch of Pavlova. Public domain

Fokine to music by Saint-Saens. This was her signature dance and Laura pictured it as early as 1912. Laura's association with Pavlova meant that she became much sought after as a primary source of information about this enigmatic dancer. In Chapter 28 of *Oil Paint and Grease Paint* she writes: 'I found Pavlova to be the sort of person you had got to look at all the time, whatever happened – you just could not help it. I can imagine her being almost lonely – she did not belong to this world … Although I was almost near enough to touch her when performing, I felt she was not there in the flesh but only in spirit'.

Nonetheless Pavolva could and did act the *prima donna*. Once, when Laura was distracted by the back-stage colour and activity, a note was sent: 'Madame Pavlova asks will Mrs Knight please confine her attention to the stage', meaning of course Madame Pavlova expected all attention to be directed towards herself. There was a fierceness about the ballerina that is captured in Laura's well-known ink portrait of her and several drawings which

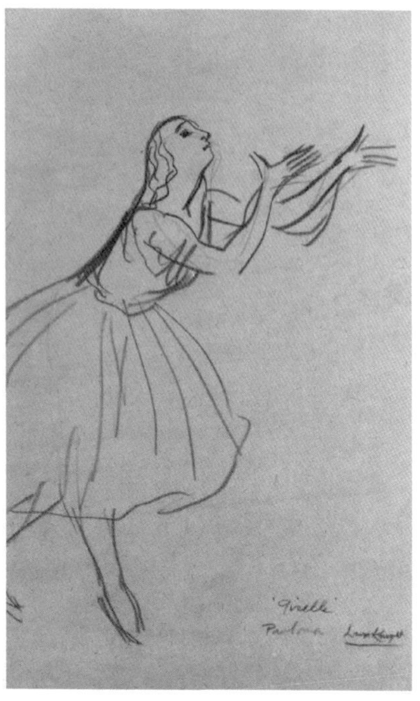

A study of Pavlova in *Giselle* by Laura Knight c.1925. Nottingham Archive

show a drawn, even hawkish mask. Yet there was also a companionable aspect to the relationship between artist and ballerina. When work was finished for the day at Ivy House, Pavlova would accompany Laura in the car that took her back to her studio. On one occasion, Laura recalls, Pavlova took off her shoe for Laura to examine her perfectly formed foot – strong and yet delicate so that one's 'finger and thumb could meet behind the tendon above the heel'. It makes a good story.

Whatever her balletic strength, the dancer's physical frailty was obvious when, exhausted after a performance, she could be seen in the wings, clinging to the theatre curtain for support. A painting Laura made of this intimate moment was lost at sea while being shipped to New Zealand in the *Manuka* disaster of 1929. For several weeks in the summer of 1920 Laura went every day to Ivy House to sketch Pavlova as she practised at the *barre* and instructed her numerous pupils. It was a magical period that ended abruptly. Pavlova was to go on a European tour and they arranged to meet again on her return to Britain. After some months she returned and the

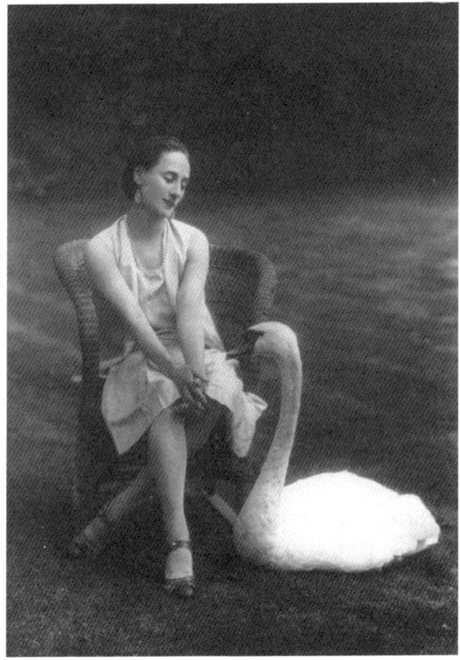

Anna Pavlova at Ivy House, with her pet swan. Public domain

invitation came once more. As arranged, Laura turned up at Ivy House only to be denied access by a Russian door keeper who spoke no English and refused to take a note inside. Typically, Laura was affronted and at once turned on her heels. She was never to see Pavlova again.

The magic of the *Ballet Russes* was also to dissipate after the failure of the extravagant full-length production of Tchaikovsky's *The Sleeping Princess* in 1922. It had been a staple of the Marinsky Theatre productions of the Russian Imperial ballet, but the London audiences (now used to short intermezzos) neither had the stamina nor the taste for such a heavyweight performance. Audiences were poor and the dancers themselves were rebellious since the extravagantly decorated costumes, specially commissioned and paid for by the impresario Oswald Stoll, proved to be too cumbersome to wear. It was a fiasco. From then the *Ballet Russe* declined, burdened with debts and by the ill-health of Diaghilev himself. However, its demise did not mean the end of Laura's association with the stage or with spectacle. A new act in the grand drama of her life in art was about to begin.

On first re-locating to London, Laura had found it difficult to adjust to the cityscape and closed skies of the metropolis. She missed the sea, the coastline, the fish bought and cooked fresh from the quayside, but above all she missed the companionship of her good friends in Newlyn and Lamorna. However, those friends did come up to London occasionally and kept in contact through the post. Laura was always an enthusiastic correspondent if a haphazard one, her letters often giving the impression of multi-tasking. Her tone can seem dismissive even rude – as in the case of a written note of 1911 in which she brusquely excuses herself for not visiting some American visitors newly arrived in Newlyn, because 'I am a very busy woman and do not pay calls'.

However, when writing to old friends in Cornwall, Laura was always affectionate, at times effusive. She and Ella Naper regularly exchanged letters and Laura was always grateful to hear from her friend and even more grateful for the parcels that Ella sent up to London. These were more often than not gifts of food: a grey mullet that Laura baked in butter – 'it was perfect'; Cornish cream that was impossible to obtain in London; flowers and herbs from Trewoofe garden, and, touchingly, in the spring a posy of primroses. Ella also sent Laura pieces fabric she had found in local markets locally for her to make up as curtains, special pieces of jewellery that she had made and also small items of pottery. Around the time that the Knights located to London, Ella, together with a newcomer to Lamorna, Kate Westrup, had set up a pottery at Lamorna. They made small and colourful bowls and pots. Ella also experimented with figurines. One pair represented herself and Laura in perfect juxtaposition: Ella balletic and stylish while Laura, recognised by her black hat and cape, stands stolid, hand on hip.

It was not too long before both Harold and Laura started to extend their social circle in London. While Harold did not enjoy what he called 'gang life', he did enjoy conversation and a drink with fellow artists. He was sought out in company for his objective grasp of political events and international affairs, his 'astringent wit' (Laura's words) and the capacity to see through cant and pretention of all kinds. He and Laura were often to be seen together at the Café Royal (from the 1860s the haunt of artists, poets and celebrities) or the Chelsea Arts Club on the King's Road and they themselves held parties at the Queen's Road studios. At the Café Royal artists of their acquaintance such as Augustus John, Jacob Epstein and the Sitwells would be regularly seen as well as old friends A.J. Munnings and Barry Jackson. The Knights were becoming part of the "London set". In an after-dinner speech given in 1932 at a dinner in Wellington, New Zealand, the art dealer Murray

Fuller reminisced about the Arts Club, Dover Street and the Chelsea Art Club, where 'on a Saturday night, one will meet practically every member of the Royal Academy' In this context he mentions Harold and Laura Knight, Arnesby Brown and S.J. Lamorna Birch as some of the 'eminent painters' he had met. While Harold went to these places as much to watch as to fraternise, Laura, naturally gregarious, was an active participant, for now she was becoming a celebrity in her own right.

It was in 1923 that Paul Konody suggested that the Knights join him and his daughters on a summer tour of the Italian Tyrol. Neither Laura nor Harold had seen a mountain range before and the spectacular scenery of the region as well as the charming people delighted them both. As usual Laura took her sketching tools – pencils, pad, paints and easel – and made the most of the picturesque subjects of the region. Staying at the village of Madonna di Campillo, in rooms over a café, while the Konody party were in the hotel, the Knights had a very good time. On arrival, they made friends with a Sicilian housepainter who, accepting them as fellow artists, took them on walks and introduced them to the local back-street cafés where music played and there was dancing. Harold was happy walking and relaxing in the sun and Laura sketched everything she saw – it was all so new to her. However, before they returned home, she destroyed most of her efforts, judging them to be of little worth. A great success was the visit to Florence that they fitted in on the return journey.

According to Laura they 'reveled' in the art galleries and yet little is said about them or their impact. What appears to have been foremost in their Florentine experience was their re-connection with an old Newlyn friend Pino Orioli, who had arranged their accommodation. Pino had left Cornwall and returned to Italy to run an antique book shop by the Ponte Vecchio and he took pleasure in introducing them to fellow collectors and book lovers, chief amongst whom were the writer Norman Douglas and Dr and Mrs Leroy Crummer from Omaha. Pino Orilio published a number of Douglas' books as well as works by other English authors, most notably – publishing laws being more relaxed in Italy- the first edition of D.H. Lawrence's *Lady Chatterley's Lover*. In another instance of fortuitous meetings, it was through Dr Crummer that both Harold and Laura were to visit America in 1927. It was all a very pleasant sojourn, only spoiled by learning on the way home that their home had been burgled.

Despite being penniless on their return, enough money came through over the following year to allow them to take a trip to Czechoslovakia in 1925. They travelled by cargo boat to Amsterdam. It was a sentimental visit, returning to old haunts of theirs such as the Café at the Hotel Krasnapolski and of course to the galleries that had opened their eyes to the tradition of Dutch art and provided them both with inspiration in the Laren days. They sought out familiar sights in the streets, but while pleased to see little change in the buildings and canals, they were disappointed to see so few peasants wearing traditional dress. Travelling on by train to Berlin and Dresden, they reached Prague where they were impressed by the mighty river Vlatava, fairy-tale castles and low-eaved houses, carved and decorated with bright ornamentation inside as well as out. Motoring through the Czech countryside they discovered the village of Prachovski Skàly, a place much beloved of artists. There, Laura, always sociable and readily making friends, got to know a local family and through them found accommodation, where Harold quietly smoked his pipe and enjoyed the sunshine while Laura sketched.

It was in Prachovski Skàly that Laura became very excited by the sight of 'peasants in gorgeous costume, with baskets full of flowered shawls and embroideries'. The colour and patterns attracted her eye and affirmed her taste for ethnic design which had been awoken by the visual spectacle of the *Ballet Russes* productions in the first London seasons, and had pleased her when she saw traditional costumes on their visit to the Tyrol. After Czechoslovakia she began to favour the dirndl skirt, fitted bodice and embroidered blouses that, with her hair in plaited earphones, were to fashion her public image from the mid- 1920s until the end of the Second World War

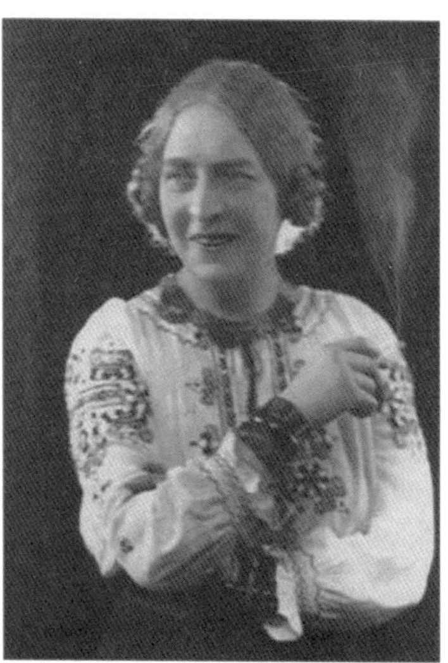

Laura Knight photograph by Bassano studio, showing embroidered blouse and 'earphones'

Around this time the Knights met the young virtuoso pianists Rae Robertson and his fiancé Ethel Bartlett. Rae and Ethel were to become internationally famous as a piano duo, performing in Europe and America until the late 1970s. Harold and Laura were present at the start of their career, sponsoring their first professional recitals at the Wigmore Hall and organising private concerts. At one time Laura even hired a second piano so that they could give a concert in their house at Langford Place. It was to be a long and happy friendship and through the Robertsons, Laura and Harold met and enjoyed the company of many musicians. Ethel played piano at John Barbarolli's violin-cello recitals in the 1920s and "Tito" as he was known to his friends, was a frequent visitor to the Knights' home. On one occasion, he turned up for a party with a string quartet in tow. The atmosphere that night must have been heavy with cigarette smoke, music and song, mingling with the smell of oil paint and linseed, intensifying with the heat – a heady brew.

The Knights also got to know the pianist Harriet Cohen who was the doyen of contemporary British music. Ralph Vaughan Williams, John Ireland, Béla Bartók, all wrote specifically for her, as did her lover Arnold Bax. Harold and Laura regularly attended her salons at which interesting people from the world of the arts would meet: musicians, painters and writers. Often, after concerts there would be evening parties and suppers at private homes. In the Royal Academy of Music archive is a letter written on 5th June 1928 from Arnold Bax's mother, Ellen Ridley Bax to Ethel Robertson, expressing thanks for inviting her to a post-recital evening party, when she met the Knights for the first time: 'I was so happy – both in hearing your wonderful music and in being so cordially and graciously welcomed into your lovely home circle. How splendid Mrs Knight is! Both she and Mr Knight have such strong and arresting personalities'. We must note here that *both* Harold and Laura are described as being 'arresting personalities', which puts a different slant on their relationship and on Harold himself, too often presented as a shy, retiring man in Laura's shadow.

Laura liked Arnold Bax, as she writes in *The Magic of a Line*: 'between Arnold and me a tie existed'. While they were very different in character – Laura noting that he disliked 'displays of any kind'– one of the reasons for the 'tie' was his connection with Cornwall and all things Celtic. His symphonic poem *Tintagel*, composed in 1919, offers 'a tonal impression of the castle crowned cliff of Tintagel, and, more especially, of the long distances of the Atlantic, as seen from the cliffs of Cornwall on a sunny but not windless summer's day'. The words are those of Bax himself, as quoted in a review by Neville Cardus in the *Manchester Guardian* (7th November 1922). In *Oil*

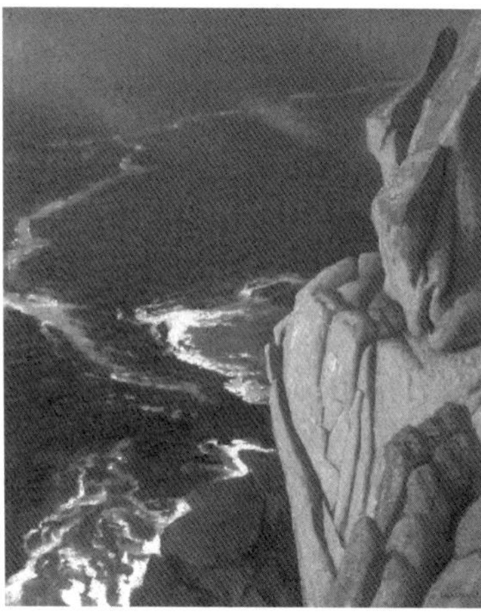

The Cruel Sea, 1967, b/w photographic reproduction. Public domain

Paint and Grease Paint, Laura writes of how his music expressed 'the still and balance of granite rock' in a medium that was, like the sea, fluid and expressive. No wonder therefore that her own rock and sea pictures, painted at Sennen Cove which the Knights had made their summer painting base, appealed to him. She was receptive to his compliment: 'Laura, if the objective in your work could be fused with the subjective in mine, what a perfect combination it would make'. This was a perceptive insight that matched her own.

Ethel Robertson (Bartlett) was a muse for both the Knights, Laura remarking that her beauty was such that 'most of her work' at that time had 'something of Ethel in it'. Harold painted her and Laura's beautiful portrait, exhibited at the Royal Academy in 1926, perfectly conveys the 'simple lines of her beauty'. This picture has become familiar as the signature image for the National Portrait Gallery's exhibition: *Laura Knight Portraits* in 2013. Janet Dunbar, who has a tendency to make unsubstantiated claims, suggests in Chapter Ten of her biography that Ethel was more than a muse for Harold. In a repeat performance of his unrequited "love" for Ella Naper, maintaining that several friends noticed that Harold had fallen 'deeply in love with Ethel'. It is, I suggest, another instance of a "spiced up" narrative which was deeply hurtful. Certainly, when Ethel herself came upon this insinuation in the book, she was incensed and contemplated legal proceedings.

Such an extension of their social and cultural life marks this period as a very positive one for both Laura and Harold. Each was in many ways independent, with separate studios and the necessity for Harold and occasionally

Laura to travel away from home on commissions. However, they preserved their Cornish connections and took a shared pleasure in entertaining guests at their home in London. One such was the "tramp" poet W.H. Davies. He was introduced to the Knights at the Café Royal in 1919 and they were friends from the start. Davies had come to public notice with the publication in 1908 of *The Autobiography of a Super Tramp* and by the time the Knights made his acquaintance he was a well-known poet and personality on the London scene. Davies' poverty-stricken childhood had led him to the life of a vagrant at a young age. Happy on the open road, he had begged his way around the kingdom, lived as a hobo in America and lost a leg "riding a train". Many of these elements of his experience appealed to Laura who could empathise with his adventures.

He invited them to tea in his room in Great Russell Street, and to their surprise provided an elegant tea-table with porcelain cups and thin bread and butter. What entranced them above all, however, was his conversation – he was a philosopher and well as an adventurer which suggested to Laura that she had indeed discovered a kindred spirit: 'From the very start, it appeared we were akin – more or less the same sort of thinking persons in lots of ways.' Harold, also taken by Davies' charm, wanted to paint him. So the "super tramp" became a regular visitor to Harold's studio where he appropriated the old Windsor chair that Harold had bought at Sneinton Market for his first studio and had kept with him since Nottingham days. It was a comfortable association and, in the summer of 1920 when the Knights left London to spend some weeks back at Lamorna Cove, Davies joined them.

On moving to London, the Knights had retained the use of their painting huts at Lamorna and they returned there regularly, sleeping on camp beds and cooking *al fresco*. When they were there, a young friend Pog (Phyllis) Ygelsias always came over to join the fun. Pog was the daughter of the Catalan painter Vincent Yglesias who had been associated with the art colony of Walberswick in Suffolk. On her father's death Pog had migrated to Newlyn together with her mother and siblings where she had trained as a sculptor and worked in wood. Fearless and unconventional, she earned the affection of members of the Newlyn community such as Lamorna Birch and his family, Ella and Charles Naper, the Walkes and the Knights. 'Golly', as Laura preferred to call her for her shock of dark hair, was very much the 'wild child' that Laura cherished within herself.

It was in the summer of 1920 (not 1922 – Laura's failing memory confuses the date in her second autobiography) that Davies, the Knights, the Napers, Dod and Ernest Procter (just demobbed), the family of Algernon

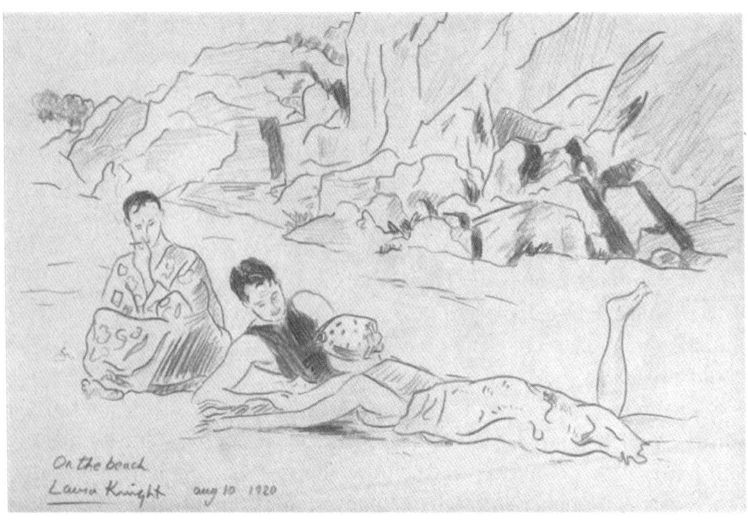

Laura Knight *On the Beach*, Sennen Cove, 1920, pencil drawing. Private collection

Newton (of Windsor and Newton, the paint and brush manufacturers) and Pog regularly gathered around the painting huts in the Cove. Each night a companionable crowd were drawn to the bonfires which Davies, with his superior knowledge of outdoor survival techniques, had expertly constructed. 'Behind the crowd of us', Laura remembers, as we sat round the bonfire, were to be seen countless pairs of bright sparks, the eyes of field mice (although these are 'rats' in Laura's later version) reflecting the fire'. This was the "gypsy life" that Laura enjoyed. She was again in her element and infected others with her enthusiasm, succeeding in her bid to get Harold and Davies to cast off any vestige of formal wear by loosely tying a neckerchief round their necks. Life was simple.

In all the weeks spent in Lamorna over that summer, the Knights never saw Davies put pencil to paper to compose a poem and that was disappointing. However, there is a poem titled *Lamorna Cove* which Davies published in his collection *The Hour of Magic*, 1922 that is addressed to his hosts:

> I see at last our great Lamorna Cove,
> Which, danced on by ten thousand silver feet,
> Has all those waves that run like little lambs,
> To draw the milk from many a rocky teat,
> Spilt in white gallons all along the shore.

Who ever saw more beauty under the sun?
I look and look, and say, 'No wonder here's
A light I never saw on earth before -
Two heavens are shining here instead of one.'
And, like the wild gulls flashing in my sight,
Each furious thought that's driving through my brain
Screams in its fresh young wonder and delight.

It was certainly a glorious, hot summer with a quality of light and depth of colour that Laura distilled in *Lamorna Cove* – a painting suffused with brilliant gold and azure light. It was, she says, an 'excessively bright canvas' paradoxically completed 'one black foggy week by electric light' back in the Hampstead studio the following winter. The painting has become well-known through the print reproduction of 1935.

At the summer camp Laura and Harold re-affirmed the links that had bound their circle of Newlyn friends together in earlier days. But none of this was nostalgic. For Laura it heralded future development since her friendship with Dod Procter in particular was to prove mutually supportive and professionally stimulating over the coming years. Ernest Procter (a Quaker) who in the War had been in France with the Friends' Ambulance Unit, had come back safely much to the relief and comfort of his wife. We last heard of them in the period of the Knight's arrival in Cornwall, when Dod was at the centre of the Myrtage girls and one of the foremost women artists in Forbes' School. She had married Ernest Procter at Paul Church on the hill above Newlyn harbour in 1912. Self-absorbed and highly strung, Dod had stayed on in Newlyn throughout the War with her small son, Bill. While she found the perceived privations and loneliness difficult and depressing, she did enjoy gardening, growing flowers which she adored (she was an accomplished flower painter) and vegetables to offset war-time shortages. She made the occasional visit to the Newlyn cinema (where she found Charlie Chaplin 'rather fetching'), socialised a great deal and continued to work in a desultory way.

On Ernest's return from the war, within weeks they were both off to Burma, where Ernest had a commission to decorate the Kokine Palace in Rangoon, leaving their son behind with a nurse and his grandparents. Dod found the exotic richness of the East 'extraordinarily thrilling' – a phrase that so epitomises the decade. It was certainly a great contrast with her life in wartime Newlyn and Dod immersed herself in the culture. On their return to Cornwall, the Procters were able to buy their own home, settling at North

Corner off Trewarveneth Street in Newlyn. But, in order to supplement their income Ernest set up a painting school with his fellow-artist Harold Harvey that had some success. Dod herself, inspired by her experiences in the East and her studies of the serene images of Buddhist temples, set her mind on developing a new style of figure painting: sculptural monolithic forms and a restricted tonal range. In 1927 she was to have the first example of the technique hung in the Royal Academy: *Morning*. It created a sensation.

The subject of the painting is Dod's favourite Newlyn model, fisherman's daughter Cissie Barnes who is shown asleep on a rumpled bed in colours of 'oyster-white and stone'. This canvas, says Alison James in her biography of Dod, *A Singular Vision,* 'united the modern and the classical with its drapery and form, while her adoption of sober grey and flesh- coloured tones were reminiscent of some Cubist art'. Contemporary critics perceived the image as the prototype of the "painting of the future" and so popular was it that the *Daily Mail* purchased it for the nation. It toured in the States for 2 years before being placed in the Tate Gallery (now Tate Britain), London. Both Harold and Laura were impressed when they first saw *Morning* in Newlyn before its London exhibition: 'That's a noble–looking picture' said Harold and Laura's response was just as positive. This was precisely the effect that she too had sought to achieve over several years – a representation that in its purity and simplicity ennobles and dignifies the female form as simply that – physical form. In many ways her studies in the dynamics of the body and obsession with *rhythm* had diverted her from that aim and produced a proliferation of almost abstract linear studies. Now was the time to return to the problem or rather the challenge of the representation of *mass*.

Laura was warm in her congratulations and in assessing Dod's new-found style, reassessed her own. As a result, when in Cornwall in the late 1920s she painted a series of studies of women dressing, washing, or just seated, that reveal the influence of Dod's work. Not everyone liked what they saw, for example the critic A.L. Baldrey, writing in *Creative Art* magazine in 1928, remarks churlishly: 'Mrs Knight's aggressive nudes are ponderously commonplace and too laboriously realistic to be aesthetically acceptable'. One painting though did earn a consensus of approval as well as satisfying Laura's aspirations. This was *Susie and the Wash Basin* of which she writes: 'I was determined to get the last fraction of richness in the modelling, and a three-dimensional quality, such as had not previously accomplished.' It is true that there is a difference in quality between Dod's marmoreal figure in *Morning* and Laura's *Susie*. The first remains a personification, while the second addresses us as a personality. Laura has indeed managed to invest the 'modelling' with 'richness' and Susie has life and presence in our space and time. When it appeared at the Royal Academy in 1929 *Susie and the Wash Basin* earned Laura the accolade of the "most outstanding" artist of the show.

But we are accelerating ahead way too fast and must return to the year 1922 when something unexpected changed the parameters of Laura's life. She was approached by one of the Directors of the Carnegie Institute in Pittsburgh, Homer St Gaudens, asking if she would be willing to join Lucien Simon, a renowned painter and teacher from Paris, as the European judges for the next International Exhibition. From 1912 Laura had regularly sent pictures there and was committed to enhancing her international reputation, so, although much caught up in preparations for an exhibition at the Alpine Club, organised by Ernest Brown, she agreed to go. Mystified as to why she of all possible contenders for the honour had been chosen, she was told: 'You had less bricks thrown at you than anyone else'. It was the kind of back-handed compliment that she was used to from Harold and was not put out. Having selected paintings in Paris and London to take with them, Laura and Lucien Simon sailed first class on the RMS Olympic, the first of the White Star Line's Olympic class and sister ship of the ill-fated Titanic. With two small suitcases and a "posh" frock which she had run up the day before with a piece of Indian fabric bought in an antique shop for ten shillings, she boarded at Southampton in rough weather, sleeping on deck in her old musquash coat until the ship picked up French passengers including Simon, at Cherbourg.

Travelling first class on the Olympic was luxurious, its scale beyond anything that Laura had known to date. Lord Winterton, travelling on the same liner in 1912, described the amenities in his journal. The Transcript of which is reproduced in Richard Davenport-Hines book *Titanic Lives*: 'She really is a fine ship. Exceeds one's imagination. Racquet Court, Gymnasium, Swimming Bath, Restaurant and Public Rooms are splendid. Decorations all over in real and not (as generally at sea) in tawdry taste. Food in Restaurant quite excellent'. While the liner is long gone, it is possible to gain at least an idea of this opulent floating hotel and imagine Laura as she sipped a cocktail and enjoyed a cigarette in the First-Class Passengers' Lounge. For when the liner came out of service in 1935 and her fittings and contents dispersed, the interior of the First Class Lounge and a section of one of the grand staircases were purchased and installed in the dining room at the White Swan Hotel, Alnwick, Northumberland by the then owner, Algernon Smart, Something of the ambiance of the lounge that was enjoyed by Laura can therefore be appreciated today, if not that of the top deck to which she was lured by an importunate American with 'diamond studs' on the pretext that she would find the best subjects to sketch up there. Not to be churlish, she went and in the complete darkness had to fend off his embraces and request for 'a little bit of love'. It was then that she made the famous riposte: 'It's not in my line'.

Arriving in New York harbour, where the Statue of Liberty appeared as a 'lonely figure' in the cold blue of dawn, Laura goes on to describe the 'lemon and rose' sky against which the silhouettes of skyscrapers were 'fused in the pearly mist'. She is moved by the scale of things – the 'vast dock', the height of the Olympic as it towers over smaller craft and the sight of her two little suitcases on the luggage escalator 'a pair of fleas on a mammoth's back'. Then they were transported out of the port and into a car to speed off on a helter-skelter tour of New York: Fifth Avenue, the Brooklyn Bridge, the Woolworth Building (at that point the highest skyscraper in Manhattan). Laura was booked into a "Ladies Club" where she was impressed by the food – an 'enormous breakfast' and 'the best coffee I had ever tasted poured hot over cream!' she exclaims in the 'America' chapter of *Oil Paint and Grease Paint*. Over the next few days, they were 'sumptuously feted' and the always hungry Laura was very impressed. This was a land of plenty and excess. When attending the various luncheon parties and dinners, Laura wore her striking Indian dress and a pair of patent leather boots of which she was exceedingly proud, until at one reception an American lady commented: 'What charming rubber over-shoes those are you're wearing'. That she records the remark at all shows something of Laura's ability to rise above the discomfort of a deflated ego and see the humour.

They were taken on whirlwind visits to mansions housing the art collections of fabulously rich connoisseurs, seeing walls crowded with the works of Goya, Degas, Manet, Monet and El Greco. One such New York mansion had been built by the industrialist Henry Clay Frick. He had died in 1919, leaving the house and its contents in trust, together with an endowment for the maintenance of a gallery to be called the 'Frick Collection'. Such riches seemed unreal, beyond Laura's wildest dreams, but the dream continued unbroken. Without time to take breath, they next travelled up to Boston on a bitterly cold day and took in Harvard, motoring so many miles that she lost track in the endless snowy landscapes. Turning to the present tense, she allows us to share with her the days and nights 'spent on trains swinging through wild country' to arrive at last in Pittsburg where the party is greeted by the press. All are eager to know what this lady English artist made of America: 'Wonderful' was all she could reply for, totally disorientated, tired and apprehensive, all she wanted was a hot bath and something to eat.

The actual judging of the submissions at the Institute is given little attention in either of Laura's accounts. More important for her is to record the next stage of their tour as they transferred in warm spring sunshine (her musquash coat and patent boots becoming something of a disadvantage) to Washington. 'Rushing' from place to place, day and night, they were taken to all the sights of the capital, including the newly erected Lincoln Memorial and George Washington's house, although all she says about it is that the great man had cut a hole in the door to let his cat through! They came back to the coast exhausted, having been it was calculated through fourteen states in 10 days, and very hot, for summer had come to New York with a vengeance and the musquash coat and patent boots were a definite liability.

Returning across the stormy Atlantic on the French liner *La France*, she and her companion the famous Frenchman Lucien Simon were feted. This time Laura 'enjoyed the bad weather; it was exhilarating' and when she landed at Le Havre felt very important as an experienced traveller. She crossed the Channel by boat and took the train to Waterloo Station where she was met by Harold. There was so much to tell, so many experiences to re-live. However, when they returned to Queen's Road, she found the house stripped of portable goods. In her absence Harold had found himself financially embarrassed and had pawned many items. When she recounted to him

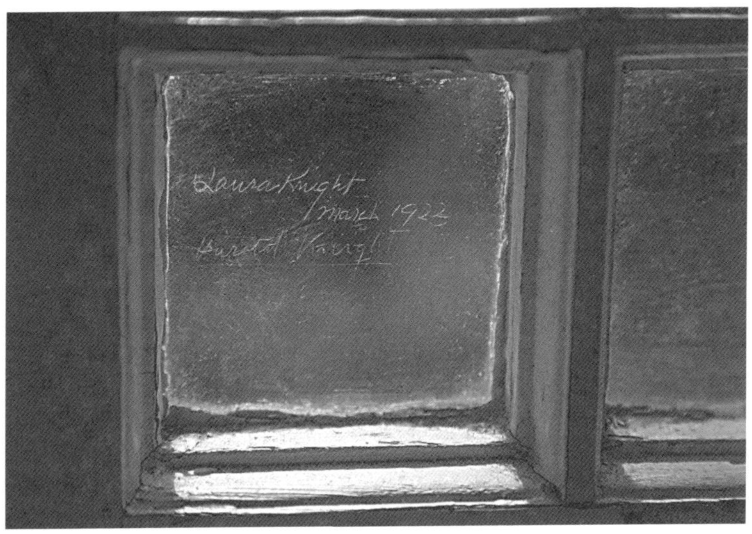

Inscription in the window glass at 16 Langford Place, 1922. Private collection

stories of the extravagance and riches she had encountered in the States, they 'roared with laughter' at the irony of their situation and somehow that put it all into perspective. Within days though, Harold's weak constitution gave in and he went down with 'flu that developed into pneumonia. They were just in the process of moving from Queen's Road which, while having some charm, had several disadvantages. For instance, the somewhat primitive guest-accommodation involved having to climb a circular open stairway and wash in a tin bath. Barry Jackson sampled these facilities and Laura admits it was the first and only time he chose to do so! The new rented property in St John's Wood was a "better address" with ample facilities. Nonetheless, their circumstances were such that the move was only achieved through the help of their friends and neighbours Kenneth Forbes and his wife (Forbes was a Canadian who, like Laura, had been commissioned to paint for the Canadian Government in the War) and a loan from Barry Jackson (then a major name in the theatre word both in London and in Birmingham). Number 9 (later renumbered 16), Langford Place was to be the Knight's London home for the next 50 years.

Various Newlyn friends came to stay with the Knights at their house in Langford Place: Ber Walke, Golly Yglesias, Ella and Charlie Naper and Dod Procter. Laura and Dod now hared a model, Eileen Mayo. Eileen was a friend of Ethel Robertson and an artist in her own right. Her cool blonde looks lent themselves to the "monumental" treatment of physical form that Laura and Dod were exploring at that time. A 2-minute silent newsreel made by Pathé in 1927 can be accessed online, showing what was dubbed a "famous artist's studio", in which Laura acts out the process of painting Mayo in the picture *Blue and Gold*. Somewhat tongue-in-cheek, she describes the experience of being filmed in Chapter 35 of *Oil Paint and Grease Paint*: 'The studio did not bear much resemblance to my workshop over Butler's garage' she writes. What is more she 'never ever stood an inch or two from the canvas', as she is here so that (in an unconscious parody of her *Self Portrait*) the camera could take in the artist, the model and the canvas 'all in together'. It was all rather ridiculous, made more absurd when the producer suggested that Mayo's shoulders be draped in pink chiffon for modesty and that they pretend to have a tea-party! Here we see the nuances of Laura's world in the 1920s, when the old-fashioned niceties and conventions were colliding headlong with a new world.

Talking of New Worlds, there was to be another trip to America in 1926. This time, as result of the meeting in Florence with the Leroy Crummers, it was Harold who was invited across the Atlantic to undertake portrait commissions for the John Hopkins Memorial Hospital in Baltimore. Undoubtedly this was an honour that affirmed Harold's international reputation as a portrait artist of distinction. Laura, one feels, was left sulking at home – although she had Golly and Dod Procter staying with her as well as an invitation from the Duke and Duchess of York to attend an evening party at St James' Palace (she was now it seems on the "A list" of VIPs). She took a taxi there and, since she did not know any other guests to speak to, took the opportunity of strolling through the Royal apartments on her own – except for the odd footman of course. Underlying this episode there seems to be a slight petulance – a chip on the shoulder perhaps – illustrated by her decision to make the return journey home on a "No.2 bus" with a 3d ticket. Her good spirits returned, however, when Harold, who was being paid well, sent money for her to join him in the States. Then she decided to go first class – 'to be impressive'. She sailed at Christmas on the new German liner, the *SS Hamburg*. Not quite as impressive as the *Olympic* or *La France*, nonetheless, Laura thoroughly enjoyed herself aboard. The company was jolly, the food was good and plentiful and she indulged to such an extent that over the voyage her clothes became noticeably tight.

They stayed at the Waldorf Astoria and Harold bought Laura a new fur coat (the musquash having seen too many better days) at what she calls in local parlance a 'swell' store. From there they travelled to Baltimore where they stayed with the orthopaedic surgeon Dr Baer, whose portrait Harold was to paint. This Laura records was 'one of his finest'. It was Dr Baer who gave Laura permission to go onto the segregated wards to draw and paint.

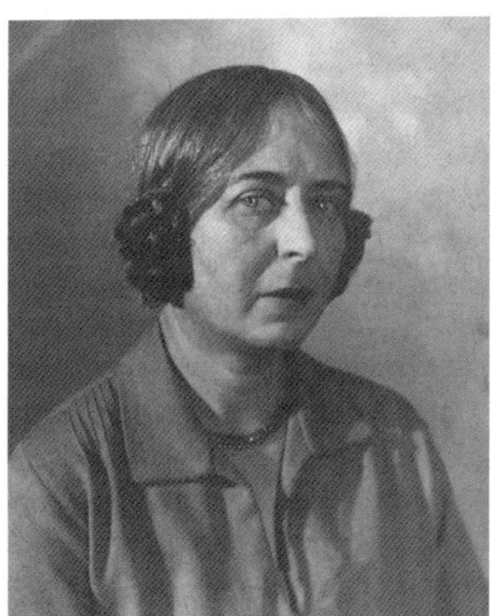

Press photograph of Laura Knight, *Baltimore Sun*, January 1927. Public domain

Caroline Fox suggests that in seeking out negro subjects, Laura was emulating Dod Procter who had made a study of Burmese children. However, any assumptions that she may have had about discovering in the negro community a 'world apart' that would open up a fresh direction for her art, as the Far East had done for Dod, were quickly dispelled.

When she went rummaging around local markets looking for evidence of what she expected to be a completely different culture and when she met and talked to representatives of what she thought was a tribal people, she was destined to be frustrated. Meeting Dr Bauer's highly competent negro staff, nursing assistant Pearl Johnson and her sister Irene Dodson, she was brought up sharply in the realization that these were women very much like herself, hard-working, committed and Western. What she had omitted to consider was that these African Americans were many generations away from Africa. They were pragmatic, engaged and politically aware. Pearl and Irene were both active members of the Inter-racial Fellowship Group that campaigned against racial segregation in the state of Maryland. Taking Laura under their wing, they introduced her to negro art clubs and concerts, and she was taken to a social evening at a "negro newspaper" where she heard a lecture on civil rights. Meeting them Laura discovered people engaged with the realities of the modern world, with hopes and aspirations she understood.

As a result, the portraits she painted of Pearl and Irene are direct and thoughtful, and the studies she made on the maternity and children's wards at John Hopkins and Baltimore Children's Hospital, constitute some of her most successful work. Laura always had a gift for portraying children, despite having none of her own. Perhaps because of that and because she never lost her own 'inner child', she is able to see and portray them physically and emotionally from their perspective and at their level. It was with a sense of pride that she brought her pictures back to England, a selection of which can be observed in the background of the Pathé newsreel of 1927.

Once Harold's commissions were complete, the ever-hospitable Dr Baer and his wife took their visitors on a tour of Maryland and Virginia before their return to England. In the summer 1927 they arrived back in London to find Dod Procter the talk of the town for her painting *Morning*. Laura was warm in congratulating her old friend and it was not long before she too was the centre of attention, being elected in that year to the position of Associate Royal Academician. A.J. Munnings had put her name forward several times but the male-dominated Academy was reluctant, several members persisting in the belief that women artists were inferior, too superficial in their art to merit such distinction. However, one woman painter, Annie

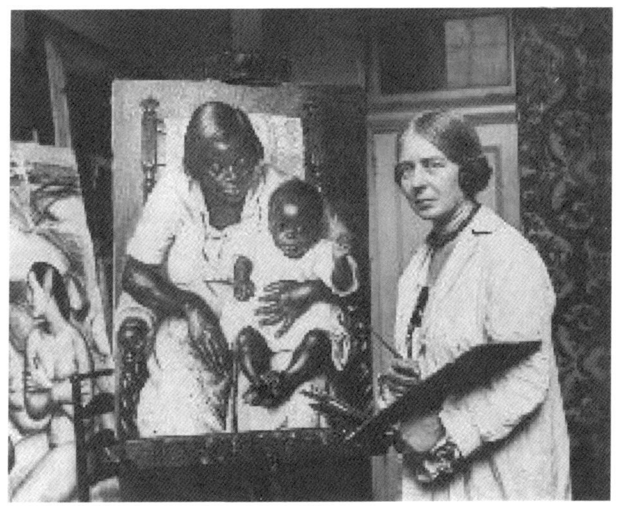

Studio photograph, 1927 showing *Madonna of the Cotton Fields*

Swynnerton, a feminist and active suffragette, had set a precedent by being elected as Associate 1922. The only previous female members had been Angelica Kauffman and Mary Moser who had been founder members of the Academy in 1768. So, when Laura's name was put forward in 1927, after much lobbying from old acquaintances such as A.J. Munnings and William Reid Dick the sculptor, her election was historic. The telephone message from Munnings came through to Langford Place while the Knights were having dinner with Rae and Ethel Robertson. The rejoicing was great.

Some suppose that Harold, who had not been elected RA, although he was to be the following year, must have been resentful. Harold had been hailed as the most gifted student Nottingham Art College had produced and he had been Laura's idol, mentor and partner for decades. So, it is presumed he must have felt bitter. There is no evidence to suggest so. However, Janet Dunbar, imagining his discomfort and distress, suggests that his feelings could only have been truly understood by ever-sensitive Ethel Robertson, Laura, in her euphoria, being oblivious. That would be unlikely, for, despite their independent professional lives, as a couple they were close through long association and mutual affection. That Harold has little mention in *Oil Paint and Grease Paint* is not a sign of alienation. It is due to his request to be 'kept out of it'. For such a private man public exposure was not appropriate. Following the announcement of Laura's election, he managed the stream of telegrams, phone calls and crowd of journalists that appeared outside Langford Place with good humoured resignation, as he did the press notices that referred to him as 'the husband of Laura Knight' who also happened to be an artist.

The achievement of ARA after her name was the fulfilment of Laura's Mother's prophecy that one day, she 'would be famous'. But Laura was not content to rest there. She had to maintain her momentum, find fresh stimulus: new territories and alternative communities to befriend and paint. In the *Cornishman* newspaper there is an article based on an interview given by Laura in early 1929. The reporter informs readers that: 'She has decided to seek new types in the Caledonian Market (an antiques and 'flea' market in Islington), that strange sale-ground where bargains can be picked up by the connoisseur for a mere song … (she) is convinced that she can find there many interesting types among the stall-holders – faces that may tell of a life of struggle, a life with which the artist was herself not unfamiliar in her early days'. That statement says so much. Once more she was seeking 'a place and a people apart' that would not only provide subject matter but offer the embrace of a community that understood life's 'struggle'. And that explains the alacrity with which in 1929 she accepted an invitation from Bertram Mills to join the circus!

CHAPTER NINE

"To understand, to grasp life with both hands"

In the early 1920s Laura broke her wrist in a fall caused by attempting to do an extra high kick in a rather tight skirt. This meant she was unable to hold her palette. However, rather than accepting this as a set-back, she accepted it as an opportunity to develop her skills and widen her repertoire. She teamed up with an old friend from Laren days, John Everett, and together they set out to learn the art of engraving and, although their equipment was initially primitive and held together by parts picked up on market stalls, they soon mastered the basic techniques. Laura's earliest successful prints were to include *A Crowd* and *A Dancer Resting*, both of 1921. She then bought a redundant press that had belonged to fellow artist Sir George Clausen and, together with Harold learned how to master the art of aquatint in earnest – the acid, black varnish – the printers' ink. Altogether Laura successfully produced some ninety prints of good quality.

Through the practice of engraving Laura discovered a new-found enthusiasm for the *line*, and a fresh understanding of *light* and *shade*, *mass* and *contrast*: 'I have never been so ingrained with black', she writes, it was a 'glorious period' and she '(I) was pleased to say, executed many plates that have since been successful'. These included many familiar favourites: *At The Follies Bergeres, Dressing Room No.1, Spanish Dancers, Bank Holiday, Hampstead Heath,* and *A Fair* – all produced in 1923. Her biggest and most important aquatint was, in her opinion, *Five Clowns* of 1925. So proficient was she that in 1925 she exhibited at the Royal Society of Painter-Etchers. She was to become a full member of the Society in 1932 and in the same year *The Studio* published a selection of her work in No 19 of their series *Modern Masters of Etching*. The novelty of printmaking wore off in due course, but not before she had tried her hand at the whole range of the printer's art including linocuts, woodcuts, lithographs, soft ground and dry point etchings,

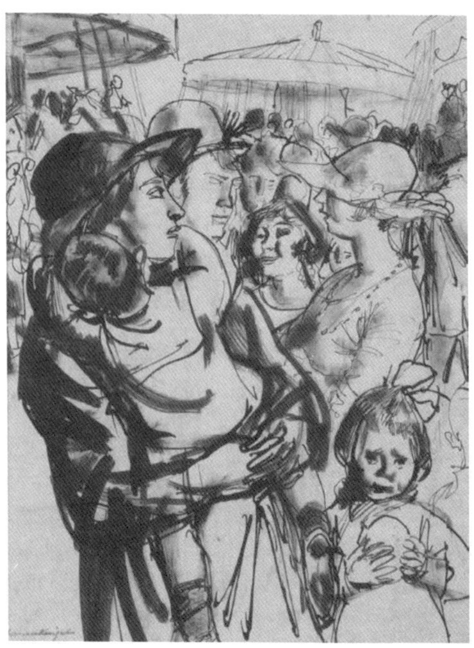

At the Fair, c.1920, ink drawing. Private collection

mezzotints as well as aquatint. That she continued to undertake the occasional print (her last, *Carting Corn* was produced in 1943) is indicated in the authoritative book on the subject: *The Graphic Work of Laura Knight* by C. Fredric Bolling and Valerie A. Withington which catalogues over a hundred plates over the period 1921–43.

What is distinctive about much of the subject matter of Laura's prints in the 1920s is that they display a spirit of carnival: the ballet, flamenco dancers, faces in a crowd and the delightful studies of Bank Holiday on Hampstead Heath. Just as at Penzance Fair in past years, when on Hampstead Heath Laura familiarized herself with the show people who invited her into their wagons and behind the stalls to sit and sketch: 'Fair life has always had for me a great fascination, the bands all playing different tunes at one time, the gilt and the colour, the worn grass, the sun and even the rain and wind. I love mingling with a big crowd'. It took her back to Nottingham days when as small children the Johnson girls could glimpse the racetrack and fairground beyond and hear the muffled sounds of the fairground organs and hurdy-gurdies or at Goose Fair – a world so very different from that of Noel

Street. Yet she was at ease in that world and was readily accepted by them for the simple reason that her manner was direct and she had no pretentions. 'I always liked show people and got on well with them. They are clean-living, with a great deal of self-respect' she writes.

By contrast, while she enjoyed the life of a "celebrity" in London society, perhaps as a result of her background, she had a habit of attention seeking and at times was loud and coarse. Critics sometimes described her and her work as 'vulgar' (and some still do), but that word implies something other than 'tasteless'. In other contexts and returning to its Latin roots, it means "of the people". This would be a perfect way to describe Laura's knack of gaining the trust and loyalty of groups outside the norms of conventional society. Laura Knight's absorption into the life of the Circus, for instance testifies to her uncanny ability to win the confidence and acceptance of groups outside the mainstream, those whom conventional people perceive as living "on the edge".

Laura's introduction to a "real old-fashioned circus" was on the recommendation of a railway porter at Paddington Station who directed her to Swallow's Circus, then showing at the Royal Agricultural Hall in Islington. From the start she was enthralled and stayed there several weeks sketching: 'I drew everything in sight from Salt and Saucy the elephants (Plate 13) to the trapeze artists in their dressing-rooms, and made many friends – Mr Swallow, Johnny Regan, Randy, Comical Walker – her introduction to the "inside"'. Such friends were lifelong. So too was the long black cape 'which I am supposed always to wear' – that she made for herself to provide warmth against the perishing cold of the Agricultural Hall over the Christmas period.

In describing the circus people Laura makes comparison with the fishing folk of Staithes. This is another 'race apart', displaying the same endurance, loyalty and indomitable spirit: 'I never felt a stranger among them; their acceptance of me as one of themselves has always seemed a miracle, for usually, like fisher-people, they are difficult to know intimately.' Yet, in a short time Laura did get to know them intimately. This was a community which drew her in, recognising in her a fellow spirit. She worked hard and could be depended upon and that was enough to prove she was one of their own. As a result she was accepted into the 'big family party' that was the circus.

After the First World War the ritual of a Christmas Circus was revived – its exoticism, colour and sparkle a welcome tonic after years of khaki and hardship. The elephants, lions, liberty horses, sea-lions, acrobats, high wire performers, tumblers and clowns offered diversion and, above all, laughter. One of the best loved circuses in the early 20th century was Bertram Mills'

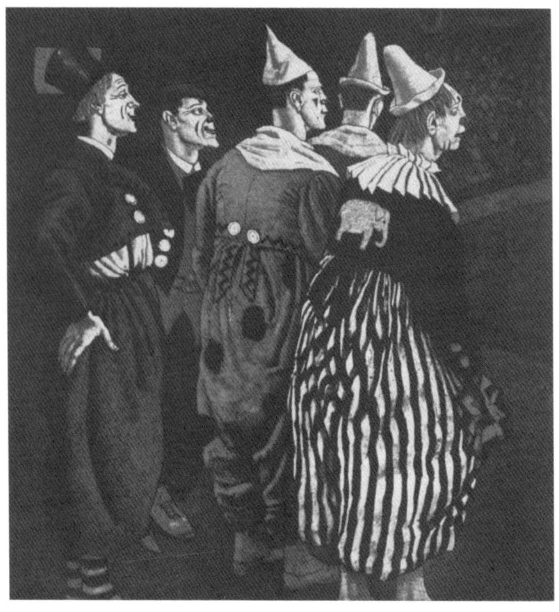

Five Clowns, 1926, etching and aquatint. Laing Art Gallery, Tyne & Wear Museums

Circus at Olympia. In 1927 through her friend Munnings, Laura got to know Captain Bertram Mills himself, the premier name in early 20th century circus. The son of a funeral director, Bertram Mills' role in the family firm had been, amongst other things, to wash down the hearses and look after the horses, and as a result he had a life-long passion for equines. During the War he rose to the rank of Captain in the Royal Medical Corps and he retained that title of rank all his life. His interest in circus was triggered by his seeing Fred Wilkins' *Great Victory Circus and Allied Fair* at Olympia, the first post-war entertainment to be put on there at Christmas 1919–20. High quality as this was, Mills wagered: 'If I could not give the people a better circus than that for their money, I'd eat my hat'. As a result, the following Christmas the first Bertram Mills Circus had been staged at Olympia – the first of a long tradition of festive performances there.

A.J. Munnings made the introductions and gained Laura access behind the scenes. Once again she was overwhelmed with promising subject matter and in both her autobiographies waxes lyrical. As she takes in the excitement and sensuous extravagance of the spectacle, she describes the colours and textures, the spangles and tossing plumes, the prancing horses and lumbering elephants as they parade the ring. While she frequently dined with the Captain, just as frequently she was invited to eat with the performers: 'I shared their eats and cups of tea; and, with sketchbook in hand, made swift notes'. As with the ballet, sitting in dressing rooms of the clowns Whimsical Walker and Joe Cranston, it was the paraphernalia of performance that attracted her as she describes this in the 'Circus Inspiration' episode in *The Magic of a Line*: 'discarded costumes of all tints hung on the walls, together with daubed huge head masks – ridiculous as they hung from strings upside down ... dummy ladies to dance with, dummy animals, huge parti-colour play balls. Here someone's performing dog (she tells us that the proper name for such a dog is a 'buffer') reached up to lick a plate from among the contents of a dressing-shelf: make up of all sorts, wigs, perhaps a red shoe, and a teapot.' This bizarre clutter was unified by an atmosphere, a spirit, a soul, which she had never before experienced, even in the ballet, and Laura embraced it as her own.

In the first part of the 20th century many artists painted clowns, acrobats and the harlequinade. For instance, Walter Sickert and his third wife Thérèse Lessore painted Swallow's Circus at the Royal Agricultural Hall in Islington. And in the wider European context, Picasso took circus folk, acrobats and clowns ("Saltimbanques") as his subject. These were to mutate over 10 years from being recognizable human figures as in the *Family of Saltimbanques* of 1905 into the fractured abstraction of *Harlequin* of 1915. These represent a paradigm of the ideological shift that was Modernism – conscious artistic and political statements. In his poem *An Eclogue for Christmas* of 1933, Louis MacNeice summed up their significance, regretting the loss of representational art in favour of an abstraction in which the human model is 'sifted and splintered in broken facets ... anything but soul and flesh'. Laura Knight never went down such a road, maintaining the human face of circus – always the personal rather than the conceptual.

She was very much at home in the company of the clowns, as she admits, for being 'a bit of a clown myself I have always had a particular fancy for that Profession'. In them she saw a reflected image of her own live performance and valued their friendship. Whimsical Walker had been clowning in pantomime and circus since the age of eight when he performed in Pablo Fanque's circus (the most popular in mid-Victorian England) in the late 1850s. Experienced in all aspects of the circus business as tumbler, acrobat, equestrian and clown, over his lifetime he undertook three world-tours and visited the United States seventeen times. In 1874 he was contracted to John Murray's Railroad Circus in America and stayed there for 7 years, negotiating

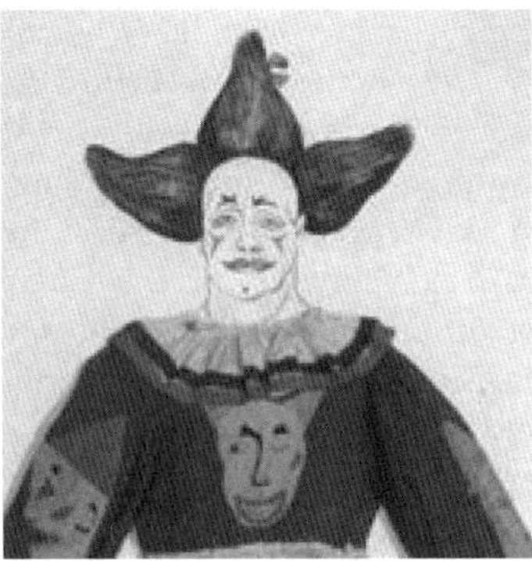

'Whimsical Walker' costume,
now at Museum of London.
Public domain

the purchase from London Zoo of the famous elephant Jumbo for Barnum and Bailey in 1882. Barnum transported the elephant across America in the famous circus-trains until, struck down by a railway engine, Jumbo died in 1885. After the elephant's unfortunate death, the skin (preserved by a taxidermist) and its skeleton were exhibited for several more years by Barnum as a lucrative public spectacle.

Whimsical's own act showcased a variety of animals including at one stage a singing donkey (its party-piece was 'Home Sweet Home'), which at the first Royal Command Performance in 1886 misbehaved in front of Her Majesty the Queen. She was not amused. When Laura knew Whimsical in the 1920s his canine partner was "Bill" who aided and abetted him in the traditional clowning routines: a string of "sausages", a "goose" and a "red hot" poker. His clown wig comprising three black cones with a threaded, red-braided plait behind was modelled on that of the great Grimaldi. It was made for him by Clarksons of Wardour Street who charged a guinea per year for the hiring. In 1934 Laura visited the 88-year-old Whimsical on his deathbed in hospital. Still ready with a wry quip, he is reported to have told her: 'I shall be in a different sort of theatre this time'. His distraught widow was looked after by Laura, who personally wrapped up Whimsical's clowning suit, bought his wig from Clarksons for a mere 2/6 and took them both straight to the Museum of London where they can be seen to this day.

Joe Cranston, another old trouper, had begun his career with the travelling menagerie of Wombwell and Bostock, which Laura would have come across in the 1880s at Nottingham Goose Fair. Joe was a true "sad" white-face clown, known in the trade as a *blanc* – with a tight white cap and black curl atop, scarlet lips and a slit down the eyes and a teardrop too. The *blanc* type was and continues to be a serious and aloof, sometimes sad, authority figure.

He acts as a foil to the apparently witless, clumsy *auguste* or "red" clown with his exaggerated red and white make-up, false nose, huge feet and baggy pants held up by braces. She listened to the tales of Joe Cranston for hours, for his telling them was often pure 'poetry'. Then there was "Goliath", just tall enough to pinch the bottoms of the circus girls. Laura writes of his other habit of placing his bowler hat upside down on the ground and then, straight-legged, bending over to fit his head inside before coming upright – 'for the sheer joy of it'. Goliath features frequently in Laura's circus sketches.

Laura got to know the liberty horses by name and by nature, being especially fond of the "Knapstropers" – black and white spotted 'plum puddings' she calls them, all with exotic and romantic names: Hassan, Blitz, Sulieman, Klingo and Tully. She painted them often. Captain Anker, the equestrian director, instructed her on their anatomical and choreographed positions, just as Signor Cecchetti had done in the practice room of the ballet. In fact, the horses were equine dancers, forming a corps in synchronized movement with 'the line and subtleties of the modelling … as entrancing as those of the human form'. Laura loved those horses and admitted being prone to a 'Horse-sickness' for them long after she had moved on. It was a similar story with the lions (Plate 14). In learning the lore of the 'cats', she was told hair-raising as well as moving tales of loyalty and affection. 'I have never known anything more beautiful than the mutual worship of Paris and Togare his trainer' she reflects. She delineates the muscular torso of the star, Togare, 'tall, powerful, handsome as they make 'em', and his beast Paris in many a sketch and in Chapter Twenty One of *The Magic of a Line* narrates the dangers and the dramas of their life together as well as the poignancy of their final separation. She viewed the acrobats and trapeze artists with the admiration of one who as a child and even as a grown woman had tumbled and somersaulted – not well but with a will.

The world of circus in all its variety is found in a painting that she was commissioned to paint for a Major Evelyn Atherley, a circus-lover who had read of Laura working at Olympia. His first request was for a painting of Whimsical that was to include Atherley's own pet terrier. Soon, however, he wanted more – Joe Cranston the white-faced clown, the ring master Mr Schumann, the Liberty horses, further clowns including Goliath, the elephants and performing seals, trapeze and high-wire artists, acrobats … Laura said 'yes' to everything. She liked the Major and they shared not only the delights of visual spectacle but also the visceral thrill of the circus ring. They were great pals, as Laura would say. It was Goliath who gave the name to the composition: *Charivari*. The word means a disorderly rout and was used in the nineteenth century as the title of a satirical French newspaper and as the moniker of *Punch* magazine: 'the London Charivari'. Despite those somewhat negative connotations, Laura thought the title perfect for this jigsaw of a picture and the Major was delighted. Harold was not impressed, intimating that this was another example of Laura's exhibitionism. But she enjoyed doing it – it had been self-indulgent and fun. Before she knew it, the painting had gone public, was the basis of caricature in *Punch* (substituting political figures for the circus performers) and she had earned for herself the reputation of being a "Circus Painter".

When Bertram Mills' Circus joined up with The Great Carmo's outfit to undertake their first tour in the spring of 1929, without hesitation, she joined them. Carmo (real name Harry Cameron and not to be confused with Fred Karno, the music hall impresario) was an illusionist who had worked the major theatres in Britain. His act featured a number of animals, the climax of which was to make Mary the elephant disappear. Laura was to get to know Mary well. (Plate 15: *Mary and the Shetland Ponies*) The combined Mills/Carmo Circus was to be on the road for several weeks. It was a commitment and Laura appears to have decided to go without discussing it with Harold. Used to Laura's impulsive character and knowing that she was happiest when following her inclinations wherever they might lead, Harold

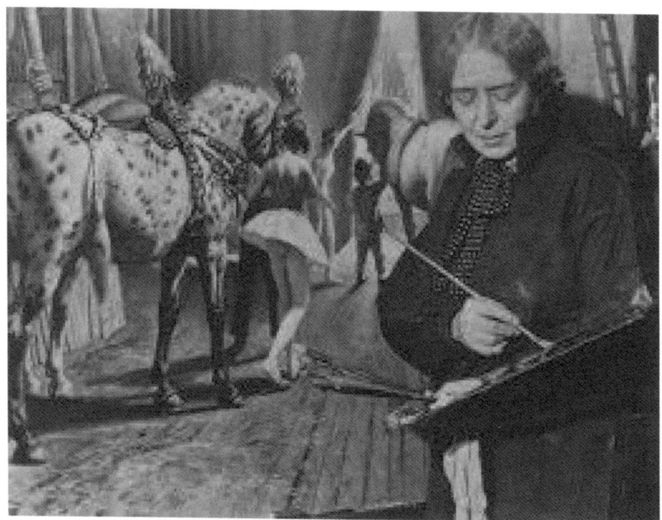

Photograph of Laura painting the 'plum puddings' backstage in the Big Top, Bertram Mills' Circus. Public domain

did not formally object. He was not a sentimental man and was busy with his own work.

He made one visit to see her during this tour of the south coast in the company of Rae and Ethel Robertson whose sister, Edith De Peyer lived with her husband and family – also musicians – at Middleton-on-Sea. Laura and Harold were to get to know them well and her painting of them, another bearing the title *The Beach* was exhibited at the Academy in 1932. Not one of them, however, was impressed by the conditions under which she was living in the circus. Harold's comment that she was 'circus crazy' was of course correct. Laura typically counters this with: 'No one outside could understand my happiness in the life we led'. The use of pronouns here – '*my* happiness' and 'the life *we* led' illustrates her own position as an independent artist and that her loyalties are with her new family. For however independent Laura might seem to be at times, she needed a sympathetic context, a "community" or "family" that met her own needs and endorsed her sense of self.

On this her first Circus tour of 1929–30, Captain Mills, having been called away, offered her the use of his travelling wagon, but Laura declined. She did not want to put an artificial distance between herself and her subject matter. She wanted to be integrated into their world. So, she elected to share lodgings with two new friends: Joe and Ally Bert. Joe had begun his career as a boy tumbler and had also been an accomplished acrobat and an equestrian, but now that he was beginning to feel the physical effects of years of contortions, had turned to clowning. It is Joe Bert, the white-faced clown, who appears on the right of her *Three Clowns* painting, alongside the *august* Marba and her old friend Randy whom she had met at Swallows circus in Islington.

Joe's wife, Ally Bert, had been a bare-back rider and an acrobat but no longer performed and at that time was in charge of the refreshment stall at Carmo's. The couple had met on board ship as they travelled East with their respective troupes. It was a love-match from the first. 'She had a neck like a swan', said Joe, 'we married and I first trained her as a high-school rider. Many years later, we made a special act together with a lovely little dog we called Flippy'. Found as a puppy in a Glasgow pet-shop, Flippy was greatly loved and a natural performer, indeed a star. The climax of their act had been the formation of a pyramid with Joe on Ally's shoulders and then, by running up their backs to sit on Joe's head, Flippy completed the apex. All three would then 'do a simultaneous forward somersault' with all landing on their feet to rapturous applause.

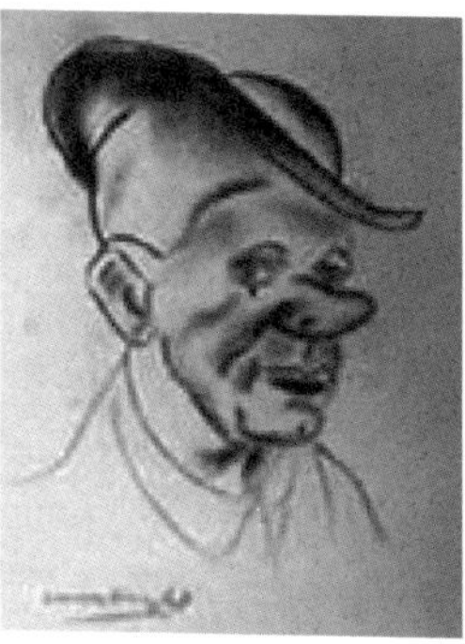

Laura Knight, drawing of Joe Bert.
Private collection

'Without either Joe or Ally I would have been at a loss', Laura writes, 'Joe proved my guardian in the stables – Ally gave of herself in providing what comfort was possible in our lettari (lodging), as well as searching the shops for the best food; she even fed me with cigarettes while I painted'. Ally's help to Laura was unconditional and was to last 'through the thick and thin of endeavour' until she died in 1961. As for Joe, it was his early life that provided Laura with the material for *A Proper Circus Omie* ("omie" is circus-speak for "man"). This she published in 1962 as a tribute to a soulmate. Out of season the Berts lived in a wagon at a Mr Sully's Garage in Brixton and every Saturday afternoon Laura would visit them to hear Joe's life story. She implies that she never did hear it all, only the first sequence, because he fell ill and died in 1936 at the age of 59. This meant that Joe was never able to fulfil his promise to recount the myriad of adventures

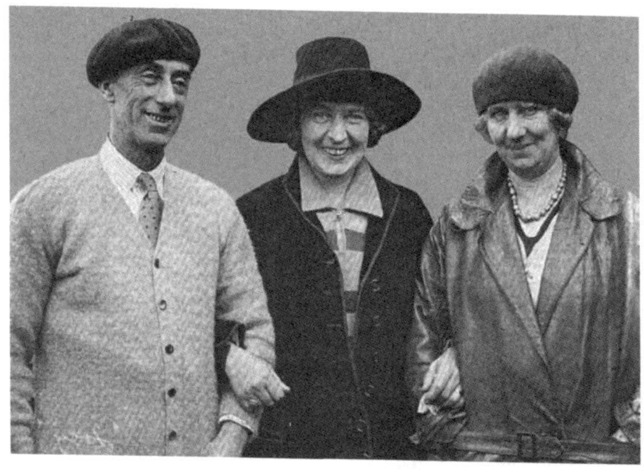

Laura with Joe and Ally Bert. Nottinghamshire Archives

that he and Ally had experienced over their lives. However, in the National Archive there is a set of notes which describe (at Joe's dictation) a sequence of subsequent events that were never written up by Laura. These typed sheets concern Joe's life from joining the circus up to 1920: his marriage and travels in the UK, in India, Ceylon, Malaya, Java, China (where he was present during the Boxer Rising in 1900), Australia, New Zealand, Africa and South America as well as his wartime experiences as part of a burial party in the trenches. The archived records state that the sheets are numbered 1–95 but that these are inaccurate, some are missing, and there are alterations in pencil. Other loose sheets are partially numbered but 'fragmentary'. These include definitions of circus terms and material describing her impressions when sketching in the circus as well as further tales to be interpolated whose titles run: 'Tent Tale', 'Indian Tale' and 'Snow and Fire'. This last describes the two main fears of the circus on tour that Laura features in Chapter 40 of *Oil Paint and Grease Paint*. When Laura published what we have of *A Proper Circus Omie* in 1962, she was eighty-five, and already considering her second autobiography *The Magic of a Line*, published in 1965. It might therefore be that the narrative of Joe's story was dropped to make way for her own. However, it is not quite so simple, because we can see there the emergence of her latest persona.

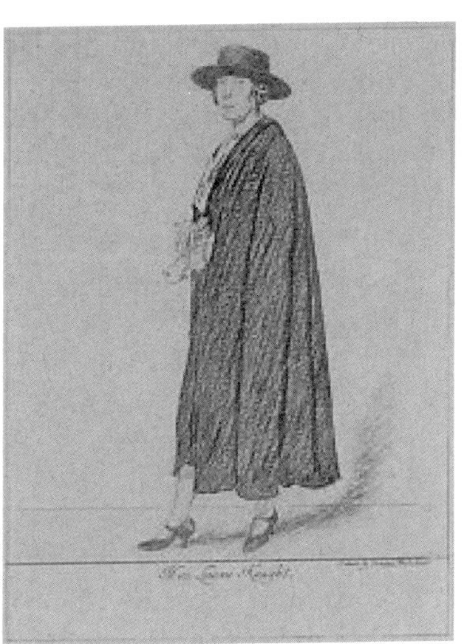

George Belcher R.A. (1875–1947) 'Mrs Laura Knight'. Charcoal, watercolour and ink. c.1925. Possibly intended for Mr Punch's Personalities. Public domain

A Proper Circus Omie is a first-person narrative, and from the start Laura identifies herself with the young Joe. She speaks for him, adopting his voice and at times imprints her own childhood experiences on his. As an instance, early in his story, the oddly fanciful and physically restless boy is described by neighbours: 'Something's wrong with the child's head', they'd say, 'he ought to have it looked at by a doctor'. This is just what they had said about young Laura in her wilder moments: 'She ought to have a doctor – 'look at 'er – she must 'ave an abscess growing in 'er 'ead!' It appears from this that in starting to write Joe's life, Laura felt a compulsion to return to and review her own, supplementing and continuing her own story beyond where she had left off in 1936.

Joe had a poetic streak and Laura responded to his lyricism when observing the sensuous and visual detail of day-to-day life on the *tober* (the circus site): 'When the grass is green below and the canvas is white above, it makes an old performer open his nostrils wide', he would say. In her chapter 'Circus Inspiration' in *The Magic of a Line*, she writes of 'the gold dust atmosphere of sunlight gleaming through canvas' and once again we sense the dust that had fallen on her in the barns at Laren or when the theatre footlights beamed through resin and cigarette smoke. These moments were all rolled into one when the band started up to mark the start of the performance. Then the sawdust rose in the limelight shaft, silhouetting the beasts and their riders in procession round the ring and she was consumed by the glamour and the controlled wild energy of it all.

After a short visit home to retrieve more paints, Laura rejoined the circus at Margate. It was there that Ally Bert began to take full responsibility for Laura's welfare, relieving her of unnecessary worries so that she could concentrate on the task in hand. Always, as we know, interested in food although not much of a cook herself as she admits, Laura retrospectively savours Ally's culinary triumphs created in the clowns' dressing van: chops, tomatoes and potatoes – the 'savoury smell' mingling with that of burning oil from the stove. Ally extended her duties by taking charge of Laura's paints, easel and brushes. This was often necessary in the approaches to the ring, where animals and performers jostled for space, and Laura was often in danger of being trampled on, her painting materials scattered and ground into the dust, or more often, mud.

Painting the circus was stressful. Since everything happened at speed, a glance at a subject had often to be enough to register line, movement and its effect. However, as she had found with the ballet, that could be an advantage, saying: 'I am never sure that my best work is not done under these difficult circumstances'. Even so, she found that the artistes in the main had great patience, never resenting her being there. She describes discovering 'a real sensation of painting power that season', attacking canvases without any preliminary preparation of sketches, driven into oblivion by the end of the day. She often set her easel near to the lions, the elephants and the zebras and got to know their ways and habits, developing respect for them. Her pleasure in the animals was unbounded and she painted and sketched them with vigour. She loved the set of their heads and the patterns of their coats, especially the zebras (bad tempered though they were) and, although always careful to keep her distance, was very fond of the elephants June and Mary (of disappearing fame) who was always accompanied by Tiny the Shetland pony. The subject matter was rich and Laura worked intensely over long hours. It was Ally who would remind her that it was time give over painting and talking into the small hours – she needed some sleep. Sleep, or rather the lack of it, in such a nomadic lifestyle could become a major preoccupation – you had to snatch it as and where you could. Laura was often found curled up in a corner having a desperately needed brief nap and in *A Proper Circus Omie*, 'Sleep' is the title of the final chapter.

The disconcerting lack of permanence, the continual putting up and pulling down of the Big Top took its toll. It was subject to the vagaries of the weather as autumn winds found their way beneath the canvas, and then as winter approached the weight of rain and snow strained the guide ropes and threatened collapse. But the worst fear at any time of year was fire. When winter came Laura did not continue with the Circus and returned to London. Carmo, however, decided to continue the tour, investing in a 'super-strong tent' to withstand the weather. The late winter of 1930–31 saw seriously bad weather and letters arrived from Ally describing deep mud and heavy snow, so heavy that it weighed down the big top and brought it to the ground. Nothing daunted, a new one was ordered but that too was destroyed in a matter of weeks, this time by the scourge of fire. Ally and Joe's letters from Birmingham described catastrophic scenes of great suffering. Flames had whipped through the stands and the 'wallings' (the canvas sides of the tent), up into the big top itself, then out into the stable tent where the animals were tethered and caged. There was panic and destruction everywhere: the lions got loose, Mary the elephant charged, the zebras were decimated. Laura writes of the disaster with a sense of drama and deep sorrow: the whole 'pretty show was down'.

When she rejoined Carmos in Hanley, Staffordshire, Carmo himself was facing bankruptcy, there was little feed for the animals and no wages.

Worse, they were playing to half-empty houses since it seemed that Potteries people hadn't much liking for circuses. The "Great Carmo" collapsed with exhaustion and had to take to his bed. At such times of distress, to "send in the clowns" was the solution. And so they did. By the time the circus was in Blackpool in the following spring, there had been a resurrection of both tents and spirits. Laura responds with enthusiasm and with the first chords of the band once more she cheers – 'The show is on!' But from this time on the Great Carmo's Circus was in decline, audiences further shrank and a series of disasters meant that by 1933 all performers and keepers were laid off and animals dispersed. Paris the lion was separated from Togare and Mary the elephant from her little Shetland pony, Tiny. It was heart-breaking.

Laura never travelled with the circus again, although she remained close to Ally and Joe and kept in regular contact with Captain Mills and the Christmas Circus at Olympia. Every year she and Harold would go to the Circus People's Reunion Dinner to meet old friends and they were members of the Circus Fans Association. In December 1934 the Knights were present at the inaugural dinner of the re-named Circus Friends Association. The celebrations started at midnight in the enormous circus ring at Olympia. It was hosted by the President, the writer and publicist for circus companies, Lady Eleanor Smith. The toasts were firstly to the *Cause of circus in England* and the second *To the Animals*! And to this last an elephant present trumpeted its response.

Laura was 2 years with the circus and the body of work she produced over that time was prolific. She herself acknowledges that to others her focus appeared to be narrow, and that her exhibitions contained 'too many red and blue tent poles, too many spreads of canvas, too many green and white stripes'. In 1931 some of her circus pictures were seen at the annual exhibition at the Carnegie Institute in Pittsburgh. A review of that exhibition by Harvey Gaul in the *Pittsburgh Post-Gazette* of 11th March 1931 begins with a hearty cheer for the artist, a 'familiar name here' he writes, and 'perhaps the most distinguished woman painter in that three-island circus, England'. Her latest collection on display at the Institute is, he continues, 'given over to glorifying saw-dust life and people who perform under the "Big Top" (and) much is made of the elephants … and Shetland ponies'. His general analysis is that Knight is a 'virile' and 'vigorous' craftsman – her work 'refreshing' after 'run-of-the-atelier' subject matter so often displayed.

Laura's work was most certainly not 'run-of-the-atelier' because critics and the public alike never knew what she would do next in terms of genre, style, subject and technique. Her circus work falls into three main categories: sketches and drawings, engravings, and full-bodied oil studies like *Three Clowns,* painted in 1930, which display her accomplishment as a *colourist.* Laura had explored this technique in the 1920s in the occasional ballet picture, such as her 1920 version of *Carnaval* showing the dancers assembling on stage before the curtain rises. This "behind the curtain" assembly of dancers in character sings loud with opaque primary colours – rich reds, emerald greens and peacock blues. In *Three Clowns* too there is strong and confident *moulding* of the figures through colour. They have substance (*mass*) and stand three-square solid and yet they also have a dynamic, existing in time as well as space as the scarlet, purple and dark blue of their costumes apparently folds, leans and settles into place.

Beneath the plush and richness of their costume and the make-up that identifies their roles as *tumbler, auguste* and *blanc,* these are recognizably Randy, Marba and Joe Bert, discussing a matter of some seriousness in the daily 'battle with circumstances'. A review in the *Nottingham Evening Post* under the headline 'Colourful Circus Studies in London Exhibition' (referring to the Leicester Galleries exhibition of 1932), describes the way the painting 'catches their transient poses, their moments of abstraction, and even their fleeting, self-revealing expressions to perfection, and fixes them for all time in virile line and tone' (11th March 1932). She must have been mightily pleased with these notices, although the re-iteration of the word 'virile' could well have been becoming tedious!

For a good while, the circus provided Laura with all she needed – a world where art and performance became as one, absorbing her just as she absorbed it: 'I became Circus – accepted in Circus as Circus for good and all – proud of it. I never wanted to do anything else again'. But she was to do other things. Like the circus she was always moving on, trying something new or revisiting a favourite place but with a different set of criteria and sense of purpose. When she was in Blackpool she first discovered ice-skating, fast becoming popular both as a sport and as entertainment as a result of the first Winter Olympics of 1924. Ice dance at first seemed to offer the grace of ballet matched with the spectacle of circus (it was often an act within the circus programme) and it appealed to her inclination for quick-fire sketches of figures in movement. But the images produced were often clumsy and unsatisfying and the task was not one that promised her personal fulfilment.

Laura's most fulfilling work was when her subject brought with it the gift of social integration and emotional identification. Some recent critical comment has described her circus work in particular as "sentimental" – in the sense of trite and kitsch. I would agree that they are "sentimental" but rather in the sense of showing empathy with the individuals beneath the costumes and make-up. Laura herself, who from childhood was always a performer, who kept her show on the road, adjusting to and riding over obstacles, identified with the Circus, just as she had identified with the dancers of the *Ballet Russes*. These were working metaphors for her life-experience. But now the question arises: where to and what next? The answer was plain: join the Gypsies.

Alfred Munnings had first introduced Laura to the Gypsy life early in the Newlyn days. Having an eye for horseflesh, he frequented country horse fairs and often took off on a whim to travel with the Romany people he met there. His painting of them and their horses was all consuming – they were his sort – nomadic, living beyond the pale of conventional social norms and yet true to their own. It was through his paintings of Gypsies that Munnings made what he considered to be his fortune, when in 1919 the two Connell brothers who owned a gallery in Bond Street, made an unexpected bid of several thousand pounds for a selection of his Gypsy paintings.

Munnings' interest in the turf and love of horses as well as the travelling folk who gathered at race meetings meant that he was a regular at Ascot and Epsom. Sometime around 1926 he placed the idea in Laura's head that these were the places to go for subject matter. She did in fact go to Epsom and to Ascot too, but not in AJ's company. In 1931 she went to stay with her friends Mr and Mrs Arnold Palmer and visited the races at Newmarket for Derby Day. Being Laura, she went fully prepared with her painting equipment just as she was when she went with Mrs Palmer to Epsom for the Oaks in the same year. In 1932 she was asked by Lord Astor to paint his winning horses *Mannamead* and *Pay Up*. Laura liked horses and, having studied so many in the circus stables and ring, was a highly competent painter of equines. However, she decided that her first interest was people and from 1934–40 regularly went to race meetings but not to paint the horses, instead 'it was the Cockney crowd, the bookies and their stands, and the gypsies I was after'. This was her introduction to another community and the start of a new obsession.

At first Ally and she went to Ascot by train – in all weathers – until Laura decided that an alternative form of transport was necessary. She hired a car that was big enough (only just) to hold her, Ally, the canvases and her painting equipment. Once she was on site, she 'perched on the roof' and fended off interference and inanities from the crowds as she painted, but it was not an ideal outdoor studio. So, in 1934 she persuaded Mr Sully, who ran the wedding and funeral transport business in Brixton next to where the

Berts lived in their wagon, to drive them to the racecourses of both Epsom and Ascot in his Rolls Royce. It was spacious – 'big enough to hold a thirty by twenty-five-inch canvas' as well as a generous picnic basket prepared by the Knights' House-keeper Mrs Molyneux. Even so, often the painter's view from the Rolls was restricted by the crowd that always gathered round to watch – each member in their way a critic, one spectator commenting: 'it'll look better when it's photoed'. Despite such distraction, with Ally mounting guard on the running board and fending off inquisitive folk and pestering children, over the several seasons Laura successfully 'painted more than sixty Canvases in that Rolls-Royce', including *The Paddock at Ascot* and *Rain at Ascot* both from 1936.

In fact, it was the artist, not the paintings, 'that was photoed'. The press took delight in her eccentricity and made her headline news. Laura Knight had been awarded an honour for services to the Arts in 1929 and was now addressed as a "Dame Commander of the British Empire". What did it matter that her new friends had no real idea of what the title meant? That they thought she might be a "Pantomime Dame" made it all the more special! Dame Laura Knight was riding high, secure in her natural element: with 'the sky for a ceiling' – the phrase she employs as the title for Chapter Twenty Five of *The Magic of a Line*.

The Gypsy paintings, the first of which, *The Gyppos*, was painted and exhibited in 1934, are as fresh and bright today as the finery worn by her subjects on those auspicious race days. They were willing to stand and pose for their portraits, that is, if she crossed their palms with silver! In *Romanies at Epsom* for example, *Gaudy Beggars* and *Ascot Finery* (Plate 18) the girls are pictured in close-up against a wide expanse of the racetrack. Since the format of these images was determined by the aperture of the door of the Rolls, there is focus but not confrontation between the artist and her subjects. She manages to capture both their wariness and vulnerability as they ply their trade, wheedling a piece of silver in return for a fortune cast in the crystal ball. Responding to the circumstances, Laura was employing a more sketchy technique than is evident in many of the Circus paintings. Nonetheless there is *plein air* clarity here – as intense as the song of the larks that she heard above her early in the morning before business began on the racecourse. Late at night she and Ally would return to St John's Wood, having shared supper with the Gypsies and sung songs around the campfire.

Laura was as robust and energetic as ever and game for any experience that would enhance and consolidate her grasp of this latest subject. So, when she was invited by the venerable Gypsy Queen, Granny Lilo Smith, to visit the permanent Gypsy camp at Iver in Buckinghamshire, she jumped at the chance. This was an opportunity to engage with a whole community – all ages – babies, middle aged and old – all settled in one place. In around 1936 she arranged for Mr Sully and the Rolls to take her and Ally and the picnic basket to the Common at Iver as he was regularly to do over the next years until war intervened. She describes the site in her own way, once again bringing past memory into the dramatic present: 'sweet is the scent of this wide-open space – foul is the smell of London streets on our way back … It was one of the most inspiring times of my working life'. The following image is redolent of the spirit of the Gypsies and of Laura at this time. She writes of an 'immense wild rose bush, gaudy with bloom, that flourished on the common' which for her 'typified the gypsy in its freedom of bloom and thorn'. There were indeed 'thorns' and she does not obscure the hardships. The dark moods, the 'aloof resignation' and the lassitude of the Romany people, she recognizes and understands, just as she also identifies with their gaudy extravagances and their love of display: 'I was at home with these people – found them kindly'.

Granny Lilo Smith was painted several times in her 'gypsy splendour' – the title of Laura's portrait of her in her best Ascot outfit, 1939. Now to be seen at Nottingham Castle Museum and Art Gallery, the painting is gloriously rendered. Finely formed, beautiful (despite her broken nose: 'Me 'usband – twice') and regal, she sits enthroned on the steps of her wagon. Laura painted the generations of the Smith family, from small children to grown men but she was most taken with the deaf-mute Beaulah (although her real name was Freedom), the wife of one of Granny Smith's sons, Harry. Painting the young woman several times, she found in her an instinctive creature with an unfathomable soul, a beauty that also held the 'marks of tragedy'. Beaulah, she writes was 'typical of her race in her aloofness and resignation to whatever happened'. Perhaps the most affecting of her portraits is that of a terminally ill Gypsy who insisted she paint him. Having once been painted by Munnings he told her he was a 'proper' artist's model. So, he left his sick-bed, got dressed in his good clothes and sat for his picture, while the rest of the camp kept an eye on the proceedings, aware that he was dying. He passed away the morning after the picture was finished.

These Gypsy studies are highly successful as Caroline Fox affirms: 'Perhaps because she was able to concentrate on painting one or two individuals' (the result of a narrow perspective given by the Rolls' door) and spend considerably more time on the sittings, Laura's paintings of the Gypsies 'are on the whole more interesting and satisfactory' than her Circus work. There was a major exhibition of her 'Gypsy' pictures at the Leicester Galleries which opened in April 1939. But those later paintings of travelling folk, painted on the racecourse, in the hop-fields, in their wagons take us well ahead in the narrative of Laura's life. We must return to another community that engaged her professional and personal interest at this time: the theatre.

During the First War Laura had been asked to design a programme for a play devised by E.V. Lucas of *Punch* in aid of the war effort and featuring the great Ellen Terry. Rightly in awe of the great actress, she describes her appearance. Wearing a blue silk dress, her 'grey hair loosely piled on the top of her head; she was still beautiful – age would not spoil the magnificent bone structure of her face'. It seemed to Laura that it was inappropriate when others urged the old lady to lie down and rest and reacts with anger 'I felt like shrieking: "Let her live while she is here".' It was a consideration that she herself was to request in old age.

With the departure of Diaghilev's *Ballet Russes* from London after the failure of the *Sleeping Beauty,* Laura became involved with a smaller ballet company run by Stanislas Idzikowsky at the Coliseum. Always competent with a sewing-machine, designing and making her own clothes as well as for amateur productions at Newlyn, Laura had her first taste of designing costume for the professional stage with Idzikowsky's production of *The Roses* in 1924. Her designs show a mix of conservatism and elements of abstract modernity, using striking primary colours. At the same time she was developing her etching and aquatint skills in images of the dressing-room that are dramatic, highly decorative and appealing, such as the etchings *The Dressing Room 2* and *Powder and Paint*, all produced in 1923–4. These intimate studies are essentially of women rather than performers – women dressing and applying make-up in readiness for a performance. Linking ballet and the theatre with her desire to portray the female form without embarrassment, these works contribute to a body of work that was building up in the 1920s. They can be cross-referenced with iconic paintings such as *Dressing for the Ballet* of 1927 that shows Eileen Mayo in the role of "ballerina" in the company of her "dresser". This striking image was submitted to the Royal Academy in that year and to the Paris Salon in 1928. However, when it is compared with *Ballet Dancer and Dressmaker* of 4 years later in 1932, the earlier painting seems awkward and contrived. That the artist reworked the earlier painting in 1947 shows that she herself was not convinced by it.

Like the Mayo picture, *Ballet Dancer and Dresser* was deliberately set up by the artist, this time in response to a commission from an American patron, H. Earl Hoover, the vacuum cleaner magnate. The sitters were one of Laura's favourite models Barbara Bonnar and her own dressmaker, Miss Ferguson. Unlike *Dressing for the Ballet,* this painting displays no self-conscious artifice. The dancer is caught mid-glance looking left, her body arrested in movement, while her dresser fixes a flounce on the skirt. Notwithstanding the delicate colour harmonies, the pink tights and ballet shoes and petal-like net of the skirt, here there is authority, power and control. This is no fragile ballerina but an athlete in repose. The dresser, while sharing the blue-black harmonies of the background drape, does not recede into it. Her head is at an equal level with that of her companion, their equally prominent hands connected through the sightline that moves from the dresser's elevated elbow, down through her right hand to connect with the dancer's left and to the toe of her ballet-shoe. Significantly, the line continues beyond the shoe downwards with the fabric to the cotton-reel at the margin to bring in the artist (and by implication the viewer) into their time and space and to complete the triangle. This is a set piece that affirms physical and professional equality. Like her *Self Portrait* of 1914, it testifies to another stage of her growing confidence and self-belief as well as to her professional status.

A Dame of the British Empire, Laura's status was further enhanced when the University of St Andrews awarded her an honorary degree of Doctor of Laws in 1931. She was impressed both by the ceremony and by the elaborate black and scarlet academic gown in which she processed. Harold was not present and she did not return to London directly from Scotland but to her friends at Carmos's circus which was then in Blackpool. When in 1929 she went to her investiture as DBE at St James' Palace, Harold had not gone, being occupied with a commission. It was their friend Barry Jackson who drove her to the Palace in his car, waited for her and brought her back in style. Harold's absence may indeed have been due to obligations relating to his work. More likely it was occasioned by his not being invited, having been marked as a conscientious objector in 1916.

On the way to the palace Laura had been somewhat discomforted when, on putting on her new gloves, talcum powder was dispersed liberally over her (dark) outfit. Once there, she was overcome by the protocol and ceremony but comforted to see an acquaintance in the crowd. This was Lillian Bayliss, there to receive the Companion of Honour. Bayliss had become manager of the Old Vic Theatre in 1912 and through her tireless efforts it had become a successful centre for theatrical experiment. Over the years 1914–1921 the Old Vic mounted the whole of the First Folio of Shakespeare's plays with Sybil Thorndyke as the leading lady. Other leading actors who made their debut there include John Geilgud, Edith Evans, Ralph Richardson and

Laurence Olivier. In 1929, Lillian Bayliss was working towards a revival in fortunes for the Sadlers Wells Theatre – a project that was to merge the two theatres. The "Vic-Wells" company was to seed-corn highly distinguished theatre and ballet companies in London. Significantly, the Bolshoi, performing for the first time out of the USSR since the Revolution, visited London in 1936 and Laura was there sketching and painting in the wings. This was an exciting and progressive period for dance and theatre. For Laura it marked a change of pace and direction.

The Knights, if we remember, had first met Barry Jackson, the son of a wealthy Birmingham grocer, in Newlyn in 1914 just as he was establishing the Repertory company in his native city of Birmingham. Previous to that in the early 1900s he and his friends Herbert Milligan, John Drinkwater and C.R. (Tim) Dawes had performed short plays at the Jackson family home, The Grange in Moseley, Birmingham. Becoming more ambitious, the group formed themselves into "The Pilgrim Players", performing adaptations of Shakespeare, some works by Ibsen and Galsworthy as well as plays they themselves had written. They were first based at the Edgbaston Assembly Rooms, but aspired to build a new theatre, the Birmingham Repertory Theatre in Station Street. Funded by private monies, it opened in February 1915 with a production of *Twelfth Night*.

It was not until after the First World War that the Knights were to come across Jackson again, when they accidently met him outside Lord's Cricket Ground in London. By that time he was a well-known producer and director in the theatre world, in London and in Birmingham. He invited them to his home in Birmingham and to see the Repertory project, and from then on they were firm friends. In fact their friendship with Barry Jackson and his partner the actor Scott Sunderland was to be one of the main supports of Harold and Laura for almost half a century. They understood each other and appreciated the driving force lying behind their artistic endeavour. When in 1932 Laura, Harold, Ethel Robertson, Scott Sunderland and Barry Jackson went on holiday together to Switzerland, it was essentially a "family outing" uniting all the arts – painting, music and the theatre. Writing at the close of *Oil Paint and Grease Paint* in 1936, she makes that clear, since it is the arts which 'make the world a richer place' – the visual artist, like Turner or Rembrandt, makes us see; the musician opens our ears and in the theatre our heart is touched by the highs and lows of humanity. It was indeed her joy to be able to project herself into all of them.

The Knights were present at many memorable performances at "The Rep" and at the Regent Theatre in London. Jackson conceived the idea of

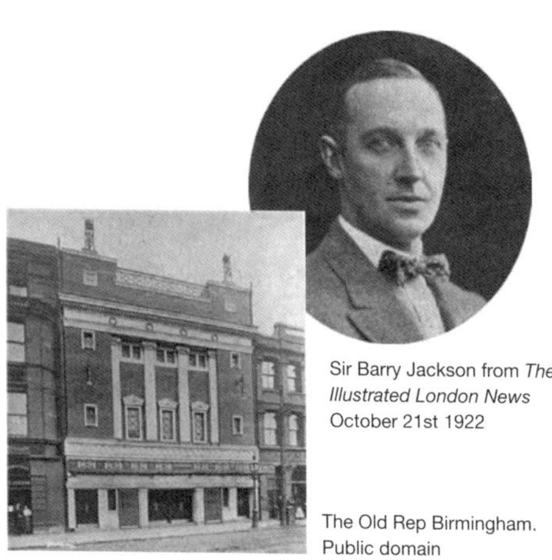

Sir Barry Jackson from *The Illustrated London News* October 21st 1922

The Old Rep Birmingham. Public domain

performing Shakespeare in modern dress (a trend led by Gordon Craig after the Great War) and in 1923 produced *Cymbeline,* that was dubbed "Shakespeare in Plus-fours".

It was directed by H.K Ayliff and designed by Paul Shelving who was to have a long and successful career at "The Rep" as designer of over three hundred productions. As impresario, Jackson facilitated the premieres of many important works, such as Pirandello's *Six Characters in Search of an Author* in 1922, a play that he had faith in ('the best play I have ever known' he told the Knights) but which attracted little interest or popularity. It closed after 3 weeks. The opposite was true of George Bernard Shaw's epic *Back to Methuselah* which was premiered in 1923. For then Shaw held the attention of the nation with works that entertained and wore their erudition lightly, works that combined wit and humour with social comment and philosophy. To stage a Shaw play attracted public attention, anticipation and curiosity – you could not lose.

Birmingham Repertory Theatre was to see the emergence of some of the most important actors and actresses of the 20th century stage, whose performances Laura saw from the auditorium as well as sketching them in the dressing room. Audiences and critics alike were entranced by Gwen Ffrangcon-Davies (1891–1992). Laura met the young actress in 1922 when Jackson transferred his production of Rutland Boughton's operetta *The Immortal Hour* to the Regent Theatre in London. The dress she wore in the character of the heroine Etain, was a make-do one devised by Laura in silver and it was highly effective. Laura loved being busy behind the scenes, making herself useful as well as recording characters, events and off-stage business.

In one of her watercolours, now in the Victoria and Albert Theatre Collection, Gwen Ffrangcon-Davies is shown being laced into her Juliet costume by her dresser for the production of *Romeo and Juliet* that opened at the Birmingham Repertory Theatre on 27 May 1922 with Ion Swinley as Romeo. As with her ballet pictures, Laura was ready to acknowledge the support structures backstage that make the theatrical illusion possible: the application of make-up and the process of dressing, or rather being dressed for a part by the "dressers" who are allowed their place alongside the "stars". The production was revived at London's Regent Theatre on 24th May 1924, with John Gielgud playing Romeo to Ffrangcon-Davies' Juliet (below).

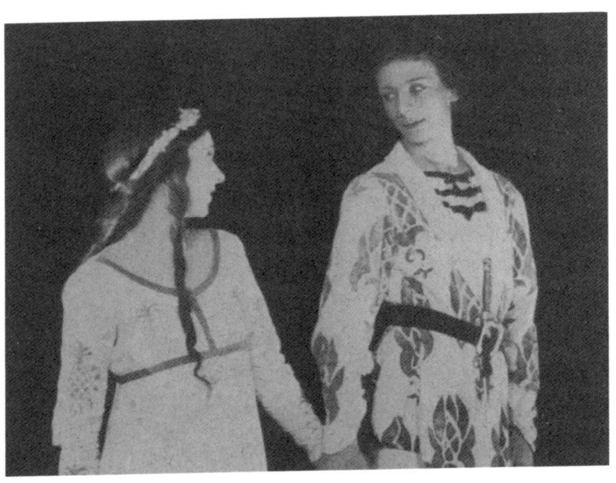

Regent's Theatre, London, 1924. Public domain

Laura followed the production to London and there drew Gielgud in his dressing room, nonchalant, 'wearing the robe for his next entry, a small velvet hat on his head, a cigarette in his mouth, as he stands manicuring with an orange stick'. These rapid sketches are essentially of the moment and once again testify to the artist's interest in 'the polarity between the fixed image and the flux of life', as Wilcox says in *Laura Knight at the Theatre*. They also display at times the contested area between the actor and the role. That was a space that Laura inhabited very comfortably.

In the years after the Knights moved to London, when Laura made a name for herself as a painter of ballet, circus, gypsy life and the theatre, so many markers were set and so much publicity was generated, that by the

1930s Laura had celebrity status at home and abroad. This period was the one that established and consolidated her reputation in the public sphere, and gave her much excitement, satisfaction and good companionship. Life was 'rich' – her own favourite adjective for whatever was special and satisfying – and applicable as much to curtains as to people and places. Not that this was a cue for complacency. At all times, as she says towards the close of her first autobiography, it was her 'joy of joys' to 'go on, to see in some common thing interest that has never been seen before, to understand, to grasp life with both hands'. Therefore, the following years were to be equally interesting and fulfilling, with a settled and bright horizon for them both – and that horizon was to be articulated by the 'flow of the Malvern Hills'.

CHAPTER TEN

"A panoramic view ... like a half-rolled map"

The 1930s was a decade of professional consolidation for the Knights. In 1931 there was a major exhibition of Laura's work at the Art Gallery of Toronto in Canada as well as at the Usher Gallery in Lincoln, England. In 1932 she was elected President of the Society of Women Artists and a Fellow of the Royal Society of Painter-Etchers and Engravers. In 1933 there was a joint exhibition with Harold at the Laing Art Gallery, Newcastle and at the Castle Art Gallery, Nottingham the following year. In March 1935 some of her work was exhibited in Wellington, New Zealand, organized by the highly pro-active art dealer Murray Fuller whose mission was to bring contemporary British art to the Antipodes.

In 1929 Fuller had brought a collection of paintings including works by William Orpen, George Clausen as well as by Laura Knight for exhibition in Melbourne, Australia. Unfortunately, the Manuka, the ship that was carrying them from Melbourne to Wellington, was shipwrecked on a reef in the Catlins, South Otago, with the loss of almost all cargo, including Laura's painting of Pavlova and her portrait of Irene Dodson from Baltimore. The total financial loss to Fuller was in the region of £25,000. Undaunted, he continued to arrange for exhibits to be brought over for exhibition and sale. This explains the number of Knight's works now in New Zealand, including the self-portrait which Laura painted c.1921 (Plate 1), showing her at her easel, with palette and brushes and wearing her characteristic hat and a smile that none could ignore. Originally purchased by the collectors Mr and Mrs D.A. Ewen, they gifted it to the New Zealand national museum Te Papa Tongarewa in 1936.

In 1936 Laura was appointed a full Royal Academician and Harold, who had been elected President of the Nottingham Society of Artists (a position he held for 10 years) in that year, was created a full Royal Academician in 1937. As the first married couple to be nominated Royal Academicians, they made the newspapers at home and abroad. In 1936 Laura sat on

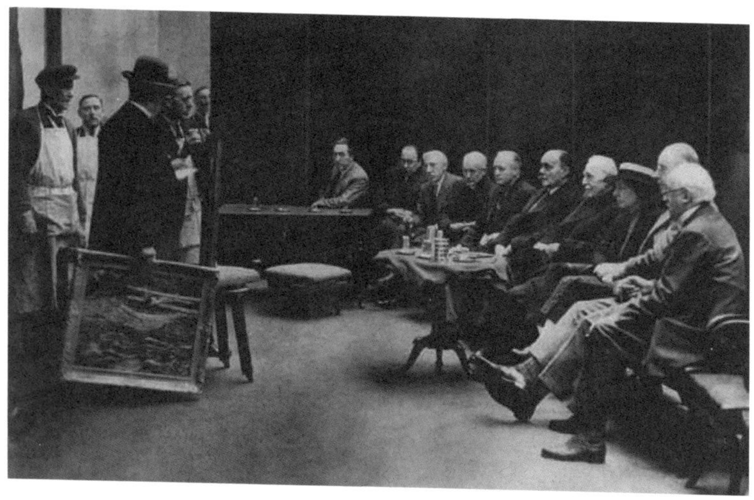

Royal Academy Selection Committee. Agency Press photograph.
Laura seated third from the right

the hanging committee at the Academy for the first time. Newspapers as far-flung as Baltimore in the United States and Sydney, Australia featured a photograph with the headline: "Unique Honour for Famous Woman Artist". To mark her election as a full Academician Laura had professional photograph portraits taken at the studios of Bassano Ltd – photographers to royalty and society figures for over 80 years. These photographs (now held by the National Portrait Gallery) are an interesting archive of the image Laura wished project at this time. In one study she wears her artistic ethnic costume, influenced by the visits to the Tyrol and Prague. She holds a lit cigarette and, it appears, wears full make-up, thereby combining the image of the bohemian artist with the socialite. In another she appears in profile, looking highly sophisticated in a gown inspired by the art-deco Egyptian revival. Here she is presented as a woman of style and of some wealth. A *Daily Herald* press photograph from 1937 shows Dame Laura and Dod Procter (whose husband Ernest had died prematurely in 1935), standing on the steps of the Royal Academy. Laura, wearing a smart ocelot coat and pork pie hat, has clearly grown into her role as Dame of the British Empire and Royal Academician and it suits her. Both Dod and Laura's names were generally recognised by the public. This, however, was not so much for their painting but increasingly through the commercial application of their work.

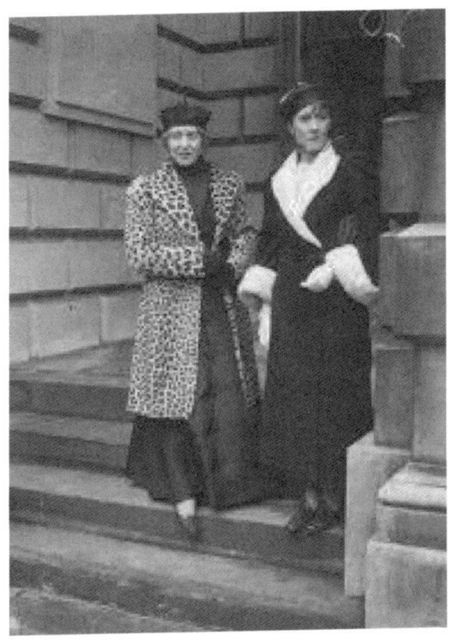

Daily Herald, 30 April 1937. Public domain

The '30s saw an easing of the Knights' financial circumstances. When Uncle Arthur Peter died in 1931, Laura benefitted from the Will as did her sister Sis. Family records describe how shortly before his decease there had been a family dispute over the inheritance. One branch of the Thers (Thirs) claimed that they should have had a portion of Aunt West-Ther's estate and went to see Uncle Arthur Peter Bates (then living in Kent) about it. There was a major row, Uncle Arthur giving short shrift, saying that the Thers 'would not get a penny, he would sooner leave it to a home for cats'. He died soon after, and Dame Laura and Sis got the lot!

In 1934, in a less controversial transaction, Harold inherited a legacy of the large sum of £12,000 from an aunt. Lamorna Birch wrote to Ella Naper: 'He (Harold) tells me it (his inheritance) makes him feel easier, as he and Laura never had much of a gift in the way of saving'. It was around this time that Laura bought tenement property in Brixton which, rented out, brought in regular income and in 1938 Harold was persuaded by his solicitor, Mr Pettit, to purchase (with a small mortgage) the freehold of numbers 12, 14, and 16 Langford Place for the sum of £8,000. Numbers 12 and 14 were to be rented out while the Knights continued at number 16, rent-free. Langford Place was convenient and the accommodation highly suitable with studios for both Laura and Harold. There was also space for Laura's circus friend Ally Bert, who, after Joe's death, lived in two rooms next to Laura's studio. Ally remained with the Knights for the next 30 years (with a break during the War) as Laura's loyal assistant and companion. Then there was Mrs Molyneux, the housekeeper and her husband – both trusted house-staff who looked after the place when the Knights were away. This was especially important since in the 1930s the Knights increasingly spent the summer months at Malvern in Worcestershire.

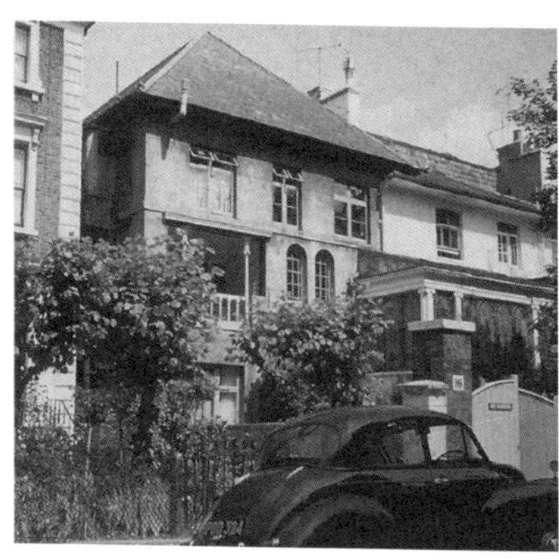

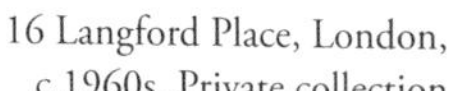
16 Langford Place, London, c.1960s. Private collection

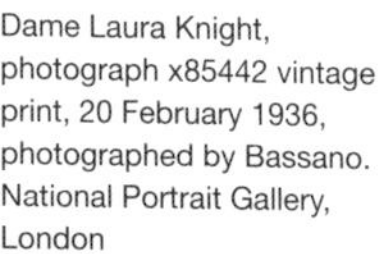
Dame Laura Knight x168788, bromide print, 1930 photographed by Walter Stoneman. National Portrait Gallery, London

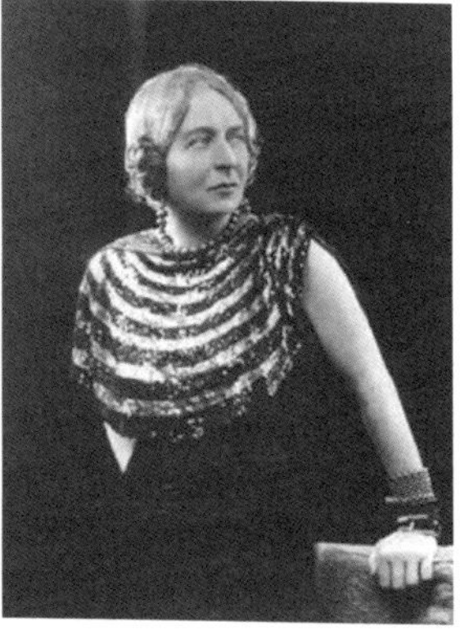
Dame Laura Knight, photograph x85442 vintage print, 20 February 1936, photographed by Bassano. National Portrait Gallery, London

Initially they stayed at Blackhills, the house of Sir Barry Jackson (he was knighted in 1925) which he had built on the slopes of the Herefordshire Beacon but later they took hotel rooms at The White Horse Inn or the Mount Pleasant Hotel, Malvern. From there they were able to join Jackson's other friends for the annual Malvern Theatrical Festival which he had established in 1929. In the early years the Festival scene was presided over by the playwright and larger-than-life celebrity George Bernard Shaw. A number of his plays were performed at the Festival over the years, and many were premiered there, including in its first season *The Apple Cart* and *Too True to be Good* in 1932.

There is a group photograph, taken in 1936 on the steps of Lawnside School in Malvern which was occasionally used to house guests, showing the Knights, Shaw, Jackson and his partner the actor Scott Sunderland (who was to play Colonel Pickering in the film version of Shaw's *Pygmalion* in 1938 and appear in the film *Goodbye Mr Chips* in 1939) along with other 'notables from all walks of life' – poets, novelists, playwrights and politicians. In the photograph Laura can be seen at the end of the second row, right. Harold with spectacles is in the back row, centre, next to Scott Sunderland on his left. Shaw, centre, is unmistakable with the dramatist, poet and first Manager of the Birmingham Repertory Theatre, John Drinkwater on his left. Barry Jackson sits at the end of the front row right.

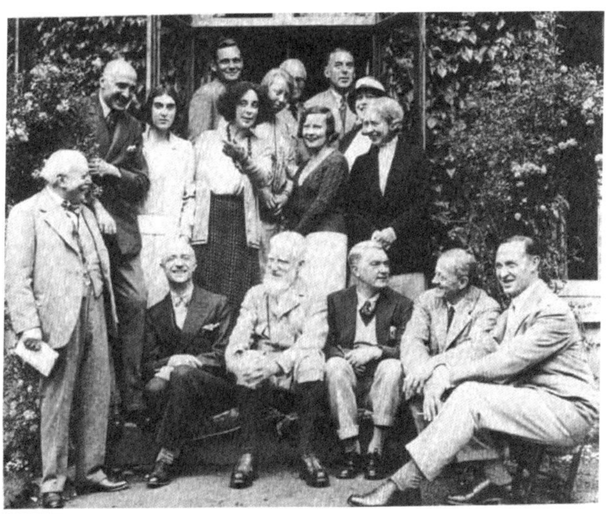

Guests at the Malvern Festival, Lawnside, 1936. Private collection

When at the Festival, Laura writes of mornings walking the hills before meeting others in the group on the terrace at Lawnside – 'to take the waters or a cup of coffee and discuss the play of the night before'. Harold and Laura would stay on after the Festival 'for the sake of the scrambles and walks that we loved'. Amongst friendships forged in Malvern, was that with Maurice and Marjorie Averill, who farmed locally and were to possess the largest collection of Laura's works held in private hands. Then there was the university academic and theatre historian Allardyce Nichol and his wife Josie. The Nichols were closely involved in the Festival until 1933 when, having been awarded a Professorial Chair at Yale, they left for the States. After the War, Nichol was Head of the English Department at Birmingham University and the Founding Director of the Shakespeare Institute, posts held until his retirement in 1961. Their house, Wind's Acre situated on the hillside to the West of the Herefordshire Beacon at Malvern, was rented out during their absence and Laura was to take over the garage-stable building there as her studio.

As you approach the Malvern Hills, they rise up from rich agricultural loam with the counties of Worcestershire and Herefordshire on either side and the Severn Valley to the east. On a good day you can see thirteen counties from the topmost ridge. The 360-degree view expands from the Lickey Hills near Birmingham to the north and Cannock Chase to the north-east; west from the Wrekin to the mountains of Wales and beyond to the Bristol Channel; south west are the 'blue remembered hills' of Shropshire and due south are the Cotswolds, while the three cathedral spires of Worcester, Gloucester and Hereford can be spied on the plains below. When she visited Malvern, Laura always sought out a hotel room that gave her, on waking, at least a partial view of this panorama.

The town of Great Malvern is situated at the northern end of the Malvern range, beneath the Worcestershire Beacon and North Hill. An ancient track runs the length of its spine and along this Laura often scrambled between the gorse and bracken, meeting on the way the local 'character' Alice Betteridge with her pony and the donkeys which carried children and less able visitors up the hills to take in the view. In 1939 Laura painted Alice, her pony and one of the donkeys against the extended landscape in a small oil *On the Top of the Hill*. At the Royal Academy exhibition of that year, just before war was declared, she showed another landscape featuring the Betteridge animals: *Harvest*. Bathed in golden light, they stand in the foreground while the patched fields and rolling hills recede into the distance.

This expanding landscape meant much to Laura and is best described in her own words from Chapter 44 of *Oil Paint and Grease Paint*:

'In panoramic view from north to south, like a half-rolled map, fertile England's beauty lies in sunlit patch of stubble, farm, copse and snug woolly tree and countless spires of churches among distant towns' blue slates … Thunderous cumuli in solemn majesty show against intensest blue, rounded mountains of glowing white modelled with both tender and heavy tones of grey, all more static and solid seeming than land itself, as in glorious game shadow chases shadow'.

The effect is of a movie camera panning across the landscape to strains of Elgar – the composer who is most associated with a particular kind of "Englishness" and with the Malverns. He died there in 1934, too old and sick for Laura to have known much of him other than as a presiding genius of the place.

There was one other presiding genius in Malvern and that was George Bernard Shaw. GBS (as he was commonly known) with his wife Charlotte (Laura describes her as rather 'crabbie') stayed in Malvern every year and was the focus of the Festival. He was very much up to the role and Malvern reciprocated, taking him to their hearts so that on his 80th birthday in 1936 there was a celebration and the official planting of a mulberry tree in the town. When in public, Shaw always played to the gallery, or a camera, and enjoyed his notoriety – although at times he could be short-tempered, especially with autograph hunters. In the company of GBS, for once Laura found her own exuberance over shadowed. Their first meeting in Birmingham had not been auspicious. GBS had been introduced to her as 'Mrs Knight' and he had passed by. But, having been advised as to just who she was, he shortly returned with: 'I hear you are Laura Knight. I didn't realise that … you could have been any Mrs Knight'. When in Malvern she and Harold were often in the company of the Shaws and met the visitors who constantly came to the door of the great man. One day GBS introduced a stranger to them, without any qualification, as the 'other Mr Shaw'. Mystified they conversed pleasantly on general topics and it was only when they left that Harold realised just who this person was. 'Mr Shaw' was then the pseudonym adopted by T. E. Lawrence of Arabia.

It appears that while Laura was to some extent awed by GBS's overbearing persona, she also understood and enjoyed his mischievous ways. In *The Magic of A Line* she writes about his physical and personal idiosyncrasies,

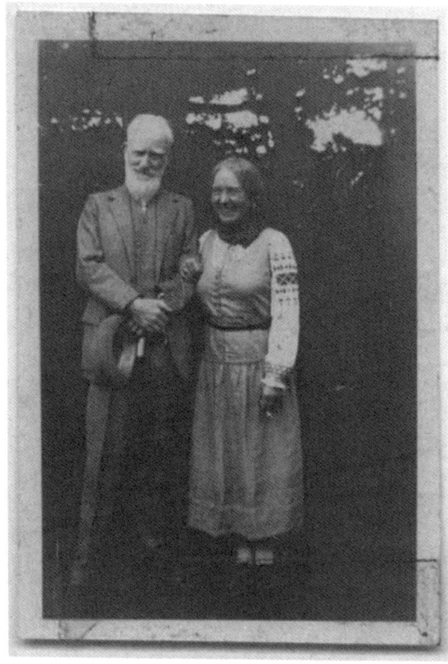

Laura Knight and GBS at the Malvern Festival. Public domain

witnessed in 1933 when she attempted, at his request, to paint his portrait. First there was the shape of his skull which he announced was the same as that of Catherine the Great and denoted, he archly claimed, 'excessive sexual development'. Then there were his ears: 'When I was a child, my nurse used to cling on to my petticoats for fear my ears might act as sails and carry me away!' This puckish sense of humour was at times disconcerting and totally missed by the Hungarian sculptor who was modelling a portrait bust at the same time as Laura was working on the picture. Once the sculptor had gone, Shaw settled down and was a good, if over-mobile, sitter, talking and singing operatic scores throughout.

The finished portrait exacted differing responses. Mrs Shaw thought the portrait the worst she had seen. GBS was unconvinced: 'you made me a sincere man, and all my life I have been an actor'. Perhaps that final observation explains why a recent reviewer in *The Guardian* describes the portrait as "frankly terrible" (14th July 1913). Agreed, the image is benign, neither mercurial nor abrasive enough for some tastes, but it does capture one of the less well-known aspects of Shaw's capricious personality. He was, Laura says, a 'strange character, with an extraordinary care to be no bother to others'.

In life, it is very satisfying when events take a turn that completes a circle. In 1933 Laura was invited to Haddon Hall, in Derbyshire, the summer residence of the Manners family. She was to paint the portrait of Violet, Duchess of Rutland. That came about through an introduction made through the Dowager Duchess, who, a great lover of music, was a friend of Rae and Ethel Robertson. Duly, Laura made the pilgrimage to the Hall where over 50 years ago she and her sisters had been taken by their Mother on sketching holidays. It was an emotional experience, like 'coming back home'. During the 5 weeks she was there, Laura was treated royally: her studio was in what had been Queen Elizabeth I's bedchamber and she had her personal footman behind her chair at meals. In conversation with him, Laura (always democratic in social exchanges) told him how she and her sisters had engraved their names on a pane of glass with Mother's diamond ring. The footman at once set about looking for it, but the house had been a ruin then and the old glass had been re-set when the Hall was refurbished. It was not found. Meanwhile, the painting went well: the Duchess, small-boned, elegant, dressed in silver and black with a white fur wrap, standing composed alongside "John Bull" the bulldog, whose 'ugly mug' Laura went to great pains to represent successfully.

Another odd juxtaposition occurred when the Dowager Duchess took Laura to meet the Duchess of Devonshire at nearby Chatsworth House. There, amidst all the grandeur of this most priceless example of Britain's great houses, Laura was shown one her own paintings that hung in the Duchess' bedroom. To her surprise the subject was of one of the daughters of the destitute miner's family that she had painted in 1905–6 at Staithes. Laura records the conversation:

'That's Elizabeth Alice!' said I.
'What a lovely name', answered the Duchess, 'and where did you find Elizabeth Alice?'
I just stopped myself in time, and only said, 'In a fishing village called Staithes on the north-east coast … where did you get it?' 'At an exhibition you held at the Leicester Galleries years ago'.

It might have spoilt her enjoyment of Elizabeth Alice had I told her that she, one of six children born to her father and mother, all suffered the most hideous poverty it has been my experience to know'.

Perhaps it was this concatenation of events that suggested to Laura that she should revisit her past and attempt an autobiography. On her return to London she began but her first attempts were so confused and disappointing that she burned her notes in her studio fireplace. The project was further set back in November 1933 when she slipped on the bathroom floor. The accident was a serious one – her left leg was broken. Across the world column space was given over to the news that the 'famous artist' had fallen but was 'comfortable'. This was highly unlikely given the seriousness of the break. Initially bed rest was recommended but with no improvement over some weeks, it was decided that a surgeon be sought to re-set the bone. The surgeon vouchsafed that it was most unlikely that she would walk again and rumours circulated that her painting days were over. For one of Laura's temperament, such a diagnosis was catastrophic. However, it was 'Harold who saved me from being the cripple that Mr Broster had expected'. He transported Laura and her plaster to Malvern where he instituted a regime of exercise, 'giving up his time to support me, step by step, eventually giving me the courage to walk again'. That spring, fearful and in discomfort, in her imagination Laura returned to Cornwall. 'Are the primroses out on the steps?' she wrote to Ella Naper, 'Dear Trewoofe, I can see it so plainly'.

The view from the window of the hotel room at the Mount Pleasant Hotel where she was forced to spend much time, offered an eastern prospect which excited her imagination: 'I got a rage for painting dawns', she writes – especially in September when autumnal 'strands of grey mist wreathe the landscape'. The American writer, poet and close friend of W. H. Davies, Conrad Aiken, who was in Malvern in 1935 (he was to be especially useful in helping Laura with the proofs of *Oil Paint and Grease Paint*), called these 'Laura's Lyrics'. This lyricism was enhanced by her friendship with the Head Mistress at Lawnside School, Miss Winifred Burrows. Together they spent many hours reciting, discussing and writing poetry. With words and rhythms on her mind, now the time was propitious to return to her autobiography.

She did not find the writing of *Oil Paint and Grease Paint* easy (an alternative title – *Canvas and Backcloth* (suggested by the typist at her publishers, Ivor Nicholson & Watson) was rejected – it was without the neat parallelism of the final title). While she had a host of anecdotes and a deal to say, a chronology to give structure to these was difficult to re-construct from memory – and memory can be deceiving. In both Laura's autobiographies, as she herself admits, timescales do become confused and events blur. For some readers this quality is frustrating and confusing, while others find it revealing of her personality with its own charm. For Laura's prose in *Oil Paint and Grease Paint* has great directness and vibrancy and it also has passages of pure poetry. In these lyrical moments remembered visual and aural impressions coalesce into passages of striking beauty. An example is this sequence from her Staithes memories in Chapter 5:

> An early winter morning: here comes a woman just back from the mussel-beds; she has been miles away over the rocks at low tide, balanced on her head is about a hundred-weight, she walks with an easy stride as if carrying nothing. Her face is dark and stern – unapproachable – her carriage superb. She wears a tubful of bait for a crown.
>
> Now is a summer evening: the sun is down behind the hills, deeptoned and sharp against the gold of the sky; shadow lies over the village, quay and beach, down which rush hurried figures. A man is half-hidden under a heap of purple blackish nets; another balances a pair of oars; a boy carries a string of coloured bladders used to buoy up the nets, they look like enormous bunches of grapes strung back and front. One woman swings a "tommy tin" containing a man's food for the night – a bundle of oilers hung over her arm; another woman has a bucket of coals on her head for the bogie fire. Cobles slide over the timbers with grating sound, here and there they are launched – a sea-booted figure wades and pushes – "She's afloat!" as he flings himself over the stern.
>
> During this, the herring season, one often sees such a scene, darkly rich against the sea, turquoise splashed with indigo in the last rays of the sun…

Here we have the immediacy of the dramatic present that, while projecting detail with a clear focus, sets it within a melange of sense perceptions where light, shadow and jewel-like hues come to the fore and recede. Taking care not to be over-precious (Laura was never, ever precious herself), what is interesting to notice is that in such a passage temporal and spatial relationships are telescoped as in the cinematic technique of montage. This liberates the sequencing of images from the restrictions of a single, fixed point of view. It is a technique we have met before. Neither Laura's panoramic views from the heights of Malvern or such sequences of her writing in *Oil Paint and Grease Paint*, offer the viewer/reader a formulaic composition structured according to conventions of landscape or the rules of syntax. Instead they are an 'assemblage' of parts, open to re-assembly as they are re-read and re-viewed.

Charles Marriott in his review of the book in the *Times Literary Supplement* on 7th March 1936, describes Laura's writing style as characteristically 'vivid, forcible and full of jumps'. He suggests that this is an essentially 'feminine' trait, typical of her painting as well as her writing. After all, he adds, the characteristic of a masculine style is 'control'. Such a gendered comment is paradoxical given previous comments about Laura's 'masculine', 'virile' style! But it proves the absurdity of imposing a gender paradigm on any art form. To repeat Laura's words in *The Queen* magazine in 1930: 'art should be regarded as (international and) sexless'. That there is no formal linear structure, or 'plot', to her writing does not mean irrational dislocation and confusion. Instead we have an alternative – the successful melding of image, rhythm and feeling. Whether this is feminine or masculine is irrelevant.

Throughout her life Laura Knight could be excitable and dramatic, prompting Harold's oft-heard response to the latest hyperbole: 'Oh Laura how you do exaggerate!' But she was also pragmatic and clear-sighted in her grasp not just of the aesthetic but of the financial value of her work in the marketplace. As we have seen, she always held out for her price, even if that meant she lost a buyer for a picture, on the principle that to accept less meant a devaluation of the Laura Knight "brand". She was disappointed when *Oil Paint and Grease Paint*, having sold well as a hardback edition, was published as a paperback by Penguin Books in 1941. It was a wartime edition, printed on thin paper and in three volumes of unequal length. Sales of the first volume were good but few people bothered to purchase the full set of three. That this was a blow to Laura's self-pride is evident, concerning enough for Barry Jackson to make a point of mentioning it in a letter dated Malvern 20th January 1942 to the Nichols in America. We have to remember that from her childhood in Nottingham, through the Staithes and Newlyn years to the "Great Depression" of the 1930s and beyond, she and Harold were never without a deeply rooted insecurity over money. No one could be more aware than Laura that money is more quickly lost than it is accumulated. She also knew from personal experience that women needed to assert their professional status and equality with men not merely in terms of opportunity but also in earning a living. It was in recognition of this that she became a member of the Society of Women Artists, becoming its President in 1932 and holding that position until 1967.

Laura was not a "feminist" in the political sense, although over the years she did show solidarity with the women's movement. This was inevitable, given her own early experience and the progressive social circles into which she was introduced in the 1920s and 30s. In 1928 she was present at the funeral of Emmeline Pankhurst, one of the leading figures of the suffragette campaign. The press report reads:

WOMEN'S MOVEMENT Stormiest Scene Closed
Mrs. Pankhurst Buried LONDON, June, 18.
Leaders of the women's movement, including Mrs. Baldwin, Lady Astor, Mrs. Despard, Mrs. Pethick-Lawrence, Miss (sic) Laura Knight, and Miss (sic)

Flora Drummond, attended the funeral of the late Mrs. Emmeline Pankhurst (hon. treasurer of the W.S.P.U.) at St. John's, Westminster, the closing scene of the stormiest episode in the suffragette campaign.

In the 1930s Laura was to paint portraits of two of those named alongside her at the graveside: Emmeline Pethick-Lawrence and Flora Drummond. Both had been militant suffragettes and organisers within the Women's Social and Political Union (WSPU). After the First World War both continued campaigning but with a broader remit. In the 1930s Drummond founded the Women's Guild of Empire, a right-wing league opposed to communism and fascism. Pethick-Lawrence, a pacifist, strenuously continued her work for the Women's International League for Peace which she had begun during the 1914–18 War. Another strong woman in the Knights' circle was Elizabeth Cadbury, the wife of the chocolate manufacturer, Quaker and philanthropist George Cadbury. Their Malvern house, Wind's Point, was situated close to that of Barry Jackson beneath the Herefordshire Beacon. Elizabeth Cadbury was a woman of energy with a strong social conscience, involving herself in a variety of social and educational projects in Birmingham. Created a Dame in 1934, she was President of the Union of Women Workers (later the National Council of Women), within which she held the positions of President, Convenor and Chair of its Peace and International Relations Committee. These connections were significant for Laura and Harold (remember, also a pacifist), for over the decade both were variously engaged in challenging the drift towards fascism and war.

The economic slump – known as "The Great Depression" – peaked in America and Britain in the mid-1930s. These were dangerous times throughout Europe for with the rise of mass unemployment came political instability; the threat of revolution from "socialists" and "communists" and with that the rise of Fascism. Within this context Laura and Harold's commitment was made clear. In 1935, along with artists such as Edward Ardizzone, Duncan Grant, Paul Nash and Henry Moore, they contributed paintings to the *Artists Against Fascism and War* exhibition, organised by the Artists International Association (the AIA). Formed in 1933, the AIA was originally set up as a far-left political group but its artistic aims were liberal and dedicated to furthering the principles of 'Peace, Democracy and Cultural Development'. One of the practical strategies of the AIA was to set up travelling art exhibitions and commission mural paintings to give the public more immediate access to art. In the wider context, in 1935 the AIA was raising funds in support of the left-wing Republican side in Spain and to support artists who were seeking refuge from oppression in Nazi Germany.

The Spanish Second Republic, set up in 1931 was challenged in the 1934–5 elections by a far-right coalition which set out to renege on recent legislation on land reform. This led to a general strike and insurrection, suppressed by a military force led by General Francisco Franco. In 1935 it was clear that there was a dangerous polarisation of forces – the Communist left and the Fascist right and that this would come to a crisis. Meanwhile, the rise of the Nazi party under the direction of Adolph Hitler was playing out an ominous scenario in Germany. Between 1932 and 1934 the Nazi party gained dominance in the Reichstag with Hitler appointed Chancellor in 1933. Policies were put into place to assure the furtherance of the Fascist agenda and the establishment of the Third Reich. The Gestapo or secret police was formed; Trade Unions and opposition political parties were banned; Germany re-armed and withdrew from the League of Nations in 1933. In 1934 Hitler assumed overall power as Führer and in 1935 general conscription was announced together with the institution of the Nuremburg Laws which defined German citizenship and forbade relationships between Jews and Aryans.

In retrospect it is possible to grasp the significance of these events in building the momentum towards the Second World War, but such an overview was not apparent to those living through the decade. Despite prophetic warnings, many, desperate to avoid another conflict after the Great War in Europe less than 20 years before, preferred to ignore them. Others were too occupied in finding the next meal to be alert to the signs of the times. Even artists at the height of their fame were finding it tough, as Laura admits: 'periods frequently came when we did not know where we should find the next quarter's rent'. However, if an artist was alert to new commercial outlets, the early 20th century provided opportunity and Laura was not slow to exploit them.

In his biography of Lamorna Birch, Austin Wormleighton observes that in the 1930s Birch changed his style to accommodate the public demand for colour reproductions: 'Although the market for original art was sluggish, quality fine art reproductions were selling well, underpinned by Frost and Reed's belief that their own reproductions were "indistinguishable from the original when viewed at a proper distance". Prints were affordable and harmonised with the uncluttered interior designs of the 1930s.' Frost and Reed, the pre-eminent producer of fine-art prints in the period, had outlets in Bristol, London and the United States. As well as the standard print run, they would produce around 100 proof copies, each to be signed by the artist. Many artists, feeling the financial pressures, chose to work with the technology and marketing expertise of Frost and Reed. Of the several images of Laura's that were reproduced in this way, *Lamona Cove* and *Dancer and Dresser* were the most popular. It was in this way that the name of Laura Knight became known to middle class house-owners who wanted affordable art for their suburban home interiors. Many of these were in the Metropolitan Railway's "Metroland", made famous by the poet John Betjeman, and illustrated in the popular magazines of the decade: *Good Housekeeping, Ideal Home* and *Woman and Home* or displayed in the *Ideal Homes Exhibitions* at Olympia.

While Laura was protective of her professional standing as a Royal Academician, it is clear that she was not at all averse to applying herself to commercial art. So, when, in preparation for the Christmas season in 1933, she was approached by the firm of Cadbury to design an "artistic" chocolate box that would be "strikingly different from any previously seen in the shops" (as a Cadbury advertisement announced in *Design for Today* in 1933), she was happy to become a painter of "chocolate box art". As well as Laura Knight, nine other contemporary artists were recruited by Cadbury for the task. These included Arthur Rackham, Edmund Dulac, Philip Connard, Mark Gertler, C. R. W. Nevinson, Dod and Ernest Proctor, George Sheringham, and Arthur Watts. Laura was quick to defend the initiative. It was in no way a prostitution of her art and what's more it would improve the taste of the general public to have their chocolates presented in such an artistic way. As might be expected, her colourful design, appropriate for Christmas, was on a Circus theme, with a clown, an elephant and the Liberty horses. Rackham offered a pixie picture, Dulac a stylized milkmaid and Sheringham a pastoral scene. The "chocolate box" idea was a promising one, but in the event the line did not prove popular in the shops and examples of such ephemeral objects are now very rare.

Equally ephemeral is poster art which, with the rapid growth of transport links around London and across Britain in the 1920s and '30s, became a feature of the urban and suburban scene. Several Newlyn artists responded to this opportunity including Frank Brangwyn (already an established poster artist, having produced wartime propaganda in 1914–18), the Procters and Lamorna Birch. Laura produced her earliest transport posters for the Underground Electric Railways Company Ltd. (the "Underground") around 1921. One advertises the tram service from Hammersmith and Shepherd's Bush to the rugby ground at Twickenham and is in the vigorous style of Laura Knight, "sporting artist". Another produced in 1921, bears the title of *Summer's Joy* and is in quite a different mode. While it features a bold figurative study of bathers, it also carries a quotation from Robert Browning's *Saul:* 'The cool silver shock of the plunge in a pool's living water'. This device is in line with other posters produced at the time which replicate a graphic style of book-illustration in which word and image endorse one another but are not integrated.

Different again is the image she produced in response to a commission from the London and North East Railway to design a cover for their promotional *Holiday Handbook for the Yorkshire Coast* in 1925. This design suggests the influence of the stylised frieze-like effects she had seen at the *Ballet Russes*. Different again is the poster she produced for the annual summer exhibition at the Royal Academy in 1930 which is aggressively "monumental" in its concept and *art deco* in design. However, these interesting contemporary approaches to the genre were not to be developed. In the later 1930s her lyrical style of poster design resurfaced. *September Freshness*, for example, and *Richmond Park* both designed circa 1937–8 for what was by then London Transport, illustrate a continuing interest in landscape and natural forms that are clearly influenced by time spent in Malvern.

Laura Knight's continuing interest in the commercial application of her art in the 1930s is nowhere better exemplified than in her work for the pottery industry. She was introduced to the idea by her sister Eva (Sis) who, trained in the art of pottery painting, was working with Clarice Cliff on the Bizarre project. Clarice Cliff was famous for her striking stylized designs produced for the firm of A. J. Wilkinson at the Newport Pottery in Stoke on Trent. Cliff had been given mis-shapes and seconds of ware to decorate and to these she applied random colour blocks and shapes to disguise the imperfections – hence they were "bizarre". The public liked them and so Wilkinson's went into serious production. So was born the phenomenon of Clarice Cliff's Bizarre ware.

Between 1932 and 1934, Cliff was the director of a major project to encourage good, modern design in the production of tableware. This was an initiative that had been suggested by the Prince of Wales: the *Art in Industry* project. To this end Cliff invited well-known figures of the art world such as Duncan Grant, Vanessa Bell, Barbara Hepworth and Laura Knight to participate. Clarice Cliff and Laura had met by chance when travelling on a train and, being "two of a kind", had struck up a friendship. Laura, always willing to extend her social circle as well as her artistic range, in addition to emulating her sister, agreed at once to participate.

Designs were officially to be for a standard pot shape called *Bon Jour,* but Laura was allowed freedom to design her own shape for her own design: 'Circus.' She tried out one or two demonstration items before producing the whole set of more than fifty pieces. With quirky motifs and elaborate finials and handles, its total conception, ornament and decoration were starkly contrasted with the other designs produced. The sumptuous decoration in pink, green and gold transforms a plate into a circus ring. In the centre of each plate a different circus act is shown (Plate 17) – performing seals and horses, bare-back riders, lions, tightrope walkers – and the tureen handles and lids are modelled as clowns. The set did not have universal appeal, but there were buyers. A twelve piece 'Circus' set was bought by Gracie Fields at a cost of £70 and in 1935 at the marriage of the Duke and Duchess of Gloucester, one of the wedding gifts was 'a handsome tea set' in the 'Circus' pattern designed by Dame Laura Knight.

Less well known, because rarer, is her 'Ballet' range. Here free linear 'scribbles' pirouette across each piece in colours of turquoise and red-pink, reminiscent of the costume designs she produced for the ballet *Les Roses* at the Coliseum 10 years earlier. Laura also designed for the firm of E. Brain & Co, makers of Foley china, alongside Graham Sutherland and Paul Nash. Her design of dancing *Maidens* (a variation of this pattern is sometimes known as *The Isle of Lesbos*) is highly distinctive with a sea-green and white sunray border. In her commercial designs she commemorated subjects that had over the recent years inspired her creative imagination: circus, ballet and the female form.

The completed examples of the *Art in Industry* project were displayed at a selling exhibition at Harrods store in London in 1934. *Modern Art for the Table* then toured the country and was seen in prestigious stores in locations such as Bristol, Derby and Newcastle. In 1935 it travelled to Australia and was on show in Perth at Foy and Gibson's store. In announcing its arrival, the local newspaper, *The Western Australian* featured 'A Circus Piece designed by Dame Laura Knight, the well-known English artist' (29th August 1935). The Wirth family, owners of Australia's largest touring circus, purchased a whole fifty-eight piece set which is now at the South Australia Art Museum in Adelaide.

As has been noted, Laura's sister Eva contributed to Cliff's *Bon Jour* range and today examples of her work command exceedingly high prices. Her career as a pottery designer, however, is not generally known, so we need to catch up with Sis. To reprise: on the death of Great Aunt West, she had gone to St Quentin to keep house and do the bookkeeping for Uncle Arthur. He had encouraged his niece to develop her artistic talents and paid for her to go to art school in France – the École des Beaux Arts. When the factory at St Quentin was sold, in 1908 Uncle Arthur retired to England to a house with a garden, "The Limes" in the village of Nonington in Kent. Sis was to be his housekeeper and companion. Again, with his backing, she began designing textiles, ceramics and printing, setting up as a successful designer in her own right. In May 1910 she married a local man, a chemist from Canterbury called Robart (known as 'Ro') Croft.

The couple lived close to Uncle Arthur in Nonington, just up from "The Limes" at a house called "The Firs" and Sis continued to care for him until his death in 1931. However, in *The Magic of a Line*, Laura suggests that Sis and her family lived a distance away and that Uncle Arthur was a lonely old man. Maybe this was one of Laura's pieces of poetic licence for out of it she indulges in a sentimental passage – Uncle Arthur, now over eighty, standing at his back door calling the birds (for each had a name) and feeding them crumbs. Laura does not mention her sister. And yet over the years they did see one another, wrote letters and remained close. However, when Sis would visit Laura in Cornwall, she did so alone, for Sis' husband 'Ro' and Laura did not get on. It was a situation apparently exacerbated by Laura's requesting a loan from him in 1922 when the Knights were hard up and she needed funds for her visit to America. He had refused. Nonetheless, despite suggestions to the contrary, the sisters were never estranged and their relationship never damaged. With no children of her own, Laura was always interested to hear about the progress of Eva's son Bob. In turn she became fond of Bob's son, John, and in later years paid for her great-nephew's training as a chartered accountant. Eva died on the 5th July 1946.

With the death of King George V in January 1936 and the accession of the popular Prince of Wales, to be styled Edward VIII, the pottery industry was given a boost. Now well known as an artist and designer for the industry, Laura Knight was commissioned by Wedgwood to design a loving cup for the forthcoming coronation. Wilkinsons too asked for commemorative ware. She had hoped that her design for a mug would be selected by the Palace as the official souvenir to be given to some five million children throughout the Empire. However, a letter from the Palace explained that another design submitted by the Newhall Pottery had been previously approved and hers could not therefore be considered. Convinced of her own distinction, Laura was somewhat affronted.

Of course, events took over and her disappointment paled into insignificance with the announcement of the abdication. This meant the cancelation of all of Edward VIII commemoratives and the need for a new set of designs

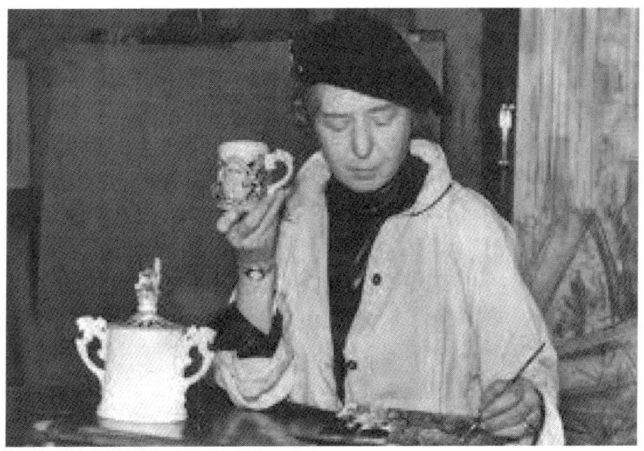

Laura Painting Coronation pieces, 1936. Public domain

to mark the coronation of King George VI. To her disgust, Laura was not paid for her original designs, and while she adapted them for the new set of circumstances, she vowed never to work in ceramics again. However, she did produce some personalised coronation mugs for the children of Compton Chamberlayne in Wiltshire, a village known to the Knights through their friendship with the local "squire" and businessman George Cross who had purchased the great house and estate – but more of him later.

Laura was always interested in young people and their artistic development and when in 1935 she met the Principal of Malvern Art School, Victor Moody, he invited her to visit. She did so frequently, encouraging and advising the 'artisan' students there. In the summer of 1936 as a full Royal Academician she was invited to Scotland to inspect the Diploma work of the students in Art Colleges in Glasgow, Edinburgh, Dundee and Aberdeen. In *The Dundee Evening*

Telegraph for 26 September 1936, there is a photograph and a summary of her report. She was favourably impressed by what she saw there. She complimented the staff for allowing students to develop in their own way instead of imposing a restricted curriculum. She recommended that all students should undertake an extra year to study 'the living head'. The transcript reads: 'A painter is not properly equipped who cannot properly construct a head either in black and white or in colour. I should wish to place very great emphasis on this point'. It is an interesting observation from one who had constantly diversified her interests from the early days at College when she was angry that it was only the 'living head' that she was allowed to study.

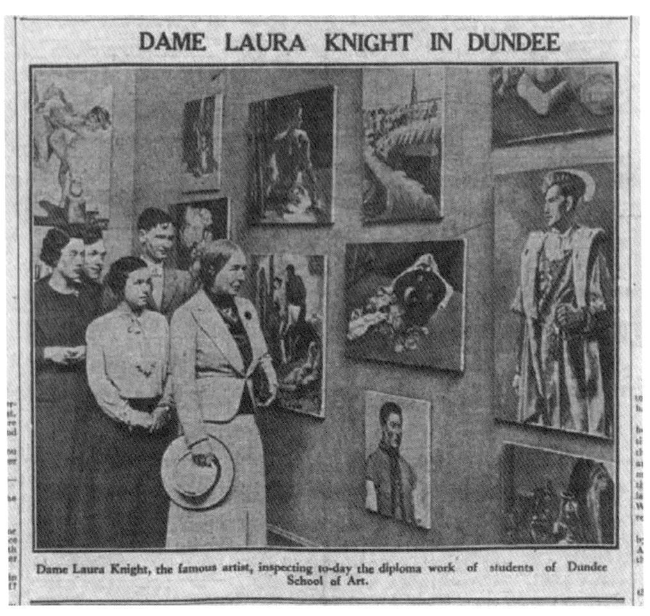

Dundee Evening Telegraph, 17 June 1936. Public domain

The years 1935–36 brought her another project. This was to join other artists in a prestigious decorative scheme for the new trans-Atlantic liner, RMS Queen Mary, sister ship of the later RMS Queen Elizabeth and flagship of the Cunard Line. Built on the Clyde, the liner was launched on her maiden voyage in May 1936 and on the Atlantic crossing won the Blue Riband. The following year she lost it to her rival French liner the Normandie, only to re-gain the Riband in 1938. The Queen Mary provided the height of luxury for passengers, with superlative interior decoration in the *art deco* style. Laura's contribution was to be a painting for a private dining room on 'R' deck. As we might expect, it has a circus theme. *The Mills Circus* features the familiar white-faced clown, liberty horses and just off-centre a figure that could just perhaps be her younger self. Today the Queen Mary is permanently docked at Long Beach, California and functions as a hotel and entertainment venue. There has been much renovation but the painting is still there, positioned at the back of the cocktail bar 'Midships'. However, this was not the first time that the painting was removed from its original context. In 1939 the liner was stripped to serve as a troop carrier for the duration of the Second World War.

In the mid-1930s the Knights stayed for periods at the Mount Pleasant Hotel in Malvern. Harold, busy on portrait commissions, was often away travelling, while Laura, continuing to paint her Gypsies at Iver, also discovered some old friends among the Gypsies who gathered at the Averills Farm in Malvern for the hop-picking. Laura sketched them and other rural subjects on the land of the Bishop family of Callow End in the Severn Valley. It is the Bishops' fields that lie patched and sunlit in the several Malvern prospects that Laura executed at this time. On their farm she pictured the sheep-shearing, and the working horses over the ploughing, sowing and harvesting seasons. These massive, sturdy, and feather-hoofed beasts were quite different in gait and style from the Liberty horses of her Circus days but Laura loved horses of all kinds.

In November 1937, Laura made headlines again – this time it was reported that the famous artist had contracted pneumonia while staying in Salisbury. Laura's illness occurred while she and Harold were staying with friends, George Cross and Heather Ealand at Compton Chamberlayne, near Salisbury (the children of which village had each received a coronation commemorative mug designed by Laura in 1936). George Cross was a very wealthy man. An astute investor, speculator and property developer, he was given the name of "Mr Edgware" because, says Wormleighton, 'he was largely responsible for developing the London suburb, right down to selecting street names.' He owned numerous smart hotels and restaurants in London and invested in land, livestock and fine-art publishing. Often seen at the Café Royal and Royal Academy exhibitions, Cross was well known to the Academicians and generous with his hospitality, regularly inviting artists down to his 1,400-acre estate for weekend painting and sketching parties. When he commissioned a portrait of himself from Harold, he invited both the Knights to Compton Park. It was the beginning of a long association. The Knights went down to Compton many times and are known to have spent several Christmas holidays there in the early 1930s. Sometimes in the summer they met up with Lamorna Birch and his wife Houghton at the invitation of George Cross. They came for the painting and sketching, but in Birch and Harold's case, mostly for the excellent fly-fishing. The cellars at Compton contained bottles of rare vintage and many a time when their host was away, Birch and Harold persuaded the butler to open a bottle or two.

Cross' mistress "Heather" (her real name was Blanche Gertrude Ealand) had been a secretary. An extremely attractive girl with vitality as well as good looks, she was of a type that Laura admired – a lovely 'creature'. Both Harold and Laura were to paint her several times, and Janet Dunbar in her biography makes much of this. She writes that not only Laura – always liable to have crushes on women with a sensual and vital personality – but that Harold too was 'smitten'. She suggests further that in the early '30s when Laura was away with the Circus and the Gypsies, he often saw Heather alone. In fact Laura herself says that at times both she and Harold would meet her without George, who, if he found out, was offended. Dunbar then makes yet another contentious claim. She writes that in conversation in the early 1970s with Laura's Malvern friend Marjorie Averill (then very elderly and perhaps a little muddled), she was told that Heather Ealand admitted to having occasionally been a lonely Harold's "mistress" during the War. This in itself is somewhat surprising, but it is woven into an even stranger scenario when Dunbar further speculates that their relationship was 'probably' consummated in 1946 at the time when Laura was in Nuremburg. Probable or improbable as this might be (after all why wait so long?), it has no basis in fact and to raise the issue is both irrelevant and sensationalist. It has no place in a serious biography. So let us get back to reality.

In 1939 Laura's major exhibition at the Leicester Galleries *Recent Paintings* comprised a selection of her work over the previous 10 years, including Newlyn subjects, Gypsy studies, landscape, ballet and circus. At the Royal Academy of that year she showed *Gypsy Splendour* as well as the portrait of Granny Smith's son, Gilderoy, with the title *The Gypsy*. The show was an eclectic mix that had mixed reviews but in the main it was well received. A reviewer in the *World of Art* described it as being 'jolly … in a fine, fresh, hefty way' But, there was a caveat: 'her vision is objective, matter of fact, commonplace'. Maybe 'commonplaceness' was what was required as the world map unfolded in 1939.

In October 1938 Laura wrote to Allardyce and Josie Nichol, just before they were due to return to England from America, expressing her relief that war may well have been avoided. The Munich Conference, she believed to have been of 'immense importance'. Now, she says with relief, the pictures which she and Harold had packed away in anticipation of war, would be unpacked again. In parallel, the precious paintings from the National Gallery, hurriedly stored to be sent out of the reach of bombs or invasion, were returned to their frames. All was going to be well. It was a hiatus that allowed both the Knights to pick up some threads of normality. At the turn of the year Laura travelled to Sussex and to Newcastle to paint portraits and then, after Harold went down with another bad dose of influenza (so many of Laura's letters are punctuated by mention of Harold's ill-health), they had a short holiday in Brighton. But however much the sun and bracing sea air might have helped Harold's recovery, ominous black clouds were gathering over Europe.

In November 1938 Laura and Harold put their names to a letter published in *The Times* protesting at the treatment of Jews in Germany, triggered by the widely reported pogrom known as "Kristallnacht" (the "Night of the Broken Glass"). Given the situation, such gestures were worthy but too little and too late. Gradually the inevitability of war was accepted, paintings were packed up again, recruitment of defensive forces began and the necessary deployment of military, naval and air-force equipment accelerated. Laura describes her state of mind in the weeks before the declaration of war on September 3rd 1939. She was, she writes at the close of Chapter Twenty Six of *The Magic of a Line*, in a 'crazy state' believing that 'I was only one of thousands of others who, by joining together, might stop war ... Send a telegram to Hitler, subtly worded, to convince him that he would gain greater kudos to himself by switching his power to the furtherance of peace'. This she did, a telegram addressed to 'Hitler, Berlin' was sent at the cost of sixteen pounds and nine shillings (fifteen pounds of that contributed, probably unwittingly, by an old man half-asleep in the drawing room of the Mount Pleasant Hotel). Whether Hitler received Laura's telegram or not, neither that nor the prayers of the nation would make a jot of difference: 'war broke out all the same I'm afraid'.

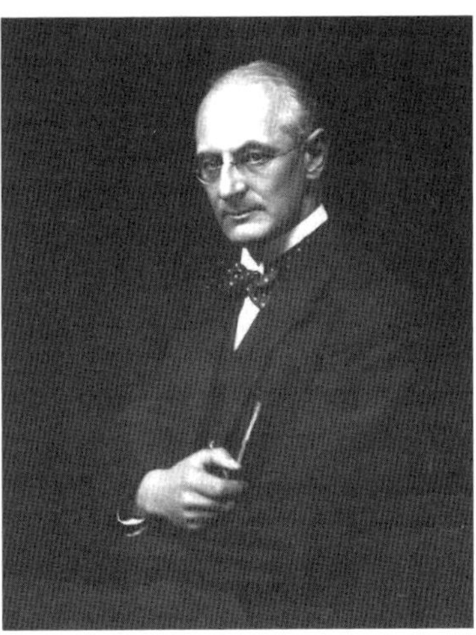

Harold Knight (Laura's favourite photograph of Harold kept by her bedside).
Private collection

CHAPTER ELEVEN

"Keep going, keep going!"

Harold and Laura were at the British Camp Hotel (now the Malvern Hills Hotel) when War was declared on 3rd September 1939. The momentous announcement was followed by a sense of deflation: 'Nothing happened!' Laura writes. This was the period between September 1939 and May 1940, during which there was no offensive undertaken either by the Allies or Germany, commonly referred to as the "Phoney War". In this hiatus, Malvern College was requisitioned by the Admiralty and Harold travelled to Scotland to begin his one remaining portrait commission, that of Edward Watt, the Lord Provost of Aberdeen. All others were cancelled. Laura stayed put and busied herself painting the garden gate at the hotel, Gypsies in the hop-fields and, as a severe winter set in, attempting to paint rural subjects. One study in particular, of two shire horses and a ploughman in a frozen cherry-orchard imprinted itself on her mind. With only some bales of straw, an 'old Burberry tied round and round me with a rope' and a thermos of hot bread and milk as protection, she braved the elements and potential frostbite.

There were several air-raid warnings in London in the first month of war and an aborted German raid over the Firth of Forth in Scotland in October. In the New Year of 1940 Laura was incensed to receive notice from Annie Molyneaux, her housekeeper at Langford Place, telling her that she and her husband had decamped from London and taken up another position at a house in the Essex countryside. Laura considered that they had acted disloyally and appeared to be in no way mollified by Annie Molyneaux' explanation: 'We thought you would be staying at Malvern, and in such a time of uncertainty and expense for you in every way it did not seem fair to stay'. There was an acrimonious dispute over the settling of monies owed which further soured the relationship. Annie was hurt at being misjudged by Laura after such a long time together – 'it does not seem like you', she wrote. It *was* out of character and can only be explained by the worry of the war which brought the Knights financial uncertainty, given that Harold's commissions for portraits had dried up and there was little expectation of sales over the coming months. The outcome was that Langford Place was closed up for the duration of the War and the Knights remained at Malvern. Writing to Allerdyce and Josie Nichol in America on the 20th January 1940, Laura advised them that she and Harold were not planning on returning to their house in London for the time being and their proposed trip to the USA would have to be postponed.

In February 1940 Harold wrote to the Nichols telling them how quiet their life was at the Hotel, with only three other guests staying there. The weather was bad with snowdrifts and sub-zero temperatures disrupting transport and communications. Nonetheless this had not prevented Laura from going to London for a Royal Academy meeting at which Augustus John, whose relationship with the Academy was always stormy, was re-admitted having resigned the year before. The next month Laura wrote to say that she had German measles but that spring was on the way and by May she was painting the peach blossom in the greenhouse at Wind's Acre, the Nichol's house which was let while they were abroad. She also celebrated spring by painting an abandoned lamb in the arms of Horace Hill, the gardener. 'I have always had a particular fancy for lambs' she writes in Chapter Twenty Seven in *The Magic of a Line*.

Her delight in sheep husbandry is also to be seen in what she describes as 'one of the best studies I ever made' (but then with Laura almost every picture she does is the 'best ever' – until the next one!). This was of Walter and Fred Bishop sheep-shearing on the farm at Colwall. Life in rural parts went on, persisting no matter what was going on in the wider world. But privations were starting to be felt in Malvern and Laura was grateful for the food parcel containing dried fruits and chocolate that arrived from Josie Nichol – one of many that were to be regularly sent from the States for the duration of the War. In the next letter in June, Laura thanks Josie for some plum jam and records that despite the fall of France 'everyone is in good spirits'. War had brought everyone together and 'sharpened' her own 'artistic appreciation'.

In May 1940 the War gathered momentum. A Coalition Government was formed and the leader Winston Churchill took control with a series of rallying orations, beginning with the famous 'Blood, toil, tears and sweat' speech which was delivered three days after the start of the German offensive in Europe. On the 4th June his 'We shall fight on the beaches' speech reported on the Panzer tanks' successful invasion of Holland, Belgium and France north of the Somme and the evacuation of the British Expeditionary

Force from Dunkirk. In July came the first German bombing raids over the Channel, attacking coastal defences prior to an intended invasion. In counter-attack, the RAF took to the skies: this was the start of the "The Battle of Britain". By then people were evacuating the capital and other major centres of population around strategic industrial bases. The "Blitz" had begun. From their elevated position just Beneath the Herefordshire Beacon, Laura and Harold, Barry Jackson and Scott Sunderland watched this theatre of war. Search-lights played over the landscape at night while enemy bombers headed north: 'Suddenly', Laura writes in *The Magic of a Line* (which is the major source for her wartime experience), 'we find ourselves in darkness and overhead brilliant clusters of light hang to slowly drop and reveal a possible target. A searchlight, bending, spots a fair hillside and in its beam a flock of scurrying sheep … And in the blackness over Coventry and Birmingham thousands of helpless people wait for their destruction.'

In August, with the threat of invasion Laura took up the offer made to a number of authors by the Librarian of St Andrews University to provide a secure holding place for their manuscripts. Laura duly dispatched an early draft, typescript and annotated proofs with corrections of *Oil Paint and Grease Paint*. They remain there in two boxes one of which has a paper cover marked *Charivari*. Meanwhile, Harold and Barry Jackson were busy with plans for the evacuation of British children to America. This was a private and not a Government initiative, supported by Quakers on both sides of the Atlantic. However, it was soon endorsed by the Government which set up the Children's Overseas Reception Board. The thought had at first been to send evacuees to the Dominions, but realising the scale of the operation, it was decided that Canada and America were the only options. With his contacts in Baltimore, Harold was well-placed to offer his assistance in arranging visas and host families. With disastrous news of German advances, by July, when the scheme had been closed, some 210,000 applications had been made by parents anxious that their children be evacuated from Britain.

Also in August, Harold's sister Ethel and her husband Mansell Dale were evacuated from Seaford on the Sussex coast. They came to Malvern and rented Wind's Acre where they lived for only a short while. Ethel was seriously ill. For a while she was nursed by Laura and a local friend Doris Tate, but when Mansell Dale was knocked down by a car, both he and his wife went into the local nursing home in Malvern. Ethel Dale died there in August 1941 and Mansell chose to return to Seaford. Both Ethel (Tet) and Agnes (Tag) Knight had maintained a close relationship with Harold and Laura over the years. Laura sketched and painted Ethel many times, which causes some confusion for many who encounter drawings bearing the name and mistake the sitter for Ethel Robertson. Agnes' daughter Mary Eady was to be a support to her uncle and aunt as they grew older and, after Harold's death, as Lady Mary Monteath (she had married the last Permanent Under-Secretary of State for India and Burma) she was a regular visitor to Langford Place and a friend to Laura in her later years.

Both the Knights enjoyed hotel life, probably because there was always something happening within or to see outside. On the 3rd October 1940 a lone German bomber successfully dropped its load on Worcester. The impact was felt at the British Camp Hotel, although the staff assured residents that the noise was only the porter dropping the ashbin! In December of 1940 tanks could be seen on manoeuvres in the fields below the British Camp Hotel, while the Knights busied themselves painting the staff of the Hotel – portraits of Mr Parish, the hotel owner and his barmaid. In the August of the following year, Laura wrote to Josie that the hotel 'was very noisy in the summer but always interesting'. To escape, she and Harold accepted an invitation to stay with friends at Hales End, a Georgian house in the middle of fields near the village of Suckley to the north west of Malvern. Laura found it 'a very rural spot' – the tone of which suggests that it was too quiet for her, whereas the Hotel offered a variety of comings and goings as well as gossip. In April of 1941, for example, there was a report of 'a row among the staff at the British Camp Hotel' and on the 15th June Barry Jackson wrote to the Nichols in America: 'The British Camp is a web of intrigue'. Laura would have been intrigued, Harold would have kept out of it, quietly amused.

Everything the Knights required was to hand in Malvern. It was on a direct railway service to London via Worcester and Birmingham. In 1940 when Birmingham came under serious bomb attack Barry Jackson made daily trips to the Repertory Theatre and managed, with rare exceptions, to keep it open throughout the war with a series of plays and readings, as well as open-air performances. Laura would often join a party to Birmingham to see productions or to go to the cinema. In January 1941, she joined a Malvern party to see Charlie Chaplin's *The Great Dictator*. 'Laura loved it' reported Barry Jackson, as of course she would, and, early in February 1942 the Old Vic Company (with the closure of the London theatre, they were now touring) came to Birmingham with a production of *The Cherry Orchard*. This received a "rapturous reception" from the audience, the Knights included.

Laura took over the stables at the Nichols' house Winds Acre as a studio, supervising its reconstruction to suit her needs. She loved it for its perfect north light and fine view west as far as the Brecon Beacons. This was

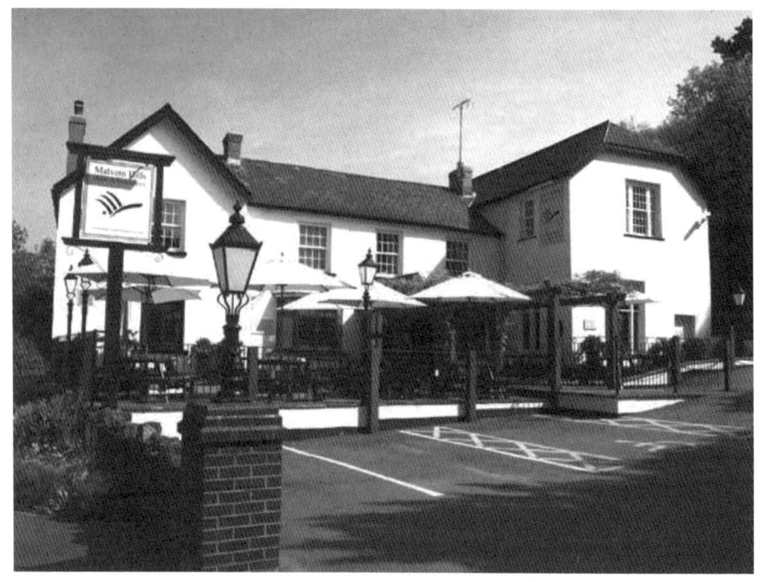

British Camp Hotel, now the Malvern Hills Hotel. Private collection

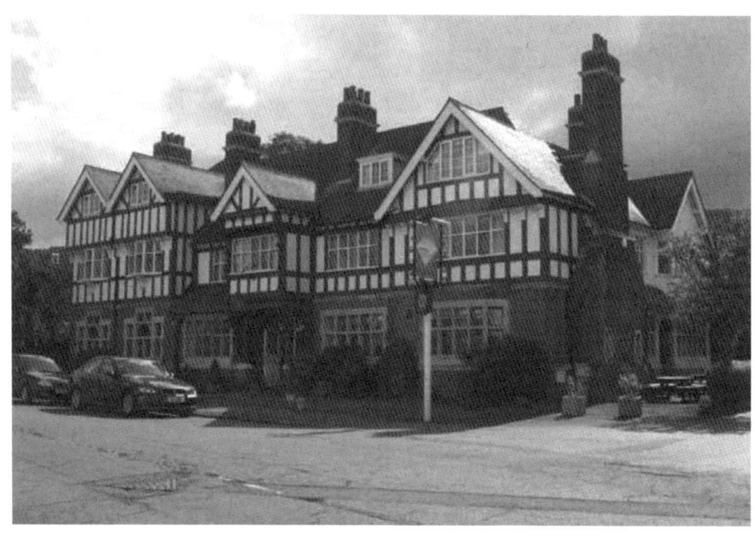

Colwell Park Hotel now. Private collection

her strategic base now that she too was on the offensive. Towards the close of 1939 she had been approached by the War Artists' Advisory Committee under the Chairmanship of Kenneth Clark, then Director of the National Gallery in London, to join the war effort. She was asked to design recruitment posters for the Women's Land Army and, given her on-going concern for women's contribution to society and culture, and as a woman artist of renown herself, she set to with enthusiasm. However, she soon realised that, even though she may well be a famous artist, she had to fulfil the criteria. A letter from R.A. Bevan, Director of the General Productions Division of the Ministry of Information, advised: 'even in the case of really distinguished artists like yourself on whose standard of work one can rely with confidence', it was necessary to provide a preliminary sketch since 'we must be able to satisfy ourselves that the artists (sic) interpretation of any subject is in accord with the policy of the campaign'. Once she had reconciled herself to this, she very effectively met the requirements of the campaign and the needs of the situation.

Even so, her first design was returned with the request that she rework it so that the figure of a Land Girl had as much prominence as the horses. She did so to everyone's satisfaction and worked up the preliminary sketches into the large landscape oil *January 1940*. This was exhibited at the Royal Academy summer show with a price of £787. It did not sell. In an article in *The Connoisseur* H. Granville Fell repeated the old saw: 'Dame Laura shows no diminution in her unceasing challenge to Masculinity'. Once again she was attacked for fighting the woman's cause and yet there was no political agenda there. The image was part of an offensive to be sure, but not a feminist one. Irritating as this gendered criticism may have been, Laura herself could play the gender card to her advantage. For instance, when she was requested in early December 1940 to paint air raids over London, not wanting to do so, she excused herself with the disingenuous reason that 'her husband' would not allow it!

Today some denigrate Laura Knight's manner of painting at that time. They describe her war art as falling within the category of "mass observation" – social research undertaken to record the experiences and opinions of men and women "in the street" – and commercial art. Quite apart from the intellectual and social snobbery implied in this assessment, what is forgotten is that this was not a time for creative innovation but for producing what was appropriate and effective within the brief: to manufacture propaganda. That Laura achieved this, while maintaining a depth of humanity in her subjects, is to her credit and our benefit.

Her portraits of operatives, both military and civilian, skilfully combine the propaganda brief with her knack of capturing something else – the remarkable resource of individuals within the extreme situation of "total war". As she wrote to Josie Nichol in the August of 1940, she was 'proud of the English spirit' and felt that her work as an artist was important to the war effort. In that year she was asked by the Artists' Advisory Committee to paint portraits of award-winning members of the Women's Auxiliary Air Force (WAAF). At first she refused on the grounds that the payment was paltry and, maintaining her ground had an on-going correspondence with Mr Dickey at the War Advisory Committee. They negotiated the fee, eventually settling on 35 guineas per picture. This set the precedent for all War Artists to be paid at this rate. As a result there is a War Office memorandum noting that Dame Laura Knight was 'a little difficult' to deal with.

The first portrait begun in 1940 was of Corporal Daphne Pearson who was awarded the Empire Gallantry Medal (later the George Cross) for saving the life of the pilot when a bomber undershot the airstrip at Detling in Kent; the second a double portrait of Corporal Elspeth Henderson and Sergeant Helen Turner, both awarded the Military Medal for bravery when their RAF base at Biggin Hill was attacked by enemy bombers; and the third of Corporal Josephine Robins, awarded the Military Medal for 'courage and coolness' in handling a direct hit on a bunker and saving lives at RAF Andover during the Battle of Britain. Painted at Malvern rather than on location, these portraits are nonetheless set within the context of the workplace and each of these women appears to be un-posed. There is a directness and authority about them that attests to their professionalism.

These images of strong and competent women echo those Laura painted in the 1930s, especially the double portrait of *Ballet Dancer and Dresser*. Laura sought to replicate that technique in these wartime portraits through the pose and apparatus of the subject's professional role: the helmets, gasmasks, radio equipment and earphones. All these create sight lines of tension and power. In the Pearson portrait, for instance, Laura wished to position the figure holding a rifle, because it 'made good line' – a line of strength and purpose. However, since the WAACs did not carry arms, Laura had to paint out the gun and replace it with a gasmask, as Kathleen Palmer observes in her book *Women War Artists*, in such a case she could not act unilaterally, but in accord with procedures. These were re-enforced when she sent details to the Minister, advising when the painting should be varnished and how it was to be framed – expensively. She was reminded politely that the standard frame used by war artists was all that was required.

In October of 1941 a request came by way of Mr Dickey for Laura to do further WAAF work. This time the subject was to be Barrage Balloon manufacture at the RAF station at Wythal, some six miles south of Birmingham. This was the Headquarters of No.6 Barrage Balloon Centre which had responsibility for the defence of the southern part of Birmingham and Coventry. She accepted, but with a proviso, expressing her hope that 'the fee will be more generous than for portraits'. It appears to have worked, for the fee for her painting *In for Repairs* was 100 guineas. Laura herself was excited by the potential offered by the location, writing that 'the balloon posed like a great silver toad with a pulse in its sides' and, as for the women themselves, she writes: 'I cannot say too much in the praise of all their consideration for me. I worked all Sundays and every other day not to take up too much time'. The picture was completed by Christmas and received with approval and a request from the Ministry of Defence for another on a similar theme, given that her pictures 'might help recruit the right sort of women for Balloon Command'. Over the next 2 years she was to travel to other balloon sites. At Coventry she painted an impressive image of a group launching a balloon against the backdrop of the partially devastated city. She also travelled to the Sheffield base of No. 33 Group RAF Balloon Command which was responsible for all sites in the industrial Midlands. This was a centre of excellence for the training of women in barrage balloon operation, thereby releasing men for other vital tasks. For many of the women volunteers working in this dangerous and unpleasant environment, this was empowering.

Laura herself felt endorsed by the fact that women were fulfilling important roles at this time. In July 1942 she accepted a commission from Mr Dickey to paint WRNS (Women's Royal Naval Service) cooks who provided mass catering for the troops. At the same time she suggested that it would be a good idea for her to paint the women who had taken over men's responsibilities in the theatre, advising him that John Gielgud was 'keen on the idea'. (DD790/167) There is no record of the response. This idea would have germinated from June 1942 when the Knights had been to Birmingham Repertory Theatre to see John Gielgud and Gwen Ffrançon-Davies play the leads in *Macbeth*. In the face of some negative criticism of Ffrançon-Davies' portrayal of Lady Macbeth, she was typically defensive. She wrote to the Nichols that Davies was certainly 'not the powerful Gorgonesque creature as is usual, but a highly strung woman of great and compelling physical attraction'. This testifies not only to Laura's acute critical sense but to her awareness of the potentially destructive power of female sexuality, to which she had been witness so many years before in the cases of Florence Munnings and

Dolly Henry. Although alien to her own nature, she understood its power.

Similarly, while she herself had no desire to be a mother, she was perfectly attuned to children and sensitive to the relationship between mothers and their babies. To have had children herself, however, would have been a distraction. She was driven by another creative drive: the labour and successful delivery of her art. This is affirmed towards the close of *Oil Paint and Grease Paint*: 'Conceived in humility and awe, born in pain – thus Art comes forth'. Her own Mother had implanted that principle and she held iconic status in Laura's memory. Harold, while tolerant of children, found them an irritant. He had no desire to be a father – after all he had not had a good relationship with his own and had no dynastic ambitions. The practical reality of family responsibilities would have been a disaster for them both.

Nonetheless the concept of parenting and family was important to Laura, especially the relationship between mother and child. At Staithes she painted numerous domestic interiors featuring mothers, sisters, infants and babies. When with the Gypsies, she was enchanted by infants and painted mothers and children with the same tenderness as is displayed in her pictures of the mothers, babies and children in the wards at the John Hopkins Hospital at Baltimore in 1927. One image in particular from that time strikes a chord – the *Madonna of the Cottonfields* – painted, as the title implies, with reverence (see chapter eight). There is a similar significance in a painting executed in March 1942: *Betty and William Jackling*. The iconography is striking, being reminiscent of the medieval emblem in which the holy Mother and Child are placed within a rose-garden, teeming with life – birds, insects, rabbits, symbolising spiritual as well as secular fecundity.

In the portrait of Betty Jackling, she, her son and the pet rabbit are composed in a tightly knit group, their closeness evoking a sense of warmth and comfort, enhanced by the texture of home-knitted woollens and soft rabbit-fur. However, the landscape in which they are placed is not a blossoming garden, but rather a winter landscape with bare trees, fitting the wartime context. Yet, directly in the foreground we have the rabbit (always a symbol of fertility), the ploughed fields are about to sprout blades of spring wheat and the pastel tones of soft green, lemon and blue promise new life. As Rosie Broadley observes: 'When it was shown at the Royal Academy in 1942, with Knight's *In for Repairs* … it would have struck a particularly poignant chord with wartime audiences enduring separation from family members amid the destruction of cities and towns'.

At the time Betty Jackling was serving as Commander of a Land Army unit on an estate in Surrey. In her excellent book on *The Women's Land Army*

(2008), Gill Clarke quotes one of the land Army girls, Madeline Barnet, who was there when Laura Knight came to paint. She tells of how the girls always knew when and where Laura was sketching and painting because she wore a red/white Fair Isle cardigan that stood out amidst the dun-coloured environment. She further recollects Laura telling the girls 'stories in the evening often until the early hours, of ballet, circus and fairs'. Once more Laura had embedded herself into a community within which she was no longer the archetypal "wild child" seeking a family, but the "wise woman", teller of tales. It was a role to which, as an independent woman of experience, she had adopted with ease, for as we know she enjoyed being at the centre of attention, was a natural storyteller and able to draw on decades of adventures to amuse her listeners.

Perhaps the most well-known image produced by Laura in the War period is that of *Ruby Loftus Screwing the Breech Ring* (Plate 21). She is shown working on a Bofors 40mm light anti-aircraft gun – a skill that was previously thought to be impossible for a woman to achieve. Ruby had been a shop-assistant in civilian life and in 2 years at the armaments works had achieved what would have normally taken a man 7 or 8 years to master. Such was her application and skill that she was identified as an "outstanding factory worker". The portrait was first suggested to Laura at the end of 1942 as part of a campaign by the Ministry of Supply to encourage women to go into factories to do war work. Since Ruby could not be spared from her work, in March 1943, Laura travelled to the No. 11 Royal Ordnance Factory, Newport, Monmouthshire. Mainly painted on site, the picture took 3 weeks to complete. When *Ruby Loftus Screwing a Breech Ring* was shown at the Academy that summer and voted "Picture of the Year", Ruby and Dame Laura made a special visit to see it and were filmed for the Ministry as part of their propaganda series *Warwork News.* The picture, says the commentator, displays that magnificent combination in wartime: 'masculine genius and feminine courage'. The painting of *Ruby Loftus* generated such popular interest that it was reproduced as a poster and hung in factories throughout the nation to boost morale.

As we have observed in Laura's portraits of other female professionals, Ruby is shown absorbed in her task. There is focus and concentration here. Surrounded by the tools of her trade – the spanners, callipers and blocks, she taps out the screw threads in the barrel with her lathe and sparks fly. The artist's eye for meticulous detail testifies to her interest in the physical and material actuality of the process which absorbs us as we too 'lean over' the workbench. But, in the spirit of the wartime slogan 'Beauty as Duty' Laura was also careful to represent Ruby as a young and attractive woman, with chestnut curls under her green snood, pencilled eyebrows and red lipstick, her hands glistening with lubricating oil. In the background other women (and one token man) busily apply themselves to their tasks. The picture was shown in 1947 at the Engineering and Marine Exhibition at Olympia as a testament to the contribution made by women to the war effort but also, as men returned to civilian life, to encourage them to return to traditional domestic roles where they could exercise their "peace-potential". This was for many women, a disappointment. The demarcation of what women could be and do was being reinstated and for Laura it seemed that all she and others had fought for to raise the status of women as being capable of work in any environment was undermined.

Laura's wish to be appropriately rewarded as an artist had led her to call Kenneth Clark's bluff in 1942 when she stated that she was frustrated by the poor pay on offer and would no longer paint for the War Artists' Advisory Committee. His reply was emollient: 'You have always given us much fuller measure than we deserved for the very meagre pay which was all we could offer', adding that he hoped that in future the Committee could be more generous. Flattered by the gesture, Laura agreed to waive her fee for a poster that was requested to warn of the dangers of fire in such flammable and dangerous environments. This was to be displayed in factories nationally.

To achieve the required effect, she went down to the Austin works at Longbridge, Birmingham where Stirling bombers were being assembled. Despite the deafening noise that caused her hearing difficulties afterwards, the end result was such a success that she writes of receiving with great glee a 'very handsome cheque' in appreciation of her work. To capitalise on this, she then suggested to the Committee that she should undertake a study of the construction of a bomber, which would, given the circumstances, have to be a watercolour. For this she requested payment of £500 and was re-buffed, again politely: 'I think it safe to say that the Ministry of Information Finance Branch would never pass the payment of £500 for a water-colour, and therefore relinquish the first refusal which you were so kind as to give the War Artists'. Unperturbed, once finished, she exhibited the picture to the Academy the following year and it was sold to a director of the Austin works.

Laura's worries about money were justified for at this time Harold was in poor health and feeling his age, his painting commissions were few and his energy low. Basically, they were once more hard-up. In order that they might have enough to cover their accommodation and living expenses in Malvern, she accepted more work for the War Artists' Committee.

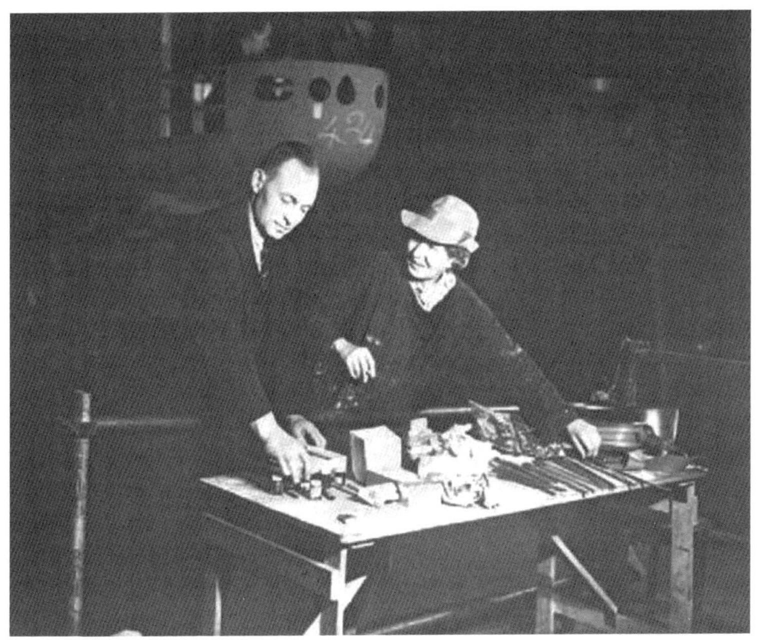

Laura Knight in the Stirling bomber factory, 1943. Public domain

At an agreed fee of £300, she travelled down to Mildenhall to paint Stirling bombers which were about to be taken out of service to make way for Halifaxes and Avro Lancasters. Once again Laura's presence was a welcome diversion from the tensions and routines of the base and, as ever she worked her magic, regaling the crews with her stories. In *The Magic of a Line* she says: 'I have today a photograph of a bomber crew watching me paint a clown emblem on their Stirling that they had named The Circus. I painted a rather big clown, in bright colour'. She was relieved to hear after the War that this had not provided a ready target for the enemy.

With no formal brief, she was able to select her own subject. This was to be a more personal painting, so having taken meticulous note of the layout and instruments within the cockpit, she also spent time listening and observing. 'I then learnt', she writes 'that there are two moments when the crew of a loaded bomber knew fear – before going down the runway and when over the target'. She selected the former. The outcome was another iconic war-time painting: *Take Off*. It is a study of a psychological moment. The viewer is confronted directly with a contained and controlled space – the cockpit within which the personnel and the equipment are drawn together in claustrophobic detail, the sight-lines taut as the engine revs and holds an uneasy equilibrium before taking to the skies. The crew can be identified: at the front Flight Sergeant Alexander Quadling, behind him the navigator Flying Officer William Escritt and the two pilots flanking the searchlight are Flying Officer Beetles and Flight Lieutenant Stuart-White. William Escritt was killed in action in 1944 and Laura made it her business to send copies of the picture to his mother – a gesture which illustrates her sense of connection with and affection for yet another extended family with whom she spent nearly 3 months, sharing their highs and lows, moments of fear and horror but 'moments of beauty too'.

Laura was making her statement and continuing to aggravate the male establishment with her interest in industrial subjects and conventionally masculine environments. However, as she was to say in relation to a painting in 1944 for the engineering and concrete manufacturers Dowsett and Mackay, she found 'painting machinery exciting and relevant to today's world'. This was modernity, human beings represented in the 'Steel, Swarf and Dirty Oil' of their context – to quote the relevant chapter heading in *The Magic of Line*. After the success of the *Ruby Loftus* picture, several other large firms wished to mark their employees' part in defending the nation. In the later stages of hostilities and post-War, Laura was asked to execute important commissions. One was for Ellison Switchgear, the leading manufacturers of aircraft components, based in Birmingham and the Skefko ball-bearing factory at Luton. Laura took pride in providing a testament to the skilled craftsmen on whom the safety and success of the troops on land, sea and air depended. She ignored any prejudice and carping about her gender and engaged with the product and the operator with respect and full attention. As far as she was concerned, women's capabilities could and should be employed (with appropriate remuneration!) in tackling demanding technical studies. Once again, she tackled every job with gusto, earning the respect and affection of the family of workers. So appalling were the conditions at Skefko, that the workforce had betted on her not lasting there a day, but she toughed it out for 6 weeks. The day she left Skefko: 'work stopped for an hour or two and they threw a magnificent farewell party. The bouquet I received was so big I had quite a struggle to get it into the taxi'.

As the War drew to its end Laura's commissions for the Artist's Advisory Committee kept coming. She was offered an opportunity to paint tank manoeuvres at Barnard Castle in County Durham for the generous fee of £300 and, for a fee of £200, to paint the interrogation of enemy pilots.

Such money was needed since the Knights were finding their circumstances severely straightened, forcing them to move from their long-established base at the British Camp Hotel in favour of a cheaper option, the Park Hotel at the village of Colwall, the historical source of Malvern Water on the Herefordshire side of the Malvern Hills. Although she did go to reconnoitre the Barnard Castle location, her driver finding her 'quite charming', she did not find the task appealing and was looking for something different.

She came up with a grand design that would in the long run be neither physically nor emotionally without cost, but which was to be the culmination of her professional life. In 1945 she wrote to the Committee: 'what about the trial at Nuremberg for a subject, instead of Tanks? It seems a pity for such an event to go unrecorded, and I feel that artistically it should prove exciting'. The War Office agreed that they would roll together the fees offered and send her to Nuremberg as a 'War Correspondent' and as a 'VIP', if 'the Americans can be persuaded'. And so at the age of 68 she prepared to go to Nuremberg to record the finale of one of the biggest dramas of history: the dark tragedy that was World War II.

Set up to examine and punish violations of the Laws of War over the period 1939–45, the Tribunal at Nuremberg was to try twenty-two of the senior political and military leaders of the Third Reich. This was unprecedented and, while not universally endorsed, undertaken in the belief that such crimes against humanity as had been committed in the name of Nazism could not go unpunished. For the first time in her life Laura kept a diary of the time she was there, as spectator and witness to the events at Nuremberg. Her experiences are therefore well documented and the diary provides a remarkable resource, not just of her personal responses to what she experienced, but as an historical record. The manuscript of the "Nuremberg Diary" provided Janet Dunbar with substantial material from which she selected and transcribed sections for her biography *Laura Knight*. It appears that Dunbar intended to edit the original for publication but this did not materialise and the whole of the "Nuremberg Diary" as well as her letters sent to Harold over the period can today be accessed in the National Archive.

On 5th January 1946 Laura flew with other officials from RAF Hendon by aeroplane to Frankfurt. There they were met by a young officer, Major Peter Casson, Chief of Staff and Deputy Assistant Adjutant General of the British War Crimes Executive. Driven in the official staff car, he accompanied the party to Nuremberg. On the road, Laura was set back by what she saw from the windows as they passed through 'the horror of total destruction'. When they reached the Grand Hotel (one of the few buildings in

Nuremberg to retain a vestige of its former structure) she had to negotiate scaffolding, duckboards and rubble to get to her quarters. She was even more shocked to be told that the 'large and luxurious' (and centrally heated) rooms allotted to her had been Hitler's after he requisitioned the Hotel for his own use. 'When I go to bed', she wrote, again in the dramatic present tense, 'I often wonder if I am laying my head on Hitler's own pillow: a full metre square and filled with the finest down … the best pillow I have ever slept on'.

The International Military Tribunal was already in session when Laura arrived and over the weeks she got to know the Allied legal contingent well, notably Lord Justice Lawrence and his wife who were extremely hospitable, holding dinner parties at their residence as well as at the Hotel for colleagues and visitors. Lawrence led the United Kingdom Judicial group, earning high praise for his patience, clarity and balanced moral perspective in conducting the Trial. The United States Attorney General and Chief Prosecutor at the Trials, Robert Jackson was a familiar face at the dinner table as was Hartley Shawcross, the United Kingdom Chief Prosecutor. Laura also got to know the alternate Judge Norman Birkett and his wife. She admired Birkett's ability to balance firmness with compassion in his dealings with the prisoners and found in his wife a congenial luncheon companion. She had admiration too for Attorney General David Maxwell Fyfe for his clarity of thought and fluent delivery in the Court: 'Again and again, the theatre comes to mind', she writes, 'good lines', 'bad lines', 'good diction', 'bad diction'. It was second nature for her to interpret what she was seeing in terms of theatre. A common trope applied to her and her work at the time was that she had mastery of "life's circus" as the *Sydney Herald* commented in 1946 in respect of her commission at Nuremberg. It was to be some circus.

When Laura first entered the Court House, which was a couple of miles out of the centre of the town, it was obvious that it had retained most of its plush magnificence. Its marble staircases and seemingly endless corridors were thronged with American, British, French and Russian personnel, all determined to put their stamp on the proceedings – some hard-faced, some vengeful, most implacable, a few compassionate. Each of the allies had its own legal team, its own VIPs – senior representatives from the armed forces, politicians and statesmen, its own press corps, interpreters and recorders. To access the Court Room necessitated several checking procedures, passes to be shown and bags – including Laura's painting materials – to be searched by American army security. Once there, she was directed at once to one of the galleries where other recording artists were sitting. As we might expect, the immediate impression she gives is one of theatre. The defendants are seated in two rows in 'sharp perspective' and lit by fluorescent strip-lighting. Opposite are the judges on similarly raked seating and at floor level the prosecution and the witness boxes. In front of the prisoners sit the German defence counsel all 'with the exception of one in a purple gown … robed in black, draping handsomely over the deep rose-coloured velvet of their chairs and the grey of the carpet'. Behind the prisoners against the oak panelling is an impassive chorus line – the 'Snowdrops' – the US soldiers with their white helmets 'immovable as wooden images'.

Laura, being Laura, declined her gallery position alongside other artists watching the proceedings through opera-glasses and speedily negotiated a "box" for herself directly overlooking the dock. This was an American press-box which she was given permission to use – although with some ill grace. It had advantages. Firstly, from there she had a good view of each of the defendants from above and could note the characteristics and mannerisms of each. Secondly, it had a glass window which, when testimonies became too harrowing, could be closed so she might be insulated from the 'horror'. She writes, once more in the present: 'Aloof as I am at work in my box – not a participant in what is taking place – I need to remind myself that the drama being enacted before me does not belong to the theatrical stage, that the performing cast in the dock do not put all matter aside at the drop of a curtain, go straight to the dressing rooms and take off their make-up.'

Occasionally, as was their right, the US broadcasters with their overwhelming smell of chewing gum would invade her space and Laura and her sketching paraphernalia would become entwined with lengths of cable. So fiercely did she defend her painting territory, however, that she became the subject of what was jokingly called an "international incident" – a crisis speedily resolved by Colonel Andrus, the American in overall charge of arrangements for the Trial. Laura calls him 'the Chief Jailor' and 'one of the kindest and most honourable men I ever knew'. He became a staunch ally, going out of his way to make her life as easy as was possible under the circumstances and explaining many of the procedures and conditions under which the prisoners were held. He told her that their food was prepared by trusted German cooks and brought to the prisoners in their cells which had been stripped of anything that might provide a means of committing suicide. Each prisoner was given fresh water daily, had US standards of sanitation and, if needed, access to medical and dental treatment. Every man was issued with extra woollen clothing, regular laundering of clothes, a daily shave, access to books, writing materials, cards and chess-sets for relaxation.

Laura, as we have noted, could be extremely astute and in her analysis of the characters in the dock (as seen through the glass of her box) as well as the speeches of the legal teams on both sides (as far as she heard them) provides a perspective on the proceedings. All this was retailed to Harold back in Malvern. His letters in return, telling her of his work on the latest portraits, news of friends and domestic issues such as problems with the boiler and the difficulties associated with letting their Langford Place properties, are

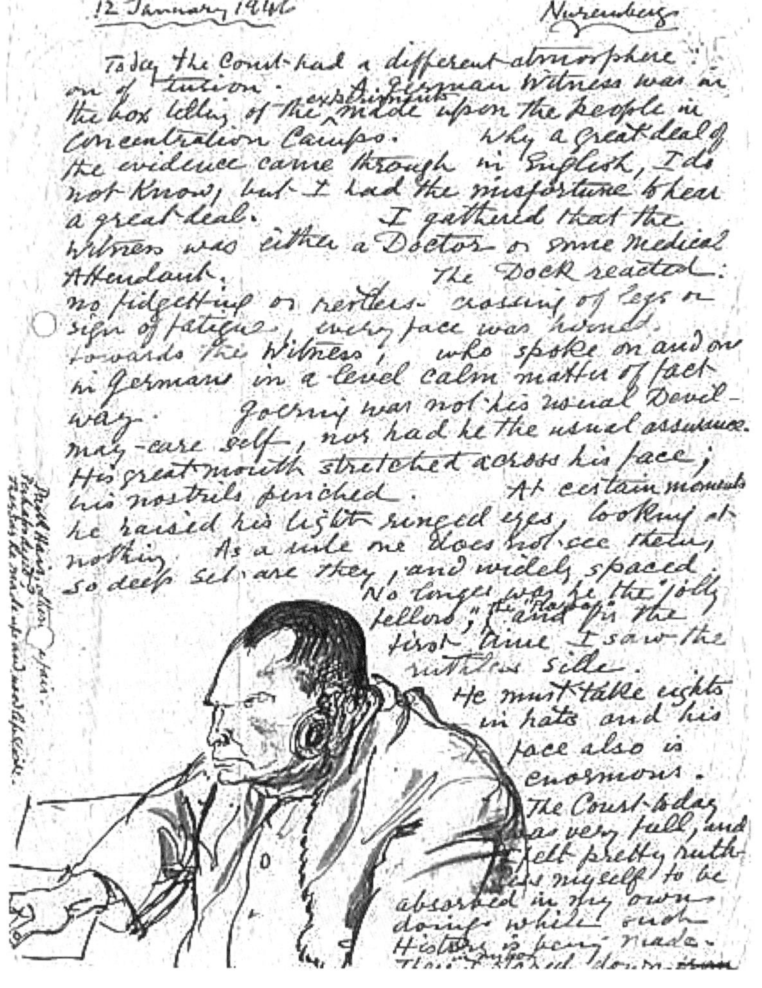

Nuremberg Diaries, 1946. Courtesy of Imperial War Museum

a world away from what Harold describes as her 'enthralling' letters. What was striking to her, and is to us as we view the painting, is that these are old men – either through age or made so by recent experience. Many had balding heads and, what was disturbing, all appeared to have conspicuously clean and well-manicured hands but their boots were clumsy, square toed and countrified. 'Do the prisoners hate artists making drawings of them?' she asks Andrus, 'No they like it' is the response with a qualification – 'especially Goering'.

Laura's catalogue of the accused can be found in letters to Harold as well as in Chapter Twenty Eight of *The Magic of a Line,* 'From my Nuremberg Diary' and they are clearly characterised in the final painting (Plate 20). At the end of the row of prisoners, with his own 'Snowdrop' sits "number one" prisoner Goering – not quite as plump as he was, the uniform of *Reichsmarschall* hangs loosely, but he retains his fresh faced 'pink and white skin' which contrasts with 'Hess's green pallor'. Goering has lost none of his arrogance and self-belief and when Laura sees him in the dock, his appearance betrays that physiological and psychological power which earned Hitler's admiration and later fear when it threatened his own. She writes home to Harold of 'a misshapen gross figure, the head of a bull, a mouth which stretches right across his great face. God gave out no frills in the making of Goering, but he gave him a fascination beyond words.' Capable of persuasive and masterly argument, he was a 'born showman' and could, once carried by a captive audience indulge in egocentric rant: 'I and Hitler decided to do …' and 'I and Hitler instructed Keitel to do'. Goering attempted to intimidate the other defendants and as a consequence was placed in solitary confinement. After sentencing, the day before he was due to be hanged, he committed suicide by taking cyanide – how he managed to access the poison is still a matter of conjecture.

Seated next to Goering is Rudolph Hess, Deputy Führer to Adolf Hitler from 1933 until 1941. Laura describes him in *The Magic of a Line* as 'tall, long neck and long legs: his head, completely bald on top, has a frizzy black surround like a monk's tonsure. He resembles a pictured saint, determined to become a martyr for some cause: heavy dark eyebrows on the bony structure of his face, his eyes deep-set in cavernous sockets: a smouldering glare this first day when, glancing up at me, our eyes met.' But Hess was lost, having retreated into an inner world of madness where not even Goering could reach him – cajoling, offering a piece of biscuit that was refused, as was any food brought to Hess. Laura senses that Goering is concerned for him, that he has 'considerable affection and sympathy for Hess', who, when cross-examined shows no response. It is only when reminded of his Mother that any flicker of recognition was detected in Hess' eyes. Ultimately, he did not go into the witness-box. His neurotic temperament had been apparent to those who saw him after his ill-fated solo flight to Scotland in 1941, on a mission (although a number of conspiracy theories still abound) to negotiate peace and an alliance between Britain and Germany against Russia. He was imprisoned in the Tower of London (the last political prisoner to be held there) and when returned to Germany, Hitler stripped him of his rank. At the final judgement at Nuremberg he was sentenced to life imprisonment and was the last Nazi prisoner in Spandau Jail where he died in 1987.

Ribbentrop, Foreign Minister to the Third Reich, sits next to Hess and Laura notes his surprising lack of distinction, marked by her repeatedly forgetting to sketch him. Some at the trial remembered him well as German Ambassador to London in 1936 but remarked that so changed was he that they would not have recognised him. To Laura's eyes he simply 'looks a wreck'. Next to Ribbentrop is Keitel, formerly Supreme Commander of the Armed Forces, 'stiffly upright' and without a crease in his uniform. Andrus commented that he was 'an ideal prisoner tidy, clean, obedient'. His defence was that of many of his co-defendants – he was merely following orders in accord with his oath of personal loyalty to Hitler. He admitted his guilt before the Court and was hanged, like Ribbentrop in 1946.

Every portrait of the accused is distinctive in terms of body language and demeanour. There is the intellectual Rosenberg who devised the main Nazi ideologies; Frank, Governor General of occupied Poland. Next is Streicher, founder and publisher of the main propaganda machine of the Reich *Der Strümer* – described by Laura as 'bulky in a checked sports suit'. Then we have the former Minister of the Interior, Frick, who had been the instrument of the policies of mass extermination in concentration camps. Next is Funk, former Minister for Economic Affairs who sits alongside the tenth prisoner on the front row, the banker and Economic Minister, Schacht. He appears, says Laura, to be 'completely self-confident; he speaks to no-one, looks at no-one, concentrating on the book he reads constantly. Kenneth Matthews, in charge of the BBC box just round the corner from mine, gets a better view of Schacht than I. "He's now reading Churchill's Biography in German", I am told'.

At the far end of the back row sits Doenitz, ultimately sentenced to 10 years in prison. He was created Commander in Chief of the German Navy in 1943, replacing the former Commander in Chief, Raeder who sits next to him. Then there is Schirach, Head of Hitler Youth and Sauckel,

General Plenipotentiary for the Employment of Labour from 1942 and responsible for the enslavement of the male population of occupied territories. Meanwhile, Jodl, in uniform, 'slackly makes himself as comfortable as he can on the hard benches, his limbs all over the place'. Next in line is the politician von Papen who Laura describes as a 'very distinguished-looking man, with finely cut features and a wealth of grey hair brushed from his forehead; the bands of his earphones over his thick hair give the aspect of a permanent wave'. Next to him is Seyss-Inquart, Reich Commissioner of the Netherlands and then Speer the architect of many iconic buildings for the Reich and Minister for Armaments. He sits next to von Neurath, a more moderate politician appointed by Hitler to give the Government respectability. He was to be sentenced to 15 years in prison but served only eight because of ill-health. Lastly, we have the journalist Fritsche of whom it was said that he was "small fry", put in the witness box in the place of Hitler's Minister of Propaganda, Goebbels, who had committed suicide along with his wife and children in May 1945. Fritsche, Schacht and von Papen were acquitted at the end of the Trial and of the others twelve were sentenced to death by hanging and seven to terms of imprisonment.

Along with the drama of life, food was always a major consideration for Laura – especially so after several years of rationing. Imported by the Americans in whose zone of occupation Nuremberg lay, food at the Hotel was more than plentiful and cheap. Dinners were enjoyed in which there was more meat than she could eat, excellent vegetables, cream for one's coffee and free-flowing wine. There were numerous parties too in the grand ballroom of the Hotel where personnel gathered at the end of the day. On 25th January an international Burns' Night Supper was held with Maxwell Fyfe presiding over a haggis, flown in by a Dakota together with two Gordon Highlanders from the British zone to "pipe it in". Laura, of course, was there, as she would be, taking every opportunity to socialise and wind down at the end of a day of harrowing pressure. As one of Colonel Andrus' party she attended one fine dinner at which, given her VIP status, she sat opposite their host, Andrus, and next to Lord Justice Lawrence on the one hand and on the other Mr Justice Jackson. After this they adjourned to the opera to watch a performance of *Cavalleria Rusticana* from Hitler's own box.

There was entertainment every evening, 'to save the young people – secretarial and such like – from nervous breakdown'. One night Laura, as usual democratic in her tastes, watched the performance of a young female tightrope walker. Imagine the utter surprise and joy she felt to be told by her mentor, and now friend, Major Peter Casson that 'this girl knows all about you'. She was living and working with the Carolli's whom Laura had known at Carmo's Circus. The pleasure in meeting was mutual. Both Laura and Casson were invited to visit the circus camp: 'We danced, we nibbled cakes, we drank glass after glass of white wine. Acrobatics were performed on the hearthrug, and in between Francesco Carolli (who was engaged to the tightrope walker) played the guitar … The hour got later and later, and then the elder Carolli, who had been working in the stables, returned saying, 'You must see the horses before you go' … These are not the same horses I painted when you were performing at Islington Christmas circus in 1938, I said. 'No, they were killed here by a bomb'.' That intrusion of the war into Laura's circus world was perhaps the ultimate affront to her sensibilities. Wherever she went she was confronted by death. DEATH IS PERMANENT she read on a placard in the road. It was an Apocalyptic sign of the times, threatening not only her own existence but everything she held dear.

When, in a gap between official duties, Peter Casson took Laura in his car to see the devastation of Nuremberg, she was assailed by the sight of the pathetic attempts of those who remained to create living space amidst the charred fragments of what had been an historic and beautiful medieval town. She writes that: 'Wherever we went we saw old and young people groping for broken pieces of timber or corrugated iron for shelter … two or three poor souls trying to light a tiny bonfire with the scraps of rubbish so ardently sought by all survivors in the hope of finding enough warmth in that ruthless wilderness to keep them alive'. As was her wont, Laura approached a group of boys with whom she forged a 'close casual friendship' who, in return for cigarettes and matches, described the destruction of the cathedral. Then, in the sub-zero temperature, she spotted a malnourished artist seated at his easel with only a thin coat to cover him. Laura was moved to act: 'I told him that I too was an artist – he allowed me to wrap the woollen scarf I was wearing round his neck.'

This was the first of many attacks upon her conscience that Laura had to manage during her time in Nuremberg. She was worried by the threadbare clothing of her chambermaid at the Hotel and was further troubled by the fact that she did not offer her one of her warm jumpers to cover her thin arms. That she did not, she tells Harold in her evening letter, is down to the fact that 'I was not a good enough Christian to do anything about it'. In her book Dunbar offers the reader one of her speculations on the moral dilemma presented to Laura at that moment and even what she 'told herself'. She talks of the artist's inborn selfishness to avoid anything that might detract from her own comfort and health and jeopardize the completion of her task. Furthermore, there is an endorsement of Laura's lack of Christian charity. As a subsequent biographer I remain neutral and refrain from moral judgement.

Laura herself says nothing in her own text about admitting an instinctive selfishness that warned her not to get involved and there is no evidence of what she told herself in self-justification. This is only supposition. What we know for certain is that she kept focused, held fast to her brief and painted what she saw. How it affected her emotionally and morally had for the time being to be put to one side. But, after the initial weeks the strain began to tell and, exhausted mentally and physically, one day in her box she found herself retreating into a daydream of the Malvern heights. The 'Horrors' had got her down, she needed to get away, to see Harold and the Malvern Hills. The proof – if proof were needed – of a profound distress is her admission that she had reached a stage when for once 'even swallowing a mouthful of food is difficult'. That, for Laura, was serious.

She was found a seat on a troop plane and returned to Britain for 'a week's peace'. Back again in England, she found herself famous. In his letters Harold had kept her informed of the on-going publicity surrounding her presence at the Trials. This was raised to a pitch when a recording of her impressions of Nuremberg that she had made for the BBC was transmitted on 7th February 1946. All the guests at the Park Hotel, Colwall had gathered around the radio to listen and Harold was 'warmly congratulated' on his wife's broadcast. Dunbar writes that he 'told Laura of this in a postcard, and she was pleased'. She then takes the opportunity to again raise the issue of Harold's being always simply "the husband" and his resentment, not just of Laura's fame but that she was considered to be "marvellous". Harold was of course the superior artist in terms of technique and, being a truthful person, held back from endorsing such uncritical praise of his wife's work. As Laura herself admits, it was for her own good, it grounded her, and she was thankful. However, in terms of her energy and commitment she certainly was "marvellous" and Harold never denied that or stood in her way.

Laura had thought that with her sketches satisfactorily accomplished, she would be able to return to Malvern and assemble the composition in her studio there. However, she realized that since 'one goes so deeply into things' she needed to realize her 'vision' on the spot in Nuremberg. Aware that she was prolonging her time away and leaving Harold to his own devices, she was apologetic and Harold, as usual, did not demur. So she organized for the large canvas intended for the final picture to be transported to Nuremberg. She had been allotted a more spacious office room with her name and "Do not disturb" on the door. There she could spread out and bring all the elements of her picture into relationship. Only then could she achieve that 'miracle of revelation' which was appropriate to her physical and emotional investment in the project. On the 12th March Laura wrote to Harold, telling him (as he requested) about her technical progress on the painting: 'I am inclined to lay in with turps an Indian-red thin foundation, because of getting that greeny weird look of the strip lighting, without painting anything real green, except perhaps the malachite marble doorway. That greenish pallor of the lighting might help the drama, and I know only too well the danger of a green scheme and how horrid it can be. Make it look green when it isn't really green, and one may achieve beauty'. Here we have the initial preparation for the canvas, the composition of which was already constructed – the 'sharp perspective' that had arrested her when she first entered the Courtroom. However, the picture was to be more than just a record of an historical event. Instead, she continues, 'I am trying out my rather crazy idea which gives me an opportunity for space and mystery. I do hope so much I can bring it off … I will not say what the idea is, only that it is not normal'.

That 'idea' was to allow into the picture all the emotion that, in her single-minded focus on the task, had been suppressed: the distress, the fear, the guilt and disappointment, the horror welling up from the abyss that had opened up at her feet. She worked with fierce concentration in taking her otherwise representational history painting to the level of the visionary. As she said to Harold, if 'Stanley Spencer could do it' (Stanley Spencer was a fellow Academician, known for his mystical realism) then so could she. As if in a mirage, the Courtroom dissolves left into the tortured landscapes of a ruined and burning city. It testifies to all the homes, communities, towns, cities and nations that had been dislocated and destroyed by the men in the dock. And those same men, quite ordinary in appearance, testify to the capacity of human beings to commit such atrocities that the moral, cultural and geographical fabric of not just Europe but the whole globe was polluted and broken. The painting of Nuremberg then takes on a profound universal significance. It also bears witness to the painter's own seared conscience. For once in her life Laura Knight had been shaken to the core.

Then one of the Snowdrops urged Laura to come down to the entrance of the Hotel to see a starling that was building its nest in a shattered tower opposite the Courtroom and a glimmer of hope broke into the darkness. She observes other signs of life returning: 'I see a young German girl outlined by the devastation behind her. She is powdering her nose and draws a cupid's bow in red on her lips. The dead city is waking to life. I have a glimpse of a prowling cat. At the doorway of one of the half-buried cellars – the entrance to some family's home – is a pot of scarlet geraniums.' Colour has returned to the wasteland. She returned to England in the final days of April 1946 to see the fields 'lush and green', the pear blossom billowing in the orchards and everything 'calm and sweet as if war had never been and sorrow never was'.

CHAPTER TWELVE
"To hold the excitement and the ecstasy"

As they picked up the threads of their professional life, the Knights made the Orchard Hotel in Portman Street their London base given that 16 Langford Place was uninhabitable as a result of structural damage and flooding. The Nuremberg paintings and the associated sketches were delivered to Kenneth Clark at the National Gallery, although Laura insisted on holding onto some of the detailed studies until she had finished her 'big work' for the Royal Academy show. As she wrote to the Secretary of the Artists' Advisory Committee before her return, Nuremberg had been a project for which she had 'never made a bigger effort' and, despite exhaustion, she was determined to make the most of it! When finished, the oil painting was shown at the Royal Academy Summer Exhibition. However, it was not received with the acclaim that Laura had expected, probably because the public and the critics too were war weary. Today, we view the painting as a remarkable record of an event that continues to resonate in the historical conscience of Europe. It and much of the preparatory work are held by the Imperial War Museum in London, while the edited typescript of the *Nuremberg Diary* is lodged in the National Archives.

After Nuremberg there were intimations of another official commission and further travel. Rumours in the press had it that three painters would accompany the King and Queen on their trip to South Africa in February 1947. Mention was made of Frank Salisbury (the highly respected society and "ceremonial" painter), Dame Laura and her husband Harold Knight. This did not materialise and nor did the £1000 fee that had been promised by the Maskew Miller Gallery in Cape Town. A projected trip to Canada, where a selection of her Nuremberg studies had been sent, was not to happen either. Ill health continued to dog Harold, who for some time had been suffering from arthritis which was becoming increasingly debilitating. What is more, Laura's own recovery from what had been a traumatic period in Germany was a slow process. 'After 1946', she writes, 'I had no adventure such as Nuremburg, Mildenhall, circus or gypsy life or the shattering noise of a factory workshop'. Nonetheless, even though entering her '70s, she would never become complacent and was determined to keep working. As she told a London Correspondent of *The Sydney Morning Herald* in July 1946: "I am still a student … and work: harder than ever I did as a youngster, hoping that someday I may do something worthwhile."

The same journalist described her appearance: 'Dame Laura's "Nuremberg" is realistic. For this small virile woman is herself realistic. The greying, golden hair, halo-like in the sunlight, belies her toughness and sturdy constitution. She looks benign, but there is a glint in her bright blue eyes that tells of something more' (23rd July 1946). It was at this time that Laura cut her hair. No more plaits or "earphones", she adopted a modern "bob" – so much easier to maintain. It suited her, especially when dressed up with a velvet hairband or slide. She was once again ready for business. Nonetheless, Harold recognised that she was not in the best of spirits and needed diversion from memories of her recent adventure in Nuremberg. The theatre offered her a resource and once again she found herself working back-stage for Barry Jackson.

At the end of the War in 1945 Jackson had been appointed Artistic Director of the then run-down Shakespeare Memorial Theatre at Stratford. His efforts (not always approved of by local supporters of the theatre) were directed towards building up its national and international status. To this end he brought in new young directors such as Peter Brook and actors such as Paul Scofield. However successful these seasons were, given the post-war economic climate, by 1948 there was a serious financial deficit. Jackson decided to leave and return to Birmingham. His short period at Stratford, however, re-introduced Laura to the joys of real theatre. What particularly fascinated her were the costume and property departments which were being run on a wartime "utility" budget. She had always been used to making much from very little, the remnants she found on market stalls being "run up" in no time into something distinctive to wear. Now at Stratford she 'found activity in the employment of needle and thread on dummy actors and actresses; cutting, pinning; the floor strewn with odd lengths of material, scissors, reels of cotton'. Many of the costumes had a history, having been salvaged from long neglected wardrobe cupboards. One day she opened a trunk of shoes that had been worn by Sir Henry Irving, only to find them shredded by mice. A striking painting that dates from this time is *The Yellow Dress* – a heavy, rich yellow gown in process of renovation by a male tailor seated at the sewing machine. This is now in Worcester Art Gallery.

Before Jackson left Stratford he presided over one landmark production: *Hamlet* performed in Victorian dress. The cast included Diana Wynyard as Gertrude, 17-year-old Claire Bloom as Ophelia and the young Paul Scofield alternating with Robert Helpmann in the title role. The critic Kenneth Tynan considered Helpmann's performance as 'correct and cold' while Scofield's was hailed as being the best he had ever seen. Laura sketched them all and, always keen to try something new, was inspired to write a play herself for Barry Jackson to consider. Never published or performed 'Time Tells' is now in the Archive. Once back in Birmingham, Jackson at the age of seventy-four went on to produce an ambitious set of productions: Shakespeare's three *Henry* plays. So successful was the run at the Repertory that the cycle was taken to the London Old Vic in 1953. Aware that this was an historic event given that these plays had not been performed in sequence like this for many years, he specifically requested Laura to make a record of what was to prove the most successful production of his career both financially and artistically. Laura's period at the Old Vic was once again productive and she had a sense of achievement, writing: 'I filled many big sketch books with perhaps the best drawings I ever did of life backstage' in the chapter titled 'Shadows Lengthen' in *The Magic of a Line*.

However, before that London season Laura was not only to record another piece of contemporary history but to realise her own mortality. In 1948 she undertook a commission at the request of the newspaper magnate Lord Iliffe, whose portrait Harold had recently painted. Iliffe was the owner of the *Birmingham Post*, the *Birmingham Mail* and the *Coventry Evening Telegraph* and he wanted Laura to paint a ceremonial picture to mark the re-building of Coventry after the depredations of the Blitz. It was to feature a visit from the Princess Elizabeth who was to open a newly built precinct in the city. Laura busied herself, going to Coventry in the September to make sketches of the Mayor and civic dignitaries who in their robes would add ceremonial pomp to the picture. She was particularly insistent that those holding the mace and sword on the edge of the group would be able to pose in full regalia. She went to Clarence

House and to what she calls an upper 'golden room' in Buckingham Palace in order to make her studies of the Princess who she found relaxed, charming and more knowledgeable than herself on the subject of art history. Afterwards she reflected on her own conduct at the sitting, concluding that in her fluster she had 'talked too much'. In return the Princess visited Laura in her Thomas Hood studio and in looking through some of the piles of stacked canvases, selected her own favourite. This surprised Laura

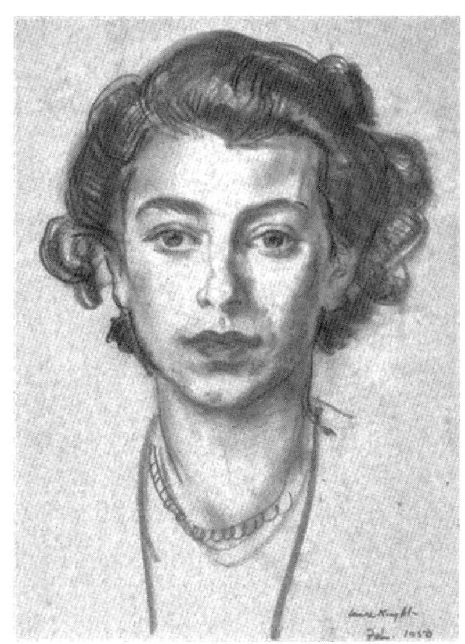

Laura Knight, preparatory sketch of the Princess Elizabeth, 1950. Public domain

greatly: it was the painting of the sick Gypsy she had made at Iver before the War.

Princess Elizabeth opening The New Broadgate, Coventry shows the moment just after a tape had been cut by the young Princess. Behind her is the bombed shell of the old Cathedral. It was not well received by the Coventry notables, annoyed because she 'had not singled out each man by painting every hair on his head'. And, when hung at the Royal Academy in 1949, it drew no compliments from either the Academicians or the public. Even she viewed it with disappointment. She was down hearted and, it turned out, seriously ill with what she describes as a blood disorder. For some time she had been suffering from weakness in her limbs and when she had attempted to lift the heavy door latch of her studio, she lost the use of her upper arms and shoulders. The doctors in London failed to come up with an explanation, but back in Colwall their old friend Dr Richardson identified the underlying problem and was able to treat her. But, she admits, 'it was many months before I could again hold a paint-brush in my right hand'. As soon as she was able to do so and with the help of Ally to hold her palette, she set out to remedy the faults she perceived in the Princess Elizabeth picture. Once again she was determined to see through a task whatever the odds stacked against her. The episode, however, alerted her to the fact that 'when one's health is not good one is in no condition to give what is needed from oneself. Great fatigue of the eye can be known, and the original vision of the whole can be lost … the picture has died under one's hands'. It was a salutary lesson and, as she suggests in *The Magic of a Line*, it is from this time that for Harold and herself the 'Shadows Lengthen'.

In 1948, Laura's painting *Sheep May Safely Graze* was hung at the Royal Academy Summer Exhibition. Inspired by Malvern, the title of this pastoral idyll was significant because in the immediate post-war period it represented nostalgic affirmation of why the nation had fought. The sentiment was implicit in the title because of its association with lunchtime music concerts, devised by Myra Hess and performed at the National Gallery throughout the War. In the empty Gallery (the paintings removed from their frames and stored in a mine in Wales for safekeeping), a wide repertoire of classical music as well as tea and sandwiches were provided for culturally starved Londoners. While a good proportion of the music was by German composers and some of the soloists were German, there was no prejudice in the audience whose enthusiasm and appreciation are legendary. Bach was a special favourite and it was his Cantata 208, *Sheep May Safely Graze* that was best remembered by

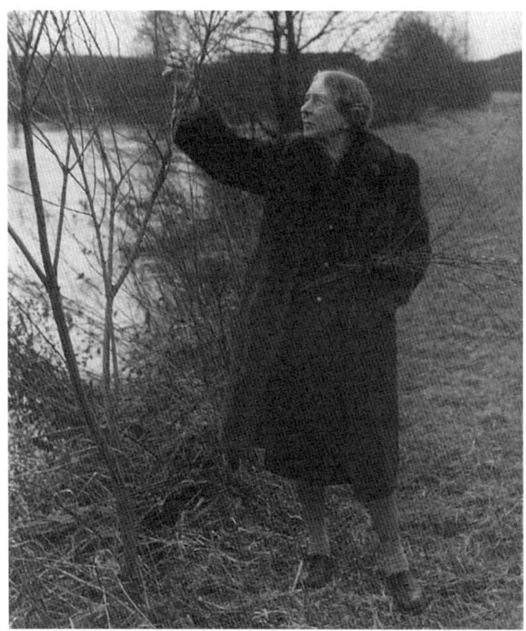

Laura Knight walking in spring c.1950. Private collection

those who flocked to hear. Laura's picture of the same name was a therefore a comforting crowd-pleaser. However, on the negative side, it was also backward looking in the context of plans already afoot to promote the future: *The Festival of Britain* which opened in 1951. With its iconic vertical feature sculpture, *The Skylon*, the Festival site on London's South Bank presented a vision of what was to come – a future in which science, technology, industry, architecture and the arts were to forge a very different world.

The post-war tension between tradition and an aggressive acceleration towards what was "contemporary" and "modern" was acutely felt in the Royal Academy. After Nuremburg, Laura was quickly re-assimilated into the bureaucracy and politics of the Academy which was going through a crisis of its own. Laura found herself in the thick of it. There were three camps – the "old guard" – those who resisted change and were fiercely protective of tradition and precedent; the "revolutionaries" who wanted to open up the Academy to modern art – experimental, non-representational, abstract; and the "shilly-shallyers" – those who couldn't decide one way or the other. A. J. Munnings was of the first persuasion. On the death of Sir Edwin Lutyens in 1944, he had been elected President on the Royal Academy, as the candidate most likely to maintain the status quo, the other being Augustus John. However, AJ was himself a loose cannon.

At the Academy Banquet in April 1949, he made his now notorious and vitriolic speech attacking "modern art". He specifically attacked Picasso, Matisse and Cezanne – all of them 'foolish daubers' – as well as Henry Moore's heavyweight 'holes'. His speech, fuelled by alcohol, was as they say "off the cuff" and became embarrassingly personal when he attacked the Keeper of the King's Pictures, Anthony Blunt, claiming that he had been heard publicly announcing a preference for a painting by Picasso over by one of Sir Joshua Reynolds, first President of the Royal Academy. He was also scathing over those Academicians who could not make up their minds on the issue of what constituted proper art. The speech trailed off into incoherence as the Academicians and their guests (who included Winston Churchill, General Montgomery, the Archbishop of Canterbury and others considered to be great and good) became first nervous, then restive and several left the room. The embarrassment was exacerbated because the proceedings were being recorded live for the radio by the BBC. The next day Broadcasting House was inundated with messages – some affronted by the choice of subject, others by Munnings' manner of presentation and use of the word 'damned'. Other messages, from quite ordinary members of the public, agreed with him. Munnings resigned his position at the end of the year.

It appears that Laura did not attend the Banquet but heard it on the radio. She must have been torn in her loyalties, between keeping faith with her old friend and the need to protect her own position in the Academy. As a result, in her chapter which deals with Royal Academy issues in *The Magic of a Line*, no mention is made of the dispute or of AJ's performance at the Banquet, and she chooses instead to focus on her own responsibilities as a member of the Hanging Committee and the selection process for the Summer Exhibition. It was, however, generally understood that, along with Munnings, it was she who was responsible for keeping adventurous modern art off the walls at Academy shows. This is understandable given that it was as a representational artist that she saw herself, painting what she saw and investing it with what she felt. At the end of *Oil Paint and Grease Paint* she makes that perfectly clear: "Above all I wish that my eyes may be opened and that I may learn to see".

By the time the war was over she had seen and felt a great deal, perhaps too much, and was increasingly content to reflect on her experience, organise exhibitions and give interviews and talks about her work and her role as a woman artist. She was much in demand as a public speaker and journalists were keen to interview her as the "Grand Old Lady" of painting. In 1952 she gave an interview on BBC television to answer questions about her life and art and in 1953 she was invited by the BBC to participate in the radio magazine programme *Woman's Hour* to talk about how she had carved out a successful career for herself in what was still a male-dominated profession and also about her experiences at Nuremberg. The talk *On being an Artist* was broadcast on the Light Programme on the 25th November 1953 and can be accessed in the BBC archives.

In February 1954 the American publication *American Artist* ran an illustrated feature on Dame Laura Knight. This repeats the now familiar story that she 'had not come by things easily. She has had to work and fight', but it also allows the artist to describe her methods and techniques. In the article she stresses that the success of her compositions is the result of careful drawing, of 'laying in' the composition with a monochrome mix of oil and turpentine before finishing with 'solid' undiluted paint. But, if the 'end result is to be a build-up', she keeps the 'brushstrokes (undiluted paint) open and well apart: 'I fill in between, modelling as I go, deepening the tone in the process if possible, until full intensity of effect is achieved'. She uses 'glazes with caution' and her 'palette is simple, mainly earth colours: white, yellow ochre, light red, Indian red, raw umber, cobalt blue, ivory black and terre verte. I rarely use anything else.' It is significant that she mentions using only natural 'earth' pigments. For instance, terre verte is based on a compound of iron silicate with clay that produces a range of colour from blue/green to yellow/green. Since medieval times it was the preferred ground for flesh tones and, along with the iron oxide pigment Indian red, was selected, as Laura informed Harold, for the Nuremburg painting.

The article finishes by mentioning that Laura 'was commissioned by the British Government to make studies of the great procession on the Coronation Day of Queen Elizabeth'. In fact, Laura's contribution to the Coronation records is not substantial – a series of charcoal sketches of the crowds and key locations on what was a cold and rainy day. *The Porch at No. 9 Carlton House Terrace, 5.30am 2nd June 1953,* for example, shows a small group of sleeping spectators in a doorway, there to get a good view of the Coronation procession as it passed. An oil, *The Queen's Coronation Ceremony passing along Oxford Street, 1953* is disappointingly colourless and without any dramatic interest – but then it was a wet and blustery day. Hers was not a predominant role at the event, the Official Painter at the Coronation Ceremony itself being Terence Cuneo, a painter best known in the later 20th century for his paintings of engineering projects (including one of the construction of the M1 Motorway) and steam locomotives.

Laura, now in her mid-seventies, was winding down, although ebullient as ever. She kept fit by continuing to practice some of the ballet steps she had learned from Dolly Snell at Trewarveneth Studio all those years ago. When this became difficult for her in her eighties, she took up yoga. That was what kept her feeling young, she said. What also kept her young were her friend-ships, old and new and, as she found herself less and less able to work with the intensity of previous decades, a deepening consciousness of what Harold meant to her. In July 1945 he had written to Laura in Nuremburg: 'This being apart is very annoying but I suppose we must make a bit of money while the going is good!' In April 1946 the pragmatic tone has changed to one of wistfulness: 'To be alone when one is working is one thing, but in between times it is not so good'. Such a confession was for Harold most unusual and marks a new phase in their relationship.

Laura herself says in *The Magic of a Line* that when at last they re-established themselves at Langford Place: 'all is comfort and intimacy: one's own chairs, beds and teaspoons; nice to touch hands with no one there to see you exchange thought without a sound … The hours still left after so many birthdays spent together are as precious as a crust of bread to a starv-ing man'. Allowing for a degree of mawkish sentiment to which Laura was occasionally inclined, we can believe her. The Hoovers, who had bought her

Ballet Dancer and Dresser picture in the 1930s, kept in regular contact, and in a letter, quoted by Dunbar, she tells them of how: 'In spite of advancing years Harold and I continue to enjoy life – in spite of Harold's slight lameness, he continues his splendid work. I, having no particular disabilities, still continue to hold the excitement and the ecstasy…'

Friendships mattered a great deal to Laura throughout her life and, as she grew older she cherished them. She kept up a regular correspondence with Munnings, now living in near-seclusion at his home in Dedham and very rarely coming up to London. He died in 1959. She kept up her associations with the circus, for although her old friend Bertram Mills had died in 1938, he was succeeded by his sons Bernard and Cyril and they

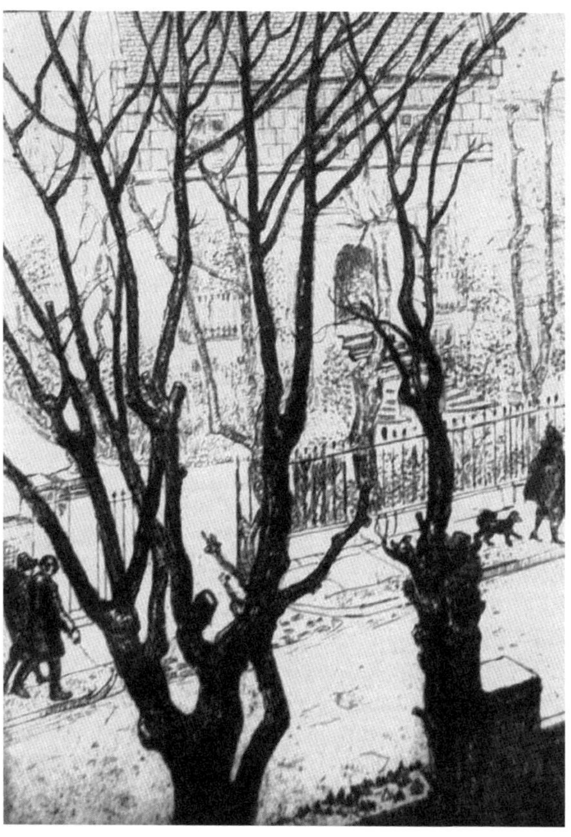

St John's Wood (view from the window, 16 Langford Place) Eva Crofts. Private collection

maintained the long-established relationship. At New Year 1951, she wrote to the Nichols telling them that over the festive period she had dined with the Mills family as well as attending a formal Academy dinner. Not long after Nuremberg she was delighted when Colonel Andrus came with his family to London and made a point of calling on the Knights, as he had promised. In addition, Major Peter Casson, her guide and mentor in Nuremberg, made a point of introducing Laura to his mother Mabel and sister Rusty. Although Peter Casson has been described as Canadian, in fact it was his father Edward Eroll Casson, the author, who was Canadian. His mother was English and the family had lived in England since 1913. Always alert and interested in current events, Harold enjoyed Casson's company and regularly invited him to the Arts Club in Dover Street as a member of what Harold and Laura described as 'the Saturday mornings Team'. For Laura, the friendship with Peter Casson was to develop into what she was to describe as 'a unique friendship – such as would be hard to match in this life'.

In the summer months Laura and Harold (as was their habit) went to the Park Hotel, Colwall, where they were able to enjoy the company of old friends, including Heather Ealand who, having settled for a while in Malvern, was able to take the Knights out and about in her car, accompany Laura to the theatre and ferry guests such as the Nichols over from their house Wind's Acre to the Park Hotel for dinner. It was a sociable and comfortable life, if only Harold's arthritis was not so bad and Laura's own energy a little depleted. Harold's leg pain was making mobility difficult to the point when in November 1953 he was fitted with a calliper, although Laura wondered at the time whether the pain associated with that procedure was worse than the underlying condition. Gradually his health was failing as was that of so many of their circle, including their great friend and ally Barry Jackson. In 1956 he built a retirement home for himself on the Hambleton Estate which he had purchased as an investment in 1919. Only a mile away from Colwall, Hambleton House had a studio which was made available for Laura who was keeping as busy as ever painting and organizing gallery exhibitions of her work.

It was Peter Casson who suggested Laura's next major project in 1955: a portrait of young woman whom he had met in Austria: the "strong woman" Joan Rhodes. In truth Rhodes was not a muscle-bound Amazon but a finely featured, attractive woman who made her living by exploiting her unusual physical strength in variety, cabaret and later on television. Known as the "Iron Girl in a Velvet Glove", in her stage routine she would bend iron bars with her hands, teeth or around her neck, tear telephone directories and lift heavy men (sometimes multiples of them) and cars. After a seriously deprived childhood, Joan Rhodes had at the age of fourteen run away to a fairground. She soon graduated to performing in vaudeville and subsequently her career took her to Hollywood. There she numbered among her friends and acquaintances Bob Hope, Marlene Deitrich and (a very close friend) Quentin Crisp. In later years she was to appear in the films *Burke and Hare* (1971), *The Pink Panther Strikes Again* (1976) and *The Elephant Man* (1980). Casson recognised in Joan Rhodes a personality with a story that would appeal to Laura. 'Can I bring her for you to see?' he had asked, 'She's lovely to look at – I am sure you will want to paint her'. She did indeed want to paint her and the outcome was a study of a head and shoulders which in no way suggests her "strong woman" reputation. Laura saw in her a quality in the moulding and modelling of her features that was essentially feminine – a quality enhanced by the delicate pastel palette. Often on completion of a painting or a project, Laura believed it to be her most successful and the one she had enjoyed the most. This was no exception. More important though, was that when the picture was hung at the Royal Academy it led to 'a number of commissions'.

In 1956 the Bolshoi Ballet came to London once more which was the signal to once again for Laura to become entrenched backstage at Covent Garden Theatre where she was given permission to paint at rehearsals. In *The Magic of a Line* she says that she was also given a good seat in the house for the performance but was going down with laryngitis at the time and was extremely ill as a result. From this acknowledgement of her own physical frailty, she shifts the tone of her narrative into a quiet memory of evenings spent with Harold at home in front of the television (a gift from one of his 'grateful' clients): 'once again every evening meant a lot – whatever the programme. Thus our partnership, made more than 50 years previously, became absolute. Never in our whole lives were we closer than during these last few years together.' It is a fitting tribute to their partnership.

In 1956, Barry Jackson's long-term partner Scott Sunderland died and in 1960 Barry Jackson's own health began to deteriorate. Having been diagnosed with leukaemia, he died in Malvern on the 3rd April 1961. The passing of such a long standing and loyal friend was a blow. Only 6 months afterwards Harold died, aged eighty-seven (which was a good count given his precarious health over the years), in the bedroom at the Hotel in Colwall on the 3rd October 1961. He was working sporadically on portrait commissions to the end. Laura wrote to Josie Nichol that she was inundated with letters of condolence and that the Park Hotel staff were a great help. She 'misses Harold' but the bond between them was so strong that 'death cannot break it'. In March 1962 she was busy sorting through Harold's work in preparation for what she hoped would be a major retrospective exhibition of his work. Triggered by Harold's loss, she was already contemplating a new version of her life story – bringing her narrative up-to-date and one in which Harold could feature, his having declined mention in *Oil Paint and Grease Paint*. That autobiography had ended in St John's Wood in the year 1935 and a great deal had happened to her since then – some of the most interesting and varied experiences of her life and, highly productive.

The Magic of a Line was published by William Kimber in 1965 and was serialised in the magazine *Homes and Gardens*. She dictated the text and was helped in the preparation of the manuscript by the publisher's wife. Perhaps because it was dictated, the narrative in *The Magic of a Line* is not as intuitive or lyrical as her first autobiography. It is uneven, in parts spare in style and at times unfocused. Read on its own, this is the narrative of an old lady whose story and sense of chronology are often a little confused. As she admitted: 'painting, theatre, circus, ballet and concerts became so mixed up it is impossible to remember consecutive events'. Taken together, however, the two autobiographies weave a texture that, while at times difficult to unpick and unravel, create a dense and rich fabric of a life. When we add another layer, the piece of literary "ventriloquism" she called *A Proper Circus Omie*, which was published in 1962, then the pattern becomes even more complicated and richer still.

She was disappointed that *A Proper Circus Omie*, which told of the early life of the clown Joe Bert, was, as she told the American writer Paul Gallico, a 'flop'. Laura's correspondence with Gallico was in relation to his purchase of the painting *The Circus Omie leaning against a tent pole*. She apologises to him for being slow in acknowledging his last communication which had enclosed a cheque in payment for £157 10/-. She thanks him for his kind words of praise and in her fulsome way adds: 'I glory in your appreciation … Never did I have happier companionship (apart from that of Harold Knight) than with my Circus pals.' She promises to send him copies of her latest books *The Magic of a Line* and *A Proper Circus Omie*.

In her later years, with the time as well as the inclination, Laura's letter writing was important to her in a way we cannot comprehend in our age of instant texting. As her physical stamina lessened, in her letters she lived intensely and with a youthful sprightliness of manner. 'Most Beloved Friend Peter', Laura wrote in May 1961, to a correspondent who was to provide her with both professional and emotional support in her final decade. Her letter invited Major Casson to come to Malvern and experience how 'every gulp of this vintage air makes you feel as boozed with its exhilaration as a bottle ful[l] of champagne.' This intoxication characterised her friendship with Casson, for despite, or perhaps because of, the age difference, he was her last "crush", the final "love" of her life: 'Ours is a unique friendship', she wrote in 1963, 'such as would be hard to match in this life'. Casson reciprocated her affection and was always loyal and attentive even as he pursued his responsibilities as a member of the United Nations High Commission for Refugees.

Initially set up as a short-term initiative, UNHCR's remit was to tackle the major problem of displaced peoples in the wake of the Second World War. However, its mandate was extended in 1956 when Soviet forces crushed the Hungarian Revolution and once again there was a major exodus of refugees in Europe. In 1959 the focus became specific with the initiative of World Refugee Year (WRY). The aim was to spread awareness of the refugee problem and to raise funds in support of the homeless and landless

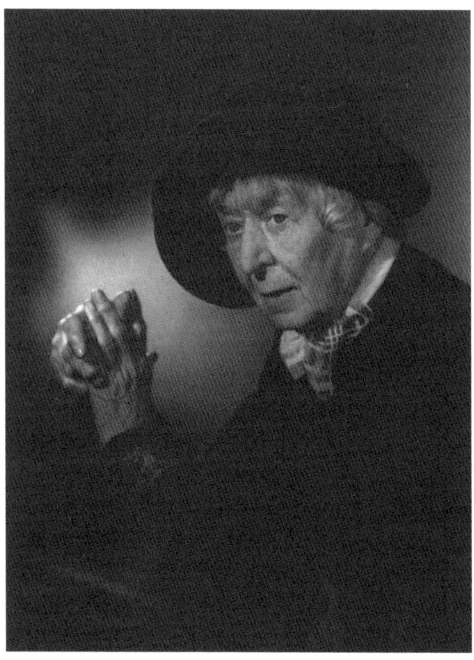

Dame Laura Knight photograph x168789 bromide print, 1964 by Walter Bird.
National Portrait Gallery

populations globally. Peter Casson was a prime mover in this. One of the founders of WRY was the athlete turned politician Christopher Chattaway, who, in an article on the UNHCR website (29/05/2013), remembers Casson, at that point UNHCR's special representative in Canada: 'He was terrific. He helped us greatly to get the thing going in Britain. And I think he played a large part buzzing around the world afterwards. He was a bundle of energy and full of ideas, galvanizing new supporters.' Casson's life was certainly frenetic. He was UN Chief Commissioner at two World Fairs, New York 1964–5 and Montreal in 1967 ("Expo '67") and throughout the 1960s travelled in response to a series of refugee crises – in Africa, the Near East, Asia and Latin America. From 1961 to 1969 he sent Laura a postcard from every destination he visited. 'We're off!', he wrote to her in April 1964 as he prepared for another round of diplomatic missions, 'By means of postcards from everywhere I'm going to take you right around the World with me'.

He was as good as his word. Postcards came from his Headquarters in Geneva, New York and Ottawa; from European cities, Munich. Bonn, Vienna; in 1963 from Saudi Arabia, Qatar, Lebanon, Hawaii, Rangoon, back to Bonn and Oslo; to Jordan, Kuwait, Iran, Afghanistan, Karachi, Delhi, New Zealand, Tokyo and the Philippines in 1964. In October 1964 he was in Africa when the United Nations took responsibility for the humanitarian programme of restoration at the end of hostilities in the Congo. In 1965 he was in Prague, Budapest and Warsaw, then in 1966 in Bahrain, Qatar and Jeddah. Postcards to Laura track his movements and the humanitarian emergencies of the decade. 'I am travelling much too fast', he writes. 'However the mere thought of our divine friendship is a great morale booster!' Laura writing in April 1964 affirms the mutual benefit of their correspondence: 'It has been wonderful to get your picture post-cards – through them I have in imagination journeyed through marvellous countries of all sorts and seen through your own eyes all the strange characters you have encountered.'

Laura looked forward to his visits to London with girlish excitement. '(W) what I really want you to know is the joy in my heart at the prospect of seeing you again so soon', she writes in April 1963 and again in June 1964: 'I am all in a beautiful glow at the thought of seeing you again so soon … Here's the biggest welcome and Hug ever…' Reciprocating the sentiments, in the following May came a postcard from Santiago in Chile: 'Just to let you know that I'm thinking of you here, my Darling Laura, and everywhere!'

In the final decade of Laura's life, it seems that Peter Casson was the recipient of all the romance and adolescent longing that had been foregone in her early years of poverty and hunger. She eagerly awaited his postcards and, anxious for his health, was worried when they did not arrive. In her long letters which increasingly dominate the correspondence, she tells him of her own triumphs: in the autumn of 1965, the exhibition at the Upper Grosvenor Gallery in London: *Paintings and Drawings by Dame Laura Knight, D.B.D., R.A.* and her progress with *The Magic of a Line* which was published in 1965 to complement her Royal Academy *Retrospective Exhibition* of paintings and drawings held in the Diploma Gallery at Burlington House in July of that year. On the day of the Preview of the retrospective, Peter Casson organised a celebration lunch for her and her friends. Laura was exhilarated, writing to him: "I am looking forward so much to 16th of July – already the Royal Academy has asked for the first batch of pictures. The last 2 weeks were sweaty: 48 pictures left this studio last Friday in a huge van … The book is in the hands of the printers and is supposed to come out at the same time as the R.A. Exhibition." And at the bottom of the letter is a drawing of two little figures holding hands.

Our beloved Laura's Greatest Day as it was billed, was celebrated at Overton's Restaurant in St James's Street, London: *On the occasion of the Private View of Dame Laura Knights'* (sic) *Exhibition at the Diploma Gallery of the Royal Academy on 16th July 1965*. In his Preface to the Catalogue for the Exhibition the President of the Academy Sir Charles Wheeler testified to Dame Laura's longevity and fame, she was, he wrote 'a household name for a generation'. The Introduction by Laura's fellow Senior Academician, William Russell Flint, was more expansive: 'No artist could be more delightful to write about than Dame Laura Knight. The only difficulty lies in expressing appreciation and affection well enough. On this occasion there will be no stint of either'. He goes on to testify to her achievement: 'Where in the boundless field of art, has any woman – or how many men – shown such a wide range? Strength, tenderness, quick enriching sympathy: these are hers in overflowing measure. She has used them all with inspiration and enduring courage and they have brought her a rare degree of authority and fame'. He goes on to reflect on an 'exceptionally long and industrious life' and her present 'enthusiasm, alert as in youth'. In his final tribute to her there is 'praise, deliberate, sincere, deserved' and his own pride that 'during her 88th year and in her own Royal Academy catalogue, I have the honour to express it'. The Exhibition comprised two hundred and sixty of her works – oils, watercolours, pastels and sketches, representing every stage of her life as an artist to date. She was generally pleased with the range and effect although she did express some sadness that, because of cost, it had been impossible to bring some of what she considered to be her best work over from galleries abroad. Interestingly, she had preferred her *Grand Parade: Charivari* circus painting of 1928 *not* to be included. Perhaps it was to her mind too much of a virtuoso performance – a show-off piece – not quite fitting the Royal Academy setting.

The summer of 1965 was a triumph all round and Laura was inundated with pressmen and correspondence. On the 9th August *The Times* reported an interview with her in her studio, describing her as 'a woman with the bright blue eyes, gentle manners and the enthusiasms of a child'. The story is told, with one or two elisions and occasional inaccuracies, the now familiar outline of her life story, the adventures she had and the people she met and her achievements. Then the conversation turns: 'Dame Laura, in her own estimation, is no housewife. "Why pretend? she says. "I have lived in too many caravans, tents, corners of dressing-rooms to care … I am not a tidy person", she confided. "Harold put up with a lot! I was never even able to cook a decent meal!" Even in the circus she told us, she could find people to cook for her. At home, often enough it was Harold, although not a great cook. He tried his best and took time and trouble over the dishes he pre-pared'. It is a frank admission and an endearing one, giving us an insight into the domestic life not just of Laura but of Harold Knight, of whom she says in the final pages of *The Magic of Line*: 'Whatever mistakes I made, he gave me understanding; without his sane judgment, my scatterbrain would have led me astray… He was always a surprise and always entertaining, but would never indulge in my wild enthusiasms'.

The year 1965 was Laura's *anus mirabilis*, and despite loving the atten-tion, she admitted to feeling the pressure, writing to Casson in the October: '… both Exhibition and Book are a success. I have had marvellous notices and 2 stinkers as well. The latter delight me although one is utterly destruc-tive. I've had thousands of letters … Everywhere I go, people speak of you. What a terrific impression you made on that opening day of the show! How grateful I am for all you did and for the time and thought you gave to me." She also mentions that she is thinking about getting a secretary. Matters were helped by the acquisition of a new housekeeper/ companion, Emily Worth, whose presence appears to have been a blessing from heaven. The former incumbent of the post ('Elizabeth') was less than assiduous in the housekeeping. In April 1966, she writes: 'You won't recognise No.16 when you come again. It has been scrubbed from top to bottom by Mr Beau Bailey [the handyman] and herself [Miss Worth]. The worst trouble with Elizabeth was that she only knelt down in church – never on the floor. God and a scrubbing brush did not join knees and hands in her religion.'

Laura Knight and Emily Worth were to enjoy the happiest of relationships. Miss Worth was efficient domestically and an excellent cook, promising Casson that on his next visit she would make him a steak and kidney pie the like of which he would never get 'in foreign parts'. That they were fellow spirits is undeniable as is proved by Laura's letter of December 1966, recounting the story of some 'gents' from Sotheby's who had come to see her. Laura was delighted to hear from them that her pictures were 'fetching good prices' and that they would be 'pleased to handle' her work. The charm of the letter lies in the image that follows: 'They seemed to be absolutely thrilled with the drawings … Miss Worth and I went screeching mad in a dance after they left!' Here we have the essential Laura, ever ready to break into a dance for the sheer joy of her life and art.

At times Laura resented being thought of as an old lady, even if a marvellous one. Writing in August 1967 to Casson, she says: 'I had what has been called my ninetieth birthday a week or so ago. It's a bit shattering to suddenly become an antiquity … I'm not going to fall into a decline, and cannot give up hard work or the enjoyment of life itself'. One memory of her great nephew John Croft is of a party in her studio when from across the room she spotted a cabal of interested parties: her accountant, her solicitor, her doctor and John himself. The doctor was expressing his concern about her drinking habits at her advanced age (she so enjoyed a glass of wine or whisky) and was suggesting that she should be persuaded to cut back. At once she intuited the nature of the conversation and made a bee-line over to them. That, she said, would be a very misguided plan since, without her tipple, she would become 'de-picklified' which, as they say, would be curtains!

She still painted and planned for the future. When visiting her, Janet Dunbar writes of seeing an unfinished painting in Laura's studio. She enquired of Laura if it was one of Harold's only to be rounded upon sharply: 'Harold? I'm painting that head for my coming exhibition'. To hold a paintbrush in her hand made her 'feel 20 years younger'.

The subject of that painting was a 'crazy Scottish lad', called John Campbell, who 'aiming at being a pop clarionetist comes most mornings to hoover and dust'. John, like Emily Worth was a treasure and a great help to her when in June 1969 the Upper Grosvenor Galleries arranged a major exhibition: *Laura Knight: 75 Years of Painting*. At the age of ninety-two she was able to look forward to yet another celebration. To mark the occasion the BBC asked her to be interviewed for a television programme. The programme was made but not before the production team had been alerted to the fact that Dame Laura had been in a car accident. She had been thrown about in the car and by her own acknowledgement was concussed.

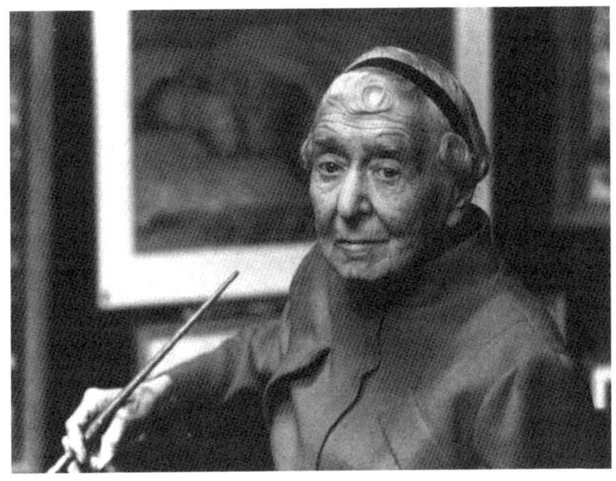

Dame Laura Knight, aged 92 years photographed 1970 by Stanley Devon.
Nottinghamshire Archive

The decision was made to abandon the event and the story continues in the words of the interviewer, John Noakes: '"Oh no, dear, don't do that" came a voice, and in she came, insisting that we carried on at once, just as she was. So on film she went, at ninety (sic) scotch in one hand and cigarette in the other'. At the Private View of her exhibition *75 Years of Painting* she took great care with her appearance. She appeared in a magenta-coloured gown, her white hair 'modelled by Miss Worth, you know' bound by a black velvet ribbon. Sitting in a blue satin chair, she received her guests – friends and artists, politicians, society figures, dancers, celebrities – all came to congratulate her and bestow on her the affection due. She had resisted the title for years, but this time she accepted her role as the "Grand Dame of Painting" with grace, good humour and the greatest satisfaction.

It seemed to be fitting that the next exhibition planned would be hosted by the Castle Museum in Nottingham, the place where Laura and Harold had been brought up, had attended art school, had seen examples of Newlyn painters' work for the first time and exhibited themselves many times over the years. David Phillips, the then fine art collection curator at the Gallery, has remarked that at that time Laura was insistent that the diverse paintings on display had one theme: "modern life". Hers was a life that spanned over 90 years and the concept of what was modern had over that time been transformed, but Laura kept up, kept going and at every stage she was able to say: 'I paint Today'. Whatever her subject and whatever the context, her response was immediate – of the present, never retrospective. She died the night before the show opened on the 7th July 1970, a month before her ninety-third birthday, from what *The Times* correspondent had diagnosed in 1965: 'that incurable disease *joie de vivre*'. Working at a pace and with an intensity that few today would be able to emulate or even understand, she was (in phrases used by Nottingham folk who we met early in her story) "an unexpected" and an "irrepressible".

The Memorial and Thanksgiving Service, arranged by Peter Casson and attended by a large congregation of those who knew, loved, admired and respected her, was held at St James Church, Piccadilly, London on the 28th July 1970.

"A rainbow shone right into our back yard"

Can this be the end? After a life lived to the full and with art in abundance, we need the band to start up and the orchestra to play not a dirge but a fanfare. The life of Laura Knight cannot be concluded simply with a memorial service and an obituary, just as her art cannot be contained within a single genre, technique, style or medium. Those who attempt to pin her down find that she has slipped out of their grasp. In the spirit of irreverence and wilfulness that demolishes pretention and over-rides dullness, like Harlequin, she has transformed and escaped through the trapdoor. In the telling of her life story, there has been no respite, no inertia, and even in her final chapter, the comment was: 'I still keeps goin' on, goin' on'.

At the beginning of this *Life* I noted that Laura Knight only infrequently presents her full face to the viewer, she turns away, glances sideways, out and beyond: 'it's as if to say "They shan't touch me" and they can't, no matter how close I am." But we set out do just that, to catch her unawares and probe the shadows and depths of her character. Was she, as one critic of her first autobiography wrote 'free from self-distrust and misgivings'? Beneath the bravado, as in childhood, we have discovered hints of insecurity, usually triggered by fears of poverty and hunger and the need to keep healthy and be self-reliant. But raw vulnerability does not come to the surface. Just now and then there is a moment of self-doubt. In the final chapter of *The Magic of a Line* she writes: 'I think perhaps I have tried too much; too many different forms of activity and the use of too many different media… I don't know. I could not help that fault in my nature: I had got to try something different'. It was a nature that acknowledged the 'spirit that protects a mishap' and transforms it into a new opportunity. As *The Times* correspondent wrote of Laura in 1965: 'Her spirit of adventure … never failed her and when things were low it was in character for her to organise a party. Her parties were legendary'.

I first became aware of Laura Knight as an artist through two paintings in the Laing Art Gallery, Newcastle: *The Beach* (Plate 7) and *A Dark Pool* (Plate 22). The first, painted in 1908, with its glancing light and breezy surface capturing the simple joys of summer and childhood. The second can only be loosely dated to somewhere between 1908 and 1918, but that matters little. What is important about it is the way that the colour, composition and the technique evoke a complex play of emotion and feeling. On the surface, the chromatic effects of this painting illustrate the artist's desire to explore the relationships and contrasts of primary colours in the representation of light and shade. Here the blue of sea and sky on the left opposes the red of the girl's dress, a hue that is carried through the rocks on which she stands in the middle-right sector. On closer inspection it can be seen that these colours bleed into one another, the varying density of pigment suggesting the shadows on the girl's legs and the movement of her dress, the surface movement and under-currents of the water.

The technique informs the subject: a girl isolated, exposed on the rock above the "dark pool" and staring into its depths. There is on the one hand a feeling of intense heat and warmth and on the other a sense of chill and sadness, drawing the viewer into a deep and lonely place. We have been aware of that place and even looked into it on occasion, most notably with her *Nuremberg* painting. But we cannot stay there long. Life is too full of possibilities – colour, music and laughter and as she said there is a rainbow in every back yard if we choose to look.

So perhaps in concluding we should return to Laura's healthy irreverence for the "expected". Look for the repeated motif in her paintings in which a small child, a girl or boy, engages us unexpectedly with a cheeky grin and a sly nudge from the margins, breaking the spell. He/she is present in the laughing child in right hand corner of *The Beach*, in the androgynous character putting his/her tongue out at the viewer at *Penzance Fair* and in the schoolboy winking at us from out of *A Crowd*. While Laura gave little away about her private self, it is these children who reveal her free spirit and sense of fun. They are 'imps' and 'sprites'. In folklore those are often lonely little creatures driven by a need for attention and friendship but if you believe in them they will work hard for you and bring good fortune. Does this sound familiar? If so, then you and I share the same understanding of our artist. Laura Knight was essentially 'impish' – sprightly to the end. I hope her spirit stays with you.

'A rainbow shone right into our backyard yesterday ...
I am truly thankful that I have known joy and despair.
Without darkness how can one appreciate the light?'

Dame Laura Knight

263

DAME LAURA KNIGHT: EXHIBITIONS

1901: The Royal Institute of Oil Painters
1903: Royal Academy Summer Exhibition, also in 1906 and then regularly from 1909
1906: Dutch Life and Landscape, Ernst Brown & Phillip's Leicester Galleries
1907: Life and Landscape, Ernst Brown & Phillip's Leicester Galleries
1910: Venice Biennale, and again in 1914 and 1924
1912: Leicester Galleries, also 1926, 1928, 1932, 1934 and 1939
1912: Carnegie International, Pittsburg, and in 1914 and 1922
1915: Fine Art Society, with Ella Naper and Lamorna Birch
1918: Camp Life and Other Paintings, Leicester Galleries
1920: Pictures of the Russian Ballet, Leicester Galleries
1920: Pictures of Modern Artists, Manchester City Art Gallery
1922: Alpine Club Galleries
1930: Circus Folk, Alpine Club Galleries
1931: Usher Gallery, Lincoln
1931: Art Gallery of Ontario, Toronto
1933: Laing Art Gallery, Newcastle Upon Tyne
1934: Nottingham Castle Museum
1963: Upper Grosvenor Galleries, 1968 and 1969
1965: Diploma Galleries, Royal Academy

Posthumous exhibitions:

1970: Nottingham Castle Museum
1983: Edition Graphique Gallery, London
1985: Painting in Newlyn 1900–1930, Newlyn Art Gallery
1985: Painting in Newlyn 1880–1930, Barbican Art Gallery
1988: David Messum Fine Art
1989: Nottingham Castle Museum
1991: David Messum Fine Art
1996: Women Artists In Cornwall 1880–1940, Falmouth Art Gallery
2005: Painting at the Edge, Penlee House Gallery
2006: From Victorian to Modern, Djanogly Art Gallery & on tour
2008: Laura Knight at the Theatre, The Lowry & on tour
2008: The Magic of a Line, Penlee House Gallery
2012: Laura Knight: In the Open Air, Penlee House Gallery & on tour
2013: Laura Knight Portraits, National Portrait Gallery, London & on tour.
29th April–11th September 2021: *Laura Knight: a Celebration*
At the time of printing planned for 2021 at Penlee House and Museum, Penzance and later at Milton Keynes Art Gallery

Information courtesy of the Dame Laura Knight website

SELECT BIBLIOGRAPHY

Alison James *A Singular Vision: Dod Procter 1890–1972* (2007)

Alison Smith *The Victorian Nude; sexuality, morality and art* (1996)

Austin Wormleighton *A Painter Laureate: Lamorna Birch and his Circle* (1995)

Brian Foss *War Paint: Art, War, State and Identity in Britain, 1939–1945* (2007)

Caroline Fox *Dame Laura Knight* (1988)

Caroline Fox *Painting in Newlyn 1900–1930* (1985)

Caroline Fox *Stanhope Forbes and the Newlyn School* (1993)

Catherine Wallace *Under the Open Sky: the paintings of the Newlyn and Lamorna Artists 1880–1940 in the Public Collections of Cornwall and Plymouth* (2002)

Diane Filby Gillespie *The Sister Arts: the Writing and Painting of Virginia Wool and Vanessa Bell* (1988)

Elizabeth Knowles *Laura Knight in the Open Air*: catalogue Penlee House (2012)

G. Frederick Bolling & Valerie Withington *The graphic work of Laura Knight, including a catalogue raisonné of her prints* (1993)

G. Garton ed. *British Printmakers* (1992)

G.W. Bishop *Barry Jackson and the London Theatre* (1933)

Gill Clarke *The Women's Land Army: a portrait* (2008)

Gregory Flaxman ed. *The Brain is the Screen: Deleuze and the Philosophy of Cinema* (2000)

Jean Goodman *The Life of Alfred Munnings 1878–1959* (2000)

John Branfield *Ella and Charles Naper: Art and Life at Lamorna* (2003) Jonathan Smith *Summer in February* (1995)

Kathleen Palmer *Women War Artists* (2011)

Kenneth McConkey *Impressionism in Britain* (1995)

L. Newton *Cullercoats: A North-East Colony of Artists* (2003)

Laura Knight 'The Artist's Experience', *the Studio* CXLVIII, November 1954, pp.129–32.

Laura Knight: a Celebration ed. Elizabeth Knowles (2021)

Laura Newton (ed.) *Painting at the Edge* (2005)

Laura Wortley *On with the Show: Drawings of Dame Laura Knight* (1988)

Norman Garstin 'The Art of Harold and Laura Knight', the *Studio* LVII, December, pp.183–97 1912

Pamela Gerrish Nunn 'Self Portrait by Laura Knight', *British Art Journal* Vol. VIII, no.2, pp.53–7 (2007)

Pamela Gerrish Nunn *From Victorian to Modern: innovation and tradition in the work of Vanessa Bell, Gwen John and Laura Knight* (2006)

Peter Phillips *The Staithes Group* (1993)

Robert Radford *Art for a Purpose. The Artists' International Association 1933– 1953* (1997)

Rosie Broadley *Laura Knight Portraits*: catalogue National Portrait Gallery (2013)

S. Adams *The Barbizon School and the Origins of Impressionism* (1994)

Stanley Booth *Sir Alfred Munnings 1878–1959* (2010)

Timothy Wilcox *Laura Knight at the Theatre: paintings and drawings of the Ballet and The Stage*: catalogue The Lowry, Salford & Nottingham Museum & Art Gallery (2008)

Tom Cross *The Shining Sands: Artists in Newlyn and St Ives 1880–1930* (1994)

INDEX

A NOTE ON SOURCE MATERIAL

The **primary sources** used in this biography are: Laura Knight *Oil Paint and Grease Paint* (Ivor Nicholson & Watson, London, 1936); Laura Knight *The Magic of a Line*: *The Autobiography of Dame Laura Knight DBE, RA* (William Kimber, London, 1965); Laura Knight *A Proper Circus Omie* (Peter Davies, London, 1962).

Original material and information was generously contributed by Charlotte (Gaby) Bedford and R. John Croft FCA.

Letters in Chapter Seven were kindly contributed by Michael Reid, Chicago, USA. **Supplementary** material (selectively used) from: Janet Dunbar *Laura Knight* (William Collins Sons & Co Ltd, 1975).

Nottinghamshire Archives: Papers of Dame Laura Knight, Artist www.nottinghamshire.gov.uk/archives Correspondence from Harold Knight to Laura Knight and Dunbar papers – reference: DD/790 Correspondence between Laura Knight and Major Peter Casson – reference: DP/105.

Cadbury Research Library: Special Collections: birmingham.ac.uk/facilities/cadbury Correspondence of John Ramsay Allardyce Nicol (letters to and from Barry Jackson, Harold & Laura Knight): US27.

Newspaper Archives sourced:

The British Newspaper Archive www.britishnewspaperarchive.co.uk

Trove: National Library of Australia www.trove.nla.gov.au/newspaper

New York Times Archive http://query.nytimes.com/search/sitesearch

Texts consulted as **secondary sources** are listed in the **Selective Bibliography** at the end of this book.

For works of Dame Laura and Harold Knight in Public Galleries and Image Sources see The Bridgeman Art Library: *www.bridgemanimages.co.uk/en*

The following catalogues are recommended for images and further description of art works mentioned in the text:

Rosie Broadley *Laura Knight Portraits* (National Portrait Gallery, 2013)

Elizabeth Knowles *Laura Knight in the Open Air* (Penlee Gallery & Museum, Penzance, 2012)